U. S. NAVY AT WAR
1941-1945

U. S. NAVY AT WAR

1941 – 1945

OFFICIAL REPORTS TO
THE SECRETARY OF THE NAVY

BY

FLEET ADMIRAL ERNEST J. KING, U. S. NAVY

*Commander in Chief, United States Fleet
and Chief of Naval Operations*

WASHINGTON

UNITED STATES NAVY DEPARTMENT

1946

*For Sale by the Superintendent of Documents, U. S. Government Printing Office,
Washington 25, D. C.*

Table of Contents

FIRST REPORT

	Page
LETTER OF TRANSMITTAL	2
INTRODUCTION	3
I—THE PEACETIME NAVY	4
Prior to the War in Europe	4
As Affected by the War in Europe	7
II—THE WARTIME NAVY	12
Fighting Strength	12
Personnel	20
The Marine Corps	26
The Coast Guard	27
The Seabees	29
The WAVES	29
III—COMBAT OPERATIONS	31
General	31
Strategy	37
The Pacific Theater	39
The Defensive	39
The Defensive-Offensive	47
The Offensive-Defensive	49
The Offensive	70
Supporting Operations	74
The Atlantic Theater	77
The Mediterranean Theater	82
Landings in North Africa	82
Landings in Sicily	86
Landings in Italy	88
IV—TEAMWORK	89
The Navy Team	89
The Army and Navy Team	89
The Allied Team	90
V—CONCLUSION	92

TABLE OF CONTENTS

SECOND REPORT

	Page
LETTER OF TRANSMITTAL	96
I—INTRODUCTION	97
II—COMMAND AND FLEET ORGANIZATION	100
United States Fleet	100
Organization of United States Naval Forces in the Pacific	100
Organization of United States Naval Forces in the Atlantic-Mediterranean	101
III—COMBAT OPERATIONS: PACIFIC	103
Hollandia and Fast Carrier Task Force Covering Operations	104
Marianas Operations	106
Progress along New Guinea Coast	112
Western Carolines Operations	114
Reoccupation of Philippine Islands	117
Assault on Inner Defenses of Japan	129
Continuing Operations	132
IV—COMBAT OPERATIONS: ATLANTIC—MEDITERRANEAN	134
United States Atlantic Fleet	134
United States Naval Forces in Europe—The Normandy Invasion	135
Eighth Fleet—Italy	143
Eighth Fleet—Invasion of Southern France	143
V—FIGHTING STRENGTH	146
Ships, Planes and Ordnance	146
Personnel	152
Supply	155
Health	157
The Marine Corps	159
The Coast Guard	159
VI—CONCLUSION	161

THIRD REPORT

	Page
LETTER OF TRANSMITTAL	166
I—INTRODUCTION	167
II—COMBAT OPERATIONS: PACIFIC	173
The Capture of Iwo Jima	173
Assault on Okinawa and its Capture	175

TABLE OF CONTENTS

	Page
Fast Carrier Force Operations in Support of Okinawa Invasion	180
Joint Operations in the Philippines and Borneo	183
Fast Carrier Force Pre-Invasion Operations against Japan	188
Contributory Operations	190
The Surrender and Occupation of Japan	192
III—LOGISTICS AND BASES—PACIFIC	196
IV—SUBMARINE OPERATIONS	201
Attacks on Merchant Shipping	201
Attacks on Naval Vessels	202
Special Missions	203
V—ATLANTIC OPERATIONS	205
Antisubmarine Operations	205
Tenth Fleet	206
U. S. Naval Forces in Europe	207
U. S. Atlantic Fleet	211
VI—SHIPS, AIRCRAFT AND PERSONNEL	213
Shipbuilding Program	213
Aircraft	214
Personnel	216
Health	219
The Marine Corps	221
The Coast Guard	222
VII—NAVAL RESEARCH AND DEVELOPMENT DURING WORLD WAR II	225
VIII—CONCLUSION	231
APPENDIX A—Status of major combatant ships of Japanese Navy at the conclusion of hostilities	233
APPENDIX B—Major combatant ships added to United States Fleet, 7 December 1941—1 October 1945	252
APPENDIX C—Losses of United States naval vessels from all causes, 7 December 1941—1 October 1945	287

First Report

TO THE
SECRETARY OF THE NAVY

*Covering our Peacetime Navy and our Wartime Navy
and including combat operations up to 1 March 1944*

BY

ADMIRAL ERNEST J. KING
COMMANDER IN CHIEF, UNITED STATES FLEET,
AND CHIEF OF NAVAL OPERATIONS

(*Issued 23 April 1944*)

UNITED STATES FLEET

HEADQUARTERS OF THE COMMANDER IN CHIEF
NAVY DEPARTMENT
WASHINGTON 25, D. C.

27 March 1944

Dear Mr. Secretary:

In view of the importance and complexity of our naval operations and the tremendous expansion of our naval establishment since we entered the war, I present to you at this time a report of progress.

It is of interest to note that the date of this report happens to be on the 150th anniversary of the passage by Congress of a bill providing for the first major ships of the United States Navy—the 44-gun frigates CONSTITUTION, UNITED STATES, PRESIDENT and CHESAPEAKE, and the 36-gun frigates CONSTELLATION and CONGRESS.

This report includes combat operations up to 1 March 1944. I know of no reason why it should not be made public.

Ernest J. King

Admiral, U. S. Navy,
Commander in Chief, United States Fleet
and Chief of Naval Operations

The Honorable Frank Knox
    Secretary of the Navy,
        Washington, D.C.

Introduction

FOR more than two years, the United States has been engaged in world-wide war. Our geographical position, our wealth, resources and industrial development, combined with an unfaltering will to victory have established and enhanced our position as one of the dominant powers among the United Nations. As such we have been closely and deeply involved with our Allies in all the political, economic and military problems and undertakings which constitute modern war. Historically, the conduct of war by allies has rarely been effective or harmonious. The record of the United Nations in this regard, during the past two years, has been unprecedented, not only in the extent of its success but in the smooth working and effective cooperation by which it has been accomplished. As one of the United Nations, the United States has reason to be proud of the inter-Allied aspects of its conduct of the war, during the past two years.

As a national effort, the war has shown the complete dependence of all military undertakings on the full support of the nation in the fields of organization, production, finance, and morale. Our military services have had that support in a full degree.

The Navy has also had full support from the nation with respect to manpower. Personnel of our regular Navy, who, in time of peace, serve as a nucleus for expansion in time of war, now represent a small portion of the total number of officers and men. About ninety per cent of our commissioned personnel and about eighty per cent of our enlisted personnel are Naval Reserves, who have successfully adapted themselves to active service in a comparatively short time. Thanks to their hard work, their training, and their will to become assets their performance of duty has been uniformly as excellent as it has been indispensable to our success.

As to the purely military side of the war, there is one lesson which stands out above all others. This is that modern warfare can be effectively conducted only by the close and effective integration of the three military arms, which make their primary contribution to the military power of the Nation on the ground, at sea, and from the air. This report deals primarily with the Navy's part in the war, but it would be an unwarranted, though an unintended, distortion of perspective, did not the Navy record here its full appreciation of the efficient, whole-hearted and gallant support of the Navy's efforts by the ground, air and service forces of the Army, without which much of this story of the Navy's accomplishments would never have been written.

During the period of this report, the Navy, like the full military power of the Nation, has been a team of mutually supporting elements. The Fleet, the shore establishment, the Marine Corps, the Coast Guard, the WAVES, the Seabees, have all nobly done their parts. Each has earned an individual "well done"—but hereafter are all included in the term, "The Navy."

✸ ✸

I
The Peacetime Navy

PRIOR TO THE WAR IN EUROPE

THE fundamental United States naval policy is "To maintain the Navy in strength and readiness to uphold national policies and interests, and to guard the United States and its continental and overseas possessions."

In time of peace, when the threats to our national security change with the strength and attitude of other nations in the world who have a motive for making war upon us and who are—or think they are—strong enough to do so, it is frequently difficult to evaluate those threats and translate our requirements into terms of ships and planes and trained men. It is one thing to say that we must have and maintain a Navy adequate to uphold national policies and interests and to protect us against potential enemies, but it is another thing to decide what is and what is not the naval strength adequate for that purpose.

In the years following World War I, our course was clear enough—to make every reasonable effort to preserve world peace by eliminating the causes of war and failing in that effort, to do our best to stay clear of war, while recognizing that we might fail in doing so. For a number of years, the likelihood of our becoming involved in a war in the foreseeable future appeared remote, and our fortunate geographical position gave us an added sense of security. Under those circumstances, and in the interest of national economy, public opinion favored the belief that we could get along with a comparatively small Navy. Stated in terms of personnel this meant an average of about 7,900 commissioned officers, all of whom had chosen the Navy as a career, and 100,000 enlisted men more or less.

This modest concept of an adequate Navy carried with it an increased responsibility on the part of the Navy to maintain itself at the peak of operational and material efficiency, with a nucleus of highly trained personnel as a basis for war time expansion.

For twenty years in its program of readiness, our Navy has worked under schedules of operation, competitive training and inspection, unparalleled in any other Navy of the world. Fleet problems, tactical exercises, amphibious operations with the Marines and Army, aviation, gunnery, engineering, communications were all integrated in a closely packed annual operation schedule. This in turn was supplemented by special activities ashore and afloat calculated to train individuals in the fundamentals of their duties and at the same time give them the background of experience so necessary for sound advances in the various techniques of naval warfare. Ship competitions established for the purpose of stimulating and maintaining interest were climaxed by realistic fleet maneuvers held once a year, with the object of giving

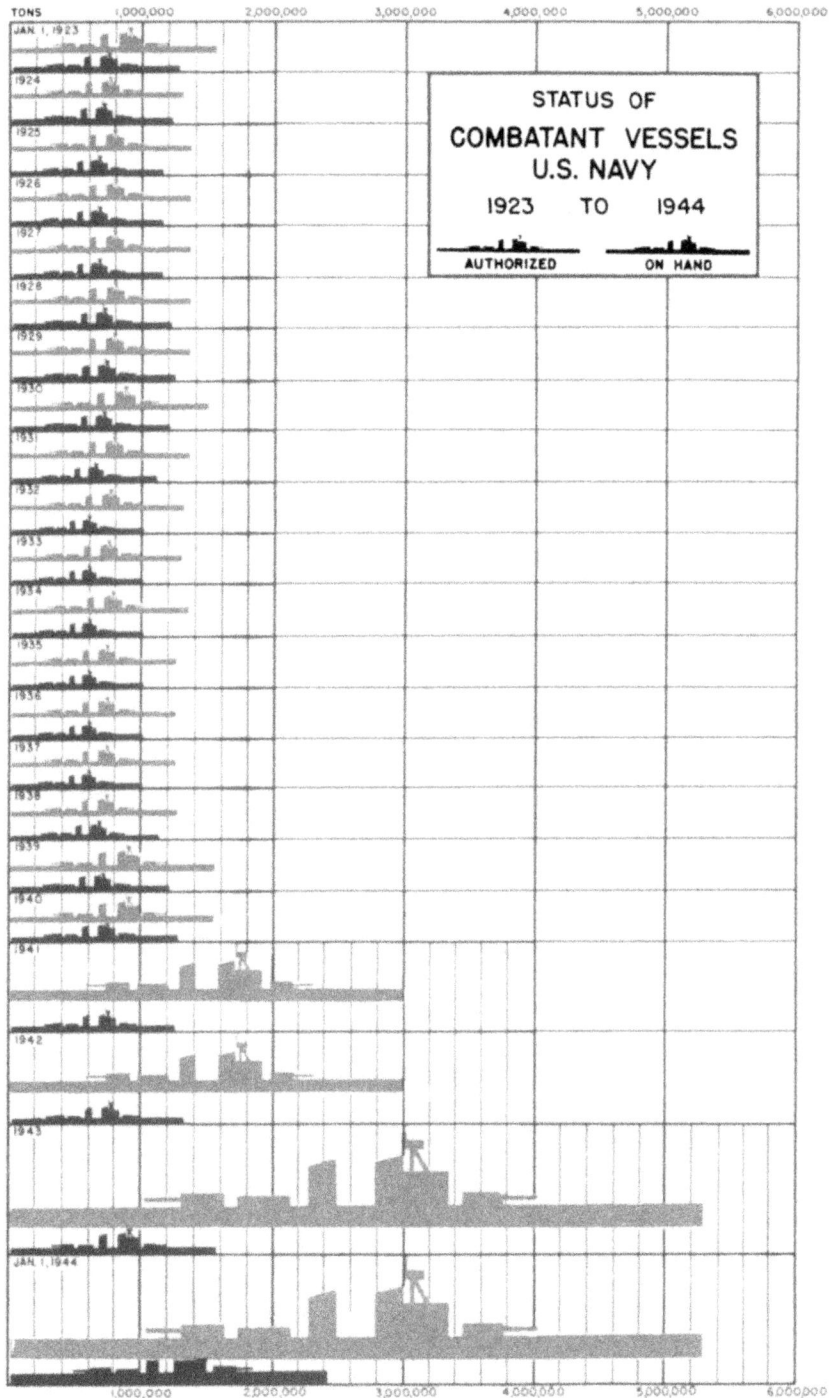

Plate 1.

officers in the higher commands experience and training in strategy and tactics approximating these responsibilities in time of war.

Our peacetime training operations, which involved hard work and many long hours of constructive thinking, were later to pay us dividends. For example, it would be an understatement to say merely that the Navy recognized the growing importance of air power. By one development after another, not only in the field of design and equipment, but also in carrier and other operational techniques—such as dive bombing—and in strategic and tactical employment, the United States Navy has made its aviation the standard by which all other naval aviation is judged and has contributed its full share to the advances which were to make aviation the *sine qua non* of modern warfare. It may be stated here, with particular reference to naval aviation, that the uniform success which has characterized our naval air operations is unmistakably the result of an organization which was based on the conviction that air operations should be planned, directed and executed by naval officers who are naval aviators, and that in mixed forces naval aviation should be adequately represented in the command and staff organization.

Size and Composition

The effects of treaty limitations on our Navy are too well known to require more than a brief review. In 1922, under the terms of the Washington Arms Conference, limitations upon capital ships and aircraft carriers were agreed upon, the ratio established being five for the United States, five for Great Britain, and three for Japan. Pursuant to that treaty, the United States scrapped a number of battleships, but was permitted to convert LEXINGTON and SARATOGA, then under construction as battle cruisers, to aircraft carriers. Whatever the other effects of the treaty, that particular provision has worked to our advantage because those two ships, as battle cruisers, would now be obsolescent, and as aircraft carriers they were—and SARATOGA still is—effective units of our fleet.

In 1930, at London, the parties to the 1922 treaty agreed upon further limitations, this time with respect to cruisers, destroyers and submarines. As a result of these two treaties, which reflected world conditions at the time, and also because of our decision to maintain our Navy at considerably less strength than that allowed by the treaties, we experienced a partial building holiday that threw our small construction program out of balance. Except for cruisers, hardly any combatant ships (no battleships or destroyers) were added to our fleet during that period, and few were under construction. In size, therefore, our Navy remained static, with certain types approaching obsolescence. Moreover, advances in the science of naval construction were hampered by the lack of opportunity to prove new designs. As the accompanying chart (Plate 1) indicates, our naval strength was at low ebb during the year 1927.

Our failure to build progressively was a mistake which it is to be hoped will never be repeated. When a total building holiday in any type of ship is prolonged, and there is no opportunity to proceed on a trial and error basis, our designers are placed under handicaps taking years to overcome.

In 1924, and again in 1929, in response to representations to the effect that we were dangerously deficient in cruisers even in a world at peace, the Congress authorized the construction of a number of cruisers. These were appropriated for from time to time, as were ships of certain other types (except battleships), usually one or two at a time.

In 1933, our building program was stepped up materially by the authorization for the construction of two new aircraft carriers, four more cruisers, 20 destroyers and four submarines. The two carriers were considerably different in design from those previously built. The other types were more evolutionary as to new features, with the possible exception of the BROOKLYN class of cruisers, which were to a degree a departure from former light cruisers, both as to ship design and armament. These cruisers were notable for their six-inch guns which combined light but strong construction with rapid loading, giving them a volume of fire far greater than any other light cruisers then—or now—in existence.

In the previous year, eight destroyers of the FARRAGUT class had been laid down. These were the first of a long series of new designs which had been improved in each succeeding class up to the latest type laid down in 1943. The 1933 program, which was considered large at the time, used the FARRAGUT type of armament, not only for destroyers but for the broadside batteries of the larger ships, because of the five-inch 38 caliber dual purpose gun which, because of its power, reliability and extremely rapid loading, proved to be the best naval antiaircraft gun of comparable caliber.

In March 1934, the Congress authorized but did not appropriate for a Navy of treaty strength.

In 1935, in anticipation of making replacements under the terms of the treaties, work was begun on the design of battleships of the NORTH CAROLINA class. Original designs (completed in 1937) included many features which have proved to be of great importance in the war; namely, increased armor protection against bombs and gunfire, heavy fragment protection around important control stations, modern five-inch antiaircraft weapons, good torpedo protection, and excellent speed and steering qualities for rapid maneuvering. Contract designs for the SOUTH DAKOTA and IOWA classes were completed in 1938 and 1939, respectively. Most of these ships did not come into service until after the war had been declared.

The 6000-ton ATLANTA class cruisers, featuring powerful antiaircraft batteries, were designed in 1937.

In 1938, foreseeing the submarine menace, an experimental program for patrol vessels was started. At the same time the motor torpedo boat was started through a series of developmental stages.

In 1938, it had become apparent that in spite of all efforts on the part of the United States to reach an agreement covering limitation of armaments, and thus to establish at least the probability of world peace, other nations were increasing their navies at an accelerating rate. At that time, in spite of the fact that there was a general desire on the part of most people everywhere in all countries of the world to remain at peace, about one-fourth of the world's population was engaged in war, and civilians were being driven from their homes and subjected to bombing attacks. In view of the situation, the President, in his message to the Congress, recommended an increase of 20 per cent in our naval strength, exclusive of replacements permitted under the Vinson-Trammel Act of 1934. In May 1938, the Congress authorized the recommended program, giving us, on paper, what appeared to be reasonably adequate naval strength.

The so-called agreement at Munich was such as to require an upward revision of the defense requirements of this country. Subsequent events in 1939 resulting in the outbreak of the war in Europe not only confirmed those estimates, but made our building up to them a matter of urgency. A great increase in design activity, in preparation for later building programs, began at this time. War had become a distinct possibility.

AS AFFECTED BY THE WAR IN EUROPE

As a result of Germany's policy of expansion by political, economic and military aggression, culminating in the invasion of Poland, the European war began on 3 September 1939. While our position was for the time being not clearly established, it was nevertheless apparent that this war would affect the United States in a degree which might extend to our becoming involved in a war for our national existence.

The Limited Emergency

The first step taken by the United States was the declaration of the limited emergency by the President on 8 September 1939. The immediate effect of this, so far as the Navy was concerned, was to fix the authorized enlisted personnel strength of the Navy at 191,000 instead of 131,485, and to authorize the recall to active duty of officers and men and nurses on the retired and reserve lists of the Navy and Marine Corps. Other direct effects were that the procurement of materials and equipment, and the taking over of land needed for military purposes, could be accomplished more readily. Also, the Coast Guard could be made a part of the Navy if it appeared desirable, by Presidential order. Indirectly, the limited emergency was responsible for changes in contracting authority which eliminated competitive bidding, and for the suspension of certain labor provisions relating to hours of work on government contracts.

Neutrality

On 2 October 1939, the Congress of American Republics assembled at Panama agreed upon a resolution which established a neutral zone surrounding the Americas, with the exception of Canada, at an average distance of 300 miles. By the terms of the resolution, belligerent raiders and submarines were to be prevented from operating close to the Western Hemisphere, as they had done in World War I, the thought responsible for the resolution being that if belligerent operations took place in that area, the United States and her Latin American neighbors might well become involved in the war. The United States Navy being the only armed force equal to the task of maintaining patrol in this extensive area, the primary responsibility for the implementation of the proclamation was obvious. The patrol was in fact taken by the United States Navy, and at that time a portion of the 111 decommissioned destroyers were recommissioned for the purpose of making it effective.

Preceded by heated debates, during which it was argued that, for insufficient reason, we would be abandoning our traditional policy of freedom of the seas, the Neutrality Act of 1939 became law on 4 November 1939, and American vessels and citizens were thereby prohibited from entering combat zones. The Act also established a so-called cash and carry policy, under which all belligerents were required to do their own transporting of goods purchased in the United States, and pay for them before being granted clearance. In addition, it authorized the President to place restrictions on the use of ports and territorial waters of the United States by submarines or merchant vessels of foreign states (pursuant to which he prohibited their use by foreign submarines of belligerent states, except when there by *force majeure*) and prohibited the use of United States ports as bases for furnishing men and supplies to ships of belligerent states lying off those ports. Other consequences of the Neutrality Act were to make effective certain laws previously enacted, having for their purpose the maintenance of neutrality. These included prohibitions against sending our armed vessels for delivery to belligerents, and contained provisions for detaining armed vessels or vessels manifestly built for warlike purposes or conversion thereto. Included, also, insofar as detention and permissible length of stay were concerned, were laws covering the use of our ports by foreign vessels.

Naval Expansion

In view of the situation, our requirements as to naval strength were again presented to the Congress, in January 1940. At that time, the part the United States was to play in the war was still not clear, but with due regard for our national safety and with aggressor nations disregarding treaties and pacts without hesitation—the immediate result being rapid changes in the international situation—Congress recognized that our security would be measured by our ability to defend ourselves. Coupled with this uncertainty was the knowledge that the international situation had been very difficult to predict. Many keen observers were certain that no European war would break out in 1939, and there were others who felt that we would be able to stay out of the war.

Pursuant to the recommendation of the Navy Department, and following a careful examination of world conditions, the Congress authorized an expansion of 11 per cent in our combatant ships, and the President signed the bill on 14 June 1940.

Meanwhile, the aggressor nations had succeeded in imposing their will upon numerous European countries. Germany had disposed of France and had overrun the Netherlands, Belgium, Norway, Denmark and Poland, and stood on the Channel coast, poised for an all out attack on Britain. In view of that alarming situation, the Congress passed the so-called Two-Ocean Navy Bill, which was signed by the President on 19 July 1940. The increase in our naval strength authorized by this Act was 1,325,000 tons of combatant ships—by far the largest naval expansion ever authorized. This authorization was followed by the necessary appropriations in due course, and, in the making, we had a Navy commensurate with our needs.

The Destroyer—Naval Base Exchange

During the summer of 1940, the Battle of Britain was in its initial stages and the German submarine campaign had been prosecuted with telling effect. At the beginning of the war Great Britain had suffered severely from the general attrition of operations at sea, particularly in destroyers in the Norwegian campaign and during the retreat from Dunkirk. Faced with this situation, Great Britain entered into an agreement with the United States, under the terms of which 50 of our older destroyers no longer suited for the type of fleet service for which they had been designed, but still adequately suited for antisubmarine duty, were exchanged for certain rights in various localities suitable for the establishment of naval bases in the Atlantic area, and essential to the national defense. In addition to the bases acquired in return for the 50 destroyers, we were granted "freely and without consideration" similar rights with respect to the leasing of bases in Newfoundland and Bermuda.

This acquisition of bases operated to advance our sea frontier several hundred miles in the direction of our potential enemies in the Atlantic, and as the bases were leased for a term of 99 years, we could profit by their strategic importance to the United States not only immediately, but long after the crisis responsible for the exchange.

The bases thus obtained by the United States were briefly as follows:

Location	Facility Established
Antigua, B.W.I.	Naval Air Station (Sea Plane Base)
British Guiana, S.A.	Naval Air Station (Sea Plane Base)
Jamaica, B.W.I.	Naval Air Station (Sea Plane Base)
St. Lucia, B.W.I.	Naval Air Station (Sea Plane Base)
Bermuda, B.W.I.	Naval Air Station (Sea Plane Base)
Great Exuma, Bahamas	Naval Air Station (Sea Plane Base)
Newfoundland	Naval Operating Base
	Naval Air Station (Sea Plane Base, Air Field)
Trinidad	Naval Operating Base
	Naval Air Station (Sea Plane Base)
	Lighter-than-Air Base
	Radio Station

Lend-Lease and its Implementation

On 11 March 1941, the so-called "Lend-Lease" Act was signed by the President. The provisions and effects of that Act are too well known to require comment in this report. Naturally, we were unwilling to see a large part of the material built with our labor and money lost in transit, and our only recourse was to give the British assistance in escorting the convoys carrying that material within North American waters.

Incident to our decision, the United States entered into an agreement with Denmark on 9 April 1941 relative to the defense of Greenland, and on that day our Marines were landed there to prevent its being used by Axis raiders. The Coast Guard cutter CAYUGA had already landed a party there to conduct a survey with respect to airfields, seaplane bases, radio stations, meteorological stations and additions to navigation, and on 1 June, the first of the Greenland patrols was organized, consisting chiefly of Coast Guard vessels and personnel.

On 27 May 1941, an unlimited national emergency was proclaimed by the President.

On 7 July 1941, United States Marines were landed in Iceland and relieved some of the British forces stationed there.

On 11 August 1941, on board the United States cruiser AUGUSTA, the President and Prime Minister of Great Britain agreed upon a joint declaration covering the principles of mutual interest to the two countries.

For some months, for the purpose of ensuring safe passage of goods shipped under the provisions of the Lend-Lease Act, our naval forces had been patrolling waters in the vicinity of the convoy routes, and had been broadcasting information relative to the presence of raiders. On 4 September 1941, GREER, a four-stack United States destroyer was enroute to Iceland, with mail, passengers and freight. When about 175 miles south of Iceland, she detected a submarine ahead. The submarine fired a torpedo at her and missed, whereupon GREER counterattacked with depth charges. Another torpedo was fired at GREER but it also missed, and GREER continued to Iceland. As a result of this incident, our naval forces were ordered by the President to shoot on sight any vessel attempting to interfere with American shipping, or with any shipping under American escort.

On 15 October, KEARNY, a new destroyer, one of a number of vessels escorting a convoy from Iceland to North America, was torpedoed amidships. Eleven of her crew were killed and seven were wounded, and the ship was badly damaged but able to make port.

On 30 October, the naval tanker SALINAS was hit by two torpedoes about 700 miles east of Newfoundland. There were no casualties to personnel, and SALINAS reached port safely.

On 31 October in the same vicinity REUBEN JAMES, another old destroyer, was struck amidships by a torpedo. The ship was broken in two; the forward part sank at once, but the after part stayed afloat long enough to enable 45 men to reach the deck and launch life rafts from which they were rescued. About 100 men were lost in this sinking.

Whatever the situation technically, the Navy in the Atlantic was taking a realistic viewpoint of the situation. During the month of November, further steps were taken to enable our naval forces to meet the steadily growing emergency. On 1 November the Coast Guard was made a part of the Navy. Prior to that time ten Coast Guard cutters were transferred to the British. On 17 November sections 2, 3 and 6 of the Neutrality Act of 1939 were repealed by an act of Congress, thereby permitting the arming of United States merchant vessels and their passage to belligerent ports anywhere.

Another effect of the European war, of major importance to the United States, was the alliance by which on 27 September 1940 Japan became one of the Axis powers.

For many years it had been predicted and expected that eventually Japan's policy of expansion would conflict with our interests in the Pacific. Recognition of that possibility, plus Japan's growing naval strength, were indicated by her being a party to the 1922 treaty on limitation of armaments, and to subsequent treaties dealing with that subject.

At the time of the 1922 treaty Pearl Harbor and Manila were fortified bases, and Guam was being fortified. None of our other Pacific territories and possessions was fortified. When, therefore, the parties to that treaty agreed to maintain the fortification of certain Pacific islands in *status quo*, the fortification of Guam was halted. Subsequently conforming to the treaty provisions, we maintained the *status quo* at Guam and Corregidor, and confined our precautionary measures in the Pacific to the strengthening of Pearl Harbor and our west coast bases.

Our foresight in developing Pearl Harbor and our west coast bases has increased, immeasurably, our ability to carry on the war in the Pacific. Whether or not Guam could have been made sufficiently strong to withstand the full force of enemy attack is of course problematical, but we appear to have had an object lesson to the effect that if we are to have outlying possessions we must be prepared to defend them.

When, in the winter of 1935–1936, the Japanese declared themselves no longer willing to abide by existing treaty provisions or be a party to further negotiations, it gave rise to a feeling of uneasiness concerning the trend of Japanese policy and activities. Unfortunately, the full import of that move did not become apparent until later.

In 1931, Japan had embarked on a policy of aggression by the seizure of Manchuria. This was followed by other conquests in China, and as we have since learned, was accompanied by the fortifying of certain islands mandated to Japan by the League of Nations, in direct violation of the treaty provisions. A complete history of our relations with Japan during the period 1931–1941 was issued by the State Department in the so-called "White Paper" dated 2 January 1943.

Continuing her aggression, Japan moved into French-Indo China in 1940. In 1941, the United States was engaged in protesting these and other moves, and while conversations with the Japanese were being held, the German offensive in Russia was being successfully pressed. It seems likely that this influenced the Japanese decision to attack Pearl Harbor.

Whatever the reasons, Japan, while her representatives in Washington were still engaged in discussions, presumably with a view to finding a means of preventing war, on the morning of 7 December 1941 attacked our ships at Pearl Harbor. The attack was essentially an air raid, although there were some 45-ton submarines which participated. The primary objectives of the Japanese were clearly the heavy ships in the harbor and our grounded Army and Navy planes were destroyed in order to prevent them from impeding the attack. Damage done to the light surface forces and the industrial plant was incidental. Of the eight battleships in the harbor, ARIZONA was wrecked, OKLAHOMA capsized and three other battleships were so badly damaged that they were resting on bottom. The damages to the other three were comparatively minor in character. A total of 19 ships was hit, including three light cruisers which were not seriously damaged. Three destroyers were hit and badly damaged. (All three were later restored to service.) Of the 202 Navy planes ready for use on that morning only 52 were able to take the air after the raid.

Personnel casualties were in proportion to the material damage. The Navy and Marine Corps suffered a loss of 2,117 officers and men killed and 960 missing.

The Japanese losses were about 60 planes, attributable mainly to antiaircraft fire, and it is probable that others were unable, on account of lack of fuel, to return to the carriers which composed the striking force.

A few hours later a similar but less damaging attack was made on the Philippines. (The situation in the Far East is described elsewhere in this report.)

On the following day we declared " . . . that a state of war which has thus been thrust upon the United States by the Imperial Government of Japan is hereby formally declared." On 11 December a similar declaration was made concerning Germany and Italy.

II

The Wartime Navy

FIGHTING STRENGTH

Armaments

THE world diplomatic situation had been deteriorating for some years, and Europe had been at war since September 1939. For those reasons, we had been adding to our fleet from time to time, beginning in 1933, but our decision to prepare ourselves fully for the inevitable conflict may be considered to have been made when the so-called Two-Ocean Navy Bill became law on 19 July 1940. At that time, we had to consider the possible disappearance of British sea power. England itself was threatened and its capture by the Germans would have meant the loss of the Royal Navy's home bases and the industrial establishments. These, we could readily see, would become very tangible assets indeed, in the event that we were drawn into the war.

In round numbers, provision for a "two-ocean Navy" meant an expansion of about 70 per cent in our combat tonnage—the largest single building program ever undertaken by the United States or any other country.

Upon the outbreak of war in Europe in September 1939, the Navy Department initiated expansion of naval shipbuilding facilities in private yards and in Navy yards. In many instances, particularly in Navy yards, the expansion provided facilities which were to be available for repairs as well as new construction.

By 19 July 1940, when the two-ocean Navy was authorized, the program for expanding facilities was well started, and it continued thereafter at an accelerating rate until the early part of 1943. Early in the period of the shipyard expansion, it was apparent that as the new programs for cargo ships, tanks, planes, and Army and Navy equipment of all kinds started to pyramid, the country's latent manufacturing capacity would soon be overloaded. Thus the problem became not merely one of expanding shipyards, but of expanding the manufacturing capacity of industry as a whole to meet the needs of the Navy shipbuilding program.

Expansion of general industry to meet the requirements of this shipbuilding program began with plants producing basic raw materials. Next to be enlarged were plants capable of manufacturing the component parts of a modern man-of-war ranging all the way from jewel bearings to huge turbines. So comprehensive was the building program that nearly every branch of American industry was affected either directly or indirectly. Manufacturers were encouraged to let out their work to subcontractors, particularly to plants which had been producing non-essential materials. An automobile manufacturer, for example, was given the job of producing extremely intricate gyroscopic compasses, and a stone finishing concern undertook the manufacture of towing machines and deck winches. Early in the building program an acute situation in the construction of turbo-electric propulsion machinery was solved by the construction of an enormous new plant in a 50-acre corn field. As an illustration of the speed with which the whole program was undertaken, the construction of that particular plant was not begun until May 1942, and by the end of the year the first unit had been produced, completed and shipped.

The rapidity of this naval expansion has had a profound effect upon our military strategy. As a result of it, we were enabled to seize and hold the initiative sooner than

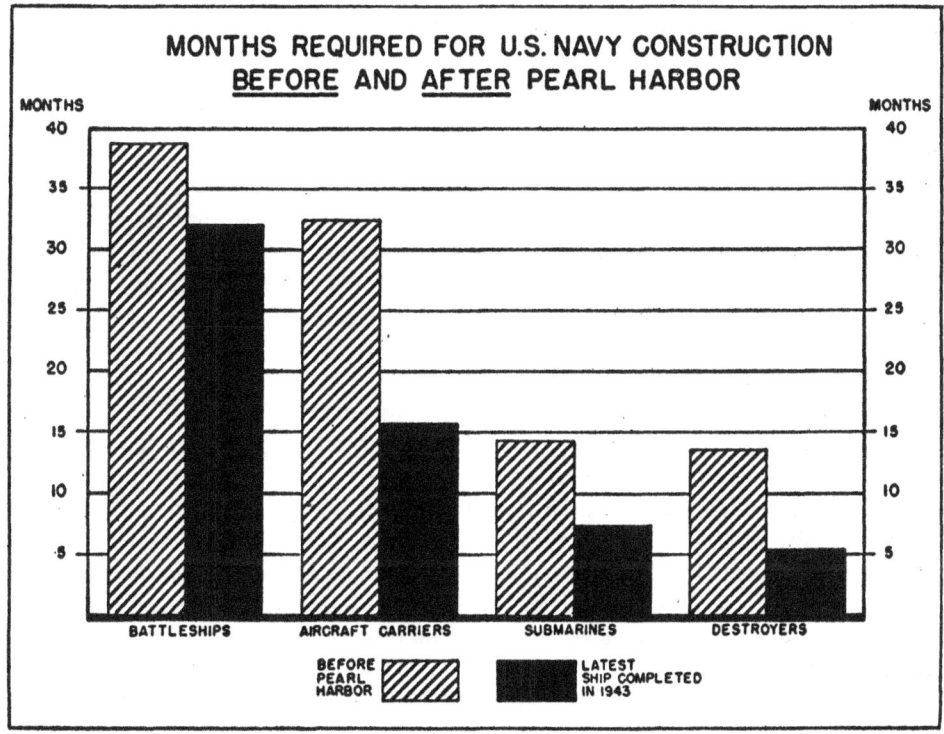

Plate 2.

we had originally anticipated, and to deal successfully with the submarine situation in the Atlantic. The former has, of course, meant a vast improvement in our military situation everywhere, and the latter was of great benefit to the shipping situation, which was very serious in the early months of the war and threatened to become more so with the prospective increases in overseas troop movements and their support. (See Plate 2.)

Immediately after the passage of the Two-Ocean Navy Bill, corresponding contracts for new construction were let and there were soon more warships and auxiliaries on the ways than had ever been under construction anywhere in the world at any one time. Simultaneously with this new construction, the conversion of merchant ships was being accomplished, one of the most important of these being the escort carriers which later proved so effective in combatting the German submarine campaign in the

Atlantic. It is interesting to note that the conversion of these ships was superimposed upon the shipbuilding effort following enactment of the Two-Ocean Navy Bill, it having been long appreciated that sea-borne aircraft would play a dominant role in overseas campaigns if and when war came.

With a construction program well under way, it was most important to keep alterations in design at a minimum in order to avoid delays. Nevertheless, changes which would increase military effectiveness or give greater protection to crews were not sacrificed for the sake of speeding up construction. Another consideration which industry had to take in its stride was the evolution of strategic plans and changes in the type of operations which made it necessary, from time to time, to shift the emphasis in construction from one type of ship to another. For example, when the war began our carrier strength was such that we could not stand much attrition. When, therefore, we suffered the loss of four of our largest aircraft carriers in the Coral Sea engagement, at Midway, and in the South Pacific, it was imperative that the construction of vessels of this category be pushed ahead at all possible speed. Shortly after we suffered the heavy loss in battleship strength at Pearl Harbor our battleships under construction at the time were given top priority. At another stage of the war, when the submarine situation in the Atlantic was a matter of great concern, emphasis was placed upon escort carriers and destroyer escort vessels. At the moment, major emphasis rests with the construction of landing craft, because we intend to use them in large numbers in future operations.

The production of aircraft quite naturally assumed proportions commensurate with the building program. Thanks to the research and experimentation that had been done in improving and perfecting the various types of airplanes, and thanks also to the genius of United States industry in the field of mass production, our air power increased with almost incredible rapidity as soon as our airplane factories were expanded and retooled for the various models of planes we needed. In view of the delays to be expected from changes in design when on a mass production basis, it was apparent that a nice timing in changes of design would be necessary, so that the performance of our aircraft would always be more than a match for anything produced by the enemy. A notable example is the change-over from the Grumman *Wildcat* to the Grumman *Hellcat*.

In order to obtain a properly balanced navy, the construction of combatant ships was supplemented by building patrol vessels, mine craft, landing craft and auxiliary vessels of all types. Some 55 building yards and yacht basins, located in practically all areas of the United States served by navigable waters, have participated in the patrol craft construction program.

No maritime nation has ever been able to fight a war successfully without an adequate merchant marine—something we did not have when the two-ocean Navy was authorized. The Maritime Commission therefore began a vast program of merchant ship construction at the same time we were expanding the Navy, and the merchant shipbuilding industry, too, faced an enormous expansion. Furthermore, the supply of materials necessary to complete the huge program had to be carefully allocated, in view of the country's other needs that had to be met. The Navy needed material to build ships and manufacture planes and equipment, the Army required the material for military purposes, and civilian needs could not be neglected. In order to control the allocation of material, the War Production Board was established by the President and decisions as to priorities have since been made by that agency.

Naturally, such a great undertaking involved thousands of business transactions on the part of the Navy Department, with the contracting builders and manufacturers. These transactions have been continuous, and have been entered into on the basis of statutes which limit the profits permissible, and provide for the negotiation and renegotiation of all contracts. This part of the program has, in itself, been a colossal job.

Battleships

At the beginning of the program ten battleships were under construction. By the time Pearl Harbor was attacked only two, NORTH CAROLINA and WASHINGTON, were in service, but since that time, six more have joined the fleet. These include SOUTH DAKOTA and three sister ships, INDIANA, MASSACHUSETTS, and ALABAMA, and two of a larger class, IOWA and NEW JERSEY. A third ship in the latter class, WISCONSIN, was launched 7 December 1943, appropriately enough, two years to the day after Pearl Harbor was attacked. In speed, in fire power, particularly antiaircraft fire, in maneuverability, and in protection, these ships represent a great advance over previous designs.

Aircraft Carriers

Construction of aircraft carriers represents one of the most spectacular phases of the naval shipbuilding program. The carrier strength of the Navy on 7 December 1941 was seven first-line vessels and one escort carrier, a converted merchant ship. Contracts had been placed for several large carriers of the new ESSEX class, and some of these had been laid down. Conversion of a number of merchant vessels was under way. The pressing need to add to our striking power in the air and to replace losses suffered in the Pacific during 1942 led to a great expansion of the construction program for first-line carriers. Concurrently, an even larger expansion of the escort carrier program was undertaken. By the end of 1943, more than 50 carriers of all types had been put into service in our Navy, and in addition a large number of escort carriers had been transferred to Great Britain.

This remarkable record in construction enabled us in a single year to build up our carrier strength from the low point reached in the autumn of 1942, when SARATOGA, ENTERPRISE and RANGER were the only ships of our fleet carrier forces remaining afloat, to a position of clear superiority in this category. The rapidity with which new carriers of various types were put into service in 1943 influenced naval operations in many important respects. Availability of several ships of the ESSEX class and of a considerable number of smaller carriers, completed months ahead of schedule, contributed to the success of our operations in the Southwest Pacific, aided materially in checking the submarine menace in the Atlantic, and enabled us to launch an offensive in the Central Pacific before the end of the year.

A large proportion of the ESSEX class carriers have joined the fleet. Excellent progress is being made on construction of the remaining ships in the original program and of the additional vessels in this class authorized after the Pearl Harbor attack. Nearly all of the carriers of the INDEPENDENCE class, converted from light cruisers, have been completed. These ships, though smaller than the ESSEX class vessels, are first-line carriers. It is planned to supplement these two basic types of carriers with a third, substantially larger than any of our present classes, which will displace 45,000 tons, and will be capable of handling bombing planes larger than any which heretofore have operated from the decks of aircraft carriers. They will be far more heavily armed than smaller carriers and will be much less vulnerable to bomb and torpedo attack.

The Navy's first escort carrier was the LONG ISLAND, converted early in 1941, from the merchant vessel MORMACMAIL. When experiments with this ship proved successful, a sizeable conversion program was initiated, using Maritime Commission C-3 hulls, and a number of oilers. In 1942, because of pressing need, this program was greatly expanded.

The "baby flat-tops" have three principal uses. They serve as antisubmarine escorts for convoys; as aircraft transports, delivering assembled aircraft to strategic areas; as combatant carriers to supplement the main air striking force of the fleet. Although their cruising speeds are lower than those of our first-line carriers, these auxiliary carriers can be turned out more rapidly and at a fraction of the cost of conventional carriers. These ships have proved invaluable in performing convoy escort and other duties for which larger and faster carriers are not needed.

Cruisers

The BALTIMORE class heavy cruisers, a number of which are now in service, were designed during the period from 19 July 1940 to 7 December 1941. These cruisers are considered as powerful as any heavy cruisers afloat, particularly as recent technical developments have made it possible to improve their fighting characteristics. The CLEVELAND type of light cruiser (a development of the BROOKLYN class) was approved for a large part of the cruiser program, its design having been completed just before the expansion was authorized. The design of the large ALASKA class was the result of a series of studies commenced when treaty limitations went by the board and we were no longer bound by any limitations on the size of ships.

Destroyers and Destroyer Escorts

The FLETCHER class of destroyers designed just after the outbreak of the war in Europe, formed a large part of the new destroyer building program. As compared with earlier destroyers, they are larger and have greatly increased fighting power, made possible by the same technical developments that permitted similar improvements in our cruisers.

Destroyer production has been highly satisfactory, and it has been possible to expand and accelerate this part of the program in an orderly manner. Although some new yards were engaged in building destroyers the increases were made possible by expanding facilities in yards which had had experience in destroyer construction. An idea of the acceleration in the rate of delivery of destroyers may be had by comparison with the figures for 1941 and 1943. In 1943, the rate was approximately eight times that of 1941. (See Plate 3.)

Contracts for the first destroyer escorts were let in November 1941. In January 1942, the program was increased, and as Germany stepped up the construction of

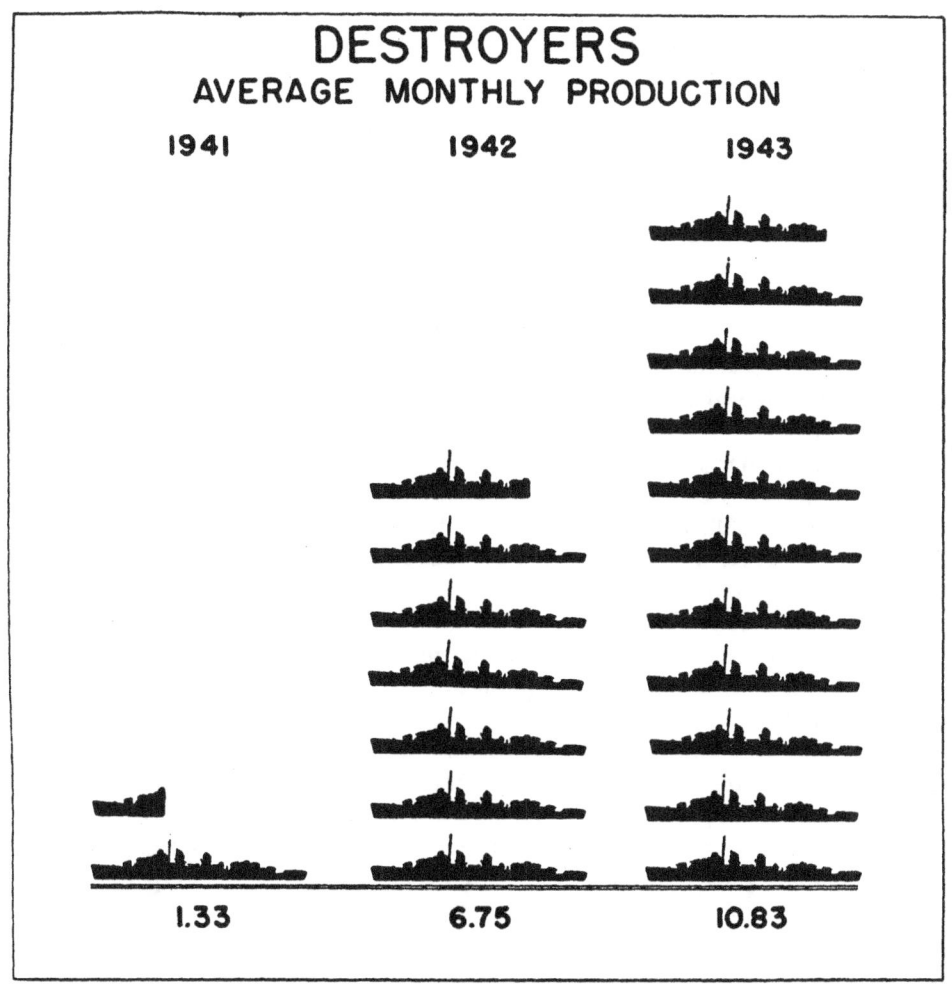

Plate 3.

u-boats several more increases were found necessary. Because of priorities the commencement of a large building program was delayed, but after delivery of the first vessel of the class, in February 1943, mass production methods became effective in the 17 building yards concerned. The result was a phenomenal output of those very useful vessels.

Submarines

As a result of the orderly progress which had been made in the construction of submarines, involving continuous trial under service conditions, the main problem to be solved in building more submarines was the expansion of facilities. For a period of 15 years or more, there were only three yards in the United States with the equipment and the know-how to build submarines. These were the Navy yards at Portsmouth, New Hampshire, and Mare Island, California, and the Electric Boat Company at Groton, Connecticut.

In addition to the expansion that took place at these yards, two other yards went into the production of submarines. One of these was the Cramp Shipbuilding Corporation of Philadelphia, Pennsylvania, and the other was the Manitowoc Shipbuilding Company at Manitowoc, Wisconsin. The building at the latter yard is a further testimonial to the ingenuity displayed throughout the entire program, in that submarines are built at Manitowoc, tested in the Great Lakes, then taken through the Chicago drainage canal, and down the Mississippi River to New Orleans, where they are made ready for sea.

Landing Craft

One of the most important achievements has been the landing craft construction program. Although the Navy had begun to experiment with small landing craft in 1936, we had only a few thousand tons in this category when we entered the war. In 1942, a billion dollar program for the construction of landing craft was superimposed on the already heavy building schedule, and the work was given top priority until the desired quota was filled. The facilities of existing public and private shipyards were given part of the burden. New yards were constructed, many of them in the Mississippi Valley, where bridge-building and steel-working companies which had had no previous experience in shipbuilding put up new plants and swung into production. In the second half of 1942, almost a quarter of a million tons of landing craft were produced, and the figure increased to well over a third of a million tons for the first half of 1943.

This production included a tremendous variety of vessels from small rubber boats to tank landing ships more than 300 feet in length. Within this range are small craft designed to carry only a few men, and ships with a capacity of 200, tracked craft capable of crawling over coral reefs or up beaches, craft for landing tanks or vehicles, craft for landing guns, craft for giving close fire support—in fact, all types necessary for success in that most difficult of military operations, landing on a hostile shore.

Airplanes

As a natural consequence of the importance of aviation in war, there has been a tremendous growth in the number of aircraft in the Navy.

Lessons learned in battle have been incorporated in the design of combat planes. New naval aircraft have larger engines and more power, increased protection for both crew and plane, and greater firepower than the models in service at the time of Pearl Harbor. The Grumman *Wildcat*, which served with distinction through the first year of the war, has been largely replaced by two new fighters—the Chance-Vought *Corsair* and the Grumman *Hellcat*. These two fighters were born of the war. While the *Corsair* existed as an experimental model before Pearl Harbor, it was so modified before going into production as to represent virtually a new plane. Offering greatly increased speed and firepower, the *Corsair* went into production in June 1942, and large numbers were being sent to the war fronts by the end of the year. The *Corsair* was followed, but in no sense succeeded by the *Hellcat*, which carries more armament and has greatly increased climbing ability. In production since November 1942, and in service with the fleet since September 1943, the *Hellcat* rounds out a powerful striking force for naval aviation. These two planes are superior to anything the Japanese have.

The Douglas *Dauntless* scout and dive bomber, in service when this country entered the war, has undergone successive modifications but is still in use. A new plane in this category—the Curtiss *Helldiver*—is now ready for the fighting front. This plane can carry a greatly increased bomb load, has more firepower, and is speedier than the *Dauntless*.

Twelve days after the attack on Pearl Harbor the Navy approved the final experimental model of a new torpedo bomber, the Grumman *Avenger*. Six weeks later, this plane began coming off the production line. Undergoing its baptism of fire at the Battle of Midway, it gradually replaced the Douglas *Devastator* and has now become almost an all-purpose plane for the fleet. The *Avenger* is a speedy, strongly protected, rugged aircraft capable of delivering a torpedo attack at sea or a heavy bomb load on land targets. Since it was first put into service, its defensive armament and auxiliary equipment have been improved, and a new model introducing other improvements is almost ready for volume production.

No field of aviation has been more important to the Navy than that of long range reconnaissance and patrol. After two years of war, the Consolidated *Catalina* flying boat remains in active service, having proved its usefulness in performing such varied tasks as night bombing patrol, rescues, antisubmarine warfare, and even dive bombing. Since Pearl Harbor, the *Catalina* has been supplemented by the Martin *Mariner*, a larger plane, which has likewise proved to be versatile in this field.

The Navy has made increasing use of land-based patrol airplanes because of the greater speed and range of newly developed models of this type and their greater defensive ability as compared with seaplanes. With more land bases becoming available, it has been possible to utilize them effectively for long over-water operations. Their superior offensive and defensive power makes them more valuable in antisubmarine warfare and for combat reconnaissance photography and patrol.

Two principal types of land-based patrol planes are now in service with the Navy—the four-engine Consolidated *Liberator* and the two-engine Vega *Ventura*. The Navy's version of the *Liberator* is an extremely useful plane for fast, long range reconnaissance, search and tracking. A new version, with more powerful defensive armament and greater offensive strength, soon will be available. The *Ventura* is a strongly armed aircraft which carries a heavy bomb load. It has proved a powerful weapon, particularly in the war against the submarine. Two other land-based bombers—the Lockheed *Hudson* and the Douglas *Havoc*—have seen limited service with the Navy and a third—the North American *Mitchell*—is in use by Marine air squadrons.

The principal plane used by the Navy for scout observation work during the war has been the Vought-Sikorsky *Kingfisher*. A newer plane in this field, now in service, is the Curtiss *Seagull*.

The field of air transport has been enormously expanded since the beginning of the war. The Naval Air Transport Service now operates, either directly or through contract with private airlines, more than 70,000 miles of scheduled flights to all parts of the globe, helping to maintain the Navy's long supply lines. Thus far, standard type transport planes have been used. In December 1943, however, the Martin *Mars*, world's largest flying boat, was accepted by the Navy after exhaustive tests which proved its ability to carry heavy loads at long range. Manufacture of the *Mars*, under a prime contract with the Navy, is now under way, and the first production planes of this type recently entered actual service as cargo carriers.

Auxiliaries

The tremendous increase in the number of fighting ships and the global nature of the war required the acquisition of a commensurately large fleet of auxiliaries. These ships were obtained by construction, by conversion of standard Maritime Commission commercial hulls and by acquisition and conversion of commercial vessels. A considerable number of conversions of standard Maritime Commission types have been accomplished under the supervision of the Maritime Commission. Probably the most important vessels produced under the auxiliary program during 1943 were those which take part in actual landing operations, consisting of attack transports, attack cargo vessels and general headquarters ships. The demand for repair ships of standard and special types, which increased many-fold during 1943, was met by new construction and conversion.

Patrol Craft

As previously stated, patrol vessels were necessary to a properly balanced Navy. The first group of patrol craft, whose design was developed before the war, was completed in the spring of 1942, and more than 600 vessels of this type were completed in 1943. Motor torpedo boats (which have been employed to good advantage in several different theaters) were produced at intervals in accordance with military requirements. The classification "Patrol Craft" includes the 110-foot sub-chaser and the 136- 173- and 184-foot steel vessels. The greatest emphasis on this type of ship prevailed prior to and during the German submarine offensive off our Atlantic Coast and in the Caribbean.

PERSONNEL

The expansion program and the additional requirements following the outbreak of war resulted in increases in personnel as follows. The figures given include officers and men and the Women's Reserve, but not officer candidates or nurses:

	8 September 1939	7 December 1941	31 December 1943
Navy	126,418	325,095	2,252,606
Marine Corps	19,701	70,425	391,620
Coast Guard	10,079	25,002	171,518

Taking the number of men indicated into an organization was in itself an enormous undertaking. Training them was an even greater undertaking, in spite of their high intelligence and the other characteristics which make the American fighting man the equal of any in the world.

Procurement of Officers

In time of peace the Navy is manned almost entirely by officers of the regular Navy, most of whom are graduates of the Naval Academy. Several years before the war, knowing that the Naval Academy would not be able to supply officers in sufficient quantities for wartime needs, the Navy established Naval Reserve Officer Training Corps units at various colleges throughout the country. Under the system set up, students were given the opportunity to take courses in naval science (which included training at sea during the summer months) and, upon successfully completing them, were commissioned in the Naval Reserve. When the limited emergency was declared, these officers were ordered to active duty, but when the war broke out it became apparent that the combined supply of commissioned officers from the Naval Academy and from ROTC units would not be sufficient to meet our needs for the rapidly expanding Navy.

In February 1942, therefore, offices of naval officer procurement were established in key cities throughout the country. Hundreds of thousands of officer candidates went to these offices and there presented their qualifications. With the requirements of health, character, personality and education duly considered, the applications of those who appeared qualified were forwarded to the Navy Department for final consideration. Under this procedure some 72,000 officers were commissioned in the Navy directly from civil life, to meet immediate needs.

Meanwhile, educational programs designed to produce commissioned officers had been established in numerous colleges throughout the country. Included were the aviation cadet program (v-5) principally for physically qualified high school graduates and college students, and later the Navy college program (v-12) which absorbed undergraduate students of the accredited college program (v-1) and of the reserve midshipman program (v-7). At the present time there are 66,815 members of the v-12 program in some 241 different colleges.

From the foregoing, it will be seen that high school graduates are now the Navy's principal source of young officers. Their training is described elsewhere in this report, but the various programs for Naval Reserve officers have supplied the fleet with large numbers, many of whom have already demonstrated their ability and the wisdom of the policy calling for their indoctrination and training before being sent to sea. Officers of the regular Navy are universally enthusiastic over the caliber of young reserve officers on duty in the fleet.

In general, procurement of officers has kept up with the needs of the service, with the exception of officers in the medical, dental, and chaplain corps and in certain highly specialized fields of engineering. As graduates of professional schools are the chief source of commissioned officers in the various staff corps and as there must be a balance between military and civilian needs, we are at present somewhat short of our commissioned requirements in certain branches of the service.

By comparison with the increase in size of the Naval Reserve, the increases in the regular Navy have been small. The output of the Naval Academy is at its peak, however, having been stepped up by shortening the course to three years and by increasing the number of appointments. In addition, during 1943, 20,652 officers have been made by the advancement of outstanding enlisted personnel.

Recruiting of Enlisted Personnel

When the President declared the existence of a limited emergency on 8 September 1939, the personnel strength of the Navy had been increased by calling retired officers and men to active duty and by giving active duty status to members of the Naval Reserve who volunteered for it. At the time the large naval expansion was authorized in July 1940, however, there were still only slightly more than 160,000 men in the Navy and by the end of that year only 215,000. As late as June 1941, the total was still well below 300,000, and it was apparent that a radical increase over and above the existing figure was an immediate necessity. Various measures were therefore taken to stimulate recruiting, by virtue of which the Navy strength stood at 290,000 on 7 December 1941. In other words, we doubled our personnel in two years.

Immediately after the attack on Pearl Harbor there was a large increase in enlistments, and by the end of that month some 40,000 additional men had been accepted for naval service. This heavy enlistment rate, however, experienced in December 1941 and January 1942, subsequently fell off at a time when the requirements were still mounting. In order to meet the situation and to provide an adequate method of recruiting the large numbers of men needed, our recruiting system, which had already been expanded, was fortified by a field force of officers commissioned directly from civil life, and by the fall of 1942, we were accepting each month a total equivalent to peacetime Navy strength.

On 5 December 1942, the voluntary enlistment of men between the ages of 18 and 37, inclusive, was ordered terminated as of 1 February 1943, on which latter date the manpower requirements of the Navy were supplied by operation of the machinery of the Selective Service system. During the period of active recruiting about 900,000 volunteers were accepted. Since 1 February 1943, 779,713 men have entered the Navy through Selective Service. During the same period voluntary enlistments within the age limits prescribed totalled 205,669.

On 1 June 1943 the Army and Navy agreed on joint physical standards which were somewhat lower than those previously followed by the Navy, but still sufficiently rigid to permit all inductees to be assigned to any type of duty afloat or ashore.

Training

Strictly speaking, it is probably true that training is a continuous process, which begins when an individual enters the Navy and ends when he leaves it. In time of peace the number of trained men in the Navy is relatively high. In time of war, however, particularly when we experience a personnel expansion such as has been described, trained men are at a premium. It is not an exaggeration to state that our success in this war will be in direct proportion to the state of training of our own forces.

When we entered the war we experienced a dilution in trained men in new ships because of the urgency of keeping trained men where fighting was in progress, and initial delays in getting underway with the huge expansion and training program had to be accepted. As the war progressed, and as the enemy offensive was checked, we were able to assign larger numbers of our trained men to train other men. Our ability to expand and train during active operations reflects the soundness of our peacetime training and organization. With that as a foundation on which to build, and with the tempo of all training stepped up, adequate facilities, standardized curricula, proper channeling of aptitude, full use of previous related knowledge, lucid instructions, and top physical condition became the criteria for wartime training.

Generally speaking, the first stage in the training of any new member of the Navy is to teach him what every member of the Navy must know, such as his relationship with others, the wearing of the uniform, the customs of the service, and how to take care of himself on board ship. The second stage involves his being taught a specialty and being thoroughly grounded in the fundamentals of that specialty. The third stage is to fit him into the organization and teach him to use his ability to the best advantage.

Commissioned Personnel

The over-all problem of training officers involves a great deal more than the education of the individual in the ways of the Navy. The first step is classification according to ability, which must be followed by appropriate assignment to duty. This is particularly true in the case of Reserve officers, who must be essentially specialists, because there is insufficient time to devote to the necessary education and training to make them qualified for detail to more than one type of duty.

As previously stated, ROTC units, which were part of the V-1 training program, had been established in various colleges, and courses in naval science, which included drills and summer cruises, were worked into the academic careers of the individuals enrolled. With the approach of war, the training of these students was shortened in most colleges to two and one-half years, and eventually they became part of the Navy college training program (V-12).

In 1935, the Congress authorized the training of naval aviation cadets, and that statutory authority was implemented by a program for their training, known as the V-5 program, which was open to physically qualified high school graduates and college students. Under the methods adopted, a decision as to whether or not a candidate would be accepted for the V-5 program was made by Naval Aviation Cadet Selection Boards, who were guided by high standards covering the educational, moral, physical and psychological qualifications of each individual. The period of training normally requires from 12 to 15 months, exclusive of additional college training required for 17-year-old students. Of this time, six to eight months are spent in preliminary training in physical education and ground school subjects at pre-flight schools. The remainder of the training consists of primary, intermediate and advanced flight training. Upon successful completion of the full flight training course, an aviation cadet is commissioned ensign in the Naval Reserve or second lieutenant in the Marine Corps Reserve and is then ordered to active duty as a pilot.

The V-12 (Navy college training) program was established on 1 July 1943. It consisted initially of students who were on inactive duty in the Naval Reserve, new students from civilian life, and young enlisted men especially selected. The new students from civilian life consist of selected high school graduates or others with satisfactory educational qualifications who can establish by appropriate examination their mental, physical and potential officer qualifications. These students are then inducted into the Navy as apprentice seamen or as privates, United States Marine Corps, placed on active duty, and assigned to designated colleges and universities to follow courses of study specified by the Navy Department.

v-12 training embodies most of the features of preceding Naval Reserve programs. Depending on training requirements, and with the exception of medical and dental officers, engineering specialists, and chaplains, length of courses vary from two to six semesters. The courses of study include fundamental college work in mathematics, science, English, history, naval organization and general naval indoctrination for the first two terms for all students. This is followed by specialized training in a particular field, assignment of a student to special training being based upon his choice and upon his demonstrated competence in the field chosen, subject to available quotas. Upon satisfactory completion of college training, students are assigned to further training in the Navy, Marine Corps or Coast Guard, and if found qualified after completion of that training they are commissioned in the appropriate reserve.

So far, the v-12 program has worked well. It permits the selection of the country's best qualified young men on a broad democratic basis without regard for financial resources, and the induction and training of those young men who show the greatest promise of having superior ability and the other qualities likely to make a good officer.

The link between the College Training Program and the fleets is the Naval Reserve Midshipman Program. The Navy college graduates who are going to deck and engineering duties with the forces afloat are sent to one of the six reserve midshipman schools for a four months' course. Upon the successful completion of the first month's study, they are appointed reserve midshipmen, and after the remaining three months' intensive training, they are appointed ensigns in the Naval Reserve.

Originally four Reserve midshipmen schools were established, located at Columbia University, Northwestern University, Notre Dame, and the Naval Academy. The program has been such an outstanding success, and the demand for its graduates has so increased, that two additional schools recently have been put into commission, at Cornell and at Plattsburg, New York, with the result that there are nearly 9,000 men in this training program at any one time. The combined result of the College Training Program and the Reserve Midshipman Program is to meet the need of the fleets for thoroughly trained young deck and engineering officers.

Enlisted Personnel

Recruit training, in addition to the instruction given the individual in the ways of the Navy, consists of his being fully informed of the training opportunities open to him. This is followed by a series of tests designed to determine the ability of each recruit. These tests are based on the type of duty to be performed in the Navy, and in addition to such tests as the general classification test, consists of a systematic determination of aptitudes in reading and mechanical ability and any knowledge of specific work. Through a system of personal interviews these tests are supplemented by considering the background and experience of the individual, so that the special qualifications of each recruit may be evaluated. This information is then indexed and recorded and used in establishing quotas for the detail of men to special service schools or to any other duty for which they seem best qualified.

While the recruit is learning about the Navy, therefore, the Navy is learning about him. A practical application of this system was the assembly of the crew for NEW JERSEY, a new battleship. While the ship was fitting out, a series of tests and a thorough study of the requirements of each job on board were conducted. For example, special tests determined those best fitted to be telephone talkers or night lookouts or gun captains, and as a result, when the crew went aboard each man was assigned to a billet in keeping with his aptitude for it.

As permanent establishments, we had four training stations—Newport, Rhode Island; Norfolk, Virginia; Great Lakes, Illinois, and San Diego, California. As soon as we entered the war it became apparent that it would be necessary to expand these four stations radically and to establish others. By November 1942, we had expanded the four permanent training stations and established new ones at Bainbridge, Maryland; Sampson, New York, and Farragut, Idaho.

The training in the fundamentals of the specialty to be followed by a newcomer to the Navy is carried on ashore and afloat. Recruits showing the most aptitude for a particular duty are sent to special service schools designed to give the individual a thorough grounding in his specialty before assuming duties on board ship. If he hopes to become an electrician's mate he may be assigned to the electrical school; if a machinist's mate, to the machinist's mate school; if a commissary steward, to the cook's and baker's school, and so forth. Approximately 32 per cent of those who receive recruit training are assigned to special service schools.

An advanced type of training is given men who are already skilled in a specialty by assembling them and training them to work as a unit. This is known as operational training, and in addition to the special meaning of the term as applied to aviation training, it encompasses such special activities as bomb disposal units as well as the training of ship's crews before the ship is commissioned.

When the individual goes on board ship, he discovers that his training has only begun, because he must learn how to apply the knowledge he has already gained and how his performance of duty fits into the organization of the ship. This is another form of operational training—conducted, of course, by the forces afloat—which is a preliminary to the assignment of that ship as a unit of the fleet. This does not mean that the ship is fully trained, but it means that the training is sufficiently advanced to fit the crew for the additional training and seasoning that comes only with wartime operations at sea. With the proper background of training, the most efficient ship is very likely to be the one which has been in action. In other words, actual combat is probably the best training of all, provided the ship is ready for it.

Health

The health of the personnel in our naval forces has been uniformly excellent. In addition, the treatment and prevention of battle casualties has become progressively better.

The Medical Corps of the Navy has not only kept up with scientific developments everywhere, but it has taken the lead in many fields. The use of sulfa drugs, blood plasma and penicillin, plus the treatment of war neuroses, probably represent the outstanding medical accomplishments of the war, but all activities requiring medical attention have been under continuous study.

For example, the conditions under which submarines must operate have been found to require special diet, air conditioning, sun lamps, special attention to heat fatigue, and careful selection of personnel. Similarly, in the field of aviation medicine, such matters as supply of oxygen, decompression treatment, acceleration stresses, air sickness, and fatigue, require the closest attention. In the case of aviation medicine, flight surgeons, who are themselves qualified naval aviators and therefore familiar with all aviation problems, have been instrumental in keeping our aviation personnel at the peak of their efficiency.

Naval mobile hospitals were developed shortly before the war. These are complete units, capable of handling any situation requiring medical attention. Each unit contains officers of the Medical Corps, the Dental Corps, the Hospital Corps, the Nurse Corps, the Supply Corps, the Civil Engineer Corps and the Chaplain Corps, and in addition, enlisted personnel of a wide variety of non-medical ratings such as electricians, cooks, and bakers. Mobile hospitals are organized and commissioned, and being mobile as the name implies, are placed under the orders of the Commander in Chief, United States Fleet, for such duty as may be deemed desirable, the same as a ship. These mobile hospitals have proved invaluable in all theaters.

While it is hardly possible to single out any one activity as outstanding, the practice of evacuating sick and wounded personnel from forward areas by plane to be treated elsewhere has been estimated to have increased the efficiency of treatment by about one-third. The beneficial effects of this practice on our ability to carry on a prolonged campaign, such as in the Solomon Islands, are obvious.

There have been many more contributions to our military efficiency having to do with not only medicine, but health in general. The question of malaria control in the Solomon Islands, protective clothing, the survival of personnel in lifeboats, the purification of drinking water, the treatment of flash burns, the recording by tag of first aid treatment received in the field, and periodic thorough physical examinations are a few of the progressive measures which, collectively, have been responsible for marked increases in our military efficiency.

THE MARINE CORPS

Statistics previously given indicate the personnel expansion of the Marine Corps. In terms of combat units those figures represent a ground combat strength of two half-strength divisions and seven defense battalions expanded to four divisions, 19 defense battalions and numerous force and Corps troop organizations and service units; 12 aviation squadrons expanded to 85; and increases in ships detachments to keep pace with the ship construction program. Under the leadership of Lieutenant General (now General, Retired) T. H. Holcomb, USMC, the Marine Corps successfully met the greatest test in its history by forging a huge mass of untrained officers and men into efficient tactical units especially organized, equipped, and trained for the complicated amphibious operations which have characterized the war in the Pacific.

Training of the expanding Marine Corps personnel had to be conducted by stages because existing bases were inadequate in housing, space, and facilities. Basic training for all Marines was continued at the established recruit depots at Parris Island, South Carolina, and San Diego, California. Specialized advanced training for ground and aviation personnel before being assigned to combat units was conducted chiefly at Camp Lejeune, New River, North Carolina; at Camp Elliott, near San Diego, California; and at Camp Pendleton, Oceanside, California. Improvised facilities were used at those three bases until they had been developed into centers capable of affording training in all the basic and special techniques required in amphibious warfare. The final stage of training began with assignment of personnel to combat units and ended with the movement of those units to combat areas. (The effectiveness of individual and unit training of the Marine Corps was first demonstrated at Guadalcanal and Tulagi, eight months after the beginning of the war. That first test showed Marine Corps training methods to be sound and capable of producing combat units in a minimum of time.)

The commissioned personnel of the expanding Marine Corps were initially obtained from reservists and graduates of the Marine Corps Schools at Quantico. Later, commissioned personnel were obtained by including the Marine Corps in the Navy v-12 program, by selecting candidates from graduates of designated colleges and universities, and by increasing the number of enlisted men promoted to commissioned rank.

Marine Corps aviation, while expanding to a greater degree than the Corps as a whole, has continued to specialize in the providing of air support to troops in landing or subsequent ground operations. Training and organization in the United States and excellent equipment have made it possible to operate planes from hastily constructed airfields with limited facilities. The generally excellent performance of Marine aviation squadrons operating from forward bases in the Central and South Pacific areas in successful attacks against enemy aircraft, men-of-war, and shipping attests the soundness of the organization.

In November 1942, the Marine Corps Women's Reserve was established, the authorized strength being 1000 commissioned and 18,000 enlisted women, to be reached by 30 June 1944. By 31 December 1943 there were 609 officers and 12,592 enlisted women in the organization, all of whom have released male Marines for service in combat areas. The remarks relating to the performance of duty of the WAVES, contained in that part of this report covering their organization and training, are equally applicable to women in the Marine Corps.

Participation of Marines in combat is covered in Part III of this report.

THE COAST GUARD

The duties of the Coast Guard under naval administration consist of the civil functions normally performed by the Coast Guard in time of peace which become military functions in time of war, and the performance of naval duties for which the personnel of the Coast Guard are particularly fitted by reason of their peacetime employment. The organization operates separately with respect to appropriations required for Coast Guard vessels, shore stations, and personnel.

The increase in the size of the Coast Guard was necessitated chiefly by additional duties in connection with captain-of-the-port activities in the regulation of merchant shipping, the supervision of the loading of explosives, and the protection of shipping, harbors, and waterfront facilities. In addition, the complements of Coast Guard vessels and shore establishments were brought up to wartime strength; certain transports and other naval craft, including landing barges, were manned by Coast Guard personnel; and a beach patrol (both mounted and afoot) and coastal lookout stations were established. The Coast Guard also undertook the manning and operating of Navy section bases and certain inshore patrol activities formerly manned by naval personnel, and furnished sentries and sentry dogs for guard duty at various naval shore establishments.

Coast Guard aviation, which is about three times its previous size, has been under the operational control of sea frontier commanders for convoy coverage and for antisubmarine patrol and rescue duties. Other squadrons outside of the United States are employed in ice observation and air-sea rescue duty. Miscellaneous duties assigned to Coast Guard aviation include aerial mapping and checking for the Coast and Geodetic Survey and ice observation assistance on the Great Lakes.

The assignment of certain Coast Guard personnel to duties radically different from those they normally perform required numerous changes in ratings. This resulted in extensive classification and retraining programs designed to prepare men for their new duties. The replacement of men on shore jobs by SPARS, both officer and enlisted, has been undertaken as a part of this retraining program. Approximately 10,000 SPARS—whose performance of duty and value to the service is on a par with that of the WAVES and the women of the Marine Corps—will be commissioned and enlisted when the contemplated strength of that organization is reached.

The present strength of the Coast Guard was attained by the establishment of the Coast Guard Reserve and by commissioning warrant officers and enlisted men for temporary service. Other increases in the commissioned personnel of the Coast Guard have been accomplished by appointments made direct from civil life in the case of individuals with particular qualifications, such as special knowledge in the prevention and control of fires, police protection and merchant marine inspection.

A feature peculiar to the Coast Guard is the Temporary Reserve, which consists of officers and enlisted men enrolled to serve without pay. Members of the Temporary Reserve have full military status while engaged in the performance of such duties as pilotage, port security, the guarding of industrial plants, either on a full or part-time basis. At the present time there are about 70,000 members of the Temporary Reserve, but it is anticipated that it will eventually be reduced to about 50,000. The Coast Guard Auxiliary, which is a civilian organization, has contributed much of its manpower to the Temporary Reserve, the result being a substantial saving in manpower to the military services.

Under the general direction of Vice Admiral (now Admiral) R. R. Waesche, USCG, Commandant, the Coast Guard has done an excellent job in all respects, and as a component part of the Navy in time of war, has demonstrated an efficiency and flexibility which has been invaluable in the solution of the multiplicity of problems assigned. The organization and handling of local defense in the early days of the war were particularly noteworthy.

THE SEABEES

For some months before the Japanese attacked Pearl Harbor we had been strengthening our insular outposts in the Pacific by construction of various fortifications. When these islands were attacked by the Japanese, the construction was only partially completed, and the civilians who were employed there by various construction companies were subjected to attack, along with our garrisons of Marines.

In that situation, the civilians were powerless to aid the military forces present because they lacked the weapons and the knowledge of how to use them. Furthermore, they lacked what little protection a military uniform might have given them. As a consequence, the Navy Department decided to establish and organize naval construction battalions whose members would be not only skilled construction workers but trained fighters as well.

On 28 December 1941 authorization was obtained for the first contingent of "Seabees" (the name taken from the words "Construction Battalions") and a recruiting campaign was begun. The response was immediate, and experienced men representing about 60 different trades were enlisted in the Navy and given ratings appropriate to the degree and type of their civilian training.

After being enlisted these men were sent to training centers where they were given an intensive course in military training, toughened physically, and in general educated in the ways of the service. Particular attention was paid to their possible employment in amphibious operations. Following their initial training, the Seabees were formed into battalions, so organized that each could operate as a self-sustained unit and undertake any kind of base building assignment. They were sent to advance base depots for outfitting and for additional training before being sent overseas.

The accomplishments of the Seabees have been one of the outstanding features of the war. In the Pacific, where the distances are great and the expeditious construction of bases is frequently of vital importance, the construction accomplished by the Seabees has been of invaluable assistance. Furthermore, the Seabees have participated in practically every amphibious operation undertaken thus far, landing with the first waves of assault troops to bring equipment ashore and set up temporary bases of operation.

In the Solomon Islands campaign, the Seabees demonstrated their ability to outbuild the Japs and to repair airfields and build new bases, regardless of conditions of weather. Other specialized services performed by the Seabees include the handling of pontoon gear, the repair of motor vehicles, loading and unloading of cargo vessels, and in fact every kind of construction job that has to be done.

At present the Seabees number slightly more than 240,000, nearly half of whom are serving overseas at various outposts. Fleet commanders have been and are generous in their praise and appreciation of the work done by construction battalions everywhere. There can be no doubt that the Seabees constitute an invaluable component of our Navy.

THE WAVES

Early in 1942, when the need for expansion of naval personnel became acute, the Navy Department proposed to the Congress that there be established, as an integral part of the Navy, a Women's Reserve. The stated purpose of the proposal was to employ women in shore billets, so that men could be released for sea duty. Acting on that recommendation, the Women's Reserve was established on 30 July 1942, and the organization became known as the WAVES, the name being derived from the expression "Women Accepted for Volunteer Emergency Service." In November 1943, certain statutory changes were made which provided for women becoming eligible for all allowances or benefits to which men are entitled, and made certain alterations in the composition of the organization, chiefly with respect to promotions.

Initial plans called for 1000 officers and 10,000 enlisted women, and immediately upon obtaining the necessary statutory authority for the organization, officer training schools were established, at Northampton and South Hadley, Massachusetts, utilizing the facilities of Smith and Mount Holyoke Colleges. At the same time, a training school for yeomen was established at Stillwater, Oklahoma, one for radio personnel at Madison, Wisconsin, and one for storekeepers at Bloomington, Indiana. Under the procedure followed at that time all WAVES went to one of these schools immediately after joining the Navy, and upon the successful completion of their training, to duty somewhere in the continental United States where they could take the place of men.

All officer candidates now go to Northampton for their indoctrinational training and may then receive further training elsewhere—there are 16 schools for special training—in communications, supply, aerological engineering, Japanese language, radio and electronics, chemical warfare, general ordnance and photographic interpretation, and many others, including air navigation, air gunnery, and ship and aircraft recognition.

All enlisted WAVES now go to a general indoctrination school at Hunter College in New York City, and there receive their basic training. Further training at some other school—there are now 19 of them—designed to train them in their chosen specialty, is now standard practice. Enlisted personnel are trained as radio operators, yeomen, storekeepers, for various aviation ratings, and for many others, including pharmacist's mate. Approximately one-fourth of all enlisted women are now on duty with naval aviation activities.

On 31 December 1943 there were 6,459 commissioned WAVES and 40,391 enlisted WAVES serving in various capacities. Present plans call for nearly 100,000 WAVES by the end of 1944.

The organization has been a success from the beginning, partly because of the high standards WAVES had to meet to be accepted, partly because no effort has been spared to see that they are properly looked out for, and partly because of their overpowering desire to make good. As a result of their competence, their hard work, and their enthusiasm, the release of men for sea duty has been accompanied in many cases, particularly in offices, by increases in efficiency. The natural consequence is an *esprit de corps* which enhances their value to the Navy, and it is a pleasure to report that in addition to their having earned an excellent reputation as a part of the Navy, they have become an inspiration to all hands in naval uniform.

III

Combat Operations

General

ORGANIZATION OF THE UNITED STATES FLEET

ON 1 February 1941, command afloat in the high echelons was vested in three Commanders in Chief, one of whom commanded the Asiatic Fleet, one the Pacific Fleet, and one the Atlantic Fleet, provision being made whereby one of these three, depending on the circumstances, would act as Commander in Chief, United States Fleet, chiefly for purposes of standardization. In case two or more fleets operated together, he would coordinate their operations. At the time Pearl Harbor was attacked, the Commander in Chief of the Pacific Fleet was also Commander in Chief of the United States Fleet.

Almost immediately after our entry in the war it became apparent that for the purpose of exercising command all oceans must be regarded as one area, to the end that effective coordinated control and the proper distribution of our naval power might be realized. On 18 December 1941, therefore, the President changed this organization by making the Commander in Chief, United States Fleet, separate and distinct and in addition to the other three Commanders in Chief, and ordered the Headquarters of the Commander in Chief, United States Fleet, established in the Navy Department in Washington.

As of 1 January 1942, Admiral H. R. Stark was Chief of Naval Operations, Admiral (now Fleet Admiral) E. J. King was Commander in Chief of the United States Fleet, Admiral T. C. Hart was Commander in Chief of the Asiatic Fleet, Admiral (now Fleet Admiral) C. W. Nimitz, who relieved Admiral H. E. Kimmel late in December 1941, was Commander in Chief of the Pacific Fleet, and Vice Admiral (now Admiral) R. E. Ingersoll was Commander in Chief of the Atlantic Fleet.

In March 1942, (coincident with my appointment as such) the duties of the Chief of Naval Operations were combined with the duties of the Commander in Chief, United States Fleet. Admiral Stark, who had so ably performed the duties of Chief of Naval Operations during the vital period preceding the war, became commander of United States Naval Forces in Europe. This move was accompanied by a number of adjustments in the Navy Department organization, calculated, among other things, to facilitate the logistic support of the forces afloat by providing for its coordination. Except for the fact that the Asiatic Fleet ceased to exist as such in June 1942, that basic organization of the United States Fleet and supporting activities is still in effect. In the spring of 1942, however, and from time to time thereafter, independent commands were established directly under the Commander in Chief, United States Fleet.

Organization Within Each Fleet

In time of peace, for purposes of standardization, and to facilitate training and administration, our forces afloat operate under what is known as a type organization. Each fleet is subdivided according to types of ships in that fleet (this includes shore-based naval aircraft), and in general, the officers assigned to command each subdivision are the next echelon below the Commander in Chief of a fleet. The "type commands" are primarily for administrative purposes. For operations, vessels and aircraft of appropriate types are formed into operating commands known as "task forces."

Sea Frontiers

As of 1 February 1941, Naval Coastal Frontiers consisted of one or more Naval Districts, depending on their geographical location, and Naval Coastal Frontier forces were administrative and task organizations. Commanders of those forces were responsible to the Navy Department for administrative purposes and to the Chief of Naval Operations for task purposes.

On 20 December 1941 the operating forces of Naval Coastal Frontiers were placed under the command of the Commander in Chief, United States Fleet.

On 6 February 1942 Naval Coastal Frontiers became Sea Frontiers, and Commanders of Sea Frontiers were made responsible to the Commander in Chief, United States Fleet, for that portion of their commands comprising ships and aircraft duly allocated as Sea Frontier forces. For the portion comprising ships and aircraft allocated by the Chief of Naval Operations as local defense forces, they were made responsible to the Chief of Naval Operations.

The foregoing change in designation of Naval Coastal Frontiers is not to be confused with the designation "Coastal Frontier." The latter, of which Sea Frontiers form a part, are coastal divisions with geographically coterminous boundaries within which an Army officer and a naval officer exercise command over their respective forces and activities.

In continental United States there are four sea frontiers: the Eastern, covering the Atlantic seaboard; the Gulf, covering the Gulf of Mexico; the Western, which takes in the southern part of the Pacific Coast; and the North West, which covers the northern part of the Pacific Coast.

Advance Base Units

Early in the war the Navy undertook a large expansion of its system of advance bases, many of which represented the consolidation of gains made by combat units. Depending on the circumstances, that is to say, whether they were gained as a result of a raid or as a result of an advance, the permanency of their construction was varied to meet the situation. In the south and central Pacific, the entire campaign thus far has been a battle for advance bases where we can establish supply ports, ship repair facilities and landing fields to act as a backstop for a continuing offensive.

Advance bases range in size from small units for the maintenance and repair of PT boats, manned by a handful of officers and men, to major bases comprising floating drydocks, pattern ships, foundries, fully equipped machine shops, and electrical shops, staffed by thousands of specialists. Some of these bases are general purpose bases; others are established for special purposes. Convoy escort bases, located at terminals of the convoy routes, provide fuel, stores, ammunition, and repair facilities for merchant ships and their escort vessels. Rest and recuperation centers afford naval personnel facilities for relaxation and recreation after they return from combat zones. Air stations provide the facilities of an aircraft carrier on an expanded scale.

Once bases are built, they must be maintained. The problem of supplying the Navy's worldwide system of advance bases is one of great complexity, requiring a high degree of administrative coordination and attention to the most minute detail. Food, clothing, fuel, ammunition, spare parts, tools, and many types of special equipment must be made available in sufficient quantities and at the proper times to maintain the fighting efficiency of the fleet.

In view of the difficulties involved, the arrangements made for the procurement and distribution of supplies to advance bases have been extremely effective. New methods have been improvised and shortcuts devised to simplify procedures and expedite deliveries. Among other devices adopted is the mail order catalogue system. Through use of the Navy's "functional component catalogue," it is possible to order all the parts and equipment needed to set up any type of base from a small weather observation post to a fully equipped airfield or Navy yard.

As our forces advance, new bases must be established and economy of personnel and material demands that this be accomplished largely by stripping the old bases that have been left behind as the front is extended. This process is known as "rolling up the back areas."

FIGHTING EFFICIENCY

When Pearl Harbor was attacked, the forces comprising the Atlantic Fleet had been engaged with Axis submarines, but the forces comprising the Asiatic and Pacific Fleets had not been previously engaged in combat. In the case of all ships everywhere, the transition from a state of peace to a state of war involved a great number of immediate changes, some of which could not possibly be made until our ships had been in action. For example, we profited from experiences gained after the war started with respect to the use of certain of our weapons in actual combat. Such things as depth charges and explosive charges in torpedoes and shells were put to the real test by our forces, and all personnel have become accordingly familiar with their handling and use. We also learned from experience the best practice in such matters as the painting and preservation of the interior of ships, camouflage, deficiencies and improvement of equipment, and from time to time what new contributions were of value. The most valuable of all experience has been that gained with respect to the operational technique in such fields as air combat, amphibious operations, and escort of convoys.

The war was also the real test of the training methods we had followed in time of peace, particularly the exercise of initiative by officers. As used in connection with the exercise of command, initiative means freedom to act, but it does not mean freedom to act in an off-hand or casual manner. It does not mean freedom to disregard or depart unnecessarily from standard procedures or practices or instructions. There is no degree of being "independent" of the other component parts of the whole—the fleet. It means freedom to act only after all of one's resources in education, training, experience, skill and understanding have been brought to bear on the work in hand. This requires intense application in order that what is to be done shall be done as a correlated part of a connected whole—much as a link of a chain or the gear within a machine.

In other words, our officers had been indoctrinated and were now in larger measure on their own. Most of those officers understood perfectly the transition that becomes automatic when we passed from the peacetime to the wartime status, but it was thought desirable to define and emphasize the standards expected in time of war, not only to confirm their understanding, but for the benefit of newcomers. Without correct exercise of the principle calling for initiative on the part of the subordinate, decentralization, which is so essential, and which is premised on division of labor, will not work.

CALCULATED RISK

The ability of a naval commander to make consistently sound military decisions is the result of a combination of attributes. The natural talent of the individual, his temperament, his reactions in emergencies, his courage, and his professional knowledge all contribute to his proficiency and to the accuracy of his judgment. We have spent years training our officers to think clearly and for themselves, to the end that when entrusted with the responsibility of making decisions in time of war they would be fully qualified.

One of the mental processes that has become almost a daily responsibility for all those in command is that of calculating the risks involved in a given course of action. That may mean the risks attendant upon disposition of forces, such as had to be taken before the Battle of Midway, when an erroneous evaluation might have left us in a most unfavorable strategic position; the risks of losses in contemplated engagements, such as the Battle of Guadalcanal on 13–14–15 November 1942; the risks of success or failure dependent upon correct evaluation of political conditions, of which the North African landings are an example, and a host of others.

Calculating risks does not mean taking a gamble. It is more than figuring the odds. It is not reducible to a formula. It is the analysis of all factors which collectively indicate whether or not the consequences to ourselves will be more than compensated for by the damage to the enemy or interference with his plans. Correct calculation of risks, by orderly reasoning, is the responsibility of every naval officer who participates in combat, and many who do not. It is a pleasure to report that almost universally that responsibility is not only accepted, but sought, and that there have been few cases where it has not been properly discharged.

LOGISTICS

The war has been variously termed a war of production and a war of machines. Whatever else it is, so far as the United States is concerned, it is a war of logistics. The ways and means to supply and support our forces in all parts of the world—including

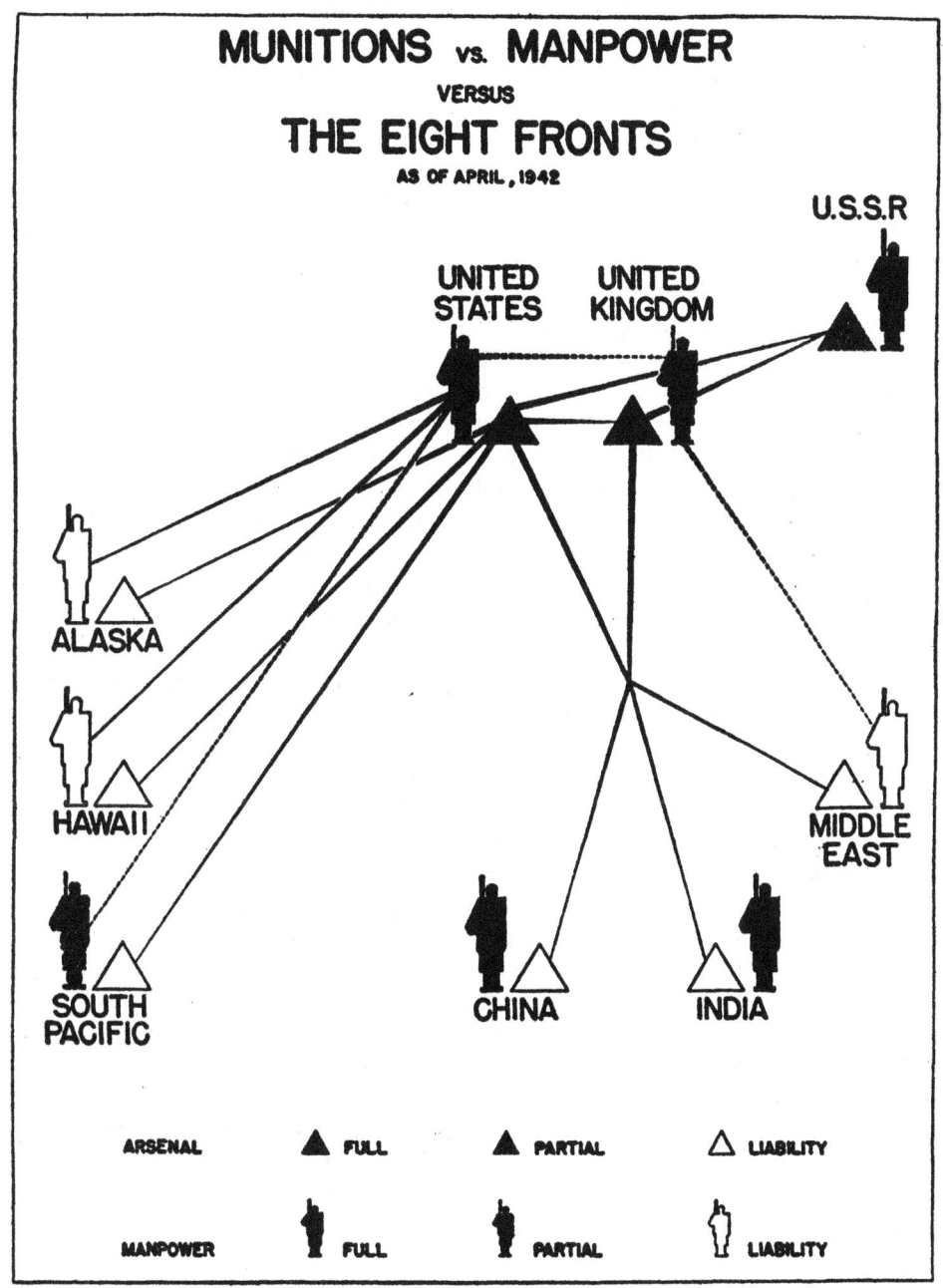

Plate 4.

the Army—of course—have presented problems nothing short of colossal, and have required the most careful and intricate planning. The profound effect of logistic problems on our strategic decisions is described elsewhere in this report, but to all who do not have to traverse them, the tremendous distances, particularly those in the Pacific, are not likely to have full significance. It is no easy matter in a global war to have the right materials in the right places at the right times in the right quantities.

Superimposed on the shipping requirements for the overhead of logistic needs has been the transportation of Army troops and the demands of lend-lease. The combination of circumstances has made shipping a question of primary importance which has been reflected in the shipbuilding industry and the merchant marine.

When war was declared, an immediate estimate of the situation with respect to material was made, as a result of which we could see that, no matter how much material was produced within the next year, it would not be enough. Therefore, with the idea of doing the first thing first, every effort was made to produce as much material as possible of all kinds, with the idea that as the war progressed our estimates could be revised to fit our needs. Stock piles of spare parts and materials needed for routine maintenance and repair of ships and aircraft were therefore established at advance bases, additional supplies being delivered under regular schedule.

Plate 4 is an over-generalization of the situation which existed in April 1942 with respect to the relationships involving munitions, manpower, and the eight fronts. From an examination of the diagram it will be seen that in order to keep our operating forces balanced in such a way as to conform to our planned operations, we had to maintain a continuous flow of munitions and manpower from sources of supply. The quantities involved, of course, had to be varied in accordance with the importance of any particular front, that is to say, the urgency of a particular campaign or operation. It is interesting to note that the United States was, and is, the only nation represented as having a full supply of both munitions and manpower.

It became possible to anticipate the needs for material much more accurately after we had been in the war a little over a year, and numerous changes were made in the methods of controlling the flow to the operating forces.

In supplying the forces afloat with the material they need, different methods are required. For example, spare parts and materials can be put on a regular schedule, but in distributing battle damage spares, which consist of complete units of pumps, turbines, boilers, turbo generators, steering gear and other assemblies, it has been found advantageous to keep them in stock at depots in the United States, and to effect immediate delivery to points where they are needed. For example, on one occasion a damaged submarine put into a distant base for extensive replacement of her main drive controls and power cables. Within thirty-six hours after receiving the information covering her needs a transport plane loaded with nine tons of parts took off for the advance base.

CHARACTER

While every kind of naval warfare has been experienced, with naval air power more often than not predominating, the war to date has to a degree become characterized by numerous amphibious operations—a method of warfare with which the Japanese had had considerable experience. Our previous conclusions that this type of warfare required a technique of its own involving the closest coordination of all forces engaged—land, sea and air—have been confirmed. The very exigencies of such operations have done much to promote effective cooperation between those forces, and they have also made all hands realize that the uniform they wear signifies first that they are members of United States forces, and second that they are members of a particular unit of those forces. The inevitable solution to successful amphibious warfare is unified command, under which system all those participating are under the command of the individual best qualified to conduct the operation regardless of his status in our armed forces.

Strategy

The trend of events during the two years following the outbreak of war in Europe indicated that the war would eventually engulf the United States and become global in all its aspects. In keeping with that trend, the growing truculence of Japan and the continuous clash of Japan's policies with the policies of the United States made it likely that that country would enter the war at the most propitious moment. Because of that attitude, we were forced to retain the major part of our naval strength in the Pacific, in spite of the unfavorable situation in Europe reflecting the possibility of the need of our naval strength in the Atlantic. We were therefore placed in an unfavorable strategic position, in that our naval forces at that time were not adequate to meet the demands in both oceans should we be forced into the war.

The sudden treacherous attack by Japan, which resulted in heavy losses to us, made our unfavorable strategic position at the outbreak of war even worse than we had anticipated. Had we not suffered those losses, however, our fleet could not have proceeded to Manila as many people supposed and there relieved our hard pressed forces. Such an undertaking at that time, with the means at hand to carry it out and support it, would have been disastrous.

Although we had made some progress, and had for some months been increasing our defenses in the Western Hemisphere, our armed forces and our production were not adequately expanded and developed to permit our taking the overall offensive in any theater. The Army ground and air forces and our shipping were not yet prepared to move overseas in sufficient strength for an offensive, and the Navy, even without the losses sustained at Pearl Harbor, could not alone carry the war to the enemy. We were therefore forced to assume the defensive in both oceans, while preparations for an amphibious war were intensified.

Our strategy in the Atlantic involved maintaining our lines of communications to Great Britain and to future bases of operations against our enemies in Europe, in addition to insuring the security of the Western Hemisphere. The control of the Atlantic was being vigorously contested by German submarine and air forces, while the Axis surface forces constituted a threat of no mean proportions. To meet the situation we trained men and manned ships and aircraft as soon as we could in order to assume the offensive. By the end of 1942, we were ready and moved overseas in force with the Army.

By the spring of 1943, the war against German submarines in the Atlantic had turned in our favor and we were fully on the offensive in that area. Furthermore, we had built up to our strategic requirements for the transportation and support of our Army ground and air forces overseas and the reinforcement of British naval forces guarding against the outbreak of the German surface forces. Coincident with this expansion and general increase in our strength, there was a rapid buildup in the forces employed in the Pacific.

At the outbreak of the war with Japan, we were initially placed on the defensive, but while we were so engaged we made all preparations to seize the initiative as soon as possible and embark on our own offensive operations. To that end, our fleet supported the operations of the Allied forces throughout the Pacific in retaining key positions and preventing further encroachments by the enemy.

In view of the absence of any well developed bases in Australia and in the South Pacific islands between Australia and the United States one of our first problems was to establish bases which would serve as links in the line of communications. Early in 1942, therefore, after surveying the situation, Efate, Espiritu Santo, and certain islands in the Fijis and New Caledonia were selected for advance bases, and developed in varying degree to suit our purposes. The establishment of those bases, which have been in constant use as fuel and troop staging stations, and as distribution points for material and supplies, was in large measure responsible for our ability to stand off the Japanese in their advance toward Australia and New Zealand. Without them we should have been at such a disadvantage that it is doubtful if the enemy could have been checked.

While essential sea and air communications to Alaska, Hawaii, New Zealand, Australia, and other intermediate positions were being established and protected, our submarines immediately took the offensive in enemy waters. Also during this period, our naval air task forces were instrumental in attacking enemy positions and in turning back enemy sea-borne forces, particularly in the Coral Sea and off Midway. The enemy succeeded in making an incursion into the western Aleutians.

The actions in the Coral Sea and at Midway did much to wrest the initiative from the enemy and slow down further advance. Our first really offensive operation was the seizure of Guadalcanal in August 1942. This campaign was followed by a general offensive made possible by increases in our amphibious forces and in our naval forces in general, which has continued to gain momentum on the entire Pacific front. At the end of February 1944, the enemy had been cleared from the Aleutians, had been pushed well out of the Solomons, had been ejected from the Gilberts and western Marshalls, was being attacked elsewhere, and was forced to adopt a defensive delaying strategy. Meanwhile, our own positions in the Pacific had been strengthened.

At the end of February 1944, therefore, we were in a position to support our submarines, which had been on the offensive from the beginning of the war, with strong naval forces, some of which were ground and air forces not needed on the European front. A similar situation exists in the Atlantic, in that the sea lanes are under our control and we are definitely on the offensive in that area.

The Pacific Theater

The war in the Pacific may be regarded as having four stages:

(a) The defensive, when we were engaged almost exclusively in protecting our shores and our lines of communication from the encroachments of the enemy.

(b) The defensive-offensive, during which, although our operations were chiefly defensive in character, we were able nevertheless to take certain offensive measures.

(c) The offensive-defensive, covering the period immediately following our seizure of the initiative, but during which we still had to use a large part of our forces to defend our recent gains.

(d) The offensive, which began when our advance bases were no longer seriously threatened and we became able to attack the enemy at places of our own choosing.

The Defensive

After the attack on Pearl Harbor, the Japanese withdrew from the central Pacific and for the time being, except for the capture of the islands of Guam and Wake, confined their major attacks to the Philippine Islands and Netherlands East Indies. Our own operations were of necessity limited to that line of enemy advance. Guam was easily taken. Our forces on Wake, after gallant resistance which took a large toll of enemy attacking forces, far superior in strength, were overcome at the end of December.

Except for the forces in the Philippine Islands under General (now General of the Army) Douglas MacArthur, our strength in the western Pacific area consisted chiefly of the Asiatic Fleet, a few aviation units, and the garrisons of marines at Guam and Wake already referred to. The small Asiatic Fleet commanded by Admiral Thomas C. Hart included the heavy cruiser HOUSTON, the light cruiser MARBLEHEAD, 13 overage destroyers, some 29 submarines, two squadrons of *Catalinas* comprising Patrol Wing Ten, and a few gunboats and auxiliaries which could not be counted on for combat. With this force (plus the light cruiser BOISE, which happened to be in Asiatic waters when the war warning was received) we undertook to delay the enemy's advance until such time as we could muster sufficient strength to put up any real resistance. In so far as completely stopping the advance was concerned, the campaign was foredoomed, but it nevertheless contributed materially to the ultimate check of the Japanese advance, and the energy and gallantry of the officers and men participating constitute a remarkable chapter in the history of naval warfare.

During the latter part of November, when the Japanese advances along the coast of Indo-China indicated the approach of a crisis, Admiral Hart had sent MARBLEHEAD and eight destroyers to Borneo. Likewise, HOUSTON, BOISE, and the destroyer tender BLACK HAWK had been dispatched to operate in southern waters. On the evening of 8 December, therefore, after the Japanese had bombed our airfields and destroyed many of General MacArthur's planes, our submarines and motor torpedo boats, which were still in Philippine waters, were left with the task of impeding the enemy's advance. On 10 December the navy yard at Cavite, which had long been recognized as inse-

PLATE 5—THE DEFENSIVE PHASE IN THE PACIFIC

1. BATTLE OF MAKASSAR STRAIT, 24 JANUARY 1942: Japanese forces moving southward are attacked by U. S. destroyers.

2. RAID ON THE MARSHALLS AND GILBERTS, 1 FEBRUARY 1942: U. S. carriers and cruisers attack enemy bases.

3. BADOENG STRAIT, 19–20 FEBRUARY 1942: Combined forces under Rear Admiral Doorman, R.N.N. engage Japanese force moving on Bali.

4. ACTION OFF RABAUL, 20 FEBRUARY 1942: Aerial engagement near the enemy's major base in New Britain.

5. RAID ON WAKE ISLAND, 24 FEBRUARY 1942: A U.S. Task Force bombards a former American outpost.

6. JAVA SEA ACTION, 27 FEBRUARY 1942: Combined forces attempt to intercept Japanese convoys. The end of organized Allied naval resistance in this phase of the war.

7. *HOUSTON* AND *PERTH* LOST, 1 MARCH 1942: The surviving cruisers of the combined force are lost in an action near Soenda Strait.

8. RAID ON SALAMAUA AND LAE, 10 MARCH 1942: Carriers attack enemy ships in recently occupied New Guinea bases.

9. RAID ON TULAGI, 4 May 1942: The opening blow of the Coral Sea actions. U.S. carrier-based aircraft attack Japanese ships in the newly occupied Solomons.

10. BATTLE OF THE CORAL SEA, 7–8 MAY 1942: Carriers exchange blows. Severe damage inflicted on the Japanese carrier force. LEXINGTON is lost, but the Japanese advance is checked.

COMBAT OPERATIONS

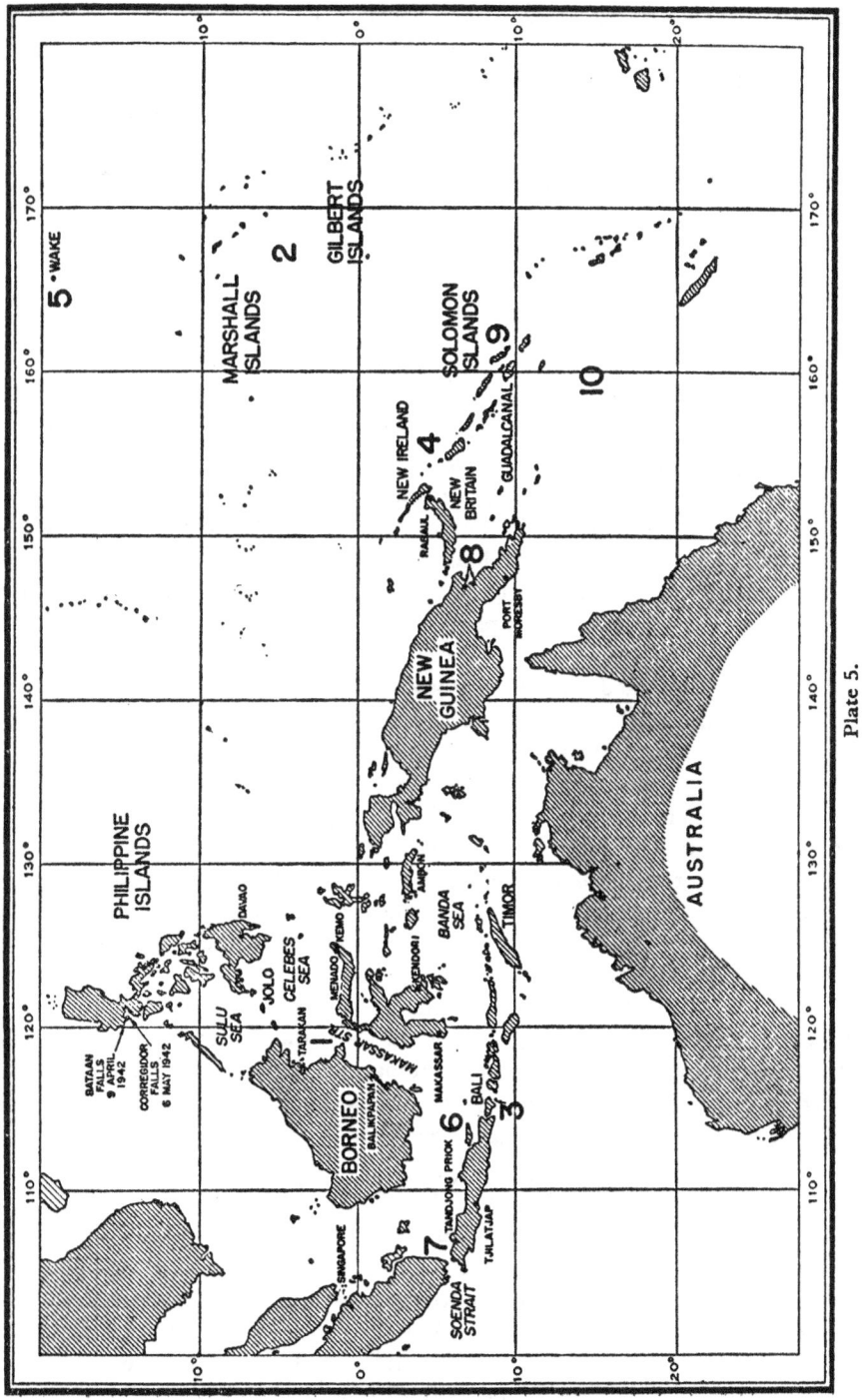

Plate 5.

cure, was practically wiped out by an air attack which also damaged the submarine SEALION and the destroyer PEARY; SEALION being destroyed by our own forces to prevent its capture. On the same day the Japanese effected landings on the islands, and thereafter all attempts to bring in effective quantities of supplies by sea proved unsuccessful. It should be noted, however, that on 10 December there were some 200,000 tons of Allied shipping in Manila Bay; most of it good, and some of it with valuable cargoes. All but one of these ships got clear, to the southward, under what amounted to cover by our surface forces, and escaped via the Sulu Sea and Makassar Strait. This was an important "save."

The holding of the Army's positions on Bataan and Corregidor became only a question of time, and Rear Admiral F. W. Rockwell, who was in command of the local naval defense forces, moved with them to Corregidor on 26 December.

Admiral Hart set up his headquarters in the Netherlands East Indies. Shortly thereafter General Sir Archibald P. Wavell, of the British Army, arrived and assumed supreme command in that theater, whereupon Admiral Hart became the Commander of the Allied naval forces. Until Admiral Hart's arrival in Java, Rear Admiral (now Vice Admiral) William A. Glassford commanded the surface ships in southern waters, assisted by Rear Admiral William R. Purnell and other members of the Fleet Staff. Up to this point (in so far as the Asiatic Fleet was concerned) the campaign was conducted in accordance with plans worked out in the Navy Department prior to the outbreak of hostilities.

The method adopted by the Japanese in making their advances through the Philippine Islands and the Netherlands East Indies was built around their air power. After building up their strength at a given base they would overcome the consistently inferior Allied air opposition at the next point of attack and then send along heavily screened amphibious forces to make landings. As a rule, the distances were too short to permit attack by our naval forces while the enemy was en route. As soon as the enemy were in control of a new area they would repair the airfields and gather forces for the next attack. These tactics were well adapted to the geography of the Philippine Islands and the Netherlands East Indies, particularly as there was almost a total absence of interior communications in the islands occupied.

In January 1942, therefore, the Japanese had overrun the Philippine Islands, and the greatest part of our strength was in the Netherlands East Indies, for which the Japanese were obviously headed. Our submarines and motor torpedo boats were engaged in slowing down the enemy advance to give us as much time as possible to get organized for the surface actions that were in prospect in the Java Sea.

THE JAVA SEA CAMPAIGN

In that situation, Admiral Hart had to plan all our operations without air support except for a few Army bombers and a few fighters based on Java. Our PBY4's of Patrol Wing Ten were not suited for the type of operations in prospect, and as a matter of fact it was only the superb work of their pilots in the face of enemy fighters coupled with the mobility of our tenders that made their use possible.

By the end of December, the Japanese were preparing bases at Davao on Mindanao, and at Jolo in the Sulu Archipelago. From these points they moved south to attack Menado on the northern tip of Celebes, Tarakan in northeastern Borneo, and shortly afterward Kema, with the obvious intention of moving down Molucca Strait toward Ambon, Kendari, and Makassar Strait. By 20 January they appeared to be ready to move against Balikpapan, on the east coast of Borneo.

Collecting the few ships at his disposal (until early February all British and Netherlands surface ships had to be used to escort troop convoys into Malaya) Admiral Hart decided upon a night torpedo attack. This was delivered off Balikpapan (the action became known officially as the Battle of Makassar Strait) early in the morning of 24 January by the destroyers JOHN D. FORD, PARROTT, PAUL JONES and POPE, under the command of Commander (now Captain) P. H. Talbot. Whatever the losses sustained by the enemy, the attack (one of four attempts by our cruisers and destroyers to come to grips with the enemy at sea) was brilliantly executed, and was responsible for the stalling of that particular force for some time at Balikpapan. Other amphibious forces, however, continued to advance eastward, and landed at Rabaul in New Britain and at Bougainville in the Solomons. New positions on the coast of Borneo were also seized by the enemy, and in the first few days of February they captured Ambon and began bombing Soerabaja and several other Javanese points.

In furtherance of the effort to delay the enemy drive, a striking force consisting of four cruisers and seven destroyers, about half of which were Netherlands and the other half American, was formed under the command of Rear Admiral Doorman of the Netherlands Navy. A large enemy convoy having gathered at Balikpapan, Admiral Doorman undertook to run up Madoera Strait into the Java Sea and deliver an attack, but our forces were discovered by Japanese planes and subjected to a prolonged bombing attack which prevented the carrying out of the plan. During this attack HOUSTON suffered one direct hit which destroyed her number three turret and MARBLEHEAD was forced to retire to the south coast of Java to effect temporary repairs.

Continuing their advance, the Japanese attacked Palembang in southeast Sumatra and entered Banka Strait. Admiral Doorman's force, in a second effort to interfere with the enemy operation, was again forced to withdraw by enemy planes. By 14 February the Japanese in Borneo and Celebes were in a position to advance on Bali and eastern Java, and Japanese forces in Sumatra were also threatening Java.

At this point in the campaign, in accordance with previous agreements providing that it would be conducted by the Netherlands, Admiral Hart relinquished operational command of Allied naval forces to Vice Admiral Helfrich of the Netherlands Navy, and a few days later General Wavell turned over his command and left the area.

Having been subjected to daily bombing at Soerabaja, our headquarters were transferred from Soerabaja to Tjilatjap on the south coast of Java. On 19 February Darwin (most of our forces basing there had been transferred to Tjilatjap because Darwin, not entirely suitable from the beginning, was becoming untenable), on the north coast of Australia, was subjected to a heavy air raid which destroyed the airport, warehouse, docks, and virtually every ship in the harbor, including our destroyer PEARY.

Enemy forces having landed on the southeast coast of Bali, and seized the airfield there, Admiral Doorman, with his composite force, attacked enemy vessels in Badoeng Strait on the night of 19–20 February. This action resulted in the sinking of the Netherlands destroyer PIET HEIN and damage to the Netherlands cruisers JAVA and TROMP and to our destroyer STEWART. Damage to the enemy in this action was impossible to assess but was believed to be considerable.

The action in Badoeng Strait was encouraging but it did little to impede the Japanese, who now controlled all the northern approaches to the Netherlands East Indies, and seemed about to move on Java. In an effort to bolster up our strength with fighter planes, LANGLEY, with planes and crew on board, and SEAWITCH, with more planes, were diverted to Java. On 26 February LANGLEY was sunk by enemy bombers. PECOS, a tanker, was sunk about the same time in the same area. SEAWITCH arrived safely at Tjilatjap but was too late.

On 27 February Admiral Doorman's composite force, consisting of two heavy cruisers, three light cruisers and nine destroyers, attacked an enemy force in the Java Sea, not far from Soerabaja. After maneuvering for position, and after having joined action, the composite force, for one reason and another, suffered a series of losses. These included the sinking of the British destroyer ELECTRA and the Netherlands destroyer KORTENAER, and damage to the British cruiser EXETER. Later that night the Netherlands cruisers DE RUYTER and JAVA were sunk by a combination of torpedoes and gunfire. This left only HOUSTON and PERTH, the American destroyers having expended their torpedoes and retired to port to refuel. Accordingly, HOUSTON and PERTH retired to Tandjong Priok. Although the Japanese suffered some damage, they were successful in preventing the striking force from reaching their convoys. The immediate problem was now to rescue our remaining vessels from the Java Sea, the exits to which were held by the enemy.

On 28 February EXETER, POPE, and ENCOUNTER headed for Soenda Strait and were never heard from again. On 1 March HOUSTON and PERTH, accompanied by the Netherlands destroyer EVERSTEN, headed in the same direction, and except for very meager reports of an engagement in Soenda Strait, they have not been heard from since. Of the entire Allied force, only the four American destroyers managed to make their way to Australia, after a skirmish with Japanese destroyers patrolling Bali Strait.

On 28 February the Japanese landed on the north coast of Java. As no port on the island of Java was tenable as a base for our surface forces, the Allied naval command was dissolved and the American ships remaining at Tjilatjap were ordered to proceed to Australia. Of the four destroyers so ordered, EDSALL and PILLSBURY were lost en route. All other craft escaped, with the exception of the gunboat ASHEVILLE. Thus ended the gallant campaign of the Java Sea, conducted against overwhelming odds by officers and men who did the best they could with what they had.

RAIDS ON JAPANESE POSITIONS

While the situation in the Far East was growing steadily worse, and the Japanese were having things their own way there and elsewhere, our Pacific Fleet, now commanded by Admiral Nimitz, carried out its first offensive operation of the war. The targets selected were the Marshall and Gilbert Islands.

To carry out raids on these islands, there was placed under the command of Vice Admiral (now Admiral) William F. Halsey, Jr., a force consisting of the carriers ENTERPRISE and YORKTOWN; the heavy cruisers CHESTER, LOUISVILLE, NORTHAMPTON, and SALT LAKE CITY; the light cruiser ST. LOUIS; and ten destroyers. Beginning 1 February 1942 bomb and bombardment damage—very severe in some instances—was inflicted by that force upon the islands of Wotje, Maloelap, Kwajalein, Roi, Jaluit, Makin, Taroa, Lae and Gugegwe. It is quite possible that because of the success at Pearl Harbor, much of the enemy's air strength originally disposed in the Marshall Islands was withdrawn before these attacks were delivered. Except for CHESTER, which suffered one bomb hit, and ENTERPRISE, which was slightly damaged by shell fragments, none of our vessels was damaged during the entire operation, and our personnel losses were slight.

The raid on the Marshall and Gilbert Islands was so successful that several other operations following the same pattern were conducted during the following weeks. On 20 February a task force built around the carrier LEXINGTON, and commanded by Vice Admiral Wilson Brown, attempted a combination air and surface attack on Rabaul, New Britain. During the approach, LEXINGTON was discovered by enemy twin-engined bombers, 16 of which were destroyed by our fighter planes and antiaircraft, five of them by a single pilot. The element of surprise having been lost and fuel having been reduced by high-speed maneuvering, the attack on Rabaul was not pressed home.

On 24 February Admiral Halsey took ENTERPRISE, two cruisers, and seven destroyers and shelled and bombed Wake Island, which had been in enemy hands since 22 December. Considerable damage was inflicted. We lost only one aircraft during that operation. Eight days later planes from ENTERPRISE bombed Marcus Island with reasonably satisfactory results. Again, we lost only one plane.

On 10 March Vice Admiral Brown, with the carriers LEXINGTON and YORKTOWN and supporting ships, raided the New Guinea ports of Salamaua and Lae, where enemy troops had landed three days earlier. A number of enemy war vessels and transport vessels were sunk or damaged, and the attack was fully successful, even though it did not appear to delay appreciably the enemy's advance toward Australia. Our losses were light.

On 18 April Tokio was bombed by army planes which took off from the carrier HORNET, the planes from ENTERPRISE providing search and fighter planes for the operation. As a carrier operation, this raid was unique in naval history in that for the first time medium land bombers were transported across an ocean and launched off enemy shores. Whatever the damage inflicted by these bombers, the attack was stimulating to the morale, which at that time, considering the surrender of Bataan, and the situation in general in the Far East, was at low ebb.

THE CORAL SEA

By the middle of April, the Japanese had established bases in the New Guinea-New Britain-Solomon Islands area, which put them in a position to threaten all Melanesia and Australia itself, and they were moving their forces through the mandates in preparation for an extension of their offensive to the southeast. Our available forces at that time were eager and ready for battle, but they were not any too strong for effective defense against major enemy concentrations, much less adequate to carry out a large-scale offensive operation.

It should be noted at this point that during the first five months of the war, nearly every engagement with the enemy had demonstrated the importance of air power in modern naval warfare. Our initial losses at Pearl Harbor and in the Philippines were the result of attack by aircraft, and the enemy's superiority in the air had been one of the controlling factors in our reverses in the Far East. Similarly, our successful though inconclusive raids on the Japanese-held islands in the Pacific had been conducted chiefly by carrier-based aircraft. The results had been excellent and the costs low. As yet, however, there had been no engagement between enemy carrier forces and our own, and although we had reason to believe that most of our naval aircraft were of good design and performance, we had no basis for comparison.

When the Japanese, on 3 May, began to occupy Florida Island in the Solomons, Rear Admiral (now Vice Admiral) Frank J. Fletcher, who was cruising in the Coral Sea with a force composed of the carrier YORKTOWN, the three cruisers ASTORIA, CHESTER, and PORTLAND, and six destroyers, proceeded north to interrupt the activity. On the morning of 4 May, about 100 miles southwest of Guadalcanal, planes launched by YORKTOWN sank and damaged a number of enemy vessels at Tulagi with loss of only one aircraft, and in the afternoon, another attack group scored additional hits, with the loss of two fighters.

On 5 May, Rear Admiral Fletcher's force had joined other Allied units, one of which was a task group including the heavy cruisers MINNEAPOLIS, NEW ORLEANS, ASTORIA, CHESTER and PORTLAND, and five destroyers. There were two flag officers in the task group, Rear Admiral (now Admiral) Thomas C. Kinkaid and Rear Admiral (now Vice Admiral) William W. Smith. The other unit, consisting of the Australian heavy cruiser AUSTRALIA, and the light cruiser HOBART, plus the American heavy cruiser CHICAGO and two destroyers, was under the command of Rear Admiral J. G. Crace, Royal Navy, and was operated in conjunction with the carriers LEXINGTON and YORKTOWN and four destroyers, which were under the command of Rear Admiral (now Vice Admiral) Aubrey W. Fitch.

On the afternoon of the 6th, enemy forces had become sufficiently consolidated in the Bismarck Archipelago-New Guinea area to indicate an amphibious operation to the southward, perhaps against Port Moresby, on the southeast coast of New Guinea. As enemy forces would have to round the southeastern end of New Guinea, Rear Admiral Fletcher stationed an attack group within striking distance of the probable track of the enemy fleet, and the remainder of his force moved northward in an attempt to locate enemy covering forces.

On the morning of the 7th, contact was made with the Japanese carrier SHOHO, which was promptly attacked and sunk by aircraft from LEXINGTON and YORKTOWN. We lost only one dive bomber in the attack, but the same morning Japanese carrier planes sank our tanker NEOSHO and the destroyer SIMS.

The next morning, contact was made with two enemy carriers, four heavy cruisers, and several destroyers. One of the carriers was attacked and severely damaged by our carrier aircraft, and as was anticipated, enemy aircraft counterattacked about an hour later. During the counterattack, both YORKTOWN and LEXINGTON were damaged, the latter rather severely. Both carriers and their planes shot down a considerable number of enemy planes during the engagement, and our aircraft losses were small by comparison, but early in the afternoon an explosion on board LEXINGTON made her impossible to control. She was therefore abandoned, and ordered sunk by one of our own destroyers. Nearly all of her personnel were saved.

Thus ended the first major engagement in naval history in which surface ships did not exchange a single shot. Although the loss of LEXINGTON was keenly felt, the engagement in the Coral Sea effectively checked the Japanese in their advance to the southward. Our losses of one carrier, one tanker, one destroyer, and a total of 66 planes were considerably less than estimated Japanese losses. Our personnel casualties totalled 543.

The Defensive-Offensive
MIDWAY

The engagement in the Coral Sea marked the end of the period during which we were totally on the defensive. There followed a lull during which both sides were preparing for further operations. Our immediate problem was to anticipate as nearly as we could what the next move of the enemy would be, as we had lost touch with the heavy Japanese forces which had participated in the Coral Sea action.

It was clear that the Japanese would not long remain inactive. Naturally enough, our various important outposts would be good targets, with Dutch Harbor and Midway offering them the best chance of success, either in the nature of a raid or of an invasion. Furthermore, an operation directed against these points would permit the enemy to retire without too great loss or complete annihilation in case their plans did not work out. At the same time, we had to consider the possibility that they might renew actions in the Coral Sea. It was a plain case of calculating the risk involved in stationing our forces. A mistake at that point would have proved costly.

Considering the chance that the enemy knew little concerning the location of those of our ships which had not participated in the Coral Sea engagement, but certainly was aware that most of our available carrier and cruiser strength was then in southern waters, it seemed reasonable to expect that the Japanese would make the most of the opportunity to strike us in the central and/or northern Pacific. Such an attack was likely because of the prospect of success in the immediate operation, and because if successful, the advance to Australia and the islands in the south Pacific could be accomplished in due course with comparative ease, once the enemy had cut our lines of communications.

Acting on our best estimate of the situation, our carriers and supporting vessels were recalled from the south Pacific. YORKTOWN was patched up temporarily, and scouting and patrol lines were established well to the westward of Midway Island. Our total forces available in the central Pacific consisted of the carriers ENTERPRISE, HORNET, and YORKTOWN, seven heavy cruisers, one light cruiser, 14 destroyers, and about 20 submarines. These were divided into two task forces, one under the command of Rear Admiral (now Admiral) Raymond A. Spruance (cruisers of this task force were commanded by Rear Admiral Kinkaid) and the other under the command of Rear Admiral Fletcher. Another flag officer, Rear Admiral W. W. Smith, was attached to the second task force. In addition, there was a Marine Corps air group based on Midway, augmented by Army bombers from Hawaii.

On the morning of 3 June, enemy forces were sighted several hundred miles southwest of Midway, on an easterly course. The composition of the force sighted was not determined at that time, but it was clearly a large attack force with supporting vessels. Late in the afternoon this force was bombed by a squadron of B-17's under the command of Lieutenant Colonel Walter C. Sweeney, Army Air Corps. While results of the attack were not definitely determined, hits on several ships were reported. On the morning of 4 June, contact was made with enemy aircraft headed toward the island of Midway from the northwest, and immediately thereafter, two carriers and the enemy main body were picked up in the same vicinity. Although the enemy aircraft were not prevented from dropping their bombs on Midway, the Japanese air attack force was nevertheless subjected to heavy fire and the enemy plane losses were large. Meanwhile, Army, Navy, and Marine Corps planes from Midway attacked carriers, battleships, and other vessels, inflicting serious damage on one enemy carrier.

At this point, our own carriers took a hand in the engagement. Having been launched from a position north of Midway, a torpedo squadron from HORNET (the now famous Torpedo Eight) without the protection of fighters, and without accompanying dive bombers, attacked a force of four enemy carriers. All planes in the squadron were shot down and only one pilot survived, but the squadron made several hits on the enemy carriers. About an hour later, torpedo squadrons from ENTERPRISE and YORKTOWN attacked the same carriers, and also suffered heavy losses, but registered hits on two carriers. These attacks were followed by dive bombers from ENTERPRISE which smothered two carriers, and by more bombers from YORKTOWN which hit a third carrier, a cruiser, and a battleship. Two carriers had been set on fire and put completely out of action. A third [SORYU] was damaged and was sunk later by the submarine NAUTILUS.

Planes from the only Japanese carrier remaining undamaged attacked YORKTOWN, and although this attack force was annihilated, it succeeded in making three bomb hits. Shortly afterward, enemy torpedo planes scored two hits on YORKTOWN, and orders were given to abandon ship. About two hours later, planes from ENTERPRISE attacked the undamaged Japanese carrier and left her a mass of flames and immediately thereafter, when a squadron from HORNET arrived, the carrier was blazing so furiously that it was possible to concentrate on a nearby battleship and a cruiser, both of which were hit.

At this stage of the engagement, it was apparent that we had won control of the air and it remained for the aircraft from Midway to put on the finishing touches. Army Flying Fortresses attacked an enemy heavy cruiser and left it smoking heavily. Other planes scored hits on a battleship, a damaged carrier, and a destroyer. By the end of the day the Japanese were in full retirement.

On the morning of the 5th, aircraft from ENTERPRISE and HORNET made an ineffective attack on an enemy light cruiser, but planes from Midway discovered two enemy cruisers, one of which they crippled, and scored a number of hits on them. Poor visibility on the 5th prevented further operations.

On 6 June, HORNET planes located an enemy force consisting of two heavy cruisers and three destroyers and made hits on the two cruisers. Planes from ENTERPRISE also scored hits on those two cruisers and later in the day HORNET planes successfully attacked two more cruisers and a destroyer. On the same day, in an effort to save YORKTOWN, which had been taken in tow, the destroyer HAMMANN went alongside to put on board a salvage party. While she was alongside, YORKTOWN was struck by two torpedoes from an enemy submarine, and HAMMANN by one. HAMMANN sank within a few minutes and the next morning YORKTOWN also sank.

The Battle of Midway was the first decisive defeat suffered by the Japanese Navy in 350 years.* Furthermore, it put an end to the long period of Japanese offensive action, and restored the balance of naval power in the Pacific. The threat to Hawaii and the west coast was automatically removed, and except for operations in the Aleutians area, where the Japanese had landed on the islands of Kiska and Attu, enemy operations were confined to the south Pacific. It was to this latter area, therefore, that we gave our greatest attention.

The Offensive-Defensive
CAMPAIGNS IN THE SOUTH PACIFIC
The Landings in the Solomons

From the outset of the war, it had been evident that the protection of our lines of communications to Australia and New Zealand represented a "must." With the advance of the Japanese in that direction, it was therefore necessary to plan and execute operations which would stop them.

Early in April, the Japanese had overrun the island of Tulagi, where (on 4 May 1942) they were attacked by our carrier-based bombers just before the Battle of the Coral Sea. In July, the enemy landed troops and laborers on Guadalcanal Island and began the construction of an airfield. As the operation of landbased planes from that point would immediately imperil our control of the New Hebrides and New Caledonia areas, the necessity of our ejecting them from those positions became increasingly apparent. Developments in New Guinea, where the enemy had begun a movement in the latter part of July, paralleling his Solomons penetrations, increased the necessity for prompt action on our part.

The counter operation—our first real offensive move in force—was planned under the direction of Vice Admiral R. L. Ghormley, who, in April, had assumed command of the South Pacific Force, with headquarters at Auckland, New Zealand. Forces participating were the First Marine Division, reinforced by the Second Marine Regiment, the First Raider Battalion, and the Third Defense Battalion, supported by naval forces consisting of three major units, two of which were under the command of Vice Admiral Fletcher. These were an air support force under Rear Admiral Leigh

*The Korean Admiral Yi-sun administered a resounding defeat to the Japanese Admiral Hideyoshi (so-called father of Japanese Navy) in 1592 off the Korean Coast.

PLATE 6—THE OFFENSIVE-DEFENSIVE PHASE IN THE PACIFIC

1. U.S. LANDING, 7 AUGUST 1942: U.S. Marines establish foothold on Guadalcanal and Tulagi in the first Allied offensive of the Pacific War.

2. BATTLE OF SAVO ISLAND, 9 AUGUST 1942: Japanese night attack on naval forces protecting landing. One Australian and three U.S. heavy cruisers lost, other units damaged.

3. BATTLE OF THE EASTERN SOLOMONS, 23–25 AUGUST 1942: Powerful Japanese naval forces intercepted by U.S. carrier-borne aircraft. Enemy breaks off action after loss of carrier support.

4. BATTLE OF CAPE ESPERANCE, 11–12 OCTOBER 1942: U.S. cruisers and destroyers in a surprise night attack engage a sizeable enemy force near Guadalcanal.

5. BATTLE OF SANTA CRUZ ISLANDS, 26 OCTOBER 1942: Blows are exchanged by U.S. carriers and Japanese carriers operating with a powerful enemy force moving to support land operations at Guadalcanal. Two enemy carriers put out of action and four enemy air groups decimated.

6. BATTLE OF GUADALCANAL, 13–14–15 NOVEMBER 1942: Enemy concentrates invasion force at Rabaul. U.S. naval forces covering reinforcements for troops on Guadalcanal meet and decisively defeat this force in a series of violent engagements in which heavy losses are sustained by both sides.

7. BATTLE OF TASSAFARONGA, 30 NOVEMBER 1942: A Japanese attempt to reinforce is defeated at heavy cost. NORTHAMPTON lost, three U.S. heavy cruisers severely damaged.

Japanese complete withdrawal, 7–8 FEBRUARY 1943.

8. FIRST BATTLE OF KULA GULF, 6 JULY 1943: U.S. cruisers and destroyers intercept the "Tokyo Express." HELENA lost.

9. BATTLE OF KOLOMBANGARA, 13 JULY 1943: The circumstances of the engagement of 6th July are repeated. Three Allied cruisers severely damaged by torpedoes.

10. BATTLE OF VELLA GULF, 6 AUGUST 1943: Japanese destroyers escorting reinforcements are intercepted by our forces. Several enemy destroyers sunk.

COMBAT OPERATIONS

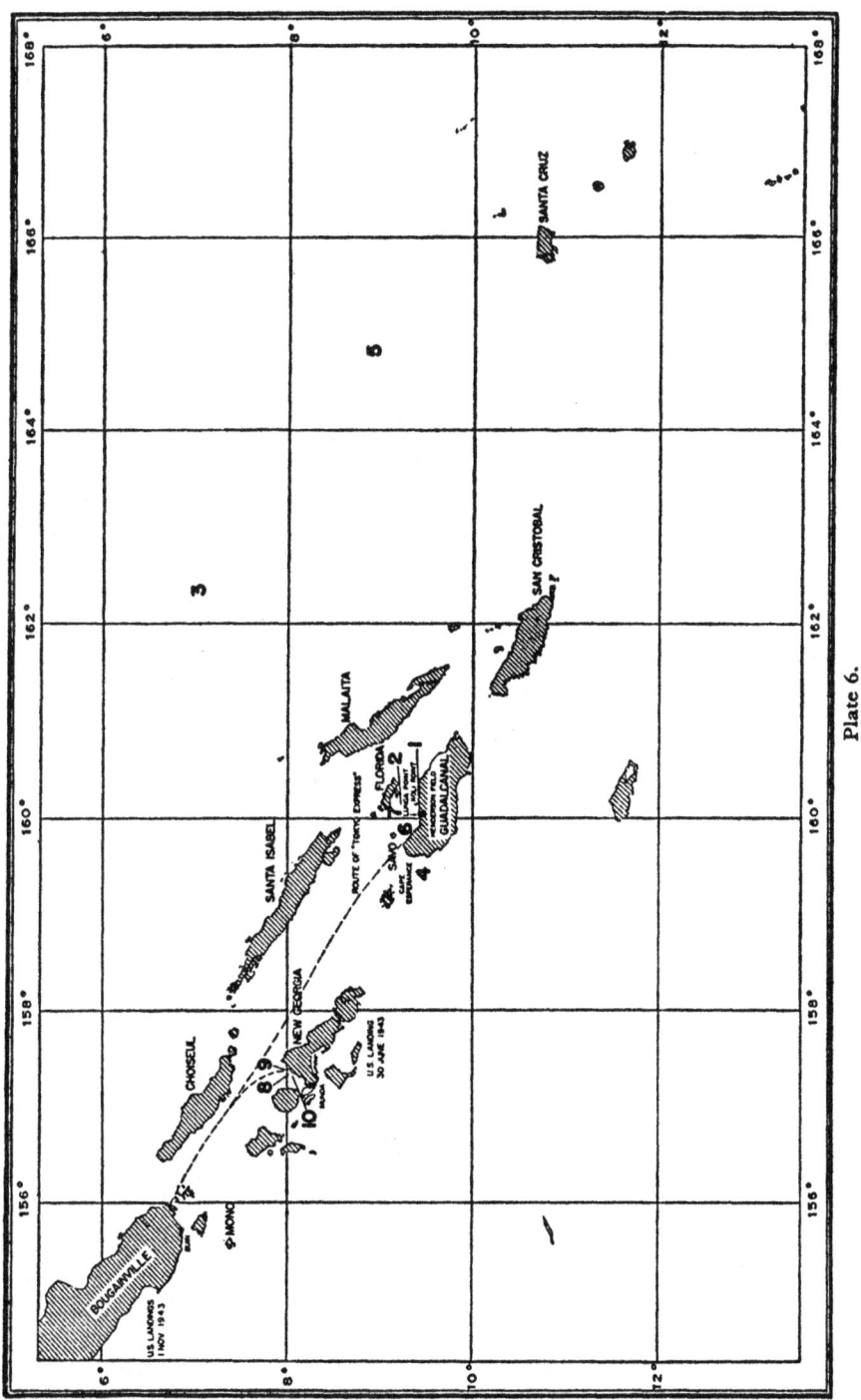

Plate 6.

Noyes, consisting of three carriers, one new battleship, five heavy cruisers, one anti-aircraft light cruiser and a number of destroyers; and an amphibious force under Rear Admiral (now Admiral) R. K. Turner, composed of six heavy cruisers (two of them Australian), one light cruiser (Australian), destroyers, and 23 transports. The third task force, under Rear Admiral (later Vice Admiral) John S. McCain (now deceased), was composed of land-based planes of various types based in New Caledonia, the Fijis, and Samoa. Under the plan, they were to cooperate closely with the planes under the command of General MacArthur in New Guinea and Australia. Marine units were formed up in New Zealand during June and July, under the command of Major General (now General) A. A. Vandegrift, USMC.

After leaving New Zealand, and after effecting rendezvous with combat units, the entire invasion force conducted a realistic rehearsal en route to their objective. On the morning of 7 August, the landing force, which took the enemy by surprise, made landings on Guadalcanal and Tulagi. There was little opposition initially on Guadalcanal, but on Tulagi the Japanese had constructed dugouts, and when they began heavy fire, progress was slow and costly. The enemy delivered an air counter-attack in the afternoon, but it was ineffective.

By the next afternoon, our Marines were in complete control of Tulagi Island and were making satisfactory progress on Guadalcanal, where they had taken possession of the airfield. The immediate objectives of the operation had therefore been obtained, at the cost of one transport sunk, one destroyer damaged and subsequently sunk, and one destroyer damaged. Plane losses amounted to 21 fighters.

Battle of Savo Island

We had repulsed air raids on the 7th and 8th with only moderate losses, but those attacks had considerably delayed the unloading of our transports and cargo vessels. Moreover, in spite of heavy plane losses inflicted on the enemy, further attacks on our vessels were a surety, perhaps by surface craft and perhaps by enemy planes based on Santa Isabel Island. At this critical time it became necessary for our carriers to withdraw from their covering position because of lack of fuel, and also because the Japanese had shown considerable air strength and were suspected of having submarines available, to which we did not care to expose our carriers.

In that situation, the cruisers of the screening forces under the command of Rear Admiral V. Crutchley, Royal Navy, took up a night disposition designed to protect the area between the Guadalcanal and Florida Islands and the channel on either side of Savo Island. The northern group covering the latter area consisted of the heavy cruisers VINCENNES, QUINCY, and ASTORIA, screened by the destroyers HELM and WILSON. The southern group consisted of the Australian cruiser CANBERRA and CHICAGO, screened by PATTERSON and BAGLEY. Two destroyers, RALPH TALBOT and BLUE, were stationed not far from Savo Island. Late in the evening of 8 August, a conference was held on board Rear Admiral Turner's flagship, MC CAWLEY. This conference included Rear Admiral Crutchley.

A force of enemy cruisers and destroyers entered the area undetected from the northwest at about 0145 and, aided by flares dropped by enemy planes, opened fire on our screening groups with guns and torpedoes. The result of the surprise and of the

Japanese fire, which was sufficiently effective to inflict severe damage on our vessels in a few minutes, was that there was little effective return fire. The action ceased at about 0215 at which time the Japanese force, having rounded Savo Island, left the area on a northeasterly course. During those thirty minutes QUINCY, VINCENNES, ASTORIA and CANBERRA were so severely damaged that they subsequently sank, and CHICAGO, RALPH TALBOT and PATTERSON were damaged.

The surprise, which was the immediate cause of the defeat, was the result of a combination of circumstances. Because of the urgency of seizing and occupying Guadalcanal, planning was not up to the usual thorough standards. Certain communication failures made a bad situation worse. Fatigue was a contributing factor in the degree of alertness maintained. Generally speaking, however, we were surprised because we lacked experience. Needless to say, the lessons learned were fully taken into account.

The immediate consequence of this cruiser battle was the retirement of the enemy force, without any attack being made on our transports unloading men and supplies on the beaches of Guadalcanal. The loss of the four cruisers, however, and the subsequent loss of two aircraft carriers left us inferior in strength for several months. The Japanese did not take advantage of this opportunity to engage in a fleet battle with the balance of power on their side, probably because they did not know—and we did not let them know—how severe our losses were.

The Fight for Guadalcanal

Except as it affected the security of the islands to the south, and Australia and New Zealand, the island of Guadalcanal by itself was not particularly important, but, having been selected by us as the point to step in and check the advance of the enemy, it became a focal point in the fighting front established. After we had landed there, the immediate situation was that of opposing ground forces on the island, and as each depended on naval forces for supplies and reinforcements it was inevitable that there would be naval engagements until the issue was decided.

After the battle of Savo Island, the Japanese began bombing Marine positions and making the adjacent waters almost untenable during the daylight hours. At night, enemy surface forces bombarded our surface installations almost at will. The Japanese, however, were unable to bring up reserve ground forces from the northern Solomons.

So far as naval activity was concerned there was a lull of about ten days. During that time the Japanese, who reacted violently to the reverses suffered in the initial landing, collected all available reinforcements near Henderson Field. The reinforced troops immediately attacked. The result was a night battle at Tenaru River in which the Marines were completely victorious.

Meanwhile, the enemy was concentrating his forces in the Rabaul area. By 23 August it was apparent that a major action was imminent.

The Battle of the Eastern Solomons

In anticipation of an enemy move in force, Vice Admiral Ghormley had concentrated two task forces southeast of the island of Guadalcanal. These were built around the carriers SARATOGA and ENTERPRISE, and included the battleship NORTH CAROLINA, the cruisers MINNEAPOLIS, PORTLAND, NEW ORLEANS and ATLANTA, and 11 destroyers. On the morning of 23 August a transport group was sighted by a search plane about 250 miles north of the island.

During the night our combined force moved north and contact was made the next morning. In the afternoon of the 24th, planes from SARATOGA sank an aircraft carrier [RYUJO] and in addition damaged a cruiser and a destroyer. While these attacks were in progress, a flight of about 75 planes attacked ENTERPRISE and her escort vessels and inflicted moderately severe damage on ENTERPRISE, in spite of the intense antiaircraft fire from escorting ships, particularly NORTH CAROLINA. That night, Marine air attack groups from Guadalcanal attacked and damaged two more enemy destroyers, and the next morning destroyed a transport. In addition to the foregoing attacks, Army planes believed they scored a hit on a cruiser, planes from SARATOGA reported hits on a battleship and two cruisers, and Marine pilots reported damage to still another cruiser. As a result of the action, the Japanese were all but stripped of carrier support and broke off the fight although their powerful surface forces were still largely intact.

* * * * * * * * *

Following the engagement in the eastern Solomons, no major action took place in the South Pacific area for a period of about six weeks. During those six weeks, however, the supply lines had to be kept open to Guadalcanal. Japanese submarines and air forces were active in the vicinity, and there were numerous scattered actions, which cost us the carrier WASP, the destroyers O'BRIEN, BLUE, COLHOUN, GREGORY, and LITTLE, and several other ships damaged. Also the Japanese made almost nightly runs of what came to be termed the "Tokio express" from the Buin-Faisi area to Guadalcanal, and enemy air forces bombed Marine positions by day and by night.

By 13 September enemy ground troops had been reinforced, and another attack was directed at Henderson Field. Although the issue was in doubt for several hours, the Marines, thanks to replacements and artillery support, succeeded in decimating the attacking force.

In spite of offensive operations directed against enemy ground troops and supporting naval forces by our ground troops and by our Marine air forces, the enemy by the end of September had succeeded in putting practically an entire new division on the island. In addition, more strong Japanese fleet units had been assembled to the northward, and the situation again was threatening. Reinforcements to the Marines had now become a necessity even though made in the face of enemy naval and air superiority. Contemplated reinforcements included Army elements available (the 164th Infantry).

Battle of Cape Esperance

After our carrier planes had attacked enemy shipping in the northern Solomons as a preliminary, our naval forces in the area were disposed in three groups. One was built around the carrier HORNET, to the westward of Guadalcanal. A second, to the eastward of Malaita Island, included the new battleship WASHINGTON. The third, under the command of the late Rear Admiral Norman Scott, was stationed south of Guadalcanal pending developments. Rear Admiral Scott's force consisted of the heavy cruisers SAN FRANCISCO, SALT LAKE CITY; the light cruisers BOISE, HELENA; and the destroyers BUCHANAN, DUNCAN, FARENHOLT, LAFFEY and MCCALLA.

On the afternoon of 11 October enemy forces were reported in "the slot" between Choiseul Island and the New Georgia group, headed for Guadalcanal. Simultaneously, Henderson Field on Guadalcanal was attacked by about 75 enemy aircraft. Rear Admiral Scott therefore headed north with his force, which rounded the northwestern end of the island about two hours before midnight. Just before midnight contact was made, and our force opened fire.

Taken by surprise, the enemy did not return the fire for nearly ten minutes, during which time our cruisers made the most of the opportunity and delivered a devastating fire on the enemy force. In less than five minutes four enemy targets had disappeared; two more were put out of action by HELENA and BOISE; and FARENHOLT, DUNCAN, and BUCHANAN each scored torpedo hits on enemy cruisers. In addition, BUCHANAN wrecked an enemy destroyer with gunfire and set an unidentified enemy ship on fire.

When the Japanese opened fire, BOISE found herself engaged with a heavy cruiser, and although the enemy cruiser soon burst into flames, BOISE was damaged. During this exchange, SALT LAKE CITY scored hits on an enemy auxiliary and destroyer. At this stage of the battle, Rear Admiral Scott ceased firing to rectify his formation, and as most of the enemy targets had disappeared there followed a short lull.

SALT LAKE CITY, HELENA, and SAN FRANCISCO reopened fire with telling effect. The BOISE damage (fire) had been brought under control, and she reentered the action, engaging a heavy cruiser and an unidentified ship, but upon receiving further damage she was forced to retire. SALT LAKE CITY, meanwhile, had covered BOISE and, assisted by SAN FRANCISCO, concentrated her fire on an enemy heavy cruiser until the action was broken off by the enemy.

During the engagement DUNCAN was so badly damaged that she had to be abandoned, and FARENHOLT was damaged. SAN FRANCISCO had been hit, and as previously stated, BOISE was severely damaged. Even so, the engagement was a victory for us, attributable in part to surprise and confusion, and in part to the accuracy of our gunfire.

* * * * * * * * * *

During the succeeding days, in spite of the reverses suffered in the Battle of Cape Esperance, the Japanese continued their attacks on Guadalcanal. Notwithstanding heavy losses inflicted on them, they succeeded in getting a number of transports through, and landed nearly another entire division. Our air attacks, however, left that division with little equipment, few rations, and inadequate artillery support. Meanwhile, support for our Marines had been arriving, and General Vandegrift had been able to improve his position. He now had better air support, made more effective by new landing strips constructed by the Seabees, but as shelling by enemy units continued, he was still in need of strong naval support, especially as the Japanese gave no signs of discontinuing their efforts to launch a full-scale attack.

Enemy submarines and aircraft renewed their efforts to interrupt our communications, and it became increasingly clear that the next Japanese move would be supported by powerful surface and air units. The destroyer MEREDITH was sunk on 15 October while engaged in keeping our line of communications open, and a few days later the heavy cruiser CHESTER was damaged by enemy submarines, but our naval forces were reinforced by the new battleship SOUTH DAKOTA, and the damaged ENTERPRISE was again ready for duty. Our naval forces were now divided into two parts, one being the WASHINGTON group under the command of Rear Admiral (later Vice Admiral) W. A. Lee, Jr. (now deceased), and the other consisting of two carriers, one battleship, three heavy cruisers, three antiaircraft light cruisers and 14 destroyers under the command of Rear Admiral Kinkaid. The former group, reinforced by the ships surviving the Battle of Cape Esperance, remained in the vicinity of Guadalcanal. The other moved northwestward in an effort to engage the enemy.

On the night of 23-24 October the Japanese began a land assault at the mouth of the Matanikau River, and although thrown back with heavy losses continued their attack the following day. On the 25th, enemy ground forces were supported by naval gunfire from two Japanese cruisers and four destroyers which slipped into Savo Sound, and on the night of 25-26 October the enemy ground offensive reached its peak. At this point the Japanese moved their naval units in force toward Guadalcanal.

The Battle of Santa Cruz Island

Early in the morning of 26 October our patrol planes made contact with three enemy forces. One of these forces included a carrier. Another consisted of two battleships, one heavy cruiser and seven destroyers. The third, which included two carriers, was attacked by the patrolling planes, and hits were scored on one of the carriers.

Simultaneously, our carriers launched three attack waves, one from ENTERPRISE and two from HORNET. While en route, the ENTERPRISE attack group encountered Japanese planes. After a short engagement during which some of our planes were shot down, it located the enemy force containing the battleships and made bomb hits on one of them. The first HORNET wave reached the enemy carrier group without interference and reported at least four 1000-pound bomb hits on a carrier. Other HORNET aircraft in that group registered three torpedo hits on a heavy cruiser. The second HORNET group discovered an enemy cruiser force and succeeded in bombing two heavy cruisers and a destroyer.

While our aircraft were delivering their attacks, our own carriers were being attacked by enemy carrier aircraft. HORNET suffered one bomb hit and was set on fire by an enemy bomber which purposely dived into the carrier's stack. Blazing gasoline was spread over the signal bridge, which was further damaged by one of the bombs carried by the plane. Resulting fires were extinguished in about two hours, but while the dive bombing attack was being delivered, a torpedo attack developed and HORNET received two hits which disrupted her power and communications. The torpedo hits were followed by three more bomb hits and another suicide plane crash which started more fires. Of 27 attacking aircraft, 20 were shot down by antiaircraft fire, but the attack, which lasted 11 minutes, left HORNET dead in the water with many fires on board and with a decided list. Our wounded personnel were promptly removed by destroyers, the fires were extinguished in about a half hour, and HORNET was taken in tow by NORTHAMPTON, but in the afternoon she was again attacked by torpedoes and dive bombers and had to be abandoned and sunk by our own forces.

Just before noon, ENTERPRISE was subjected to an attack by 24 enemy dive bombers, of which seven were shot down by antiaircraft fire in which SOUTH DAKOTA participated. Shortly after, she weathered two attacks by torpedo planes and one more attack from dive bombers.

The first dive bombing attack resulted in three hits on ENTERPRISE. Of the torpedo planes making the first attack, one dived onto the destroyer SMITH setting her on fire forward and exploding the plane's torpedo. By energetic measures, however, SMITH brought the flames under control and was able to make port. During this action dive bombers scored a hit on SOUTH DAKOTA, wounding her commanding officer, Captain (now Rear Admiral) T. L. Gatch, and inflicted considerable damage on the light cruiser SAN JUAN.

There were no further attacks and the two task forces were ordered to retire independently. During the night they were pursued by Japanese surface units, which turned back when it became clear that the enemy attacks were not succeeding.

Enemy planes estimated to have taken part in the attacks on HORNET and ENTERPRISE numbered between 170 and 180. Of that number 56 were shot down by antiaircraft fire and about the same number by our own planes. Our own losses were HORNET, the destroyer PORTER, which was torpedoed while rescuing personnel of one of our planes, and 74 aircraft. We sank no enemy vessels in the engagement, and our carrier strength in the Pacific was now dangerously low, but there were partial compensations. Two enemy carriers had been put out of action and four Japanese air groups had been cut to pieces.

Battle of Guadalcanal

For a brief period on 26 October, following the all-out enemy attack, the question of whether or not we could retain Henderson Field hung in the balance. A counterattack by Marines and by Army troops, however, restored our lines—the enemy lost 2200 men killed in that attack—and General Vandegrift took the offensive on both flanks. Except for a minor setback the following day, this constituted the last serious threat by enemy land forces on Guadalcanal.

The enemy still exercised control over the waters adjacent to Guadalcanal, and for the next two weeks our forces were engaged in scattered actions calculated to interfere with that control. Our submarines attacked Japanese supply lines, inflicting considerable damage, and on the morning of 30 October our light cruiser ATLANTA and four destroyers bombarded enemy positions near Point Cruz. On the next day the Marines, supported by naval gunfire, crossed the Matanikau River and by 3 November had advanced beyond Point Cruz. On the evening of 2 November the Japanese had landed about 1500 men and some artillery east of Koli Point but were unable to support that unit, and after our naval forces bombarded the beach heads, destroying stores and ammunition, the force was driven into the jungle and eventually exterminated. On 7 November our aircraft from Henderson Field inflicted heavy damage on an enemy light cruiser and two destroyers and shot down a number of enemy planes.

By this time it must have been apparent to the Japanese that their position was not being sufficiently improved by their continued night landings from surface craft dispatched from neighboring islands (our PT boats based at Tulagi attacked them repeatedly, sinking a destroyer and many landing craft). As evidence of that realization they again began to concentrate surface forces in the Rabaul-Buin area and by 12 November were estimated to be ready with two carriers, four battleships, five heavy cruisers, about 30 destroyers and enough transports for a decisive invasion attempt. To oppose this force we had two new battleships, four heavy cruisers, one light cruiser, three antiaircraft light cruisers, and 22 destroyers. The damaged ENTERPRISE was not ready for action and we were outnumbered in land-based aircraft.

Our troops on Guadalcanal had been reinforced on 6 November, but more supplies and reinforcements were vitally needed. Under these circumstances, Vice Admiral Halsey, who on 18 October had replaced Vice Admiral Ghormley as Commander, South Pacific Force, realized that we would have to cover our supply lines and at the same time counter the expected enemy offensive, otherwise our position in the south Pacific would be seriously jeopardized. Following this general plan, Rear Admiral Turner was placed in charge of the supply operation and the late Rear Admirals D. J. Callaghan and Scott assigned to command the covering forces. In addition, Rear Admiral Turner was to be supported by a task force commanded by Rear Admiral Kinkaid, built around the damaged ENTERPRISE and the battleships WASHINGTON and SOUTH DAKOTA.

On the morning of 11 November, three of our cargo vessels escorted by Rear Admiral Scott's task force reached Guadalcanal and began unloading off Lunga Point. Loading operations were interrupted by an air attack about four hours later which damaged the transport ZEILIN and by a second air attack two hours after that. Our protecting aircraft and antiaircraft batteries took a heavy toll of both attacking air groups. We lost a total of seven planes. Our escorts, under Rear Admiral Scott, retired to Indispensable Strait for the night.

On the morning of the 12th, the second contingent of ships with supplies and reinforcements, under Rear Admirals Turner and Callaghan, arrived and joined forces with Rear Admiral Scott. Unloading was immediately begun. As on the previous day, the enemy delivered an air attack in the afternoon but so effective was our air opposition that only one of about 25 bombers and torpedo planes escaped. One damaged enemy plane, however, dived onto SAN FRANCISCO, starting a number of minor fires and killing 30 men.

Meanwhile, our scouts had located strong enemy forces bearing down on Guadalcanal from the northwest, disposed in three groups. To meet that force Rear Admiral Turner assigned two heavy cruisers, one light cruiser, two antiaircraft light cruisers and eight destroyers to Rear Admiral Callaghan, and withdrew with the transports and cargo vessels, escorted by three destroyers. The plan was for Rear Admiral Callaghan to fight a delaying action, so that the battleship-carrier force under Rear Admiral Kinkaid would have time to intercept the Japanese landing forces believed to be en route.

After Rear Admiral Callaghan's force had escorted the transport group clear of the area, it reentered the sound shortly after midnight through Lengo Channel for the purpose of searching the vicinity of Savo Island. Near Lunga Point three groups of enemy ships were picked up to the northwestward and shortly afterward a fourth group to the northward. Our own force was a single column, with four destroyers in the van, five cruisers in the center, and four destroyers in the rear. In that situation—which was by no means as clear then as it is now, it being a very dark night with no moon—accurate identification of enemy ships was almost impossible, and in the darkness the forces nearly collided with each other before a gun was fired.

The action began when the Japanese illuminated our ships with searchlights and both sides opened fire at close range. Immediate results of the exchanges of gunfire were favorable to us. An enemy ship in the right hand group blew up within a minute under the fire from SAN FRANCISCO and other ships; and on the other side, two enemy cruisers burst into flames. Other vessels were set on fire, and ATLANTA believed she sank one of a division of Japanese destroyers crossing ahead of her. Simultaneously, ATLANTA, after suffering some hits herself, took a light cruiser under fire. At this point ATLANTA was struck by a torpedo and with all power lost, her rudder jammed. While she was circling, an enemy heavy cruiser battered her heavily, starting intense fires and killing Rear Admiral Scott and many other personnel on board.

A few minutes later SAN FRANCISCO found herself engaged with an enemy battleship in the enemy center group. In addition to the fire of SAN FRANCISCO, the battleship was attacked by LAFFEY; and CUSHING, although badly damaged, scored torpedo hits on her. LAFFEY, during this part of the action, was hit by a torpedo and later blew up. CUSHING was put out of action by gunfire.

BARTON was also torpedoed and sank almost immediately, but O'BANNON closed with the battleship and made more torpedo hits. By this time, PORTLAND had wrecked a destroyer, but had been torpedoed herself; and JUNEAU, having lost all fire control, retired from the action.

SAN FRANCISCO, assisted by PORTLAND (which responded to Rear Admiral Callaghan's radio, "We want the big ones"), concentrated fire on the battleship; HELENA, meanwhile, engaging an enemy cruiser firing at SAN FRANCISCO. At this point, a salvo from the enemy battleship smashed SAN FRANCISCO's bridge, killing Rear Admiral Callaghan, Captain Cassin Young, commanding officer of SAN FRANCISCO, and many other officers and men; but SAN FRANCISCO continued to fire, and before she was put out of action she had also accounted for a destroyer.

To recapitulate the damages sustained in the first 15 minutes of the action:

CUSHING had been put out of action by gunfire and was dead in the water; LAFFEY had sunk; STERETT and O'BANNON had been damaged; ATLANTA was burning; and SAN FRANCISCO and PORTLAND were badly holed. JUNEAU had been forced to leave the action, and BARTON had blown up. HELENA had suffered minor damage. Only AARON WARD, MONSSEN and FLETCHER remained undamaged.

The three undamaged destroyers continued the attack with gunfire and torpedoes, each scoring hits on cruisers and destroyers, MONSSEN in addition having scored torpedo hits on the damaged enemy battleship. In delivering those attacks, however, MONSSEN suffered damage which forced her to be abandoned, and STERETT, also damaged by gunfire, had to retire. The action, which lasted 24 minutes, and which was one of the most furious sea battles ever fought, was terminated when FLETCHER torpedoed an enemy heavy cruiser. During the last few minutes of the action the scattered Japanese forces had been firing at each other.

After the firing ceased, HELENA, SAN FRANCISCO, and FLETCHER joined up, proceeded out of the bay, and later fell in with JUNEAU, O'BANNON, and STERETT. At daylight the next morning PORTLAND observed a Japanese battleship [probably HIYEI, which is known to have been sunk in this action] circling slowly northwest of Savo Island, with a cruiser standing by. ATLANTA was near the beach, but her fires had been extinguished. CUSHING and MONSSEN were on fire, and AARON WARD was dead in the water. Observing an enemy destroyer south of Savo Island, PORTLAND, still turning in circles, sank it. Our planes interrupted the Japanese battleship firing at AARON WARD.

CUSHING and MONSSEN finally went down, and as the conditions on board ATLANTA were impossible to control she had to be sunk on the afternoon of the 13th.

Just before noon on the 13th, the damaged JUNEAU was attacked by an enemy submarine and sank almost immediately with heavy personnel losses.

On the morning of 13 November, ENTERPRISE launched a flight of torpedo planes which found the Japanese battleship and fired three torpedoes into it. Other attacks on the battleship were made by Army planes and other land-based aircraft from Guadalcanal and Espiritu Santo, and sometime during the evening the battleship sank.

On the morning of the 14th, a strong enemy force of cruisers and destroyers shelled Henderson Field. A few planes were destroyed, but the field was not damaged, and the bombardment was broken off when the force was attacked by our PT boats. Subsequently, planes from Henderson Field (including ENTERPRISE planes there) attacked and hit two heavy cruisers, one of which was later subjected to a second attack by ENTERPRISE planes. Other planes hit a light cruiser, and still another attack group from ENTERPRISE scored hits on a second light cruiser.

As anticipated, an enemy transport force, preceded by a heavy advance guard of battleships, cruisers and destroyers, was discovered north of Guadalcanal. This obviously was the main invasion force, and was escorted by fighter planes. Throughout the 14th, this transport group was subjected to heavy air attack by our forces, which resulted in the destruction of six transports, the probable destruction of two more, and the damaging of four. The four damaged vessels continued to Guadalcanal and beached themselves on Cape Esperance that evening. Our losses in these attacks were slight.

Rear Admiral Lee, with WASHINGTON, SOUTH DAKOTA, and ENTERPRISE, had been unable to reach the scene of the action before early evening on the 14th. Upon arrival he was ordered to conduct a search, his objective being to intercept and destroy enemy bombardment forces and the transport force itself.

Shortly after midnight a Japanese force was reported north of Savo Island, headed west. Contact was made by WASHINGTON which immediately opened fire on the leading target. SOUTH DAKOTA also opened fire, selecting the third ship as her target. Both targets disappeared and were presumed sunk. Simultaneously, four of our destroyers, which were leading the battleships, attacked an enemy group of six to ten ships, which also were taken under fire by the secondary batteries of our battleships. During this part of the action, PRESTON was sunk by gunfire, BENHAM was damaged by a torpedo, and WALKE was hit by both torpedoes and gunfire. WALKE was abandoned and sank in a few minutes. The remaining destroyer, GWIN, was damaged and forced to retire.

At this stage of the action all of our destroyers had been eliminated but neither WASHINGTON nor SOUTH DAKOTA had been hit. WASHINGTON soon located new targets, one of which was a battleship, and immediately opened fire. SOUTH DAKOTA fired on an enemy ship which had turned on her searchlights. The enemy in returning the fire concentrated on SOUTH DAKOTA. The result of this exchange was that SOUTH DAKOTA shot out all lights, and apparently sank one of the illuminating vessels, but was herself hit, suffering considerable damage to her upper works. WASHINGTON continued to fire at the battleship, and after setting her on fire and after inflicting damage on other ships, forced the enemy to retire. The enemy battleship [KIRISHIMA] is known to have been sunk in this action.

The action having been broken off, and SOUTH DAKOTA and WASHINGTON having become separated, both ships retired, and joined up the next morning. At daylight on 15 November, the four Japanese vessels which had beached themselves on Guadalcanal were bombed by aircraft from Henderson Field, and shelled by Marine artillery. The destroyer MEADE, which now exercised complete control in the area, all by herself, then completed the destruction of the beached ships by leisurely bombardment. The three day fight ended with an air engagement between ENTERPRISE fighters from Henderson Field and a flight of about 12 Zeros.

The Battle of Guadalcanal, in spite of heavy losses we sustained, was a decisive victory for us, and our position in the southern Solomons was not threatened again seriously by the Japanese. Except for the "Tokio express," which from time to time succeeded in landing small quantities of supplies and reinforcements, control of the sea and air in the southern Solomons passed to the United States.

* * * * * * * * *

After the Battle of Guadalcanal, our forces on the island retained the offensive, hunting down the Japanese in the jungles and gradually driving them westward. The 1st Marine Division was gradually withdrawn and replaced by army troops, and in December General Vandegrift turned over command to Major General (later Lieutenant General) A. M. Patch, USA (now deceased).

At the end of November, however, another powerful Japanese attempt to relieve Guadalcanal was suspected, and in order to counter such a move, Admiral Halsey placed a force consisting of the heavy cruisers MINNEAPOLIS, NEW ORLEANS, NORTHAMPTON and PENSACOLA, the light cruiser HONOLULU, and four destroyers under the command of Rear Admiral C. H. Wright.

The Battle of Tassafaronga (Lunga Point)

On 30 November, Rear Admiral Wright reached the entrance to Savo Sound, where he was joined by two more destroyers. Late that night, while crossing the sound, his force made contact with seven enemy ships, and, as the range closed, the destroyers in the van opened fire with torpedoes. Shortly afterward all ships were directed to open fire.

Immediate results of the fire appeared decidedly favorable but because of the visibility we were unable to get a clear picture of the enemy formation, and there was a temporary lull in the action.

MINNEAPOLIS and NEW ORLEANS soon engaged new targets, one of which blew up. At this time, however, both MINNEAPOLIS and NEW ORLEANS were struck by torpedoes and a few minutes later PENSACOLA and NORTHAMPTON were also torpedoed, the latter being so badly damaged that she had to be abandoned. Undamaged ships undertook to close with the enemy but were unable to regain contact.

The effect of this engagement was to break up a Japanese reinforcing attempt, but only at severe cost. Our three damaged cruisers, however, reached port safely and were repaired and refitted.

The Evacuation of Guadalcanal

With the exception of encounters with the "Tokio express," surface naval action in the Guadalcanal area ended with the Battle of Tassafaronga (Lunga Point).

On land, our forces gradually compressed and weakened the enemy, and by January the Japanese ground forces on the island, which had not been adequately supported, occupied a most unfavorable position. Under these circumstances, and bearing in mind the events of the past few weeks, it was reasonable to expect another effort on the part of the enemy to retake Guadalcanal. The Japanese had had time to repair and reorganize their surface forces and to replace their carrier air groups, and therefore when there were heavy increases in shipping at Buin and Rabaul late in January, and a stepping up of air activity, it appeared that they were ready to move. Ships available to Admiral Halsey to prevent such a move now consisted of three new battleships, four old battleships, two carriers, three auxiliary carriers, three heavy cruisers, seven light cruisers, two antiaircraft light cruisers and numerous destroyers—a force considerably stronger than any we had had in the area up to that time.

On 27 January a convoy left New Caledonia for Guadalcanal. On 29 January the heavy cruiser CHICAGO (a unit of the covering force for the convoy) was torpedoed and badly damaged by enemy planes in a night attack, and the next afternoon she was again attacked by planes, the damage inflicted being so severe that she sank immediately after being abandoned. In an effort to cover CHICAGO, the destroyer LA VALLETTE was also torpedoed.

The convoy reached Guadalcanal without damage, unloaded, and departed on the 31st. On the following day Army troops were landed behind enemy ground forces at Verahue. While engaged in covering the landing craft used in this operation two destroyers, NICHOLAS and DE HAVEN, were attacked by enemy dive bombers, and DE HAVEN was sunk.

In anticipation of another attack on the island our forces were disposed south of Guadalcanal, and aircraft dispatched by Admiral Halsey and General MacArthur carried out daily attacks on enemy air fields in the Bismarcks and northern Solomons.

The first week in February the "Tokio expresses" were increased in size, and it soon became apparent that the enemy was evacuating what little strength he had left on the island. On the night of 7-8 February 1943, exactly six months after our landing in the Solomons, the enemy completed his withdrawal. On 8 February our troops on Guadalcanal, which had been closing in on the enemy from both sides, joined forces, and the first Solomons campaign, except for incidental mopping up, ended.

NEW GEORGIA AND BOUGAINVILLE CAMPAIGNS (INCLUDES NEW GUINEA OPERATIONS)

The evacuation of Guadalcanal on 8 February 1943 was by no means an indication that the Japanese were retiring from the Solomon Islands. On the contrary, there was ample evidence that they would make every effort to retain their positions in the Solomons and in New Guinea. Conversely, having pushed them out of the southern Solomons area, our next undertaking was to push them out of the northern Solomons.

The most important enemy position in the northern Solomons was the airfield they had constructed on Munda Point on the southwest coast of New Georgia Island, but construction of a secondary base near the mouth of the Vila River on the southern tip of Kolombangara Island had begun in the latter part of December. These two airfields constituted a threat to our position on Guadalcanal, about 200 miles away, and were therefore repeatedly attacked by aircraft from Guadalcanal during January, February, and March. In addition, our surface forces conducted a series of bombardments of those positions. Munda was bombarded on the night of 4 January by a task group of cruisers and destroyers. The Vila-Stanmore district of Kolombangara Island was shelled on the night of 23-24 January. On the nights of 5-6 March and 12-13 May both airfields were bombarded simultaneously. Neither the air attacks nor the bombardments were successful in putting the airfields out of commission for more than a day or two at a time.

On 21 February our forces made landings in the Russell Islands, 60 miles northwest of Guadalcanal, and immediately began the construction of strong defenses.

On 1 March, in an attempt to reinforce New Guinea, the Japanese sent two convoys totalling 21 vessels through the Bismarck Sea. Both convoys were discovered and were almost completely destroyed by United States Army and Allied aircraft in a three day running attack.

Extensive preparations were now being made for the invasion of New Georgia, and although there were no noteworthy naval engagements for some time, aerial operations were intensified throughout the South Pacific area. Japanese raids were frequent and heavy even though carried out at severe cost to the enemy. During this period of stepped up air operations, our advance base in the Russell Islands was in constant use by our planes.

On 16 June one of the most furious air battles of the Pacific war was fought over Guadalcanal. A force of enemy aircraft estimated at 60 bombers and 60 fighters was met by slightly more than 100 United States fighters manned by Army, Marine Corps, and Navy pilots. As a result of this encounter 107 enemy planes were shot down at a cost of six United States fighters lost, one landing ship (tank) and one cargo vessel damaged.

On the night of 29–30 June, as a preliminary to the invasion of New Georgia, a task group of cruisers and destroyers under the command of Rear Admiral A.S. Merrill bombarded Vila-Stanmore and the Buin-Shortland area near the southeast end of Bougainville Island. After the operation was underway, both Munda and Vila airfields were repeatedly bombed.

On 30 June surprise landings were virtually unopposed in the Woodlark and Trobriand Island groups between the Solomons and New Guinea, and at Nassau Bay on New Guinea. On the same day landings were made simultaneously by the Army at Rendova Harbor and by Marines at Viru Harbor. Two groups of destroyers covered the landing at Rendova, and effectually silenced enemy land batteries on Munda Point. Enemy aircraft attacking our transports and destroyers were beaten off by our protecting fighters or shot down by ships' antiaircraft batteries, but not until they had succeeded in torpedoing and sinking the transport MC CAWLEY.

On 2 and 3 July landings were made on New Georgia and at Vangunu Island to the southeast of New Georgia.

During the night of 4–5 July a task group of United States cruisers and destroyers bombarded enemy positions and gun installations on the islands of Kolombangara and New Georgia, in order to support landings at Rice Anchorage. During this bombardment the destroyer STRONG was sunk by a combination of torpedo hits and gunfire from the shore batteries. Immediately after the bombardment more landings were effected for the purpose of seizing the harbors of Enogai and Bairoko.

Battle of Kula Gulf

As the "Tokio express" was making nightly runs through Blackett Strait and Kula Gulf to supply and reinforce the Japanese at Vila and elsewhere, an American task force of cruisers and destroyers, under the command of Rear Admiral W. L. Ainsworth, was dispatched to intercept the enemy. Early in the morning of 6 July contact with two enemy groups was made in Kula Gulf. Our forces opened fire with devastating effect on the first enemy group and subsequently took enemy ships in the second group under an equally effective fire. Enemy fire consisted chiefly of torpedoes. While the amount of damage inflicted on the enemy could not be accurately determined, it is probable that two Japanese destroyers were sunk in this action.

During the action the cruiser HELENA was torpedoed and sunk. Some of her personnel were rescued on the spot, and others made their way to Vella Lavella Island where they were later rescued.

Battle of Kolombangara (Second Battle of Kula Gulf)

During the second week of the New Georgia campaign our ground forces consolidated their positions at Rendova, Rice Anchorage, Viru, and began to close in on Munda. Meanwhile, the Navy continued to protect American ground troops and to prevent the enemy from reinforcing his Munda garrison.

On 12 July another task group under Rear Admiral Ainsworth again intercepted the "Tokio express." As a result of the engagement which followed (on the

13th)—the enemy was again disposed in two groups—the first enemy group was badly shot up, and one cruiser was probably sunk. The second, however, inflicted considerable damage on our forces—the cruisers ST. LOUIS and HONOLULU were damaged by torpedoes, and the destroyer GWIN was set on fire and had to be sunk. The New Zealand cruiser LEANDER suffered a torpedo hit while engaged with the first enemy group.

The two engagements in Kula Gulf were costly, but they removed a threat of naval action by the enemy which might have jeopardized our landings on the north coast of New Georgia. Furthermore, they effectively prevented the Japanese from using the Kula Gulf route to supply and reinforce their garrisons at Vila and Munda.

* * * * * * * * *

Our ground troops on New Georgia slowly converged on Munda, which was also subjected to bombardments from the sea and air. Other air attacks were delivered by Allied airplanes at Ballale, at Vila, at Vovine Cove, at Buin, at Kahili airdrome and at Shortland Harbor. The biggest single attack consisted of the dropping of 186 tons of bombs on Munda on 25 July. During the 37 days of the Munda campaign our planes destroyed an estimated 350 Japanese aircraft at a cost of 93.

Munda airfield was captured on 5 August, almost exactly one year after the first landing on Guadalcanal, and six weeks after New Georgia was invaded. The fall of Munda climaxed the central Solomons campaign, and Bairoko Harbor, eight miles to the northward, was the last remaining Japanese strong point on New Georgia Island. Vila, on the southern tip of Kolombangara Island, was virtually neutralized as soon as the Seabees and Army engineers rebuilt the Munda air strip.

The Battle of Vella Gulf

Our rapid consolidation of our control over the sea routes and the heavy ship losses sustained by the enemy during June and July made it necessary for the Japanese to support their forces at Kolombangara by barge traffic moving at night close to the coast of Vella Lavella. As our PT boats inflicted considerable damage on enemy barges and landing craft in that area, the Japanese, on 6 August 1943, undertook to send equipment and troops, escorted by a cruiser and three destroyers, into Vella Gulf between Vella Lavella and Kolombangara Islands. This operation, which was calculated to support enemy forces at Vila, led to the third surface action in the area within a month. A task group of American destroyers commanded by Commander (now Commodore) Frederick Moosbrugger took the enemy force by surprise shortly before midnight. In an engagement lasting about 45 minutes, the three Japanese destroyers were believed sunk. Our forces suffered no damage.

Invasion of Vella Lavella

Vella Lavella Island, about 14 miles northwest of Kolombangara, was selected as the next objective in the central Solomons campaign. Although the island was not occupied by the Japanese, and no opposition in force was expected, preparations were made to resist air attacks from enemy airfields to the north.

On 15 August three transport groups succeeded in making landings as planned.

The anticipated enemy air attacks materialized, but did not seriously interfere with the landings, as our own air support broke up their attacks.

Action of 17–18 August

On 17 August four enemy destroyers and a number of barges were reported en route from Bougainville on a southeasterly course. Four of our destroyers, under the command of Captain T. J. Ryan, Jr., intercepted and attacked the enemy force north of Vella Gulf at night. Our forces scored heavily with gunfire on enemy destroyers and barges, whereupon the enemy force broke off the action. Our destroyers sustained no losses.

* * * * * * * * *

The campaign on New Georgia ended successfully with the occupation of Bairoko Harbor on 25 August. The Japanese lost heavily in attempting to evacuate personnel across Kula Gulf to Vila, when PT boats attacked and sank numerous barges filled with enemy troops. As a result of the occupation of Bairoko, Kolombangara Island, which was still occupied by a Japanese garrison, was now between our forces controlling New Georgia to the southeast and those occupying Vella Lavella to the northwest. Positions secured on Arundel, which was occupied on 27 August, made it possible to bring artillery to bear on the Japanese installations at Vila.

With his air power weakened, the enemy decided to evacuate Vila during the month of September. Again barges were used for the evacuation, with costly results to the enemy. Toward the end of the month of September our destroyers conducted a particularly damaging attack on barges, which up to that time had been attacked chiefly by aircraft and PT boats. Enemy personnel losses during the evacuation of Kolombangara were undoubtedly heavy, and it was assumed that these heavy losses were the cause of increased activity to the northward shortly thereafter, particularly in the vicinity of Bougainville.

Action of 6 October

On the night of 6 October a task group consisting of three destroyers, CHEVALIER, SELFRIDGE, and O'BANNON, commanded by Captain F. R. Walker, sighted a superior force of enemy ships south of Choiseul. The enemy was disposed in two groups, one of which appeared to consist of a light cruiser and four destroyers, the other of four destroyers.

Our destroyers, in spite of their being outnumbered, closed in and attacked with gunfire and torpedoes. The result was the repulse of a superior force and the inflicting of considerable damage, at the cost, however, of the CHEVALIER, which was torpedoed and sunk.

* * * * * * * * *

By 6 October the enemy completed evacuating his troops from Kolombangara and Vella Lavella Islands, and the central Solomons campaign ended.

Bougainville Campaign

Attacks on Bougainville and the small islands to the north and south of it began about three weeks after the evacuation of Kolombangara, our air forces meanwhile having softened up the airfields of Kahili, Ballale, and Karu by daily attacks.

On 26–27 October Mono and Stirling in the Treasury Islands were invaded and occupied; on 28 October a landing was made on Choiseul Island; and on 1 November landings were made on Bougainville Island. The landings on Mono Island were preceded by bombardments by a task force commanded by Rear Admiral (now Vice Admiral) T. S. Wilkinson. Another task force under Rear Admiral Merrill bombarded enemy positions at Bonis on Bougainville and at Buka immediately preceding our landing. Rear Admiral Merrill's force then proceeded to the Shortland Islands off the southern coast of Bougainville and delivered another bombardment on Morgusaia Island.

In the meantime a landing force of Marines under the command of Lieutenant General Vandegrift (who had returned to the area following the death of Major General Barrett) landed at Empress Augusta Bay, about midway up the west coast of the island of Bougainville.

Action of 2 November

Shortly before noon on 1 November an enemy task force of four cruisers and eight destroyers was observed at the southern end of St. George's Channel, but an attempt by Rear Admiral Merrill's force to intercept was not successful, as the enemy retired before action could be joined. On the following morning, however, a Japanese force consisting of three groups of four ships each was picked up and attacked. After having suffered considerable damage, the enemy again retired. We lost no ships and sustained relatively light damage in this engagement.

The next day our ships, which had retired to Empress Augusta Bay, were attacked by enemy aircraft but suffered no appreciable damage.

* * * * * * * * * *

Army troops reinforced the Marines at Empress Augusta Bay on 8 November, and, after consolidating our beach heads, took the offensive against enemy troops on the island. On 8 November the enemy delivered an air attack on a force of our light cruisers and destroyers under the command of Rear Admiral L. T. DuBose. The attack was not successful, in that we were able to protect our transports from enemy attacks while the transports were retiring from Bougainville.

On the night of 12–13 November, while engaged in covering transports en route to Torokina Point, Rear Admiral Merrill's task force was attacked by enemy forces.

On 17 November Japanese planes attacking another of our echelons bound to Torokina succeeded in sinking the destroyer transport MC KEAN.

Action of 25 November

On 25 November four of our destroyers, patrolling the area between Buka and Cape St. George on the southern tip of New Ireland, attacked a superior enemy force with torpedoes and gunfire, inflicting considerable damage on the enemy. None of our ships was damaged.

* * * * * * * * *

During the month of December, American land-based aircraft continued vigorous operations against Japanese positions throughout the northern Solomons, with the result that enemy airfields in the Buka-Bonis areas were completely neutralized. Meanwhile, our troops and supplies continued to move unopposed into the base at Cape Torokina on Empress Augusta Bay.

On 20 December a force of American destroyers bombarded a Japanese concentration on northeastern Bougainville and on the 23rd, a task force of cruisers and destroyers bombarded the Buka-Bonis area. On the 27th, another force shelled the Kieta area.

Operations in New Guinea

Concurrently with the attacks on Japanese positions in the central Solomons, a powerful attack had been launched in the New Guinea Theater. On the night of 29–30 June Allied troops made a successful landing on Nassau Bay, about ten miles south of the Japanese base at Salamaua, and moved up the coast to Mubo and Komistum. After the landing, the Navy assisted in the new offensive by the use of planes and PT boats to harass enemy landing barges and prevent reinforcements from being put ashore. Task units of our destroyers also assisted by bombarding enemy defenses and installations.

On 3 September our amphibious forces were ready to move against the enemy's naval and air bases in the Huon Gulf area, and a task force of destroyers and smaller craft successfully landed the Australian 9th Division and other troops near Nopoi. During the following days other task forces escorted more landing craft to the beaches, successfully fighting off air attacks, and on 7–8 September bombarded positions in the vicinity of Lae. On 11 September Allied forces captured Salamaua and five days later Lae, thereby giving our naval forces additional bases.

The next objective of the Allied amphibious forces was Finschafen on the eastern end of the Huon Peninsula. On the morning of 22 September a task force of destroyers and landing craft proceeded to a beach about six miles north of Finschafen and after a brief bombardment landed a strong Australian force. Enemy air attack was ineffectual. On 2 October Finschafen was captured and our PT boats sank a number of barges loaded with enemy troops attempting to get clear of the island. On the following day our destroyer task forces suffered their first loss when the destroyer HENLEY was torpedoed and sunk.

On 2 January an Allied landing in force was made on Saidor on the New Guinea coast. There was no opposition to the landing, and there were no personnel casualties.

On 13 February a final occupation of the Huon Peninsula was completed by the meeting of Australian units coming from the eastward with the 32nd United States Division.

Rabaul

As our forces moved toward control of the Solomons and New Guinea, it became possible to strike more directly at Rabaul. This Japanese-held port was in a key position to control the general area to the south.

On 5 November a task force under Rear Admiral (now Vice Admiral) F. C. Sherman, built around aircraft carriers, delivered an air attack on Rabaul. Bombs and torpedoes directed at shipping at anchor resulted in heavy damage to enemy heavy cruisers and destroyers present. Although our planes met Japanese air resistance, we shot down about 25 enemy planes at the cost of three of our own. This carrier-based strike was supplemented the same day by a large group of Liberators, which did severe damage to Rabaul's waterfront.

A week later there was a second series of air attacks on Rabaul. This time two American task forces were engaged. Rear Admiral Sherman's ships sent in a large flight of planes, and although unfavorable weather prevented inflicting as much damage as on the prior raid, hits were scored on Japanese destroyers outside the harbor. The same day a task force under Rear Admiral A. E. Montgomery sent in a large flight of planes to attack Rabaul shipping. Heavy damage to cruisers and destroyers in the harbor was reported. Our planes shot down 24 enemy aircraft at the cost of seven of our own.

Early in the afternoon of 11 November a Japanese air attack was delivered against the carriers under Rear Admiral Montgomery. No damage was done to our ships and something over 50 enemy planes were shot down by a combination of our own planes and antiaircraft fire. We lost three planes in the encounter. Another flight of Liberators attacked Rabaul on 11 November.

During the last ten days of December the major Japanese base on Rabaul was struck by land-based planes operating from bases in the Solomons and elsewhere in the South Pacific area. On 25 December planes from a carrier task force attacked Kavieng, another important enemy base on the northern tip of New Ireland. Reports indicated the damaging of a destroyer, the sinking of two cargo ships and three barges, and damage to other enemy units afloat. Upon its withdrawal, our task force was heavily attacked by enemy planes, but received no damage. On 28 December Kavieng was again attacked, this time by our shore-based aircraft.

The attacks on Rabaul were significant in that they destroyed and damaged Japanese men-of-war (always a main objective of our aircraft), which were thereby prevented from resisting our offensive in the northern Solomons, New Guinea or the Gilbert Islands.

In the western end of New Britain island, successful landings were made at Arawe on 15 December and at Cape Gloucester on 26 December by amphibious forces from the Southwest Pacific Force.

On 1 January another carrier strike on Kavieng was delivered by a task force under the command of Rear Admiral Sherman. This task force was supported by a group of battleships under the command of Rear Admiral Lee. Primary targets were two enemy cruisers and destroyers about to enter the port. Preliminary reports indicated that the attacks on the cruisers were successful, and that both were either sunk or beached. One of the destroyers was hit by a heavy bomb and both were strafed. Information is lacking as to the effect on the destroyers, but both were believed heavily damaged. Between 20 and 30 enemy aircraft intercepted the attack. Eleven were shot down. Our losses were two fighters and one bomber.

On 4 January a task force successfully attacked two destroyers off the entrance to Kavieng.

On 8 January cruisers under the command of Rear Admiral Ainsworth bombarded the Shortlands without incident.

On 15 February an Allied landing in strength on Green Island, 120 miles from Rabaul, was virtually unopposed. On 18 February two destroyer task groups, one commanded by Captain (now Commodore) R. W. Simpson and the other by Captain A. A. Burke, bombarded Rabaul and Kavieng without suffering damage from enemy air attack. The task force making the landing was under the command of Rear Admiral Wilkinson, assault forces being composed of American and New Zealand troops. A task force of cruisers and destroyers commanded by Rear Admiral Ainsworth covered the advance and retirement of the assault forces. The aircraft task force under Vice Admiral Fitch and a support force of cruisers and destroyers commanded by Rear Admiral Merrill participated in the operation.

Occupation of the Admiralty Islands

On 29 February amphibious forces from the Southwest Pacific Force under the command of Rear Admiral W. M. Fechteler (these forces included the 1st Cavalry Division, dismounted) conducted a reconnaissance in force on Los Negros in the Admiralty Islands. As the reconnaissance revealed insufficient enemy strength to warrant withdrawing our reconnaissance forces, the island was promptly occupied. Covering forces were cruisers and destroyers under the command of Rear Admiral (now Vice Admiral) D. E. Barbey. This was a brilliant maneuver in the campaign in that part of the Pacific, conducted under the direction of General MacArthur.

The Offensive
THE CENTRAL PACIFIC CAMPAIGN

Our only operations in the central Pacific following the Battle of Midway had consisted of a diversionary damaging raid on the island of Makin, in the Gilberts, by a small party under the command of Captain J. M. Haines. On 17–18 August the submarines NAUTILUS and ARGONAUT transported officers and men of the 2nd Marine Raider Battalion to the island, where they annihilated the Japanese garrison and did severe damage to enemy installations.

Toward the end of August 1943, while Allied forces in the southwest Pacific were advancing toward the Japanese bases at Rabaul and Truk, and while other forces in the Aleutians were consolidating their positions, Admiral Nimitz organized important units of the Pacific Fleet for a series of assaults on the enemy's outposts in the central Pacific. These task forces succeeded in capturing certain islands on the eastern rim of the enemy's defenses and in diverting the Japanese from the northern

Solomons and New Guinea. In addition, these operations represented valuable combat training for new air and surface units of the fleet.

Capture of the Gilbert Islands

The Gilbert Islands are a group of coral atolls lying athwart the equator. They had been held by the British up to the outbreak of war in December 1941, when they were seized by the Japanese. Their location is of great strategic significance because they are north and west of other islands in our possession and immediately south and east of important Japanese bases in the Carolines and Marshalls. The capture of the Gilberts was, therefore, a necessary part of any serious thrust at the Japanese Empire.

In August, September, and October, carrier-based air strikes on Marcus, Tarawa, Apamama, and Wake served to soften Japanese installations and keep the enemy guessing as to where our next full-scale attack would be delivered. The attack on Wake was particularly effective as it included considerable bombardment in addition to air attacks. Enemy air opposition was overcome, and a heavy toll of enemy planes was taken, both on the ground and in the air. During October and early November, planes from our bases attacked the Japanese in the Gilberts and also the Marshalls. The Japanese retaliated by raiding our establishments in the Ellice Islands.

During October and November, various units of the Pacific Fleet were placed under the command of Vice Admiral Spruance, who was designated Commander, Central Pacific Force. Vice Admiral Spruance had commanded one of the task forces at the battle of Midway and had more recently been Chief of Staff to the Commander in Chief, Pacific Fleet. Rear Admiral Turner, who had been in command at sea during the campaigns in the Solomon Islands, was placed in charge of our amphibious forces and Major General (now Lieutenant General) H. M. Smith, USMC, in charge of the landing forces. Other forces in the command were placed under Rear Admiral (now Vice Admiral) H. W. Hill. The entire force consisted of battleships, cruisers, aircraft carriers, destroyers and destroyer escorts, transports and numerous auxiliaries and landing craft. Shore-based aircraft were commanded by Rear Admiral (now Vice Admiral) J. H. Hoover.

During the second week in November, while operations in the Bougainville area and attacks on Rabaul were in progress, the force under Vice Admiral Spruance headed west. On 19 November our cruisers bombarded Tarawa, and on the morning of 20 November our attack groups were off both Tarawa and Makin Islands.

Heavy shore bombardments by battleships and cruisers preceded the landing at Makin. Army units which landed there met little opposition at first, and although the Japanese eventually put up a stiff resistance the issue there was never in serious doubt. The capture of Makin was announced on 22 November.

The assault on Tarawa was bitterly contested. Tarawa was heavily fortified, and garrisoned by about 3,500 Japanese troops on Betio, the principal island in the group. They had been attacked repeatedly from the air for weeks preceding the assault and on the day before they had been heavily bombarded. In spite of these attacks, which silenced the Japanese heavy guns, wrecked everything above ground and killed approximately half of the enemy troops, their dugouts, pillboxes, and bomb-proof shelters were still partially intact.

The enemy was able to concentrate his forces beside the only beach where a landing was possible. In spite of fire support from the air and from ships, our casualties were heavy. The fighting which ensued was considered by many to be the most intense of any in the war, and the personnel of the 2nd Marine Division, under the command of Major General Julian C. Smith, and of the naval units which accompanied them in their landing, demonstrated magnificent courage and tenacity. The assault lasted nearly four days, at the end of which the island was captured.

During the assault period on both Tarawa and Makin, our transports, covered by their escorts, lay off the islands unloading. In some cases, ships were able to enter the lagoons and unload. During this period enemy submarine attacks which developed off Tarawa were successfully combatted, but LISCOME BAY, an escort carrier, was torpedoed and sunk off Makin. Rear Admiral H. M. Mullinnix, and the commanding officer, Captain I. D. Wiltsie, and a large number of officers and men were lost. Enemy air attacks were successfully driven off by our own aircraft.

After the completion of the assault phase of the operation, our task forces withdrew to their bases to the north and south. Carrier task groups, under Rear Admirals C. A. Pownall and A. E. Montgomery, attacked enemy air bases in the Marshalls on 4 December, the main attack being directed against the atoll of Kwajalein, where enemy naval and merchant vessels, aircraft and shore installations were heavily struck with torpedoes and bombs. A lighter attack was made on the island of Wotje. Another task force under Rear Admiral Lee proceeding southward from the Gilberts attacked the island of Nauru. Carrier planes bombed the island, and battleships subjected it to heavy bombardments, starting large fires and destroying a number of planes.

During the remainder of the year, Army and Navy land-based planes carried out repeated attacks on enemy holdings in the Marshall Islands and at Nauru, inflicting considerable damage on ships and shore installations. Enemy air attacks on our newly acquired bases in the Gilberts were delivered, but no serious damage was sustained.

Operations in the Marshall Islands

On 29 January offensive operations on the largest scale yet undertaken were directed against the Marshall Islands by task forces under the command of Vice Admiral Spruance. On that date simultaneous attacks were delivered on Kwajalein by carriers commanded by Rear Admiral F. C. Sherman, on Roi by carriers commanded by Rear Admiral Montgomery, on Taroa by carriers commanded by Rear Admiral J. W. Reeves, and on Wotje by carriers commanded by Rear Admiral S. P. Ginder. In addition, cruisers under the command of Rear Admiral E. G. Small bombarded Taroa and Wotje, and shore-based aircraft under Rear Admiral Hoover bombed all four islands, together with Mille and Jaluit.

On 30 January carrier attacks were resumed on Kwajalein by forces under Rear Admiral Reeves and the island was also bombarded by battleships. Roi was again attacked by Rear Admiral Montgomery's carrier force, and in addition was heavily bombarded by battleships. Taroa and Wotje were again struck by a carrier force under Rear Admiral Ginder and in addition were bombarded by cruisers. Forces under the command of Rear Admiral Small assisted in the bombardment of Wotje and Maloelap. Ebeye was struck by carrier forces under Rear Admiral Reeves, and Eniwetok was attacked by carriers under Rear Admiral Sherman. Mille, Jaluit and Wake were bombed by shore-based aircraft.

Other forces under Admiral Spruance's command in this operation consisted of a joint expeditionary force (southern attack group) under Rear Admiral Turner. Defense forces and land-based aircraft were under the command of Rear Admiral Hoover. Rear Admiral Hill commanded an attack group and Rear Admiral (now Vice Admiral) R. L. Conolly another (the northern attack group). Expeditionary troops were under the command of Major General H. M. Smith. The carrier task forces were commanded by Rear Admiral (now Vice Admiral) M. A. Mitscher.

On 31 January the forces commanded by Rear Admiral Hill proceeded against the atoll of Majuro, but found no Japanese present there. On the following day troops were sent ashore and the atoll was occupied.

On 2 February landings were made on Roi, Namur and Kwajalein. Roi was secured and enemy resistance on Namur was confined to the northern part of the island. By the middle of the afternoon all organized resistance on Roi and Namur was overcome and the Commanding General of the 4th Marine Division (Major General Harry Schmidt, USMC) assumed command ashore. Our casualties on these two islands were less than 100 killed and 400 wounded. Simultaneously four smaller islands were occupied. At Kwajalein our troops (7th Division, United States Army) made considerable progress against increasing resistance.

By 5 February our troops on Kwajalein had captured the island, and by the 8th, the entire atoll was in our possession.

Taroa, Wotje, Jaluit, Mille and Ponape were bombed and/or bombarded at frequent intervals during the remainder of the month.

On 17-18 February forces under the command of Vice Admiral Spruance delivered an attack on the island of Truk. The first part of the attack by carrier-based planes was followed up by battleships, cruisers and destroyers. Heavy damage was inflicted on the enemy, both in ships sunk and damaged, and in planes shot down and destroyed on the ground. This attack, which was delivered with devastating effect, was particularly satisfying as it was generally regarded as partial payment for the debt incurred when Pearl Harbor was attacked.

Forces participating in the attack on Truk included carriers under the command of Rear Admiral Mitscher (under whom were Rear Admirals Reeves, Montgomery and Sherman); cruisers commanded by Rear Admirals DuBose, J. L. Wiltsie, and Rear Admiral (now Vice Admiral) R. C. Giffen; and battleships under Rear Admirals G. B. Davis, E. W. Hanson, and Rear Admiral (now Vice Admiral) O. M. Hustvedt.

On 17 February an expeditionary task group under the command of Rear Admiral Hill (assault troops were headed by Brigadier General T. E. Watson, USMC) landed on Eniwetok Atoll, which had previously been bombarded and bombed over a period of several days. Supporting forces included carriers under Rear Admirals V. H. Ragsdale and Ginder, cruisers commanded by Rear Admiral (now Vice Admiral) J. B. Oldendorf and Rear Admiral L. H. Thebaud.

On 18 February, after extensive bombing and bombardment, Engebi Island was captured. With the capture of Eniwetok on 20 February, announced by Rear Admiral Hill, control of the Marshall Islands, which were Japanese possessions before the war, passed to the United States. The operations in the Marshall Islands carried out by the forces under Vice Admiral Spruance were characterized by excellent planning and by almost perfect timing in the execution of those plans. The entire operation was a credit to all who participated, and is a noteworthy example of the results that may be expected from good staff work.

Raids on the Marianas

On 22 February (East Longitude Date), a task force under the command of Rear Admiral Mitscher, en route to deliver attacks on Saipan and Tinian in the Marianas, was detected by enemy search planes and subsequently attacked by enemy bombers and torpedo planes. The task force suffered no damage, shot down a number of planes and proceeded to deliver attacks on the objectives stated the next day. During the attack several enemy ships were sunk and damaged. About 30 enemy planes were shot down and 85 or more were destroyed on the ground. In addition, numerous small craft were destroyed. At the same time our aircraft raided Guam.

Supporting Operations

NORTHERN PACIFIC CAMPAIGN

Since the Aleutian Islands constitute an aerial highway between the North American continent and the Far East, their strategic value is obvious. On the other hand, that chain of islands provides as rugged a theater for warfare as any in the world. Not only are the islands mountainous and rocky, but the weather in the western part of the islands is continually bad. The fogs are almost continuous, and thick. Violent winds (known locally as "williwaws") with accompanying heavy seas make any kind of operation in that vicinity difficult and uncertain. The Bering Sea has been termed a "storm factory," because during the winter months the storms form up there and, at the rate of one or two a week, travel east and southeast.

In May 1942, when we were calculating the various risks involved in the disposition of our forces, Dutch Harbor in the Aleutian Islands was considered to be a definite possibility as an enemy objective. A task force to operate in that area was therefore organized and placed under the command of Rear Admiral R. A. Theobald. His command included all American and Canadian Army personnel in the north Pacific, including sea and air units.

On 3 June 1942, just as the battle of Midway was beginning, Dutch Harbor was attacked by Japanese high altitude bombers, presumably from enemy carriers. The attacking force was not located immediately, because the fog set in, and the intention of the enemy was therefore obscure. Within a few days, however, it was discoverde that the enemy force had turned westward and effected landings on the islands of Kiska and Attu, where they were erecting buildings.

During June and July, in spite of the weather, our submarines and aircraft, by a series of attacks, succeeded in preventing the arrival of major Japanese reinforcements. Army Air Force bombardment squadrons and units of the Royal Canadian Air Force contributed notably to these operations, as they did to the operations of the succeeding months.

On 7 August Rear Admiral W. W. Smith, with a force of cruisers and destroyers, bombarded the shore installations on Kiska, but because of poor visibility the damage inflicted could not be ascertained. The bombardment served, however, to indicate the need for air bases closer to the islands occupied by the Japanese and as a consequence we occupied the island of Adak, in the Andreanof Group, at the end of August. In January 1943, we occupied Amchitka, considerably closer to Kiska, and by February our fighter planes were able to operate from there. By that time, we also had made good progress in establishing and equipping the base on Adak. Meanwhile, Kiska was attacked almost daily by planes from the Andreanofs.

Because of weather conditions and the employment of our forces in other theaters, no attacks, other than bombing raids, with the exception of the bombardment previously referred to and the bombardment of Holtz Bay and Chicagof Harbor, Attu, on 18 February by cruisers and destroyers commanded by Rear Admiral (now Vice Admiral) C. H. McMorris, were delivered on the islands until the spring of 1943.

Battle of the Komandorski Islands

In that situation, the enemy, late in March 1943, undertook to support the two garrisons by sending through a small but heavily protected convoy. Early on the morning of 26 March, a unit of our North Pacific Force, commanded by Rear Admiral McMorris, encountered the advancing enemy force, which included heavy and light cruisers, some destroyers and cargo ships, about 65 miles south of the Komandorski Peninsula. Our force, although outnumbered, closed for attack.

The engagement which followed developed into a running gunfire duel between our cruisers SALT LAKE CITY and RICHMOND and enemy cruisers. This was followed by a torpedo attack delivered by our destroyers, upon completion of which the enemy retired in the direction of Paramushiru, 500 miles to the westward. Our damage was small and our casualties were light. While the damage inflicted on the enemy is not definitely known, a superior enemy force, after being engaged for three and one-half hours, had been prevented from supporting Japanese garrisons at Kiska and Attu.

The Capture of Attu

During the month of April, severe weather interfered considerably with our operations, but later in the month a detachment of cruisers and destroyers was sent to bombard the island of Attu.

Meanwhile, plans had been completed for an assault on Attu, and a force consisting of battleships, an auxiliary aircraft carrier, destroyers, auxiliaries and transports was placed under the command of Rear Admiral Rockwell, who operated under the direction of Rear Admiral Kinkaid. In addition to Rear Admiral Rockwell's force there was a unit consisting of cruisers and destroyers under the command of Rear Admiral Giffen and another under Rear Admiral McMorris. The entire operation was to be supported by the Army Air Forces under the command of Major General Albert E. Brown. These troops were embarked in the transports.

On the morning of 11 May landings were made on the north coast of Attu, and our troops proceeded inland. In the afternoon other landings were made at Massacre Bay, and also at Holtz Bay. These landings were covered by our naval forces, and in the bitter fighting which followed, various naval units assisted Army troops by furnishing fire support and air cover. Enemy attacks on our naval forces were ineffective. On 31 May the "mopping up" stage ended, and the island was in our possession. Enemy forces there had been virtually annihilated.

Occupation of Kiska

Following the assault on Attu, preparations were made for a similar assault on Kiska. In anticipation of that assault, Kiska was heavily bombed during July and August, and on numerous occasions was also bombarded by our naval forces.

When assault troops landed on the island on 15 August it was found that it had been evacuated by the Japanese under cover of the fog. Thus, the Aleutian campaign ended, with our forces once more in possession of the entire chain of islands.

Although it had no connection with the campaign herein described, the bombardment of Paramushiru by a task force under the command of Rear Admiral W. D. Baker was carried out on 4 February 1944. Large fires were started. No damage was sustained by our forces. The bombardment is included in this part of the report because it took place in the northern Pacific.

SUBMARINE OPERATIONS

Because of their ability to operate effectively in enemy controlled waters the weakness of our Asiatic Fleet was partially compensated by virtue of the 29 submarines assigned to it—our submarines took the offensive immediately upon the outbreak of war. When our surface forces retired to the south from the Philippine Islands, submarines [under the command of Captain (now Rear Admiral) John Wilkes] succeeded in delaying the enemy's advance and in giving intermittent support to our forces remaining in the islands. As the Japanese advanced through the Netherlands East Indies and into the Solomons, submarines continued to interrupt enemy lines of communications, and since that time have continued their attacks on enemy men-of-war and merchantmen with telling effect.

At the beginning of the war Rear Admiral T. Withers was in command of the submarines in our Pacific Fleet. Rear Admiral R. H. English, who relieved him in May 1942, was killed in an airplane accident in January 1943. Since that time the uniformly excellent operation and administration of Pacific Fleet submarines has been continued under the direction of Vice Admiral C. A. Lockwood, who previously commanded submarines of the Southwest Pacific Force. Rear Admiral R. W. Christie succeeded to command of the submarines in the Southwest Pacific Force.

Atlantic Fleet submarines have been commanded since the spring of 1942 by Rear Admiral F. A. Daubin. Submarine operations in the Atlantic, which have been chiefly fitting out and training, have done much to make effective combat submarine operations possible within a minimum time after each submarine joins the Pacific Fleet.

Without adequate shipping, Japan can not hold out, much less support her forces, in the islands of the Pacific. Furthermore, the Japanese shipyards have limited capacity. Her shipping, therefore, was a natural target for our submarines, and they have taken a tremendous toll.

For reasons of security, our submarine operations throughout the Pacific can be discussed only in very general terms. No branch of the naval service, however, has acquitted itself more creditably. Submarine commanding officers are skillful, daring and resourceful. Their crews are well trained and efficient. Their morale is high, and in direct ratio to the success of submarine operations. Materially our submarines are in excellent shape, and we have kept up to the minute in all features of design and scientific development and research.

The versatility of our submarines has been so repeatedly demonstrated throughout the war that the Japanese know only too well that in no part of the Pacific Ocean are they safe from submarine attack. When the full story can be told, it will constitute one of the most stirring chapters in the annals of naval warfare.

The Atlantic Theater
GENERAL

At the outbreak of the war our operations in the Atlantic Ocean consisted chiefly of escorting convoys to Great Britain, and to Russian and Near East ports (also West Indian and South American ports) and of training. Concurrently, with these operations, it was necessary to dispose the heavy units of our Atlantic Fleet so that they would be available immediately in case ships of the German Fleet, basing at various ports in Germany, Norway, and France, attacked our shipping. From time to time, in order to maintain a satisfactory distribution of Allied strength, as insurance against such a breakout by units of the German Navy, certain of our ships operated with the British Fleet.

By agreement with the British, emphasized at the Casablanca conference and at each subsequent conference, the maintenance of the war-making capacity of the British Isles has been a continuing commitment of the United States. Obviously, such a commitment requires, as a prerequisite to the furnishing of the necessary support, the maintenance of overseas lines of communication, so that the safe passage of lend lease shipments, supplies to our own forces, and troop convoys can be accomplished.

The responsibility for those naval operations required to keep open not only those lines of communications, but, as well, all lines of communications in the Atlantic Ocean, has rested with Admiral R. E. Ingersoll, the Commander in Chief of the Atlantic Fleet. Faced with the threat of the U-boat fleet (the methods taken to combat and overcome that menace are covered elsewhere in this report) and with the possibility of attack by other enemy units, escort of convoy operations was of paramount importance.

Early in the war the attempts of the enemy to interrupt our lines of communications, while not successful, nevertheless were a matter of considerable concern. By judicious use of escorts, however, and by other means, our convoys continued to go through. The magnitude of those escort operations, which have been continuous, is not likely to be overestimated, as we have expended tremendous effort in providing the ships and training them, and in the execution of their duties. The record of safe overseas transportation of troops and material speaks for itself, in so far as the efficiency of those operations is concerned.

Direct support of units of the British Fleet in any operation requiring combined effort has been another Atlantic Fleet activity calling for careful planning and execution.

In addition, Admiral Ingersoll has had the responsibility for the defense of the Western Hemisphere by our naval forces. That has involved the stationing of air and surface forces at various points in North and South America and in certain islands in the Atlantic Ocean, and, of course, such changes in their disposition as might be warranted by the situation. The South Atlantic Force, under the command of Vice Admiral (now Admiral) J. H. Ingram, whose headquarters are in Brazil, has operated in harmony and close combination with forces of the Brazilian Navy in contributing to our control of the South Atlantic.

In order to facilitate the passage of convoys to Russia and Great Britain, and in order to provide a base for our heavy surface forces, considerable use has been made of Iceland, where we originally established a base for forces engaged in escorting lend-lease convoys. All of the bases acquired from Great Britain in exchange for the 50 destroyers have been in constant use, and of great value.

Except for antisubmarine actions and for occasional aircraft attacks, units of the Atlantic Fleet have not been in any extensive combat in the Atlantic Ocean. As covering and supporting forces, however, they have accompanied our expeditions which landed in North Africa, and later in Sicily and Italy, and in the case of the landings in North Africa, there were some engagements in the Atlantic Ocean. The details of those expeditions are covered separately in this report.

For the purpose of training the large number of newly commissioned ships on the east coast, which report to the Commander in Chief, United States Atlantic Fleet as soon as they are completed, a training command, under Rear Admiral D. B. Beary, was established as a part of the Atlantic Fleet. That command took over all ships (except submarines) as soon as they were ready for sea, and conducted such operational training as was necessary to fit each ship for duty in the fleet to which assigned. In addition to that type of operational training, the Commander in Chief, United States Atlantic Fleet was charged with extensive amphibious training.

From the foregoing it will be seen that the Commander in Chief, United States Atlantic Fleet has had a wide variety of responsibilities which have been contributory to the success of the multiplicity of operations, some of which were carried out by the Atlantic Fleet and some by other fleets. Because of the situation, there has been a continuous shift in the strength and disposition of the Atlantic Fleet, in which connection its flexibility and the manner in which adjustments and readjustments were made have been of tremendous assistance to the Navy as a whole.

THE ATLANTIC SUBMARINE WAR

The submarine war—particularly the Atlantic phase of it—has been a matter of primary concern since the outbreak of hostilities. Maintenance of the flow of ocean traffic has been, and continues to be, a vital element of all war plans.

Operating on exterior lines of communication on almost every front, the United Nations have been dependent largely upon maritime transportation. The success of overseas operations, landing attacks, the maintenance of troops abroad and the delivery of war materials to Russia and other Allies concerned primarily with land operations has depended to a large extent upon the availability of shipping and the ability to keep it moving. Shipping potentialities have been the major factor—often the controlling factor—in most of the problems with which the Allied High Command has had to deal.

The principal menace to shipping has been the large fleet of submarines maintained by Germany. Our enemies have employed the submarine on a world-wide scale, but the area of greatest intensity has always been the Atlantic Ocean where the bulk of German U-boats have operated.

The German U-boat campaign is a logical extension of the submarine strategy of World War I which almost succeeded in starving Great Britain into submission. Unable to build up a powerful surface fleet in preparation for World War II, Germany planned to repeat her submarine campaign on a greater scale and to this end produced a U-boat fleet of huge size. The primary mission of this underwater navy was to cut the sea routes to the British Isles, and the enemy undersea forces went to work on this task promptly and vigorously.

The United States became involved in the matter before we were formally at war, because our vessels were being sunk in the trans-Atlantic traffic routes. Consequently, in 1941, we took measures to assist the Royal Navy to protect our shipping. As stated in more detail elsewhere in this report these measures included the transfer of 50 old destroyers to the British, and—in the latter part of 1941—the assignment of our own naval vessels to escort our merchant shipping on threatened trans-Atlantic routes.

The submarine situation was improving as 1941 drew toward a close. Escort operations on threatened convoy routes were becoming more and more effective. British aviation had become a potent factor, by direct action against the U-boats, and also by bringing under control the German over-water air effort that had augmented the submarine offensive. Our resources were stretched, however, and we could not, for a time, deal effectively with the change in the situation brought about by our entry into the war on 7 December 1941. Our whole merchant marine then became a legitimate target, and the U-boats, still maintaining full pressure on the trans-Atlantic routes, had sufficient numbers to spread their depredations into wide areas hitherto immune. Our difficulty was that such part of the Atlantic Fleet as was not already engaged in escort duty was called upon to protect the troop movements that began with our entry into the war, leaving no adequate force to cover the many maritime traffic areas newly exposed to possible U-boat activity.

The Germans were none too quick in taking advantage of their opportunity.

It was not until more than a month after the declaration of war that u-boats began to expand their areas of operation. The first move took the form of an incursion into our coastal waters in January 1942. We had prepared for this by gathering on our eastern seaboard our scant resources in coastal antisubmarine vessels and aircraft, consisting chiefly of a number of yachts and miscellaneous small craft taken over by the Navy in 1940 and 1941. To reinforce this group the Navy accelerated its program of acquiring such fishing boats and pleasure craft as could be used and supplied them with such armaments as they could carry. For patrol purposes we employed all available aircraft—Army as well as Navy. The help of the Civil Air Patrol was gratefully accepted. This heterogeneous force was useful in keeping lookout and in rescuing survivors of sunken ships. It may have interfered, too, to some extent with the freedom of u-boat movement, but the heavy losses we suffered in coastal waters during the early months of 1942 gave abundant proof of the already well known fact that stout hearts in little boats can not handle an opponent as tough as the submarine.

The Navy was deeply grateful for the assistance so eagerly volunteered by the men who courageously risked their lives in order to make the best of available means, but there had to be better means, and to provide them no effort was spared to build up an antisubmarine force of adequate types. Submarine chasers, construction of which had been initiated before the war, began to come into service early in 1942. The British and Canadian Navies were able to assign some antisubmarine vessels to work with our coastal forces. Ocean escorts were robbed to reinforce coastal areas. These measures made it possible to establish a coastal convoy system in the middle of May 1942. Antisubmarine aviation had concurrently improved in quality and material and training of personnel. The Army Air Force had volunteered the services of the First Bomber Command which was especially trained and outfitted for antisubmarine warfare.

The effect of these measures was quickly felt in the Eastern Sea Frontier (the coastal waters from Canada to Jacksonville) where they were first applied. With the establishment of the initial coastal convoy (under the command of Vice Admiral Adolphus Andrews, Commander of the Eastern Sea Frontier) in the middle of May 1942, sinkings in the vital traffic lanes of the Eastern Sea Frontier dropped off nearly to zero and have so remained. While it has not been possible to clear those routes completely—there is evidence that nearly always one or more u-boats haunt our Atlantic Coast—submarines in that area long ago ceased to be a serious problem.

When the Eastern Sea Frontier became "too hot," the u-boats began to spread farther afield. The coastal convoy system was extended as rapidly as possible to meet them in the Gulf of Mexico (under the command of Rear Admiral J. L. Kauffman, Commander Gulf Sea Frontier), the Caribbean Sea, (under the command of Vice Admiral J. H. Hoover, Commander Caribbean Sea Frontier), and along the Atlantic Coast of South America. The undersea craft made a last bitter stand in the Trinidad area in the fall of 1942. Since then coastal waters have been relatively safe.

The problem was more difficult to meet in the open sea. The submarine chasers that do well enough in coastal waters are too small for ocean escort duty. Destroyers and other ocean escort types could not be produced as rapidly as the smaller craft. Aircraft capable of long overseas patrol were not plentiful, nor were aircraft carriers.

In consequence, protection of ocean shipping lagged to some extent. By the end of 1942, however, this matter began to come under control, as our forces slowly increased, and there has been a steady improvement ever since.

The Atlantic antisubmarine campaign has been a closely integrated international operation. In the early phases of our participation, there was a considerable mixture of forces, as the needs of the situation were met as best they could be. For a time some British and Canadian vessels operated in our coastal escorts, while our destroyers were brigaded with British groups in the Atlantic and even occasionally as far afield as north Russian waters. As Allied strength improved in power and balance, it became possible to establish certain areas of national responsibility wherein the forces are predominantly of one nation. This simplifies the problem of administration and operation, but there still are—and probably always will be—some areas where forces of two or more nations work together in a single command, and always there is close coordination in deploying the forces of the several Allies.

There is a constant interchange of information between the large organizations maintained in the Admiralty and in the United States Fleet Headquarters (in the form of the Tenth Fleet which coordinates United States anti-U-boat activities in the Atlantic) to deal with the problems of control and protection of shipping. These organizations, also, keep in intimate touch with the War Shipping Administration in the United States and with the corresponding agency in Great Britain.

Command of antisubmarine forces—air and surface—that protect shipping in the coastwise sea lanes of the United States and within the Caribbean Sea and Gulf of Mexico is exercised by sea frontier commanders, each assigned to a prescribed area. The command is naval except in the Panama area where the naval sea frontier commander is under the Commanding General at Panama.

Since aircraft and surface combatant ships are most effective when working as a closely knit team, it is the policy—in antisubmarine as well as other naval operations—to weld together air and surface forces in a single command in each area.

In the Atlantic Ocean, beyond the coastal area, antisubmarine forces—air and surface—are part of the Atlantic Fleet under the command of Admiral Ingersoll. One of the units of Admiral Ingersoll's fleet is the South Atlantic Force (Vice Admiral Ingram commanding) which guards shipping in the coastal waters south of the Equator and throughout the United States area of the South Atlantic. Vice Admiral Ingram's command includes highly efficient surface and air units of Brazil, which country has wholeheartedly joined our team of submarine hunters. This team, incidentally, turns its guns on surface raiders and other bigger game when the enemy provides the opportunity.

It is appropriate to express here appreciation of the services of Netherlands antisubmarine vessels which have operated with exemplary efficiency as part of the United States Naval Caribbean Force ever since we entered the war.

Antisubmarine warfare is primarily a naval function, but, in accordance with the general policy of working together, Army and Navy forces that are available turn to together on the enemy when need arises. Thus it happens that there are instances in which Army aircraft join in the submarine hunt. The assistance of the Army Air Force has been of great value, particularly in the early phases of the war, when naval resources were inadequate. An example of this is the formation of the Army Air Force Anti-Submarine Command in the spring of 1942, which was given the equipment and training necessary to make its members antisubmarine specialists. It operated, under the command of Brigadier General (now Major General) T. W. Larson, in the United States and abroad until last November, when the Navy obtained enough equipment to take over the tasks so well performed by this command.

It is regretted that it is not possible at this time to go into the details of our antisubmarine operations in this report. It would be a great pleasure to recount the many praiseworthy exploits of our antisubmarine forces, but to do so now would jeopardize the success of future operations. The U-boat war has been a war of wits. The submarine is a weapon of stealth, and naturally enough the German operations have been shrouded in secrecy. It has been of equal importance to keep our counter measures from becoming known to the enemy. There is a constant interplay of new devices and new tactics on the part of forces working against the submarines as well as on the part of the submarines themselves, and an important element of our success has been the ability to keep the enemy from knowing what we are doing and what we are likely to do in the future. It is, also, of the utmost importance to keep our enemies from learning our antisubmarine technique, lest they turn it to their own advantage in operations against our submarines.

Submarines have not been driven from the seas, but they have changed status from menace to problem.

The Mediterranean Theater

LANDINGS IN NORTH AFRICA

In July 1942, after several months of discussions and study by the Combined Chiefs of Staff, it was decided to effect landings in force in North Africa and there establish our troops in opposition to the German forces. The strategic significance of that move since has become apparent, in that the troops which were transported and landed in North Africa subsequently moved through Sicily to Italy, and there engaged enemy land forces.

The invasion of North Africa was a complicated operation. In the first place, in view of the uncertainty of the relationships existing between the French forces in that area and the Vichy government, the political situation in North Africa required the most careful and diplomatic handling. Obviously it was to our advantage to effect unopposed landings, and the problem therefore was to persuade the French forces not to resist. We could not afford, however, to take any chances in revealing our own plans, and the dealings with the French authorities had to be undertaken with utmost discretion. As it turned out, the French forces resisted initially, but within a few days agreed to an armistice.

In addition to the foregoing difficulty, it was agreed that the forces participating in the operations would consist of British and American units. Furthermore, the nature of the operations was such that the American units had to be both Army and Navy. Command relationships were worked out accordingly, and Lieutenant General (now General of the Army) D. D. Eisenhower, USA, was appointed Commander in

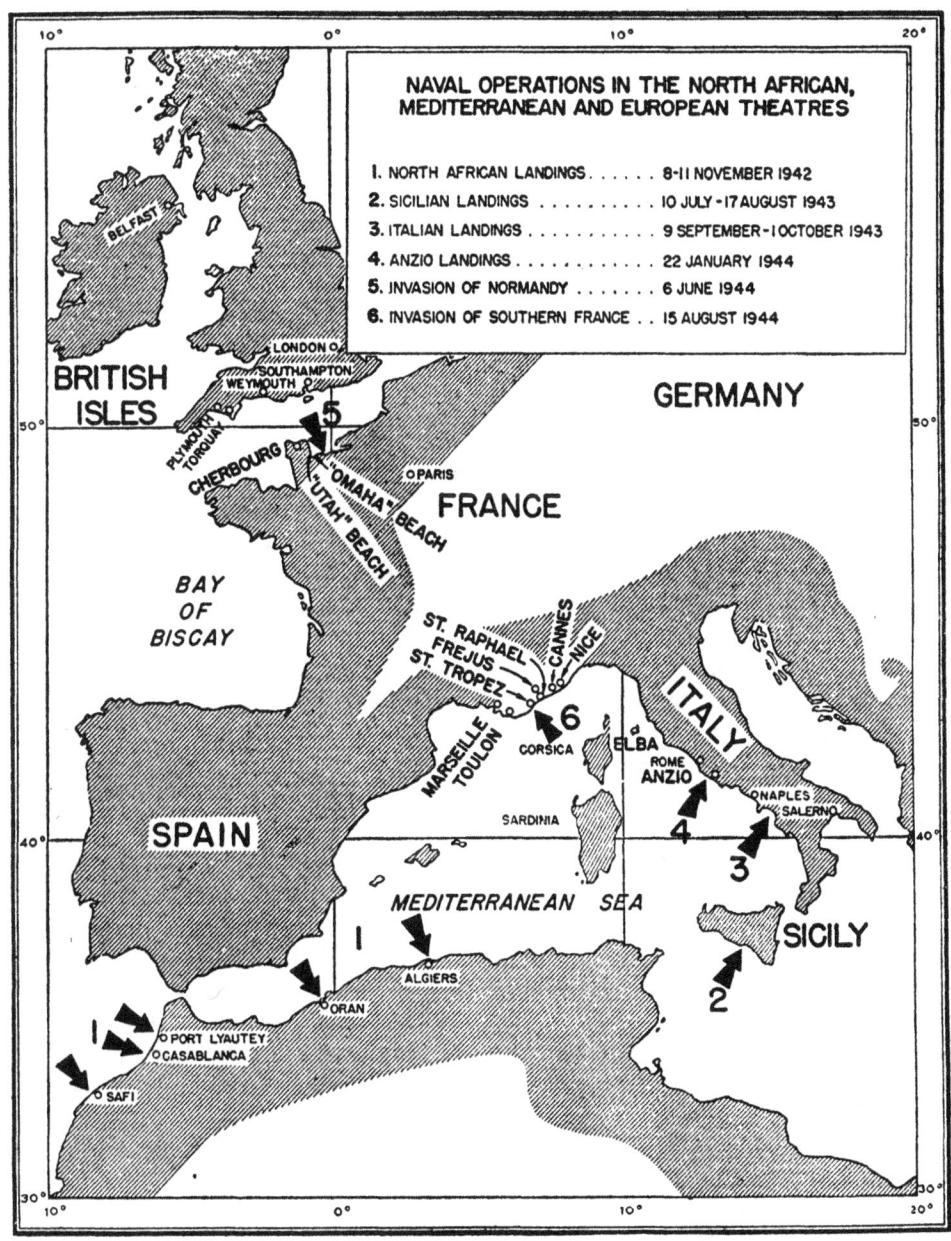

Plate 7.

Chief of the Allied force. His principal naval subordinate was Admiral Sir Andrew Browne Cunningham, Royal Navy.

The plan agreed upon called for three points of attack: Oran and Algiers, both Algerian seaports on the Mediterranean, and Casablanca on the Atlantic coast of French Morocco. The attack forces assigned to effect landings at Oran and Algiers consisted of United States Army troops supported by British naval units (with a few exceptions). The Casablanca attack force was composed entirely of United States forces. This report deals chiefly with the part played by United States naval forces in the operation.

Rear Admiral (now Admiral) H. K. Hewitt, who was placed in command of the United States naval forces designated to support the Casablanca attack [Major General (later General) George S. Patton (now deceased) commanded the Army troops in this attack] left the United States on 24 October and the movement overseas proceeded without untoward incident. On 7 November the forces separated and the three attack groups, the covering force (under the command of Rear Admiral Giffen) and the air groups proceeded independently to their assigned positions for the landing attacks.

Operations in French Morocco

Operations in French Morocco were conducted by United States forces under the unified command of Rear Admiral Hewitt until General Patton's headquarters were established on shore and he was ready to assume command. The plan called for a main landing at Fedala, 14 miles north of Casablanca, and secondary landings at Port Lyautey, 65 miles north of Casablanca, and Safi, 125 miles south of Casablanca. The object of the main landing was to capture Casablanca from the land side. The principal objective at Port Lyautey was the airfield nearby, and the objective of Safi was to capture the port by direct assault and then to assist in the reduction of Casablanca.

Early in the morning of 8 November, shortly after our troops had been landed, shore batteries opened fire on the naval forces supporting the landings at Fedala. These shore batteries were engaged at intervals during that morning by AUGUSTA, BROOKLYN, and accompanying destroyers. Early in the afternoon the shore batteries on Point Fedala were captured.

Several naval actions took place between Fedala and Casablanca on 8 November. Shortly after daylight, eight submarines left Casablanca. Three others were sunk at their moorings. Early in the forenoon, two French destroyer-leaders and five destroyers sortied and stood toward Fedala. They were taken under fire and forced to retire. Shortly afterward the French light cruiser PRIMAGUET sortied and joined the French destroyers outside the harbor. The group, which stood toward Fedala, was promptly engaged by AUGUSTA and BROOKLYN, and vessels of the covering force. With the exception of one transport, which managed to get back to the harbor, all French ships were either sunk or beached. Meanwhile, the covering force, consisting of MASSACHUSETTS, WICHITA, TUSCALOOSA, and four destroyers, exchanged fire with the shore batteries at El Hank, and the French battleship JEAN BART, which was moored in the harbor, and with the French forces that had sortied from Casablanca.

Another action took place on 10 November. Late in the forenoon the enemy vessels took up a position outside of the harbor at Casablanca and opened fire on our troops ashore, whereupon AUGUSTA and four destroyers stood toward Casablanca and engaged the two enemy vessels. While in that position, AUGUSTA was fired upon by JEAN BART. AUGUSTA and accompanying destroyers immediately retired.

Sometime between 8 November and 10 November JEAN BART was sunk at her moorings, but the water was shallow and she was able to continue to fire.

Thanks to the elimination of the French forces at Casablanca the landings at Fedala were successfully completed, but the aftermath was costly. On 11 November the transport JOSEPH HEWES, the oiler WINOOSKI and the destroyer HAMBLETON were torpedoed. The HEWES sank in an hour, and the other two ships were later taken to Casablanca for repairs. On 12 November the transports HUGH L. SCOTT and EDWARD RUTLEDGE were torpedoed and immediately caught fire and burned. All these attacks were assumed to be from Axis submarines.

The attack on Safi was made principally by two destroyers, BERNADOU and COLE, which were supported by gunfire from a covering group under the command of Rear Admiral L. A. Davidson, consisting of the battleship NEW YORK, the cruiser PHILADELPHIA, and the destroyer MERVINE. BERNADOU, carrying Army troops, and MERVINE, with naval personnel, made a daring entry into the harbor early in the morning of the 8th, and there landed their troops without serious difficulty.

The landings at Port Lyautey were made with comparatively little difficulty. Stiff resistance was later encountered south of the mouth of the Oued Sebou River, and shore batteries were not silenced until 9 November. Ships furnishing naval gunfire and naval aircraft support included TEXAS, SAVANNAH, and a number of destroyers under the command of Rear Admiral Monroe Kelly.

The Oran Operation

The naval support for the landings at Oran was furnished by the British naval forces. In order to facilitate the capture of Oran, however, it was decided to seize the harbor of Arzeu, about 25 miles east of Oran, and by a daring and well executed assault, a small raiding party, under Captain Walter Ansel, captured the harbor early in the morning of 8 November.

Also assigned to assist British naval forces was a small United States naval unit commanded by Lieutenant Commander (now Captain) George D. Dickey. This unit, together with army units, was embarked in two British ships, HMS WALNEY and HARTLAND, both of which were formerly United States Coast Guard cutters. Upon entering the harbor early in the morning of 8 November, both ships were discovered and sunk.

The Algiers Operation

Included in the naval task force assigned to assist in the Algiers landings was a division of four American transports. These vessels had proceeded from Great Britain in time to arrive on the Algerian coast simultaneously with the forces arriving on the Moroccan coast from the United States. Late in the afternoon of 7 November the transport THOMAS STONE was torpedoed. Her troops thereupon were put in landing boats about 160 miles from Algiers. After a hazardous trip, during which a number of the landing craft were lost, they succeeded in reaching the Algerian coast, but by that time hostilities had ceased

The transport LEEDSTOWN was attacked by German aircraft on the evening of

8 November and again on the following afternoon, and was sunk by torpedoes. The loss of personnel was light.

* * * * * * * * *

With the successful negotiation of the armistice on 11 November, resistance from the French forces ceased, and in so far as the immediate participation of United States naval forces was concerned, the operation ended. Meanwhile, however, a naval unit on the east coast of French Morocco was established as a Sea Frontier, under the command of Rear Admiral John L. Hall, Jr., and a Naval Operating Base at Oran, under the command of Rear Admiral A. C. Bennett, was also established.

The United States naval forces participating in these operations were taken from the U.S. Atlantic Fleet.

LANDINGS IN SICILY

By May 1943, German forces had been driven from Tunisia, and by that time our fighting strength was such that we were able to make definite plans for a major offensive move against the enemy in his own territory. Sicily was selected as the immediate objective, and an amphibious operation on the largest scale yet undertaken was planned. Generally speaking, one part of the operation was to be a ship-to-shore movement in which our troops were to be taken to the scene of the landing in transports and there embarked for the actual landing in small boats. The second part was a shore-to-shore movement, the troops being transported directly to the landing beaches from the point of embarkation.

Like the North African operation, the landings in Sicily were to be combined British and American. General Eisenhower was given command of the expeditionary force and Admiral Cunningham was given command of all naval forces participating. Under these officers were three task forces, one of which was (with the usual provisions for change-over in command) under the command of Vice Admiral Hewitt, and Lieutenant General Patton. Army air forces were under the command of Brigadier General (now General) Carl Spaatz. Under the plan agreed upon, landings were to be made at five places on the island of Sicily. Three of those objectives, namely Scoglitti, Gela, and Licata, on the south coast of Sicily, were to be attacked by the American task force.

This report concerns itself primarily with the activities of the American naval forces in the operation.

In anticipation of the operation, transports, cruisers and destroyers were assembled at Oran and Algiers. Various types of landing craft were assembled at Tunis and Bizerte. There were some exceptions to that arrangement. On 5 July the largest ships of the Scoglitti force left Oran and on the following day they were joined by the ships of the Gela force from Algiers. As the force passed Tunis and Bizerte they were joined by the small craft.

Scoglitti

The landing at Scoglitti, early in the morning of July 10, which was preceded by bombardment of shore batteries and beach positions by our naval units, was accomplished with comparatively little opposition, as the Italian troops abandoned their positions at the first attack. Landings at Scoglitti were both ship-to-shore and shore-to-shore operations, and by early forenoon all troops were on the beach.

Gela

The landings at Gela were more of a shore-to-shore undertaking than those at Scoglitti. Troops landed on schedule, and the first wave encountered slight opposition, but the second wave met stiff resistance and suffered heavy casualties until the shore batteries were silenced by the naval gunfire from the light cruisers SAVANNAH and BOISE.

Licata

The landing at Licata was almost entirely a shore-to-shore operation, practically all troops being transported in small craft. After comparatively heavy opposition was encountered, all beaches were captured by early forenoon and the unloading of supplies begun. We lost the destroyer MADDOX and the minesweeper SENTINEL in the operation, both being sunk by bombs.

After the Licata landing had been accomplished, the participating forces were subjected to intense enemy air attack which lasted three days. During that three-day period, also, the enemy launched a counterattack with tanks, which took up a position from which they could fire on the beaches and at the ships standing by. When this tank attack developed, our cruisers and destroyers moved inshore and opened fire on them, pending the establishment of anti-tank fire on the beach. So effective was naval gunfire on this occasion that the tanks were successfully repulsed at a most opportune time. Had there been no naval gunfire support, or had it been less effective, our landing force in all probability would have been driven into the sea.

By the 13th, most of our ships had completed unloading and left the area.

* * * * * * * * *

As our troops advanced inland and along the coasts from their landing points, their advance was supported from time to time by naval gunfire. During the period 12–14 July our cruisers and destroyers bombarded Porto Empedocle and Agrigento, this bombardment being one of the factors which contributed to the capture of those towns on 17 July. This bombardment was followed by a short lull, in so far as naval participation was concerned (a second contingent of transports had already arrived) and it was not until the end of the month that our forces were again employed directly in the attacks. On 31 July fresh troops were transported to Palermo. These transports were attacked by German air forces when in Palermo harbor, but were effectively protected by our destroyers.

Throughout the month of August the Navy supported the movements of land forces as they closed in on Messina. Naval gunfire destroyed shore batteries, roads, bridges, and other objectives, and on 17 August a task force of cruisers and destroyers proceeded against southern Italy.

LANDINGS IN ITALY

Landings in Italy were in logical sequence to the occupation of Sicily. Shortly after the Sicilian operation was completed, British forces began crossing the Straits of Messina, and in order to assist these forces in their progress up the Italian Peninsula, a combined Anglo-American attack was undertaken some distance in the rear of Axis troops opposing the British. The general region chosen was that portion of the Italian coast extending from Cape Circeo to the southern headland to the Gulf of Policastro and containing the important harbors of Naples, Gaeta, and Salerno. The particular part of the coast selected for the initial assault was the Bay of Salerno, which offered a number of beaches suitable for troop landings.

Although the troops employed in the landings were exclusively British or American, the naval forces supporting them were mixed. The latter were placed under the command of Vice Admiral Hewitt and divided into two parts, one of which was predominantly American and the other predominantly British. The American (southern) attack force was assigned coverage for the landings at Salerno.

The principal American convoy assembled at Oran, and British forces formed up at Tripoli, Palermo, Termini (in Sicily) and Bizerte, and from time to time, beginning 5 September, sailed from the points of assembly.

The landings were made on the morning of 9 September, and, although successfully accomplished, met immediate resistance from the Germans, who delivered a series of air attacks for the next two days. Also, enemy fire on the ground was intense, exceeding anything previously experienced and proving considerably more troublesome than had been anticipated. In spite of the resistance, however, (which included counterattacks, some of which were broken up most opportunely, as at Licata, by fire of naval vessels) the port of Salerno was captured by the 10th, and after heavy fighting on the 11th and 12th in the vicinity of Salerno, the town of Battipaglia was captured.

On the 13th and 14th, the enemy succeeded in retaking some of the ground previously gained by our troops. Our naval units, however, continued to lend reinforcements and supplies, and Allied warships, including battleships, cruisers, and destroyers, bombarded enemy positions. During the remainder of the operation, our naval forces kept up a steady flow of supplies to the various beaches, bombarded shore objectives, helped to repel air raids, and finally on 1 October took the city of Naples under bombardment.

For several months our naval forces continued to operate in the Mediterranean area chiefly in supplying our troops in that theater and in keeping open the lines of supply.

On 22 January 1944, a joint force landed at Anzio, Italy, and there established a beach head. The amphibious task force participating was under the command of Rear Admiral F. J. Lowry. Gunfire support for the operation was furnished by cruisers and destroyers.

IV
Teamwork

THE NAVY TEAM

REPRESENTING as it does intense scientific research and the development of various methods of fighting for hundreds of years, modern naval warfare is admittedly complex. Historically, any new method of fighting, whether with or without new weapons, has been productive of counter measures which are usually successful in reducing its effectiveness. This may be expected to continue. So far as new methods and weapons are concerned, we are in a position to set the pace.

The Navy, perhaps more than any other of the services, is dependent on a high quality of engineering skill and practice. All our ships and planes, the establishment which designs and builds them, and the equipment which operates and arms them could not exist without the engineer and the technical expert. We are fortunate in having in the United States in an unequaled degree the necessary engineering brains, educational facilities and technical knowledge.

Each technician on board ship must learn not only how to operate his own particular part of its machinery; he must also learn how to operate it so that it will contribute most to the efficiency of that ship as a unit. There is no better example of the necessity of team work than a modern man-of-war. In a submarine, for instance, every man in the crew and every officer has a job which directly affects the handling and operating of the ship, her hitting power, and her survival, and each depends on the other to do the right thing at the right time.

Once a unit is trained to operate efficiently by itself, the next problem is to train it to operate with other ships and planes so that all may function as parts of a powerful but smooth running machine. Each unit must learn to play its position on the team, and the whole team must be equipped, coached, drilled and taught to fight and win, anywhere in the world.

Mobility is one of the prime military qualities. The surface, submarine and air forces of the Navy possess mobility in a high degree. With the increased tempo of our operations, therefore, the question of timing—strategically and tactically—is all important. It is the basis of the coordinated striking power—the overall "teamwork" —which has been successfully used in past operations, and which we count upon with confidence for even more successful operations yet to come.

THE ARMY AND NAVY TEAM

In February 1942, the President established an agency known as the United States Chiefs of Staff (frequently called the "Joint Chiefs of Staff") whose function it is to exercise strategic control of our armed forces in the war. The members of the

United States Chiefs of Staff are the Chief of Staff to the Commander in Chief of the United States Army and Navy; the Chief of Staff of the United States Army; the Commander in Chief, United States Fleet and Chief of Naval Operations; and the Commanding General, Army Air Forces.

By effective coordination of strategic plans and their execution the United States Chiefs of Staff have in effect operated the Army and Navy as one national military force. Furthermore, by continuous exchange of information of all kinds, including that relating to operating techniques, new weapons, and strategic and tactical problems, the two services have been able to derive the maximum benefit not only from each other, but from all other agencies whose activities have a direct bearing on the conduct of the war.

In keeping with the unity of action taken by the United States Chiefs of Staff, that agency has worked out and established certain principles relating to unity of command in joint operations. Under those principles, and having due regard for the qualifications of the officer and the type of operations likely to predominate in a given theater, the supreme commander in the theater, and his principal subordinates, may be officers of any one of the services. For example, it was agreed that under certain conditions unity of command in our sea frontiers (which correspond generally to Army defense commands) would be exercised by naval officers. Under other conditions, unity of command would be vested in Army officers. Another example was the unity of command vested in General Eisenhower in the North African operation. Still another is the unity of command exercised by Admiral Nimitz in the Pacific Ocean.

The principle of unity of command as it exists within our own forces, by agreement with the British Chiefs of Staff, is extended to situations where forces of more than one nation are engaged in the same operation. The operations in the Mediterranean theater illustrate that arrangement, which has worked well.

THE ALLIED TEAM

The British Chiefs of Staff or their representatives in Washington and the United States Chiefs of Staff working together are known as the Combined Chiefs of Staff.

The headquarters of the Combined Chiefs of Staff, consisting of the United States Chiefs of Staff and representatives of the British Chiefs of Staff, are in Washington, and there the day to day problems of the war are under continuous consideration. Representatives of other Allied nations and dominions attend the Washington meetings from time to time.

At intervals the Combined Chiefs of Staff, consisting of the United States and British Chiefs of Staff, together with the heads of their respective governments, have met to discuss and decide upon the over-all conduct of the war. In meetings at Casablanca, Washington, Quebec and Cairo-Teheran during the year 1943 agreements of far reaching importance were reached. Russian representatives attended at Teheran and Chinese representatives were present at Cairo.

These international conferences, which are of sufficient duration to allow thorough presentations of matters of mutual interest, make possible on-the-spot decisions not only with respect to strategy and command relationships for combined operations but also with respect to the commitments of each country.

In addition to the foregoing, the discussions relating to the war effort in the Pacific area were made possible by the formation of the Pacific War Council. That body, over which the President of the United States presides, is composed of representatives of the United States, Australia, Canada, China, the Netherlands, New Zealand, the Philippine Commonwealth, and the United Kingdom. The Council does not meet regularly, but was established as a means to promote informal exchanges of views and information.

* *

V
Conclusion

AS this report is concluded we can look back with satisfaction on the progress of the war to date, and with just pride in the part played therein by the United States.

In the European theater, our forces have taken part in driving the enemy out of Africa, and have shared in the occupation of Sicily and in the invasion of Italy, which resulted in its capitulation. The Russian army, turning against the Germans in an irresistible offensive, has driven them back to the borders of Poland and Rumania. France has been given new hope. Instead of being a daily target for the German air forces, Great Britain has become a base for an air offensive against the heart of the Axis on a scale which dwarfs the greatest German attacks of the war. The German submarine fleet has been reduced from a menace to a problem. The encirclement of Germany is in sight.

As of 1 March 1944, the situation in the European theater is increasingly desperate for the Axis and correspondingly encouraging for us.

The German structure of satellite states is crumbling. Italy has fallen and is a battlefield in which 20 German divisions are taking heavy punishment. Rumania, Bulgaria, Hungary and Finland are weakening. The Balkans are aflame with guerrilla war, and other occupied countries await only the signal.

The Russian armies continue to advance, a massive invasion threatens in the West, and with all this, Germany is scientifically and remorselessly being bombed on a scale whose magnitude and increasing tempo have flattened her cities, wrecked her factories, and can not but be a major factor in her eventual collapse.

In the Pacific theater, the Japanese, after their attack on Pearl Harbor, advanced with impressive speed and power through the Philippines and the Netherlands East Indies into the Solomon Islands, in the general direction of Australia and New Zealand. Following these successful advances, they effected landings in the Aleutian Islands and attacked Midway. The Japanese advance was checked, however, almost as abruptly as it had begun. Our successes in the Solomons, in the central Pacific, and in the northern Pacific, are now matters of record, and we have had time to build up our strength, and to test our power. Our outposts, which two years ago were on a line running from Dutch Harbor in the Aleutians to Midway, thence to Fiji, Samoa, and Australia, now begin at Attu, on the tip of the Aleutians, and extend south through the Marshall Islands to the Bismarcks and New Guinea.

Through experience, we have mastered and improved the technique of amphibious operations, in which the Japanese were so proficient in the early days of the war. Our Army and Navy forces have learned how to fight as one team. We have learned how to make the most of what we have, but it is no longer necessary to ask our commanders to get along as best they can on inadequate means. The numerical inferiorities, which were so pronounced in the Java Sea campaign and in subsequent actions in the Solomons, have been reversed. Our submarines and planes are cutting deeper and deeper into the vital Japanese shipping, and our fleets move in the central Pacific unchallenged.

The war against Japan has gone increasingly well of late. From their posts of maximum advance in the Pacific, the Japanese have been driven back progressively by a series of offensive operations. Important as our own advances toward Japan are, they do not fully represent the improvement in our position. Japanese capacity to maintain the war at sea and in her advanced areas has suffered increasingly, due to the loss of vital shipping, while the growth of our power in the Pacific enables us to threaten attack on the Marianas and Carolines and Kuriles, which may be called the intermediate zone of defense of the Empire.

Japan will not be directly under attack, as Germany is now, until the citadel area of that empire, island and continental, is under our threat or control, but the current and prospective circumstances in the Pacific Theater present a situation which must be as dark and threatening to Japan as it is full of promise to us.

Both in Europe and in the Pacific long roads still lie ahead. But we are now fully entered on those roads, fortified with unity, power, and experience, imbued with confidence and determined to travel far and fast to victory.

Second Report

TO THE
SECRETARY OF THE NAVY

*Covering combat operations 1 March 1944
to 1 March 1945*

BY

FLEET ADMIRAL ERNEST J. KING
COMMANDER IN CHIEF, UNITED STATES FLEET,
AND CHIEF OF NAVAL OPERATIONS

(*Issued 27 March 1945*)

UNITED STATES FLEET

HEADQUARTERS OF THE COMMANDER IN CHIEF
NAVY DEPARTMENT
Washington 25, D. C.

12 March 1945

Dear Mr. Secretary:

Twelve months ago I presented to the late Secretary Knox a report of the progress of our naval operations and the expansion of our naval establishment since the beginning of the war.

Long before the war Frank Knox saw clearly and supported strongly the necessity for arming the United States against her enemies. He knew that a powerful Navy is essential to the welfare of our country, and fought with all his energies to build a Navy that could carry the attack to the enemy. How well he succeeded is now a matter of history.

The manner in which the Navy has carried the attack to the enemy during the twelve months from 1 March 1944 to 1 March 1945 is the subject of the report which I present to you at this time.

In reading this report, attention is especially invited to the significant role of amphibious operations during the entire period. In fact, amphibious operations have initiated practically all of the Allied successes during the past three years.

Ernest J. King

Fleet Admiral
Commander in Chief, United States Fleet
and Chief of Naval Operations

The Honorable James Forrestal
   Secretary of the Navy,
      Washington, D.C.

* *

I
Introduction

MY previous report presented an account of the development of the Navy and of combat operations up to 1 March 1944. This report covers the twelve months from 1 March 1944 until 1 March 1945. Within this period the battle of the Pacific has been carried more than three thousand miles to the westward—from the Marshall Islands into the South China Sea beyond the Philippines—and to the Tokyo approaches. Within this same period the invasion of the continent of Europe has been accomplished. These successes have been made possible only by the strength and resolution of our amphibious forces, acting in conjunction with the fleet.

During these twelve months, there occurred the following actions with the enemy in which the United States Navy took part:

20 March 1944	Landings on Emirau Island, St. Matthias Group, northeast of New Guinea
	Bombardment of Kavieng, New Ireland
30 March–1 April 1944	Carrier Task Force Attacks on Western Carolines
22 April 1944	Landings in Hollandia Area, New Guinea
29 April–1 May 1944	Carrier Task Force Attacks on Central and Eastern Carolines
17 May 1944	Landings in Wakde Island Area, New Guinea
19–20 May 1944	Carrier Task Force Attacks on Marcus Island
23 May 1944	Carrier Task Force Attack on Wake Island
27 May 1944	Landings on Biak Island, Dutch New Guinea
6 June 1944	Invasion of Normandy
11–14 June 1944	Preliminary Carrier Task Force Attacks on Marianas Islands
13 June 1944	Bombardment of Matsuwa Island, Kurile Islands
15 June 1944	Landings on Saipan, Marianas Islands
15–16 June 1944	Carrier Task Force Attacks on Iwo Jima and Chichi Jima, Volcano and Bonin Islands
17 June 1944	Capture of Elba, Italy
19–20 June 1944	Battle of the Philippine Sea
23–24 June 1944	Carrier Task Force Attacks on Pagan Island, Marianas Islands
24 June 1944	Carrier Task Force Attack on Iwo Jima, Volcano Islands
25 June 1944	Bombardment of Cherbourg, France
26 June 1944	Bombardment of Kurabu Zaki, Paramushiru, Kurile Islands
2 July 1944	Landings on Noemfoor Island, Dutch New Guinea
4 July 1944	Carrier Task Force Attacks on Iwo Jima, Chichi Jima and Haha Jima, Volcano and Bonin Islands
21 July 1944	Landings on Guam, Marianas Islands
24 July 1944	Landings on Tinian, Marianas Islands
30 July 1944	Landings in Cape Sansapor Area, Dutch New Guinea
4–5 August 1944	Carrier Task Force Attacks on Iwo Jima and Chichi Jima, Volcano and Bonin Islands
15 August 1944	Invasion of Southern France

31 August–2 September 1944	Carrier Task Force Attacks on Iwo Jima, Chichi Jima and Haha Jima, Volcano and Bonin Islands
6–14 September 1944	Preliminary Carrier Task Force Attacks on Palau Islands
7–8 September 1944	Carrier Task Force Attacks on Yap
9–10 September 1944	Carrier Task Force Attacks on Mindanao, Philippine Islands
12–14 September 1944	Carrier Task Force Attacks on the Visayas, Philippine Islands
14–15 September 1944	Carrier Task Force Attacks on Mindanao, Celebes and Talaud
15 September 1944	Landings on Peleliu, Palau Islands
	Landings on Morotai
17 September 1944	Landings on Angaur, Palau Islands
21–22 September 1944	Carrier Task Force Attacks on Manila, Philippine Islands
23 September 1944	Landings on Ulithi
24 September 1944	Carrier Task Force Attacks on the Visayas, Philippine Islands
28 September 1944	Landings on Ngesebus, Palau Islands
9 October 1944	Bombardment of Marcus Island
10 October 1944	Carrier Task Force Attack on Okinawa Island, Nansei Shoto
11 October 1944	Carrier Task Force Attack on Aparri, Luzon, Philippine Islands
12–15 October 1944	Carrier Task Force Attacks on Formosa and Luzon
18–19 October 1944	Carrier Task Force Attacks on Northern and Central Philippines
20 October 1944	Landings on Leyte, Philippine Islands
21 October 1944	Carrier Task Force Attacks on Luzon and the Visayas, Philippine Islands
23–26 October 1944	Battle for Leyte Gulf
5, 6, 13, 14, 19, 25 November 1944	Carrier Task Force Attacks on Luzon, Philippine Islands
11 November 1944	Carrier Task Force Attack on Ormoc Bay, Leyte, Philippine Islands
11–12 November 1944	Bombardment of Iwo Jima, Volcano Islands
21 November 1944	Bombardment of Matsuwa Island, Kurile Islands
7 December 1944	Landings at Ormoc Bay, Philippine Islands
8, 24, 27 December 1944	Air-surface Attacks on Iwo Jima, Volcano Islands
14, 15, 16 December 1944	Carrier Task Force Attacks on Luzon, Philippine Islands
15 December 1944	Landings on Mindoro, Philippine Islands
3–4 January 1945	Carrier Task Force Attacks on Formosa
5 January 1945	Bombardment of Suribachi Wan, off Paramushiru, Kurile Islands
	Air-surface Attack on Iwo Jima, Chichi Jima and Haha Jima, Volcano and Bonin Islands
6–7 January 1945	Carrier Task Force Attacks on Luzon, Philippine Islands
9 January 1945	Landings at Lingayen Gulf, Luzon, Philippine Islands
	Carrier Task Force Attack on Formosa
12 January 1945	Carrier Task Force Attack on French Indo-China Coast
15 January 1945	Carrier Task Force Attack on Formosa
16 January 1945	Carrier Task Force Attack on Hong Kong, Canton and Hainan, China
21–22 January 1945	Carrier Task Force Attack on Formosa and Nansei Shoto
24 January 1945	Air-surface Attack on Iwo Jima, Volcano Islands
29–30 January 1945	Landings in Subic Bay Area, Luzon, Philippine Islands
31 January 1945	Landings at Nasugbu, Luzon, Philippine Islands
13–15 February 1945	Bombardment of Manila Bay Defenses, Philippine Islands
14 February 1945	Landings at Mariveles, Luzon, Philippine Islands
16 February 1945	Landings on Corregidor Island, Luzon, Phillippine Islands
16–17 February 1945	Carrier Task Force Attack on Tokyo

INTRODUCTION

19 February 1945	Landings on Iwo Jima, Volcano Islands
	Bombardment of Kurabu Zaki, Paramushiru, Kurile Islands
25–26 February 1945	Carrier Task Force Attack on Tokyo and Hachijo Jima
28 February 1945	Landings on Palawan, Philippine Islands

[In the above list, all dates are given as of local time in the area of the action.]

No listing of actions with the enemy, however complete, can include the ceaseless and unrelenting depredations of our submarines in the Pacific. In the earlier phases of the war they operated by themselves far beyond the range of any of our surface ships or aircraft. Their constant presence in the westernmost reaches of the Pacific limited the freedom of the enemy's operations: their frequent and effective attacks depleted his shipping and diminished his logistic as well as his combatant strength. The rapid advance of our other forces, both sea and air, has been due in no small measure to the outstanding success with which our submarine activities have been carried on in waters where nothing but submarines could go. During the current phases of the war, our submarines are not only continuing independent operations, but are also working in concert with the task fleets which are now exerting such heavy pressure on the Japanese.

The account of combat operations in this report is based on special summaries recently made by the fleet commanders concerned. In some instances, this information will be found to differ slightly from communiques previously issued, due to the subsequent accumulation of additional facts. However, it should be understood that there has been no opportunity yet for an exhaustive analysis from an historian's point of view of the great mass of operational reports in my files. I can furnish at this time no more than outline sketches of the highlights of combat operations. The preparation of carefully documented historical studies is underway, but the results will not be available during the progress of the war.

Limits of space further require that this account of combat operations be restricted to those actions which have had a significant or decisive effect upon the progress of the war. Similarly, because of the greatly magnified scale of the operations described, it has been impossible to cite the names of individual ships and commanders in most cases. To retain any semblance of continuity, it has been necessary to omit the details of the constant activity of many naval air, surface, and shore-based units which have performed invaluable services of patrol, supply and maintenance on a vast scale. Land-based planes and PT boats have incessantly harassed the beleagured Japanese garrisons which have been by-passed in our progress across the Pacific. Seabees and other naval forces on shore have made great contributions to the conversion of islands seized in amphibious operations into useful bases for further attack upon the enemy. Countless ships and planes have contributed to the safe progress of troops and supplies along far-flung lines of communication. The operations of these forces, which have frequently involved bitter combat with the enemy, cannot, because of the nature of this report, be further elaborated upon.

II
Command and Fleet Organization

UNITED STATES FLEET

THE basic organization of the United States Fleet has remained unchanged during the twelve months covered by this report. The Headquarters of Commander in Chief, United States Fleet, located in Washington since December 1941, has continued to function as originally conceived, but with the growth in complexity and volume of work, I felt the need of assistance in matters of military policy concerning both the United States Fleet and the Office of the Chief of Naval Operations. Consequently the post of Deputy Commander in Chief, United States Fleet and Deputy Chief of Naval Operations was created, and on 1 October 1944, Vice Admiral (now Admiral) R. S. Edwards reported for duty in that capacity. On the same date Vice Admiral (now Admiral) C. M. Cooke, Jr., reported as Chief of Staff to Commander in Chief, United States Fleet, and Rear Admiral (now Vice Admiral) B. H. Bieri reported as Deputy Chief of Staff.

ORGANIZATION OF UNITED STATES NAVAL FORCES IN THE PACIFIC

United States Pacific Fleet

Operations in the Pacific Ocean Areas continue under the command of Fleet Admiral C. W. Nimitz, Commander in Chief, U. S. Pacific Fleet and Pacific Ocean Areas. As the scene of operations moved into the far western Pacific, Fleet Admiral Nimitz's headquarters at Pearl Harbor became increasingly remote. Therefore in January 1945 advance headquarters were established at Guam, from which the Commander in Chief could supervise operations more closely.

Seventh Fleet

The Seventh Fleet (Vice Admiral [now Admiral] Thomas C. Kinkaid, Commander) continues to operate in the Southwest Pacific Area. Vice Admiral Kinkaid is under the command of General of the Army Douglas MacArthur, Commander in Chief of that Area.

Sea Frontiers

On 15 April 1944 a series of changes in the command organization of waters along the Pacific coast of the United States was made. The Northwest Sea Frontier, which has been composed of the Northwestern Sector (Oregon and Washington) and the Alaska Sector, was abolished. The Northwestern Sector was incorporated into the Western Sea Frontier, and the Alaska Sector was established as the Alaskan Sea

Frontier (Vice Admiral F. J. Fletcher, Commander). At the same time the 17th Naval District was created including the Territory of Alaska and its waters. This change consolidated all sea frontier and correlated activities on the west coast of the United States under the Commander, Western Sea Frontier (Vice Admiral D. W. Bagley), and incidentally brought the jurisidictional limits of the naval sea frontiers into conformity with the Army defense organizations on the Pacific coast of the United States.

On 8 November 1944, the functions of the Commander, Western Sea Frontier, were greatly enlarged in scope in order to afford more effective logistic support for war operations of United States forces in the Pacific. On 17 November 1944, Admiral R. E. Ingersoll assumed duties as Commander, Western Sea Frontier, relieving Vice Admiral Bagley.

On 28 November 1944, Vice Admiral Bagley relieved Vice Admiral R. L. Ghormley as Commander, Hawaiian Sea Frontier.

The Philippine Sea Frontier (Rear Admiral J. L. Kauffman, Commander) was established as a separate command under Commander Seventh Fleet (Southwest Pacific Area) on 13 November 1944.

ORGANIZATION OF UNITED STATES NAVAL FORCES IN THE ATLANTIC-MEDITERRANEAN

United States Atlantic Fleet

The U.S. Atlantic Fleet (Admiral Ingersoll, Commander in Chief, until 15 November 1944, when relieved by Admiral J. H. Ingram) consists of the forces operating in the United States area of strategic responsibility, which is, roughly, the western half of the Atlantic Ocean. The Fourth Fleet, operating in the South Atlantic, is a unit of U.S. Atlantic Fleet. Vice Admiral (now Admiral) Ingram was Commander Fourth Fleet until November 1944, when relieved by Vice Admiral W. R. Munroe.

United States Naval Forces, Europe

U.S. Naval Forces, Europe (Twelfth Fleet), Admiral H. R. Stark, Commander, is an administrative command, embracing all United States naval forces assigned to British waters and the Atlantic coastal waters of Europe. Admiral Stark is responsible for the maintenance and training of all United States naval units in his area. For operations connected with the invasion of the continent of Europe, he assigns appropriate task forces to the operational control of the British Admiral commanding the Allied naval contingent of General of the Army Dwight D. Eisenhower's supreme command, which embraces all Army, Navy and Air elements involved in activities connected with the Western Front.

United States Naval Forces, Northwest African Waters

U.S. Naval Forces, Northwest African Waters (Eighth Fleet) Vice Admiral (now Admiral) H. K. Hewitt, Commander, includes all United States naval forces in the Mediterranean. Vice Admiral Hewitt is under the British naval Commander in Chief of the Allied naval forces in the area, who is, in turn, under the command of the

Supreme Commander of the area (formerly General of the Army Eisenhower, later Field Marshal Sir Henry Maitland-Wilson, at present Field Marshal Alexander of the British Army.)

Sea Frontiers

There are four sea frontiers in the Western Atlantic. The Eastern Sea Frontier (Vice Admiral H. F. Leary, Commander) consists of the coastal waters and adjacent land areas from the Canadian border to Jacksonville. The Gulf Sea Frontier (Rear Admiral [now Vice Admiral] Munroe, Commander, until 17 July 1944, when relieved by Rear Admiral W. S. Anderson) consists of the coastal waters from Jacksonville westward, including the Gulf of Mexico and adjacent land areas. The Caribbean Sea Frontier (Vice Admiral A. B. Cook, Commander, until 14 May 1944, when relieved by Vice Admiral R. C. Giffen) consists of eastern Caribbean and adjacent land and water areas. The Panama Sea Frontier (Rear Admiral H. C. Train, Commander, until 1 November 1944, when relieved by Rear Admiral H. C. Kingman) consists of western Caribbean waters, adjacent land areas, and those waters of the Pacific constituting the western approaches to the Panama Canal. The Commander of the Panama Sea Frontier is under the Commanding General at Panama. The other western Atlantic sea frontier commanders are directly under Commander in Chief, United States Fleet.

The Moroccan Sea Frontier (Commodore B. V. McCandlish, Commander) is under Commander Eighth Fleet.

★ ★

III
Combat Operations
The Pacific

DURING the year 1944, the whole of the United States Navy in the Pacific was on the offensive. My previous report, summarizing combat operations to 1 March 1944, showed the evolution by which we had passed from the defensive, through the defensive-offensive and offensive-defensive stages, to the full offensive. To understand the significance of our operations in the account which follows, the reader must be aware of the basic reasons behind them.

The campaign in the Pacific has important elements of dissimilarity from the campaign in Europe. Since the "battle of the beaches" was finally won with the landings in Normandy last June, the naval task in Europe has become of secondary scope. The European war has turned into a vast land campaign, in which the role of the navies is to keep open the trans-Atlantic sea routes against an enemy whose naval strength appears to be broken except for his U-boat activities. In contrast, the Pacific war is still in the "crossing the ocean" phase. There are times in the Pacific when troops get beyond the range of naval gun support, but much of the fighting has been, is now, and will continue for some time to be on beaches where Army and Navy combine in amphibious operations. Therefore, the essential element of our dominance over the Japanese has been the strength of our fleet. The ability to move troops from island to island, and to put them ashore against opposition, is due to the fact that our command of the sea is spreading as Japanese naval strength withers. As a rough generalization, the war in Europe is now predominantly an affair of armies, while the war in the Pacific is still predominantly naval.

The strategy in the Pacific has been to advance on the core of the Japanese position from two directions. Under General of the Army MacArthur, a combined Allied Army-Navy force has moved north from the Australian region. Under Fleet Admiral Nimitz, a United States Army-Navy-Marine force has moved west from Hawaii. The mobile power embodied in the major combatant vessels of the Pacific Fleet has, sometimes united and sometimes separately, covered operations along both routes of advance, and at the same time contained the Japanese Navy.

In November 1943 South Pacific forces secured a beachhead on Bougainville, on which airfields were constructed for the neutralization of the Japanese base of Rabaul on New Britain. Simultaneously Southwest Pacific forces were working their way along the northern coast of New Guinea.

In November 1943 Pacific Ocean Areas forces attacked the Gilbert Islands, and at the end of January 1944 the Marshall Islands—the first stepping stones along the road from Hawaii. To control the seas and render secure a route from Hawaii westward, it was not necessary to occupy every atoll. We could and did pursue a "leap frog" strategy, the basic concept of which is to seize those islands essential for our use, by-passing many strongly held intervening ones which were not necessary for our purposes. This policy was made possible by the gradually increasing disparity between our own naval power and that of the enemy, so that the enemy was and still is unable to support the garrisons of the by-passed atolls. Consequently, by cutting the enemy's line of communicating bases, the isolated ones became innocuous, without the necessity for our expending effort for their capture. Therefore, we can with impunity by-pass numerous enemy positions, with small comfort to the isolated Japanese garrisons, who are left to meditate on the fate of exposed forces beyond the range of naval support.

This strategy has brought the Navy into combat with shore-based air forces. It has involved some risks and considerable difficulty, which we have overcome. However, as we near the enemy's homeland, the problem becomes more and more difficult. During the first landing in the Philippines, for example, it was necessary to deal with the hundred or more Japanese airfields that were within flying range of Leyte. This imposed on our carrier forces a heavy task which we may expect to become increasingly heavy from time to time. While shore-based air facilities are being established as rapidly as possible in each position we capture, there will always be a period following a successful landing when control of the air will rest solely on the strength of our carrier based aviation.

The value of having naval vessels in support of landings has been fully confirmed. The renewed importance of battleships is one of the interesting features of the Pacific war. The concentrated power of heavy naval guns is very great by standards of land warfare, and the artillery support they have given in landing operations has been a material factor in getting our troops ashore with minimum loss of life. Battleships and cruisers, as well as smaller ships, have proved their worth for this purpose.

As I pointed out above, our advance across the Pacific followed two routes. At the opening of the period covered by this report, General of the Army MacArthur's forces were working their way along the northern coast of New Guinea, while Fleet Admiral Nimitz, by the capture of the Gilbert and Marshall Islands, had taken the first steps along the other route. The narrative which follows begins with the operations leading to the capture of Hollandia on the north coast of New Guinea.

HOLLANDIA AND FAST CARRIER TASK FORCE COVERING OPERATIONS

On 13 February 1944 the final occupation of the Huon Peninsula in northeast New Guinea was completed. The occupation of the Admiralty Islands on 29 February 1944 by General of the Army MacArthur's forces and of Emirau in the St. Matthias group, north of New Britain, by Admiral W. F. Halsey's forces on 20 March had further advanced our holdings. In these two operations, the amphibious attack forces were commanded respectively by Rear Admiral W. M. Fechteler and Rear Admiral (now Vice Admiral) T. S. Wilkinson. On 20 March battleships and destroyers bombarded Kavieng, New Ireland.

The enemy had concentrated a considerable force at Wewak, on the northern coast of New Guinea, several hundred miles west of the Huon Peninsula. Hollandia, more than two hundred miles west of Wewak, had a good potential harbor and three airstrips capable of rehabilitation and enlargement. In order to accelerate the reconquest of New Guinea, it was decided to push far to the northwest, seize the coastal area in the vicinity of Aitape and Hollandia, thus by-passing and neutralizing the enemy's holdings in the Hansa Bay and Wewak areas. This operation was made possible by the availability of the fast carrier task force of the Pacific Fleet to perform two functions, namely to neutralize enemy positions in the Western Carolines from which attacks might be launched against our landing forces or against our new bases in the Admiralties and Emirau, and to furnish close cover for the landing.

Carrier Task Force Attacks on Western Carolines

Under command of Admiral R. A. Spruance, Commander Fifth Fleet, a powerful force of the Pacific Fleet, including carriers, fast battleships, cruisers, and destroyers, attacked the Western Carolines. On 30 and 31 March, carrier-based planes struck at the Palau group with shipping as primary target. They sank 3 destroyers, 17 freighters, 5 oilers and 3 small vessels, and damaged 17 additional ships. The planes also bombed the airfields, but they did not entirely stop Japanese air activity. At the same time, our aircraft mined the waters around Palau in order to immobilize enemy shipping in the area.

Part of the force struck Yap and Ulithi on 31 March and Woleai on 1 April.

Although the carrier aircraft encountered active air opposition over the Palau area on both days, they quickly overcame it. Enemy planes approached the task force on the evening of 29 March and 30 March but were destroyed or driven off by the combat air patrols. During the three days' operation our plane losses were 25 in combat, while the enemy had 114 planes destroyed in combat and 46 on the ground. These attacks were successful in obtaining the desired effect, and the operation in New Guinea went forward without opposition from the Western Carolines.

Capture and Occupation of Hollandia

The assault on Hollandia involved a simultaneous three-pronged attack by Southwest Pacific forces. Landings at Tanahmerah Bay and, 30 miles to the eastward, at Humboldt Bay trapped the Hollandia airstrips situated 12 miles inland. The third landing, an additional 90 miles to the eastward at Aitape, provided a diversionary attack, wiped out an enemy strong point, and won another airstrip. Approximately 50,000 Japanese were cut off and the complete domination of New Guinea by Allied forces was hastened. The operation was under the command of General of the Army MacArthur. Three separate attack groups operated under a single attack force commander, Rear Admiral (now Vice Admiral) D. E. Barbey, who also commanded the Tanahmerah Bay attack group. Rear Admiral Fechteler commanded the Humboldt Bay group and Captain (now Rear Admiral) A. G. Noble the Aitape group. This amphibious operation was the largest that had been undertaken in the Southwest Pacific area up to that time. Over 200 ships were engaged. A powerful force of carriers, fast battleships, cruisers and destroyers from the Pacific Fleet, commanded by Rear Admiral (now Vice Admiral) M. A. Mitscher, covered the landings.

Throughout 21 April, the day before the landings, the carriers launched strikes against the airstrips in the Aitape-Hollandia area, which had previously been bombed nightly since 12 April by land-based aircraft. On the night of 21-22 April, light cruisers and destroyers bombarded the airfields at Wakde and Sawar. The amphibious landing took place on the 22nd, and on that and the following day planes from the Pacific Fleet carriers supported operations ashore, while keeping neighboring enemy airfields neutralized. Prepared defenses were found abandoned at Aitape; at Hollandia and Tanahmerah Bay there were none. The enemy took to the hills and the landings were virtually unopposed. Once ashore, all three groups encountered difficulties with swampy areas behind the beaches, lack of overland communications, and dense jungles. In spite of these obstacles, satisfactory progress was made. At the end of the second day the Aitape strip had been occupied and fighters were using it within twenty-four hours. The Hollandia strips fell a few days later.

As soon as the airstrips were in full operation and the port facilities at Hollandia developed, we were ready for further attacks at points along the northwestern coast of New Guinea.

Carrier Task Force Attack on Central and Eastern Carolines

Returning from support of the Hollandia landings, the fast carrier task force attacked Truk on 29 and 30 April. Initial fighter sweeps overcame almost all enemy air opposition by 1000 on the morning of the 29th, and thereafter over 2200 sorties, dropping 740 tons of bombs, were flown against land installations on Truk Atoll. Our planes encountered vigorous and active antiaircraft fire, but did exceedingly heavy damage to buildings and installations ashore. One air attack was attempted on our carriers on the morning of the 29th, but the approaching planes were shot down before they could do damage. Our plane losses in combat were 27 against 63 enemy planes destroyed in the air and at least 60 more on the ground.

For over two hours on 30 April a group of cruisers and destroyers bombarded Satawan Island, where the enemy had been developing an air base. Although existing installations were of little importance, the bombardment served to hinder the enemy's plans and furnished training for the crews of our ships. Similarly, a group of fast battleships and destroyers, returning from Truk, bombarded Ponape for 80 minutes on 1 May. There was no opposition except for antiaircraft fire against the supporting planes.

MARIANAS OPERATIONS

During the summer of 1944, Pacific Ocean Areas forces captured the islands of Saipan, Guam and Tinian, and neutralized the other Marianas Islands which remained in the hands of the enemy.

The Marianas form part of an almost continuous chain of islands extending 1350 miles southward from Tokyo. Many of these islands are small, rocky, and valueless from a military viewpoint; but others provide a series of mutually supporting airfields and bases, like so many stepping stones, affording protected lines of air and sea communication from the home islands of the Japanese Empire through the Nanpo Shoto [Bonin and Volcano Islands] and Marianas to Truk; thence to the Eastern

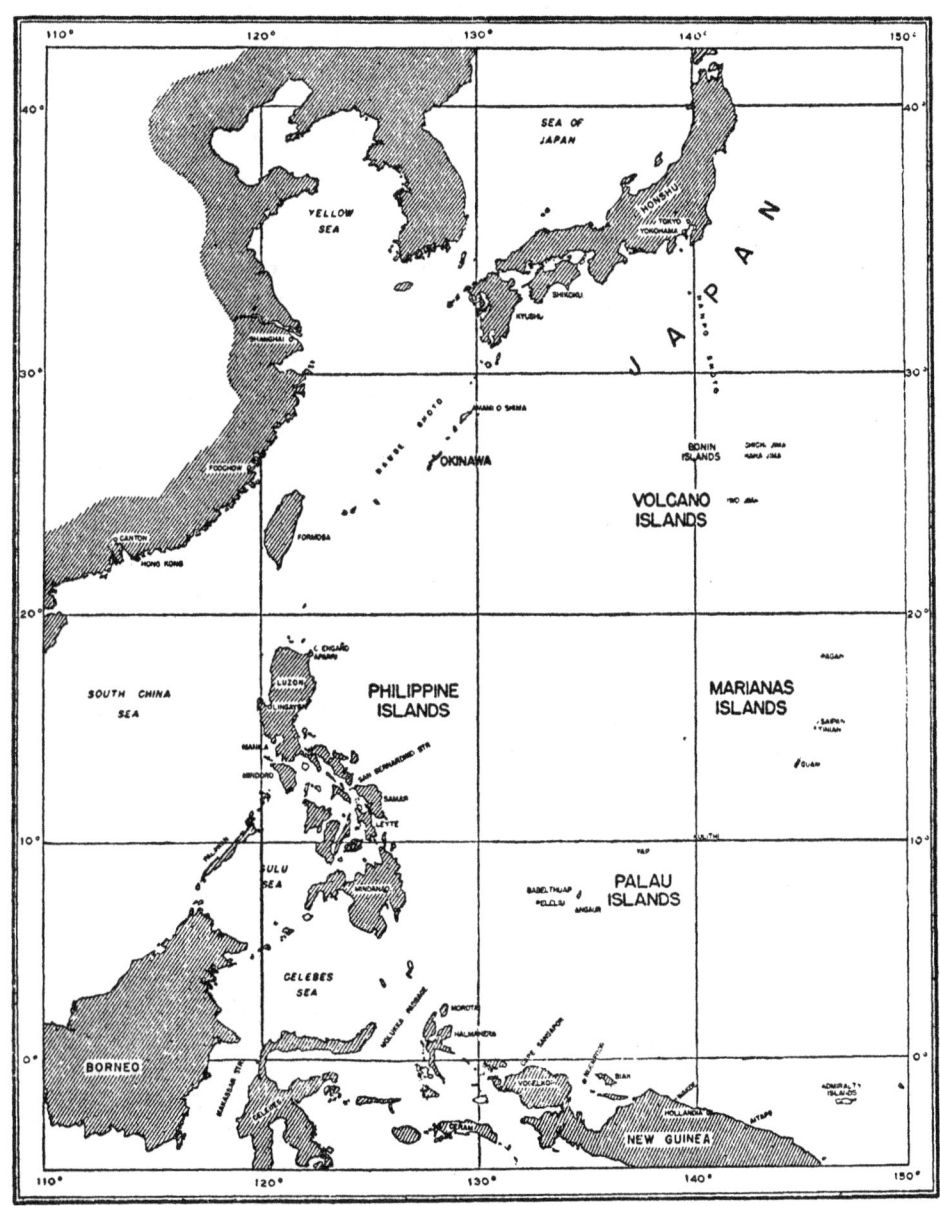

Plate 8.

Carolines and Marshalls, as well as to the Western Carolines, the Philippines and Japanese-held territory to the south and west. Our occupation of the Marianas would, therefore, effectively cut these admirably protected lines of enemy communication, and give us bases from which we could not only control sea areas further west in the Pacific but also on which we could base aircraft to bomb Tokyo and the home islands of the Empire.

As soon as essential points in the Marshall Islands had been secured, preparations were made for the Marianas operation. Admiral Spruance, who had already conducted the Gilberts and Marshalls operations, was in command. Amphibious forces were directly under Vice Admiral (now Admiral) R. K. Turner and the Expeditionary Forces were commanded by Lieutenant General Holland M. Smith, USMC. Ships were assembled, trained, and loaded at many points in the Pacific Ocean Areas. More than 600 vessels ranging from battleships and aircraft carriers to cruisers, high-speed transports and tankers, more than 2,000 aircraft, and some 300,000 Navy, Marine and Army personnel took part in the capture of the Marianas.

Enemy airbases on Marcus and Wake Islands flanked on the north our approach to the Marianas. Consequently, a detachment of carriers, cruisers, and destroyers from the Fifth Fleet attacked these islands almost a month before the projected landings in order to destroy aircraft, shore installations, and shipping. Carrier planes struck Marcus on 19 and 20 May and Wake on 23 May. They encountered little opposition and accomplished their mission with very light losses due to antiaircraft fire.

From about the beginning of June, land-based aircraft from the Admiralties, Green, Emirau and Hollandia kept enemy bases, especially at Truk, Palau, and Yap, well neutralized. The fast carriers and battleships of the Fifth Fleet, under Vice Admiral Mitscher, prepared the way for the amphibious assault. Carrier planes began attacks on the Marianas on 11 June with the object of first destroying aircraft and air facilities and then concentrating on bombing shore defenses in preparation for the coming amphibious landings. They achieved control of the air over the Marianas on the first fighter sweep of 11 June and thereafter attacked air facilities, defense installations, and shipping in the vicinity.

Initial Landings on Saipan

Saipan, the first objective, was the key to the Japanese defenses; having been in Japanese hands since World War I, its fortifications were formidable. Although a rugged island unlike the coral atolls of the Gilberts and Marshalls, Saipan was partly surrounded by a reef which made landing extremely difficult. To prepare for the assault scheduled for 15 June, surface ships began to bombard Saipan on the 13th. The fast battleships fired their main and secondary batteries for nearly 7 hours into the western coast of Saipan and Tinian Islands. Under cover of this fire, fast mine sweepers cleared the waters for the assault ships, and underwater demolition teams examined the beaches for obstructions and cleared away such as were found.

The brunt of surface bombardment for destruction of defenses was borne by the fire support groups of older battleships, cruisers and destroyers, which preceded the transports to the Marianas and began to bombard Saipan and Tinian on 14 June.

Early on the morning of 15 June the transports, cargo ships, and LST's of Vice Admiral Turner's amphibious force came into position off the west coast of Saipan. The bombardment ships delivered a heavy, close range pre-assault fire, and carrier aircraft made strikes to destroy enemy resistance on the landing beaches. The first troops reached the beaches at 0840, and within the next half hour several thousand were landed. In spite of preparatory bombing and bombardment, the enemy met the landing force with heavy fire from mortars and small calibre guns on the beaches. Initial beachheads were established, not without difficulty, and concentrated and determined enemy fire and counterattacks caused some casualties and rendered progress inland slower than was anticipated.

The 2nd and 4th Marine Divisions landed first and were followed the next day by the 27th Army Infantry Division. Although Saipan had an area of but 72 square miles, it was rugged and admirably suited to delaying defensive action by a stubborn and tenacious enemy. The strong resistance at Saipan, coupled with the news of a sortie of the Japanese fleet, delayed landings on Guam.

Battle of the Philippine Sea

This sortie of the Japanese fleet promised to develop into a full scale action. On 15 June, the very day of the Saipan landings, Admiral Spruance received reports that a large force of enemy carriers, battleships, cruisers and destroyers was headed toward him, evidently on its way to relieve the beleaguered garrisons in the Marianas. As the primary mission of the American forces in the area was to capture the Marianas, the Saipan amphibious operations had to be protected from enemy interference at all costs. In his plans for what developed into the Battle of the Philippine Sea, Admiral Spruance was rightly guided by this basic mission. He therefore operated aggressively to the westward of the Marianas, but did not draw his carriers and battleships so far away that they could not protect the amphibious units from any possible Japanese "end run" which might develop.

While some of the fast carriers and battleships were disposed to the westward to meet this threat, other carriers on 15 and 16 June attacked the Japanese bases of Iwo Jima and Chichi Jima. During this strike to the northward our carrier planes destroyed enemy planes in the air and on the ground, and set fire to buildings, ammunition and fuel dumps, thus temporarily neutralizing those bases, and freeing our forces from attack by enemy aircraft coming from the Bonins and Volcanos. The forces employed in the northward strike were recalled to rendezvous west of Saipan, as were also many of the ships designated to give fire support to the troops on Saipan.

On 19 June the engagement with the Japanese fleet began. The actions on the 19th consisted of two air battles over Guam with Japanese planes, evidently launched from carriers and intended to land for fueling and arming on the fields of Guam and Tinian, and a large scale lengthy attack by enemy aircraft on Admiral Spruance's ships. The result of the day's action was some 402 enemy planes destroyed out of a total of 545 seen, as against 17 American planes lost and minor damage to 4 ships.

With further air attacks against Saipan by enemy aircraft unlikely because of the enemy's large carrier plane losses, and with its basic mission thus fulfilled, our fleet headed to the westward hoping to bring the Japanese fleet to action. Air searches were instituted early on the 20th to locate the Japanese surface ships. Search planes did not make contact until afternoon and, when heavy strikes from our carriers were sent out, it was nearly sunset. The enemy was so far to the westward that our air attacks had to be made at extreme range. They sank 2 enemy carriers, 2 destroyers and 1 tanker, and severely damaged 3 carriers, 1 battleship, 3 cruisers, 1 destroyer and 3 tankers. We lost only 16 planes shot down by enemy antiaircraft and fighter planes. Precariously low gasoline in our planes and the coming of darkness cut the attack short. Our pilots had difficulty in locating their carriers and many landed in darkness. A total of 73 planes were lost due to running out of fuel and landing crashes, but over 90 per cent of the personnel of planes which made water landings near our fleet were picked up in the dark by destroyers and cruisers. The heavy damage inflicted on the Japanese surface ships, and prevention of enemy interference to operations at Saipan, made these losses a fair price to pay in return.

The enemy continued retiring on the night of the 20th and during the 21st. Although his fleet was located by searches on the 21st, planes sent out to attack did not make contact. Admiral Spruance's primary mission precluded getting out of range of the Marianas, and on the night of the 21st, distance caused the chase to be abandoned. The Battle of the Philippine Sea broke the Japanese effort to reinforce the Marianas; thereafter, the capture and occupation of the group went forward without serious threat of enemy interference.

Conquest of Saipan

During the major fleet engagement, land fighting on Saipan continued as bitterly as before. Between 15 and 20 June the troops pushed across the southern portion of the island, gaining control of two enemy airfields. During the next ten days, from the 21st to the 30th, the rough central section around Mount Tapotchau was captured. The Japanese, exploiting the terrain, resisted with machine guns, small arms and light mortars from caves and other almost inaccessible positions. This central part of the island was cleared of organized resistance, and the last stage of the battle commenced. By 1 July, the 2nd Marine Division had captured the heights overlooking Garapan and Tanapag Harbor on the west coast, while the 4th Marine Division and 27th Army Division had advanced their lines to within about five miles of the northern tip of the island. From 1 to 9 July the enemy resisted sporadically, in isolated groups, in northern Saipan. On 4 July the 2nd Marine Division captured Garapan, the capital city of the island. One desperate "banzai" counterattack occurred on 7 July but this was stemmed and all organized resistance ceased on the 9th. Many isolated small groups remained, which required continuous mopping up operations; in fact, some mopping up still continues.

While the campaign ashore went on, it was constantly supported by surface and air forces. Surface ships were always ready to deliver gunfire, which was controlled by liaison officers ashore in order to direct the fire where it would be of greatest effectiveness. Carrier aircraft likewise assisted. Supplies, ammunition, artillery and reinforcements were brought to the reef by landing craft and were carried ashore by amphibious vehicles until such time as reef obstacles were cleared and craft could beach. The captured Aslito airfield was quickly made ready for use, and on 22 June

Army planes began operation from there in patrols against enemy aircraft. Tanapag Harbor was cleared and available for use 7 July.

Japanese planes from other bases in the Marianas and the Carolines harassed our ships off Saipan from the time of landing until 7 July. Their raids were not large and, considering the number of ships in the area, these attacks did little damage. An LCI was sunk and the battleship MARYLAND damaged. An escort carrier, 2 fleet tankers, and 4 smaller craft received some damage, but none serious enough to require immediate withdrawal from the area.

While these activities went on in Saipan, the fast carriers and battleships continued to afford cover to the westward, and also to prevent the enemy from repairing his air strength in the Bonins and Volcanos. On 23 and 24 June, Pagan Island was heavily attacked by carrier planes. Iwo Jima received attacks on 24 June and 4 July and Chichi Jima and Haha Jima on the latter date. The 4 July attack on Iwo included bombardment by cruisers and destroyers. These attacks kept air facilities neutralized and destroyed shipping.

Reoccupation of Guam

As has been seen, the unexpectedly stiff resistance on Saipan, together with the sortie of the Japanese fleet, had necessitated a postponement of landings on Guam. This delay permitted a period of air and surface bombardment which was unprecedented in severity and duration. Surface ships first bombarded Guam on 16 June; from 8 July until the landing on the 21st the island was under daily gunfire from battleships, cruisers and destroyers, which destroyed all important emplaced defenses. This incessant bombardment was coordinated with air strikes from fields on Saipan and from fast and escort carriers. The destruction of air facilities and planes on Guam and Rota, as well as the neutralization of more distant Japanese bases, gave us uncontested control of the air. The forces engaged in the reoccupation of Guam were under the command of Rear Admiral (now Vice Admiral) R. L. Conolly.

Troops landed on Guam on 21 July. As at Saipan the beach conditions were unfavorable and landing craft had to transfer their loads to amphibious vehicles or pontoons at the edge of the reef. With the support of bombarding ships and planes, the first waves of amphibious vehicles beached at 0830. There were two simultaneous landings; one on the north coast east of Apra Harbor and the other on the west coast south of the harbor. Troops received enemy mortar and machine gun fire as they reached the beach. The 3rd Marine Division, the 77th Army Infantry Division and the 1st Marine Provisional Brigade, under command of Major General R. S. Geiger, USMC, made the landings; from 21 to 30 July they fought in the Apra Harbor area, where the heaviest enemy opposition was encountered.

The capture of Orote Peninsula with its airfields and other installations, made the Apra Harbor area available for sheltered and easier unloading. Beginning on 31 July, our forces advanced across the island to the east coast and thence pushed northward to the tip of Guam. While enemy opposition was stubborn, it did not reach the intensity encountered on Saipan, and on 10 August 1944 all organized resistance on the island ceased. Air and surface support continued throughout this period.

The elimination of isolated pockets of Japanese opposition was a long and difficult task even after the end of organized resistance. As at Saipan, the rough terrain of the island, with its many caves, made the annihilation of the remaining small enemy forces a difficult task. The enemy casualty figures for Guam illustrate the character of this phase. By 10 August the total number of Japanese dead counted was 10,971, and 86 were prisoners of war. By the middle of November, these numbers had increased to 17,238 enemy killed and 463 prisoners.

Occupation of Tinian

The capture of Tinian Island, by forces commanded by Rear Admiral (now Vice Admiral) H. W. Hill, completed the amphibious operations in the Marianas in the summer of 1944. Located across the narrow channel to the southward of Saipan, Tinian was taken by troops who had already participated in the capture of the former island. Intermittent bombardment began at the same time as on Saipan and continued not only from sea and air, but from artillery on the south coast of Saipan. A joint naval and air program for "softening" the defenses of Tinian went on from 26 June to 8 July, and thereafter both air and surface forces kept the enemy from repairing destroyed positions. There were heavy air and surface attacks on 22 and 23 July, the days immediately preceding the landing, and these completed the destruction of almost all enemy gun emplacements and defense positions. The landings, which took place on beaches at the northern end of Tinian, began early on 24 July. Beach reconnaissance had been conducted at night and the enemy was surprised in the location of our landing. Troops of the 2nd and 4th Marine Divisions landed in amphibious vehicles from transports at 0740 on the 24th. They met only light rifle and mortar fire, and secured a firm beachhead. Like Saipan and Guam, Tinian presented a difficult terrain problem, but enemy resistance was much less stubborn than on the other islands. On 1 August the island was declared secure, and the assault and occupation phase ended on the 8th.

Throughout this period, surface and air units provided constant close support to the ground troops. In addition, on 4 and 5 August units of the fast carrier task force virtually wiped out a Japanese convoy, and raided airfields and installations in the Bonin and Volcano Islands. Damage to the enemy was 11 ships sunk, 8 ships damaged, and 13 aircraft destroyed; our losses were 16 planes.

PROGRESS ALONG NEW GUINEA COAST

Before and during the Marianas operation, Southwest Pacific forces under General of the Army MacArthur engaged in a series of amphibious landings along the north coast of New Guinea. These operations were undertaken to deny the Japanese air and troop movements in western New Guinea and approaches from the southwest to our lines of communication across the Pacific, thus securing our flank. Unlike the Hollandia operation, which was supported by carriers and battleships of the Fifth Fleet, they involved the use of no ships larger than heavy cruisers.

Occupation of the Wakde Island Area

In order to secure airdromes for the support of further operations to the westward, an unopposed landing was made on 17 May 1944 by U. S. Army units at

Arara, on the mainland of Dutch New Guinea, about 70 miles west of Hollandia. Under command of Captain (now Rear Admiral) Noble, a naval force of cruisers, destroyers, transports and miscellaneous landing craft landed the 163rd Regimental Combat Team reinforced. Extending their beachhead on D-day along the coast from Toem to the Tor River, the troops made shore-to-shore movements to the Wakde Islands on 17 and 18 May. By 19 May, all organized enemy resistance on the Wakde Islands had ceased.

Occupation of Biak Island

Because of the need for a forward base from which to operate heavy bombers, an amphibious assault was made on Biak Island, beginning on 27 May. The attack force, under the command of Rear Admiral Fechteler, composed of cruisers, destroyers, transports and landing craft, departed Humboldt Bay on the evening of 25 May and arrived off the objective without detection. Initial enemy opposition was weak and quickly overcome, but subsequently the landing force encountered stiff resistance in the move toward the Biak airfields. Air support and bombardment were furnished by B-24's, B-25's and A-20's, while fighter cover was provided by planes from our bases at Hollandia and Aitape.

After the initial landing on Biak Island, the enemy, entrenched in caves commanding the coastal road to the airstrips, continued stubborn resistance and seriously retarded the scheduled development of the air facilities for which the operation had been undertaken. Furthermore, it became apparent that the enemy was planning to reinforce his position on Biak. To counter this threat, a force of 3 cruisers and 14 destroyers under the command of Rear Admiral V. A. C. Crutchley, RN, was given the mission of destroying enemy naval forces threatening our Biak occupation. On the night of 8-9 June, a force of 5 enemy destroyers attempting a "Tokyo Express" run was intercepted by Rear Admiral Crutchley's force. The Japanese destroyers turned and fled at such high speed that in the ensuing chase only one of our destroyer divisions, commanded by Commander (now Captain) A. E. Jarrell, was able to gain firing range. After a vain chase of about three hours the action was broken off.

Occupation of Noemfoor Island

On 2 July 1944, a landing was made in the vicinity of Kaimiri Airdrome on the northwest coast of Noemfoor Island, southwest of Biak Island. The amphibious attack force, under the command of Rear Admiral Fechteler, consisted of an attack group, a covering group of cruisers and destroyers, a landing craft unit, and a landing force built around the 148th U. S. Infantry Regimental Combat Team reinforced. Landing began at 0800, and all troops and a considerable number of bulk stores were landed on D-day. Prior to the landing nearby Japanese airfields were effectively neutralized by the 5th Air Force.

Enemy opposition was feeble, resistance not reaching the fanatical heights experienced on other islands. There were not more than 2000 enemy troops on Noemfoor Island and our casualties were extremely light, only 8 of our men having been killed by D-plus-6 day. Again, forward air facilities to support further advance to the westward had been secured at a relatively light cost.

Occupation of Cape Sansapor Area

On 30 July 1944 an amphibious force, under the command of Rear Admiral Fechteler, carried out a landing in the Cape Sansapor area on the Vogelkop Peninsula in western New Guinea. Rear Admiral R. S. Berkey commanded the covering force.

The main assault was made without enemy air or naval resistance. Beach conditions were ideal and within a short time secondary landings has been made at Middleberg Island and Amsterdam Island, a few thousand yards off shore.

Prior to D-day Army Air Force bombers and fighters had neutralized enemy areas in the Geelvink-Vogelkop area and the main air bases in the Halmaheras. On D-day, when it became evident that the ground forces would encounter no resistance, Army support aircraft from Owi and Wakde were released for other missions and naval bombardment was not utilized. Again, casualties sustained were light: one man killed, with minor damage to small landing craft.

This move brought our forces to the western extremity of New Guinea. It effectively neutralized New Guinea as a base for enemy operations, and rendered the enemy more vulnerable to air attack in Halmahera, the Molukka Passage and Makassar Strait. Enemy concentrations had been by-passed in our progress up the coast, but due to the absence of roads, the major portion of enemy transport was of necessity water-borne. Here our PT boats did admirable service, roaming east and west along the coast, harassing enemy barge traffic, and preventing reinforcements from being put ashore.

WESTERN CAROLINES OPERATIONS

Following closely upon the capture of the Marianas, Fleet Admiral Nimitz's forces moved to the west and south to attack the Western Caroline Islands. Establishment of our forces in that area would give us control of the southern half of the crescent shaped chain of islands which runs from Tokyo to the southern Philippines. It would complete the isolation of the enemy-held Central and Eastern Carolines, including the base at Truk.

Admiral W. F. Halsey, Jr., Commander Third Fleet, commanded the operations in the Western Carolines. Additions to the Pacific Fleet from new construction made an even larger force available to strike the Western Carolines than the Marianas. Nearly 800 vessels participated. Vice Admiral Wilkinson commanded the joint expeditionary forces which conducted landing operations. Major General J. C. Smith, USMC, was Commander Expeditionary Troops, and Vice Admiral Mitscher was again commander of the fast carrier force. Troops employed included the 1st Marine Division and the 81st Army Infantry Division.

Preliminary Strikes by Fast Carrier Task Force

Prior to the landings in the Western Carolines, wide flung air and surface strikes were made to divert and destroy Japanese forces which might have interfered. Between 31 August and 2 September, planes from the fast carriers bombed and strafed Chichi Jima, Haha Jima and Iwo Jima. Cruisers and destroyers bombarded Chichi Jima and Iwo Jima. They destroyed 46 planes in the air and on the ground, sank at least 6 ships, and damaged installations, airfields and supply dumps. Our forces lost 5 aircraft. On the 7th and 8th, planes from the same carriers attacked Yap Island.

Simultaneously, other groups of fast carriers devoted their attention to the Palau Islands where the first Western Carolines landings were to take place. In attacks throughout the group from 6 to 8 September, they did extensive damage to ammunition and supply dumps, barracks and warehouses.

The plan was for Pacific Ocean Areas forces to land on Peleliu Island in the Palau group on 15 September, simultaneously with a landing on Morotai by Southwest Pacific forces. In order to neutralize bases from which aircraft might interfere with these operations, carrier air strikes on Mindanao Island in the southern Philippines were made. These attacks began on 9 September and revealed the unexpected weakness of enemy air resistance in the Mindanao area. On 10 September there were further air attacks, as well as a cruiser-destroyer raid off the eastern Mindanao coast, which caught and completely destroyed a convoy of 32 small freighters.

The lack of opposition at Mindanao prompted air strikes into the central Philippines. From 12 to 14 September, planes from the carrier task force attacked the Visayas. They achieved tactical surprise, destroyed 75 enemy planes in the air and 123 on the ground, sank many ships, and damaged installations ashore.

In direct support of the Southwest Pacific landing at Morotai, carrier task force planes attacked Mindanao, the Celebes, and Talaud on 14–15 September. On the 14th destroyers bombarded the eastern coast of Mindanao. There was little airborne opposition and our forces destroyed and damaged a number of aircraft and surface ships.

Landings on Peleliu and Angaur

Ships and troops employed in the Western Carolines landings came from various parts of the Pacific. Three days of surface bombardment and air bombing preceded the landing on Peleliu. During this time mine sweepers cleared the waters of Peleliu and Angaur Islands and underwater demolition teams removed beach obstructions. The Peleliu landing took place on 15 September, the landing force convoys arriving off the selected beaches at dawn. Following intensive preparatory bombardment, bombing and strafing of the island, units of the 1st Marine Division went ashore. Despite difficult reef conditions, the initial landings were successful. The troops quickly overran the beach defenses, which were thickly mined but less heavily manned than usual. By the night of the 16th, the Peleliu airfield, which was the prime objective of the entire operation, had been captured. After the rapid conquest of the southern portion of the island, however, progress on Peleliu slowed. The rough ridge which formed the north-south backbone of the island was a natural fortress of mutually supporting cave positions, organized in depth and with many automatic weapons. Advance along this ridge was slow and costly. The Japanese used barges at night to reinforce their troops, but naval gunfire dispersed and destroyed many of them. Enemy forces had been surrounded by 26 September, although it was not until the middle of October that the assault phase of the operation was completed.

The 81st Infantry Division went ashore on Angaur Island, six miles south of Peleliu, on 17 September. Fire support ships and aircraft had previously prepared the way for the assault transports. Beach conditions here were more favorable than at Peleliu. Opposition also was less severe, and by noon of 20 September the entire island had been overrun, except for one knot of resistance in rough country. Prompt steps were taken to develop a heavy bomber field on Angaur. Part of the 81st Division went to Peleliu on 22 September to reinforce the 1st Marine Division, which had suffered severe casualties.

The southern Palau Islands offered no protective anchorage. Before the landings of the 15th, mine sweepers had been clearing the extensive mine fields in Kossol Roads, a large body of reef-enclosed water 70 miles north of Peleliu. Part of this area was ready for an anchorage on 15 September, and the next day seaplane tenders entered and began to use it as a base for aircraft operation. It proved to be a reasonably satisfactory roadstead, where ships could lie while waiting call to Peleliu for unloading, and where fuel, stores and ammunition could be replenished.

Marine troops from Peleliu landed on Ngesebus Island, just north of Peleliu, on 28 September, by a shore-to-shore movement. The light enemy opposition was overcome by the 29th. Later several small islands in the vicinity were occupied as outposts.

No landing was made on Babelthuap, the largest of the Palau group. It was heavily garrisoned, had rough terrain, would have required a costly operation, and offered no favorable airfield sites or other particular advantages. From Peleliu and Angaur the rest of the Palau group is being dominated, and the enemy ground forces on the other islands are kept neutralized.

As soon as it became clear that the entire 81st Division would not be needed for the capture of Angaur, a regimental combat team was dispatched to Ulithi Atoll. Mine sweepers, under cover of light surface ships, began work in the lagoon on 21 September and in two days cleared the entrance and anchorage inside for the attack force. The Japanese had abandoned Ulithi and the landing of troops on the 23rd was without opposition. Escort carrier and long range bombers kept the air facilities at Yap neutralized so that there was no aerial interference with landing operations. Although Ulithi was not an ideal anchorage, it was the best available shelter for large surface forces in the Western Carolines, and steps were taken at once to develop it.

Landings on Morotai

Occupation of the southern part of Morotai Island was carried out by the Southwest Pacific forces of General of the Army MacArthur to establish air, air warning and minor naval facilities. This action was further designed to isolate Japanese forces on Halmahera, who would otherwise have been in a position to flank any movement into the southern Philippines. It was timed simultaneously with the seizure of Palau by Pacific Ocean Areas forces. On 15 September 1944 an amphibious task force composed of escort carriers, cruisers, destroyers, destroyer escorts, attack transports and miscellaneous landing ships and craft, all under the command of Rear Admiral Barbey, approached Morotai. Practically no enemy opposition was encountered, and personnel casualties were light; difficulty was experienced, however, in beaching and unloading, due to coral heads and depressions in the reef adjacent to the landing areas.

Prior to D-day Army land-based planes from Biak and Noemfoor carried out heavy strikes on enemy air facilities in Ceram, Halmahera, northern Celebes, Vogelkop and southern Philippine areas. Carrier fighter sweeps combined with further bombing operations prevented hostile aircraft from reaching Morotai on D-day. Naval gunfire support was furnished by destroyers and two heavy cruisers. During subsequent covering operations we sustained our first naval loss in the Southwest Pacific Area, except for planes and minor landing craft, since the Cape Gloucester operations in December 1943; the destroyer escort SHELTON was torpedoed and sunk by an enemy submarine.

REOCCUPATION OF PHILIPPINE ISLANDS

After providing support for the Palau landings, the Third Fleet fast carrier task force returned to the attack on enemy power in the Philippines. From waters to the east, they conducted the first carrier attack of the war on Manila and Luzon. Under cover of bad weather the carriers approached without detection. On 21 and 22 September planes from the carriers attacked Manila and other targets on Luzon, inflicting severe damage on the enemy and suffering only light losses.

On 24 September carrier planes struck the central Philippines. They completed photographic coverage of the area of Leyte and Samar, where amphibious landings were to take place in October, and reached out to Coron Bay, a much used anchorage in the western Visayas. Many enemy planes and much shipping were destroyed. The light air opposition revealed how effective the first Visayas strikes of 10 days previous had been. Following the strikes of the 24th, the fast carrier task force retired to forward bases to prepare for forthcoming operations.

Initial plans for re-entry into the Philippines intended securing Morotai as a stepping stone with a view to landings by the Seventh Amphibious Force on Mindanao some time in November. The decision to accelerate the advance by making the initial landings on Leyte in the central Philippines was reached in middle September when the Third Fleet air strikes disclosed the relative weakness of enemy air opposition. It was decided to seize Leyte Island and the contingent waters on 20 October and thus secure airdrome sites and extensive harbor and naval base facilities. The east coast of Leyte offered certain obvious advantages for amphibious landings. It had a free undefended approach from the east, sufficient anchorage area, and good access to the remainder of the central islands in that it commanded the approaches to Surigao Strait. Moreover, the position by-passed and isolated large Japanese forces in Mindanao. The accelerated timing of the operation and choice of the east coast for landing required, however, the acceptance of one serious disadvantage—the rainy season. Most of the islands in the Philippines are mountainous and during the northeast monsoon, from October to March, land areas on the east sides of the mountains have torrential rains.

Forces under General of the Army MacArthur carried out the landings in the Philippine Islands. For this purpose many transports, fire support ships and escort carriers were temporarily transferred from the Pacific Fleet to the Seventh Fleet, which is a part of the Southwest Pacific command.

The Central Philippine Attack Force, composed of Seventh Fleet units, greatly

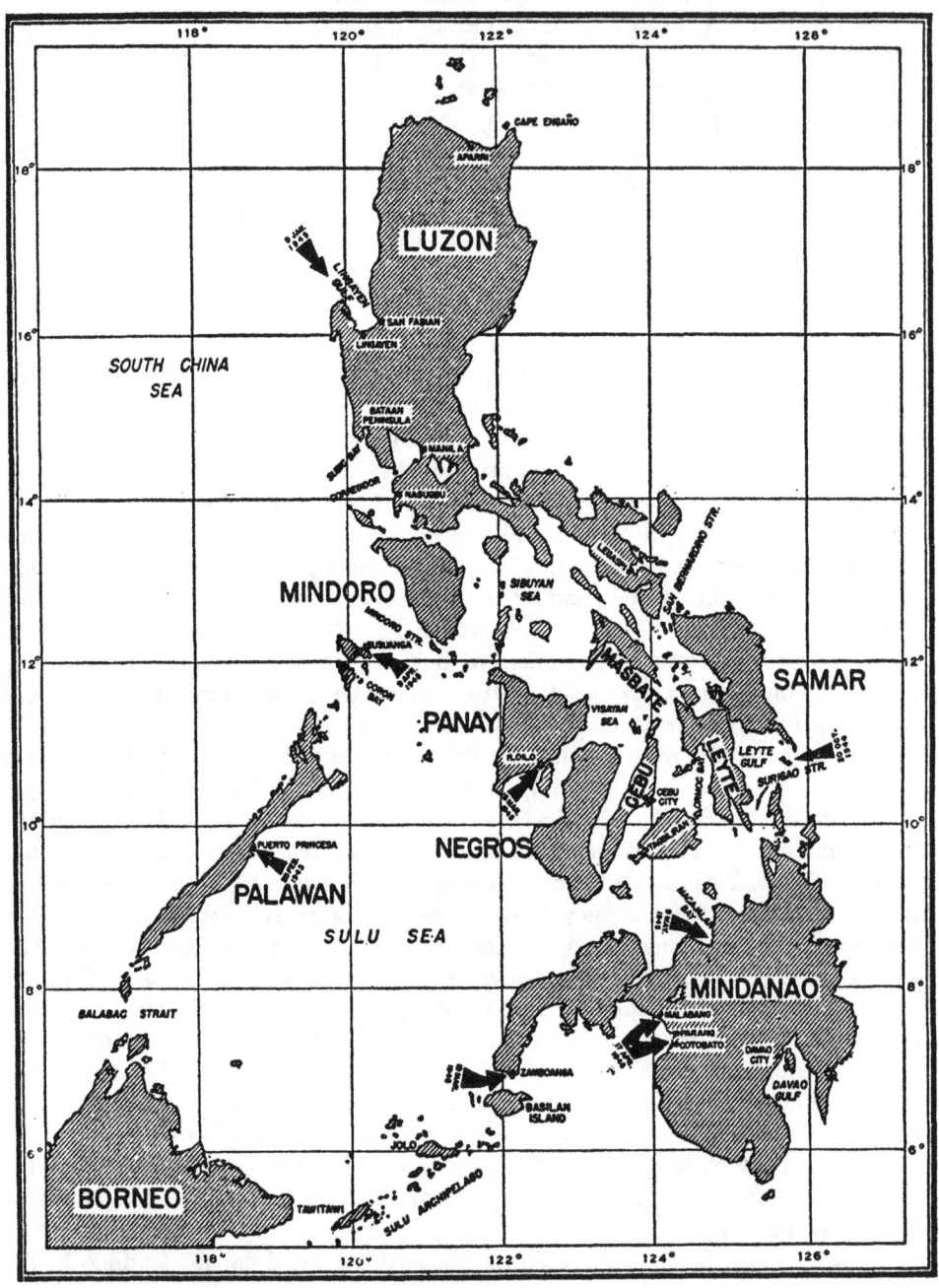

Plate 9.

augmented by Pacific Fleet forces, was under the command of Vice Admiral Kinkaid. This large force was divided into the Northern Attack Force (Seventh Amphibious Force, Rear Admiral Barbey commanding) and the Southern Attack Force (Third Amphibious Force, Vice Admiral Wilkinson commanding), plus surface and air cover groups, fire support, bombardment, mine sweeping and supply groups. It comprised a total of more than 650 ships, including battleships, cruisers, destroyers, destroyer escorts, escort carriers, transports, cargo ships, landing craft, mine craft, and supply vessels. Four army divisions were to be landed on D-day.

The Third Fleet, operating under Admiral Halsey, was to cover and support the operation by air strikes over Formosa, Luzon and the Visayas, to provide protection for the landing against heavy units of the Japanese fleet, and to destroy enemy vessels when opportunity offered.

Preliminary Strikes by Fast Carrier Task Force

Preparatory strikes to obtain information on installations, and to destroy air and surface strength which might hinder our success in the Philippines, lasted from 9 to 20 October.

While a cruiser-destroyer task group bombarded and damaged installations on Marcus Island on 9 October, ships of the fast carrier forces were approaching the Nansei Shoto [Ryukyu Islands]. Long range search-planes and submarines "ran interference" for the force, attacking and destroying enemy search-planes and picket boats, so that our heavy forces achieved tactical surprise at their objective. Carrier aircraft attacked Okinawa Island in the Nansei Shoto on 10 October. The Japanese apparently were taken by surprise. Not only was little airborne opposition met, but shipping had not been routed away from the area. Many enemy ships were sunk and airfields and facilities severely damaged.

On 11 October while the force was refueling, a fighter sweep against Aparri on the northern end of Luzon disorganized the relatively underdeveloped and lightly garrisoned fields there.

The next attack, on Formosa and the Pescadores, took place on 12 and 13 October. These strikes on aviation facilities, factory warehouses, wharves and coastal shipping, were expected by the enemy and, for the first time in this series of operations, a large number of enemy planes were over the targets and antiaircraft fire was intense. In spite of opposition, 193 planes were shot down on the first day and 123 more were destroyed on the ground.

At dusk on the 13th, part of the task force was skillfully attacked by aircraft and one of our cruisers was damaged. Although power was lost, the ship remained stable, due to prompt and effective damage control, and was taken in tow. With a screen of cruisers and destroyers, and under air cover from carriers, the slow retirement of the damaged ship began. At that time the group was 120 miles from Formosa and within range of enemy aircraft on Okinawa, Luzon, and Formosa. Enemy planes kept the group under constant attack and succeeded in damaging another cruiser on the evening of the 14th. She also was taken in tow, and both vessels were brought safely to a base for repairs.

In order to prevent further air attacks while the damaged ships retired, the carriers launched repeated fighter sweeps and strikes over Formosa and northern Luzon on 14 and 15 October.

Beginning on 18 October the carrier planes again struck the Philippines. In strategical as well as direct tactical support of the landings of Southwest Pacific forces at Leyte on the 20th, the strikes of the 18th and 19th were aimed at the northern and central Philippines. On 20 October some of the fast carriers furnished direct support to the Leyte landing and others conducted long-range searches for units of the enemy fleet. Thus, Japanese airfields in and around Manila and in the Visayas were kept neutralized during the initial assault phase of the Leyte landing, while at the same time carrier planes from the Third Fleet furnished direct support to the landings by bombing and strafing beaches and interior areas on Leyte throughout the day. On 21 October there were sweeps and strikes to southern Luzon and the Visayas, including an attack as far west as Coron Bay. Carrier planes also continued long-range searches with negative results.

Leyte Landings

During the 9 days preceding the landing on Leyte, the task groups sortied from New Guinea ports and the Admiralties and moved toward Leyte Gulf. On 17 October (D-minus-3 day) preliminary operations commenced under difficult weather conditions. By D-day the islands guarding the eastern entrances to Leyte Gulf were secured. The approach channels and landing beaches were cleared of mines and reconnaissance of the main beaches on Leyte had been effected.

After heavy bombardment by ships' guns and bombing by escort carrier planes had neutralized most of the enemy opposition at the beaches, troops of the X and XXIV Corps were landed as scheduled on the morning of 20 October. The landings were made without difficulty and were entirely successful. Our troops were established in the central Philippines, but it remained for the naval forces to protect our rapidly expanding beachheads from attack by sea and air.

In the amphibious phase of the Leyte operation, YMS 70 sank in a storm during the approach and the tug SONOMA and LCI (L) 1065 were sunk by enemy action. The destroyer ROSS struck a mine on 19 October and the light cruiser HONOLULU was seriously damaged by an aerial torpedo on 20 October.

Battle for Leyte Gulf

The Leyte landings were challenged by Japanese naval forces determined to drive us from the area. Between 23 and 26 October a series of major surface and air engagements took place with far reaching effect. These engagements, which have been designated the Battle for Leyte Gulf, culminated in three almost simultaneous naval actions, the Battle of Surigao Strait, the Battle off Samar, and the Battle off Cape Engaño. They involved the battleships, carriers, and escort carriers, cruisers, destroyers and destroyer escorts of the Third and Seventh Fleets, as well as PT boats and submarines.

Three enemy forces were involved. One of these, referred to hereinafter as the Southern Force, approached Leyte through Surigao Strait and was destroyed there by Seventh Fleet units on the night of 24–25 October. A second, or Central Force, passed through San Bernardino Strait in spite of previous air attacks by Third Fleet carrier planes and attacked Seventh Fleet escort carriers off Samar on the morning of the 25th. Finally, a Northern Force approached the Philippines from the direction of Japan and was attacked and most of it destroyed by the Third Fleet fast carrier force on the 25th.

On the early morning of 23 October, two submarines, DARTER and DACE, in the narrow channel between Palawan and the Dangerous Ground to the westward discovered the Central Force, then composed of 5 battleships, 10 heavy cruisers, 1 to 2 light cruisers, and about 15 destroyers. These submarines promptly attacked, reporting four torpedo hits in each of three heavy cruisers, two of which were sunk and the third heavily damaged. DARTER, while maneuvering into position for a subsequent attack, grounded on a reef in the middle of the channel, and had to be destroyed after her crew had been removed. Other contacts were made later in the day in Mindoro Strait and off the approach to Manila Bay, resulting in damage to an enemy heavy cruiser.

On the 24th carrier planes located and reported the Central Force (in the Sibuyan Sea) and the Southern Force (proceeding through the Sulu Sea) sufficiently early to permit aircraft from Vice Admiral Mitscher's fast carriers to inflict substantial damage.

The third enemy force, the Northern, was not located and reported until so late on the afternoon of the 24th that strikes could not be launched against it until the next morning. While these searches and strikes were being made, the northernmost of our fast carrier task groups was subjected to constant attacks by enemy land-based planes.

Although about 110 planes were shot down in the vicinity of the group, one of the enemy aircraft succeeded in bombing the light carrier PRINCETON. Large fires broke out on the damaged carrier and despite heroic efforts of cruisers and destroyers to combat them, PRINCETON suffered a series of devastating explosions which also caused damage and casualties to ships alongside. After hours of effort to save the ship, it became necessary to move the task group to meet a new enemy threat (the reported sighting of the Northern Force), and PRINCETON was sunk by torpedo fire from our own ships. It should be noted that PRINCETON was the first fast carrier lost by the United States Navy since the sinking of HORNET in the Battle of the Santa Cruz Islands on 26 October 1942.

Battle of Surigao Strait

A part of the enemy's Southern Force entered Surigao Strait in the early hours of 25 October. Seven ships (2 battleships, 1 heavy cruiser and 4 destroyers) advanced in rough column up the narrow strait during darkness toward our waiting forces. The enemy was first met by our PT boats, then in succession by three coordinated destroyer torpedo attacks, and finally by devastating gunfire from our cruisers and battleships which had been disposed across the northern end of the strait by the officer in tactical command, Rear Admiral (now Vice Admiral) J. B. Oldendorf. The enemy was utterly defeated. This action is an exemplification of the classical naval tactics of "crossing the T." Rear Admiral Oldendorf had deployed his light forces on each flank of the approaching column and had sealed off the enemy's advance through the strait with his cruisers and battleships. By means of this deployment he was able to concentrate his fire, both guns and torpedoes, on the enemy units before they were able to extricate themselves from the trap. The Japanese lost 2 battleships and 3 destroyers almost before they could open fire. The heavy cruiser and one destroyer escaped, but the cruiser was sunk on the 26th by our planes. Other ships of the Southern Force which did not engage in the night battle were either later sunk or badly damaged by aircraft attack. In the night action, the destroyer ALBERT W. GRANT was severely damaged by gunfire; our other ships suffered no damage.

Battle off Samar

Throughout the 24th the Third Fleet carriers launched strikes against the Central Force which was heading for San Bernardino Strait. This force consisted of 5 battleships, 8 cruisers and 13 destroyers. As they passed through Mindoro Strait and proceeded to the eastward, our planes launched vigorous attacks which sank the new battleship MUSASHI—pride of the Japanese Navy, 1 cruiser and 1 destroyer, and heavily damaged other units, including the battleship YAMATO, sister ship of MUSASHI, with bombs and torpedoes. In spite of these losses and damage which caused some of the enemy ships to turn back, part of the Central Force continued doggedly through San Bernardino Strait and moved southward unobserved off the east coast of Samar. Our escort carriers with screens, under the command of Rear Admiral T. L. Sprague, were dispersed in three groups to the eastward of Samar, with the mission of maintaining patrols and supporting ground operations on Leyte. Shortly after daybreak on 25 October the Japanese Central Force, now composed of 4 battleships, 5 cruisers and 11 destroyers, attacked the group of escort carriers commanded by Rear Admiral C. A. F. Sprague. A running fight ensued as our lightly armed carriers retired toward Leyte Gulf.

The 6 escort carriers, 3 destroyers and 4 destroyer escorts of Rear Admiral C. A. F. Sprague's task group fought valiantly with their planes, guns and torpedoes. Desperate attacks were made by planes and escorts, and smoke was employed in an effort to divert the enemy from the carriers. After two and one-half hours of almost continuous firing the enemy broke off the engagement and retired towards San Bernardino Strait. Planes from all three groups of escort carriers, with the help of Third Fleet aircraft, which struck during the afternoon of the 25th, sank 2 enemy heavy cruisers and 1 destroyer. Another crippled destroyer was sunk and several other enemy ships were either sunk or badly damaged on the 26th as our planes followed in pursuit.

In the surface engagement, the destroyers HOEL and JOHNSTON, the destroyer escort ROBERTS and the escort carrier GAMBIER BAY were sunk by enemy gunfire. Other carriers and escort ships which were brought into the fray sustained hits; these included the escort carriers SUWANEE, SANTEE, WHITE PLAINS and KITKUN BAY. Enemy dive bombers on the morning of 25 October sank the escort carrier SAINT LO. Approximately 105 planes were lost by Seventh Fleet escort carriers during the Battle for Leyte Gulf.

Battle off Cape Engaño

Search planes from Third Fleet carriers had located the enemy Southern and Central Forces on the morning of 24 October, and had ascertained that they were composed of battleships, cruisers and destroyers, without aircraft carriers. As it was evident that the Japanese Navy was making a major effort, Admiral Halsey reasoned that there must be an enemy carrier force somewhere in the vicinity. Consequently he ordered a special search to be made to the north, which resulted in the sighting by one of our carrier planes on the afternoon of the 24th of the enemy Northern Force —a powerful collection of carriers, battleships, cruisers and destroyers—standing to the southward.

During the night of the 24th–25th, our carrier task force ran to the northward and before dawn launched planes to attack the enemy. Throughout most of 25 October the Battle off Cape Engaño (so named from the nearest point of land at the northeastern tip of Luzon Island) went on with carrier aircraft striking the enemy force, which had been identified as consisting of 1 large carrier, 3 light carriers, 2 battleships with flight decks, 5 cruisers, and 6 destroyers. Beginning at 0840 air attacks on these ships continued until nearly 1800. Late in the day a force of our cruisers and destroyers was detached to finish off ships which had been crippled by air strikes. In that day's work all the enemy carriers, a light cruiser, and a destroyer were sunk, and heavy bomb and torpedo damage was inflicted on the battleships and other Japanese units.

Early on the morning of the 25th, Admiral Halsey received the report that the Central Force, which his carrier planes had attacked the day before, had pushed on through San Bernardino Strait, had turned southward along the coast of Samar and was attacking Rear Admiral Sprague's escort carriers. Consequently, Admiral Halsey dispatched a detachment of fast battleships and carriers to the assistance of these Seventh Fleet units. Meanwhile the Central Force had turned away and begun to retire northward to San Bernardino Strait in the face of the heroic defense put up by the escort carriers and the expectation of attack by other of our forces. Third Fleet aircraft reached this Central Force after it had begun to retire and inflicted additional serious damage. On the afternoon of 25 October our carrier planes probably sank 2 heavy cruisers and a light cruiser, blew the bow off a destroyer, and damaged 4 battleships and other cruisers and destroyers. Fast surface ships of the Third Fleet reached the scene of action after the enemy had re-entered San Bernardino Strait. However, they encountered a straggler on the 26th, which was promptly sunk. This straggler was identified as either a cruiser or destroyer.

On 26 October aircraft from Third Fleet carriers attacked the retiring Japanese forces again, doing further damage to the surviving battleships. By the end of that day, the Battle for Leyte Gulf was over and the three enemy forces were either destroyed or had retreated out of range of our ships and planes. Thus the major Japanese threat to our initial Philippine landing was averted and the enemy's total surface power severely crippled. The losses of our Third Fleet in the action amounted to 40 planes in combat, in addition to the light carrier PRINCETON.

November Carrier Task Force Strikes

While part of the fast carrier task force retired to fuel and reprovision at forward bases, the remainder continued in action in support of the Leyte campaign. During this period the fast carrier task force was commanded by the late Vice Admiral J. S. McCain. On 27 October planes from carriers bombed and strafed a cruiser and a destroyer off Mindoro.

No major naval actions developed during the remainder of 1944, but the Third Fleet was constantly active in providing vigorous support for the operations in the Southwest Pacific Area. Although Japanese installations in the Philippines and to the northward had been heavily damaged by the September and October strikes, they were not destroyed. On 2 November enemy planes attacked a carrier task group of the Third Fleet and, although 10 of the Japanese aircraft were shot down, several ships were damaged and some personnel casualties were suffered.

Carrier aircraft of the Third Fleet struck at Manila and the airfields in the vicinity on 5 and 6 November. They destroyed 439 planes, sank a cruiser, a destroyer, a destroyer escort, a submarine chaser, an oiler, 2 transports and a freighter, as well as damaging 44 vessels. They hit numerous ground installations and destroyed railroad facilities.

On 11 November planes from the fast carriers attacked and destroyed a Japanese convoy entering Ormoc Bay on the west coast of Leyte Island. They sank 4 transports, 5 destroyers and 1 destroyer escort, and shot down 13 enemy aircraft. This effectively ended one major attempt by the enemy to reinforce his Leyte garrison.

Another two-day series of strikes on Luzon by aircraft from the fast carriers occurred on 13 and 14 November. Antiaircraft fire over the targets was light on the first day, but increased the second. Carrier aircraft sank 3 transports, 3 freighters, and 3 destroyers, and damaged 43 vessels. Eighty-four enemy planes were destroyed in the two days' raid.

Another air attack on Luzon targets came on the 19th. There was little airborne opposition, only 16 planes being shot down at the target, but 100 were destroyed on the ground and with those shot down near the carriers, 124 enemy planes were eliminated during the day. Few shipping targets could be located and the total in that category was 1 freighter and 2 small craft sunk with 13 vessels damaged.

On 25 November the last strike in support of the Leyte operation was launched against Luzon. This time, a light cruiser, a mine layer, a destroyer escort, 6 freighters, and a tanker were sunk, and 29 vessels were damaged. Over the target our planes shot down 25 aircraft and destroyed 32 on the ground. Enemy air attacks on the carriers were heavier than usual, and 31 enemy planes were shot down near our ships.

During the November strikes the air combat losses of the fast carrier task force were 97 planes.

Landings at Ormoc Bay

In order to cut the enemy overwater lines of supply and reinforcement and to separate enemy ground forces on Leyte, an additional amphibious landing was made at Ormoc Bay, on the west coast of the island, on 7 December. Naval forces commanded by Rear Admiral A. D. Struble put Army troops ashore 3 miles southeast of Ormoc against sporadic resistance. The destroyer MAHAN and destroyer transport WARD were, however, so heavily damaged by enemy aerial torpedoes that it was necessary for them to be sunk by our own forces. Several days prior to the landing, the destroyer COOPER was lost in a night action, while engaged in an anti-shipping sweep in this vicinity, and on 11 December the destroyer REID was sunk during an enemy air attack on a supply convoy en route to Ormoc Bay.

Landings on Mindoro

On 15 December Southwest Pacific forces landed on the southwest coast of Mindoro Island, nearly 300 miles northwest of Leyte, in order to seize the San Jose area and establish air facilities there. Enemy air on Luzon, not having been entirely neutralized, attacked the convoy en route. Our ships suffered some damage but continued the approach. The landing was without opposition from shore but sporadic air attacks resulted in the sinking of a few LST's. In moving from Leyte to Mindoro, our forces obtained the advantages of more favorable weather for airfield construction and aircraft operations.

Occupation of southwest Mindoro presented a more serious threat to Manila and to Japan's shipping lanes through the South China Sea. As an immediate and strong reaction by the enemy was expected, carrier planes of the Third Fleet promptly began making Manila Bay untenable. Securing tactical surprise, they struck at dawn 14 December, the day before the Mindoro landings. Local air control was gained and held continuously for three days. In attacks on 14, 15 and 16 December our carrier aircraft sank or destroyed 27 vessels and damaged 60 more, destroyed 269 Japanese planes, and bombed air and railroad facilities. Enemy aircraft did not molest the carriers during this strike, but 20 of our planes were lost in combat.

On 17 December sea conditions began to deteriorate east of Luzon where the Third Fleet was scheduled to refuel: a typhoon of severe intensity developed with great rapidity along an erratic course. Although the main body of the fleet escaped the center of the storm, the destroyers HULL, SPENCE and MONAGHAN were lost.

Landings at Lingayen Gulf

The mid-December carrier strikes on Manila Bay had led the enemy to expect further landings in that area. When we by-passed southern Luzon and landed on the south and southeast coast of Lingayen Gulf on 9 January, the enemy was again taken by surprise.

Luzon, the largest of the Philippine Islands, with an area roughly the size of Virginia, is generally mountainous, but is cut by two large valleys. The central plain, extending from Lingayen to Manila Bay—about 100 miles long and from 30 to 50 miles wide—contains Manila, the capital, the major concentration of population and wealth, numerous airfields, and a network of roads and railways. Prompt seizure of this area would strike at the heart of the enemy defenses in the Philippines, provide bases for the support of further operations against the Japanese, and deny the enemy the freedom of the South China Sea. The most vulnerable part of the central plain is at Lingayen, where the low land does not offer the same opportunities for defense as do the approaches to Manila Bay.

The Luzon Attack Force, commanded by Vice Admiral Kinkaid, under the over-all command of General of the Army MacArthur, was composed of Seventh Fleet units largely augmented by Pacific Fleet forces, and numbered more than 850 ships. This was divided into the Lingayen Attack Force (Vice Admiral Wilkinson commanding), the San Fabian Attack Force (Vice Admiral Barbey commanding), a reinforcement group (Rear Admiral Conolly commanding), a fire support and bombardment group (Vice Admiral Oldendorf commanding) and surface and air covering groups (Rear Admiral Berkey and Rear Admiral C. T. Durgin, respectively, commanding). The Luzon Attack Force was to transport, put ashore and support elements of the 6th United States Army (Lieutenant General Walter Krueger commanding) to assist in the seizure and development of the Lingayen area.

The Third Fleet, operating under Admiral Halsey, with its fast carrier task force commanded by Vice Admiral McCain, was to cover and protect the operation by air strikes over Luzon, Formosa and the Nansei Shoto. Complete surprise was attained in attacks on Formosa and the southern Nansei Shoto on 3 and 4 January. There was little airborne opposition, but unfavorable weather conditions somewhat reduced the toll of enemy ships, planes and facilities destroyed. Luzon was hit 6 January, with the zone of operations extending southward to the Manila Bay area in order to give special attention to enemy airfields. Overcast weather prevented blanketing of the northern Luzon fields, and the attack was consequently renewed on the 7th.

Landings in Lingayen Gulf were scheduled for 9 January. During the passage of the attack force to Lingayen there was no enemy surface opposition. One Japanese destroyer put out from Manila Bay, and was sunk by our escorting destroyers. There was, however, intensive air attack both during the passage and the preliminary operations in Lingayen Gulf, which resulted in the loss of the escort carrier OMMANEY BAY, the fast mine sweepers LONG, HOVEY and PALMER, and considerable topside damage to other ships. For three days prior to the assault, Vice Admiral Oldendorf's battleships, cruisers and destroyers bombarded the area, while mine sweepers were at work and beach obstacles were being cleared. Immediately prior to the landings the bombardment by heavy ships and the air strikes from escort carriers were intensified; the assault waves were preceded by rocket-firing and mortar-carrying landing craft, which took up the frontal fire against the beaches, while the heavier calibre fire was directed inland and to the flanks.

The Lingayen Attack Force landed the XIV Army Corps on the southern shore of Lingayen Gulf, while the San Fabian Attack Force simultaneously put the I Army Corps ashore on beaches in the Damortis area to the northeastward. Only very light resistance was met at the beaches, and the troops advanced rapidly inland in spite of unfavorable terrain conditions. Bombardment and bombing had already silenced or destroyed the great majority of fixed defenses and dispersed their personnel.

While the troops were going ashore in Lingayen Gulf on 9 January, the Third Fleet fast carrier task force was striking Formosa. This target was chosen to lessen the enemy air strength which had been operating against Seventh Fleet forces on earlier days. As a result of this operation there was little enemy air interference with the actual Lingayen landings: the Third Fleet in addition netted 15 enemy ships sunk and 58 damaged for its day's work.

Although the troops pressed rapidly southward on Luzon, and were soon out of range of naval fire support, a heavy force of battleships, cruisers, destroyers and escort carriers remained in Lingayen Gulf for a considerable length of time to cover the landing of reinforcements and supplies and prevent enemy surface, subsurface, and air interference.

Third Fleet Covering Operations

In continued support of the Lingayen operations, the Third Fleet fast carrier task force made a thrust into the South China Sea, especially seeking the destruction of any major units of the Japanese Fleet that might be encountered there. None were found, but the air strikes of 12 January on the coast between Saigon and Camranh Bay achieved much shipping destruction. One enemy convoy was entirely destroyed and two others were severely mauled: the shipping tally totaled 41 ships sunk and 31 damaged. One hundred and twelve enemy planes were destroyed, and docks, oil storage and airfield facilities were heavily damaged. Air opposition was negligible.

Formosa was struck again on the 15th, against very slight opposition, while fighter sweeps and searches were made to Amoy, Swatow, Hong Kong and Hainan. Poor weather, however, greatly reduced the score of shipping destruction.

To complete the Third Fleet's visit to the China coast, Hong Kong, Canton and Hainan were struck in force on 16 January. A considerable amount of shipping was damaged or destroyed. Extensive destruction was inflicted on docks, refineries and the naval station in the Hong Kong area, while huge oil fires were started at Canton. Air opposition was again negligible.

In the course of this thrust into waters that the enemy had hitherto considered his own, 3800 miles were traversed in the South China Sea with no battle damage to our ships. No enemy aircraft had been able to approach the fast carrier task force closer than 20 miles.

Formosa and the southern Nansei Shoto were again attacked on 21 January under favorable weather conditions. Heavy damage was inflicted on aircraft, shipping, docks and the industrial area at Takao. On the following day Okinawa in the Nansei Shoto was struck. The destruction of enemy aircraft and airfield facilities in all these strikes led to a marked lessening of Japanese air effort against the Luzon assault forces.

Operations against Manila

During the remainder of January, General of the Army MacArthur's troops pressed steadily southward from Lingayen Gulf down the central plain. To accelerate the progress of operations against Manila and to open sea access to its harbor, additional amphibious landings were carried out in southwestern Luzon at the end of the month. On 29 January an amphibious assault force, commanded by Rear Admiral Struble, put the XI Army Corps ashore in the San Narciso area, northwest of Subic Bay. This move, which was designed to cut off Bataan Peninsula, was entirely unopposed. Mine sweepers made exploratory sweeps off the landing beaches with negative results, and as it was evident that no enemy forces were present the scheduled bombardment of the area was not carried out. The troops moved rapidly inland and reached Subic by noon. On the following day, the 30th, troops were landed on Grande Island in Subic Bay, again without opposition. Mine sweeping of Subic Bay continued, with negative results, and this fine harbor was made available for further operations against the Manila entrance.

An assault force commanded by Rear Admiral Fechteler landed elements of the 11th Airborne Division at Nasugbu, 15 miles directly south of the entrance to Manila Bay, on 31 January. In this instance the naval bombardment was confined to destroyers and smaller ships. Although the troops reached their objective without opposition, a number of small high-speed craft attacked the naval force, and PC 1129 was sunk in the ensuing action.

On 13 February a force of light cruisers and destroyers, commanded by Rear Admiral Berkey, commenced a preliminary bombardment of the entrances to Manila Bay, and on the following day continued to shell Corregidor Island and the southern portion of Bataan Peninsula. Mine sweepers began clearing Manila Bay. On the 15th, while the bombardment of Corregidor and the mine sweeping continued, troops landed at Mariveles on Bataan against very light opposition, and on the 16th landings were made on Corregidor itself.

The ability to place troops ashore in protected and mined waters was made possible by naval gunfire against the fixed defenses of Corregidor, and the sweeping of mines in the channel between Corregidor and Mariveles. In considerably less than two months from the initial landings at Lingayen Gulf, General of the Army MacArthur's forces had covered the ground that had required more than four months for the Japanese in 1942. In comparing the methods used by the two invaders for seizing positions controlling the entrance to Manila Bay, it is interesting to note that in both cases the attacking forces had control of the sea and air. The Japanese relied principally on field artillery from Bataan against our guns on Corregidor. Our method employed naval strength as the spearhead of amphibious assault, thus allowing the ground force commander flexibility in selecting the time and place of the attack.

Landings on Palawan

At the close of February various operations against enemy holdings in different parts of the Philippines were in progress, in which forces of the Seventh Fleet were participating. On the 28th, the last day covered by this report, a force of cruisers and destroyers commanded by Rear Admiral R. S. Riggs bombarded Puerto Princesa, on the east coast of Palawan. An amphibious attack group, commanded by Rear Admiral Fechteler, put troops ashore shortly after. No opposition was encountered: the town and two nearby airfields were quickly seized. This landing secured virtual control of the westernmost of the Philippine Islands, and provided the sites for air bases that will assist in hindering enemy water transport from the Netherlands East Indies.

ASSAULT ON INNER DEFENSES OF JAPAN

The amphibious operations of the spring, summer and autumn of 1944 carried our forces such great distances across the Pacific that in February 1945 they were enabled to begin the assault upon the inner defenses of the Japanese Empire itself.

The occupation of Saipan, Tinian and Guam had established shore-based air forces of the Pacific Ocean Areas in positions from which continuing air attacks could be made against the Volcano and Bonin Islands, and from which long-range bombers could operate against Japan. To operate with the greatest effectiveness and a minimum of losses, long-range bombers should be provided with fighter support. Iwo Jima in the Volcano Islands, 750 miles from Tokyo, provided three sites for airfields, and was admirably situated for the establishment of a fighter base for supporting Marianas-based B-29's operating over the home islands of the Empire. The possession of Iwo Jima would also permit medium bombers to attack Japan, deprive the enemy of an important aerial lookout station, and reduce his air attacks on our Marianas bases.

The operations for the capture of Iwo Jima were under the command of Admiral Spruance, Commander Fifth Fleet. Vice Admiral Turner was in over-all command of the amphibious forces, and the Expeditionary Forces were commanded by Lieutenant General Holland M. Smith, USMC. Major General Harry Schmidt, USMC, commanded the Fifth Amphibious Corps; Major General Clifton B. Cates, USMC, the 4th Marine Division; Major General Keller E. Rockey, USMC, the 5th Marine Division; and Major General Graves B. Erskine, USMC, the 3rd Marine Division. The fast carrier task force, operating in support of the assault, was once more commanded by Vice Admiral Mitscher.

It was anticipated that enemy resistance would be severe. Iwo Jima had been heavily fortified by the Japanese over a period of many years because it is the only island in this strategically important group which lends itself to construction of airfields. As the island is only five miles long and less than two miles wide, the enemy could cover the whole shoreline with artillery and machine gun fire and could concentrate on the only two landing beaches. There was no opportunity for maneuver to select an undefended landing place, and hence there could be no surprise once we had begun reduction of the major defenses of the island. Consequently preparations had to be made for the most intensive ground fighting yet encountered in the Pacific. Landing forces of 60,000 Marines, put ashore by a naval force of more than 800 ships, manned by approximately 220,000 naval personnel, are evidence of the scale of the attack and the determination of opposition expected.

Preliminary Air-Surface Attacks on Iwo Jima

For seven months prior to the February 1945 assault, Iwo Jima was subjected to air attacks and surface bombardments, which increased in frequency and intensity from December 1944 onward. Planes from the fast carrier task force struck the island on 15, 16, 24 June, 4 July, 4–5 August and 31 August–2 September; on 4 July and 2 September bombardment by surface ships was carried out.

Beginning just before midnight on 11 November and continuing until 0100 on the 12th, cruisers and destroyers commanded by Rear Admiral A. E. Smith bombarded Iwo Jima, making special efforts to damage air installations. There was moderate shore battery fire during the first part of the bombardment, but none of our ships suffered damage. Numerous explosions were seen and several large fires were started.

Early in December bombers of the Seventh Army Air Force, operating under the Strategic Air Force, Pacific Ocean Areas, began daily attacks on Iwo Jima, and Marine Corps bomber squadrons, based in the Marianas, began a daily series of night harassing flights against enemy shipping in the area. These constant raids were supplemented periodically by intensified air attack and surface bombardment.

On 8 December and again on 24 December attacks by P-38's, B-29's and B-24's were followed by over an hour's bombardment by Rear Admiral Smith's cruisers and destroyers. A number of large fires were started ashore during each attack. The bombarding ships suffered no damage.

On 27 December Army B-29's and P-38's bombed Iwo Jima once more, and the same surface ships returned to fire on shore targets for an hour and a half. Little opposition was encountered on either day, although one of our ships received slight damage from shore batteries. Light personnel casualties aboard one of our destroyers resulted from a hit from an enemy destroyer escort which was pursued and sunk at sea.

Chichi Jima and Haha Jima in the Bonin Islands, as well as Iwo Jima, were bombarded on 5 January 1945 by Rear Admiral Smith's surface ships, while Army aircraft of the Strategic Air Force, Pacific Ocean Areas, bombed airstrip installations on Iwo. Fire from enemy shore batteries was meager.

A battleship-cruiser-destroyer force, commanded by Rear Admiral O. C. Badger, attacked Iwo Jima on 24 January in a coordinated action with Strategic Air Force bombers and B-29's of the 21st Bomber Command. Air installations and shipping were attacked, with no interception by enemy planes and only slight anti-aircraft fire. One Japanese cargo vessel blew up and two others were left burning.

Attack on Tokyo

Carrier aircraft of the Fifth Fleet attacked Tokyo on 16 February, exactly one year after the first carrier strike on Truk. Fleet Admiral Nimitz's communique announcing the strike stated: "This operation has long been planned and the opportunity to accomplish it fulfills the deeply cherished desire of every officer and man in the Pacific Fleet."

Landings on Iwo Jima were scheduled for 19 February. Consequently on the 16th pre-invasion bombardment and bombing of Iwo Jima began, while the fast carrier task force struck Tokyo. This attack on the enemy's capital was designed to provide strategic cover for the operations against Iwo by destroying air forces, facilities and manufacturing installations, as well as to bring to the Japanese home front a disrupting awareness of the progress of the war.

Approaching the coast of Japan under cover of weather so adverse as to handicap enemy air operations, our forces obtained complete tactical surprise; our attack was vigorously pressed for two days. All enemy efforts to damage our ships were unsuccessful. Against a loss of 49 of our planes, 322 enemy aircraft were shot out of the air and 177 destroyed on the ground. A Japanese escort carrier at Yokohama was bombed and set on fire; she went down by the bow and was left lying on her side. Nine coastal vessels, a destroyer, 2 destroyer escorts and a cargo ship were sunk. Hangars, shops and other installations at numerous airfields were destroyed; the Ota aircraft factory was damaged; and the Musashine Tama and Tachigawa engine plants were heavily bombed. Upon completion of the 17 February strike, the fast carrier task force retired towards Iwo Jima to give more direct support of the landing operations.

Landings on Iwo Jima

After three days of intensive bombardment by surface ships of the Fifth Fleet and bombing by Navy carrier and Army shore-based planes, the 4th and 5th Marine Divisions began landing operations at 0900, 19 February, on the southeast shore of Iwo Jima. This bombardment and bombing made initial opposition light, except for some mortar and artillery fire at LST's and boats, but resistance rapidly developed in intensity during the day. The enemy was soon laying down a devastating curtain of artillery, rocket and mortar fire on the beaches, and the remainder of the day saw bitter fighting as the Marines inched ahead against determined resistance from heavily fortified positions. The troops who came ashore encountered an intricate system of defenses, as well as some of the most modern weapons that the enemy has employed in the present war. The defending garrison, estimated at 20,000, was emplaced in an interlocking system of caves, pillboxes and blockhouses, with both the guns on Mount Suribachi (at the southern tip of the island) and in the high northern area commanding the Marines' positions, the beaches and the sea approaches. By the end of the first day, the Marines had advanced across the width of the island at its narrow southwestern tip, isolating the Japanese on Mount Suribachi from the main enemy forces in the north.

During the early morning hours of 20 February, an enemy counterattack was broken up by the 27th Marines; by the end of the day our troops had captured Motoyama Airfield No. 1.

Desperate fighting continued during the third day: by 1800 more than 1200 Japanese dead had been counted, and one had been captured. The 3rd Marine Division landed, as reserves, and moved into line between the 4th and 5th Divisions. Although enemy air strength was generally light, it succeeded in sinking the escort carrier BISMARCK SEA. During the night of 21–22 February, the enemy counterattacked again and again, but each assault was hurled back. The following morning the Marines renewed the attack; by noon they were advancing slowly under adverse weather conditions, knocking out enemy strongpoints. During the afternoon the enemy counterattacked again, exerting maximum pressure on both flanks of the Marine spearhead which was pointed toward Motoyama Airfield No. 2; the attack was repulsed with heavy losses to the enemy.

The southern part of Motoyama Airfield No. 2 was occupied on 23 February. Simultaneously other troops stormed the steep slopes of Mount Suribachi, capturing the summit and winning gun positions which commanded the island. At 1035 the

28th Marine Regiment hoisted the United States flag over the extinct volcano. The capture of these heights eliminated some of the enemy mortar and artillery fire which had been directed against our troops on the previous days, while mortar fire from Kangoku Rock, northwest of the island, was eliminated by a destroyer. Throughout the entire period, close support was constantly furnished by carrier aircraft and naval gunfire. Unloading continued on the beaches; roads were being constructed, and the captured airstrips being restored to operational condition.

By 25 February, Marines of the three divisions, spearheaded by tanks, had captured approximately half of the island, including Motoyama Airfield No. 2, and were closing in on the main village. The advance was made against fanatical resistance from rockets, bazooka-type guns, pillboxes and interlocking underground strongholds. On one flank alone, 100 caves, 30 to 40 feet deep, had to be knocked out one by one.

By the end of February, Marine Corps observation and artillery spotting planes were operating from Motoyama Airfield No. 1; the 3rd and 4th Marine Divisions had captured hills which further reduced the enemy's fire power and allowed a freer supply flow on the beaches. The Japanese, despite heavy losses, continued to offer maximum resistance, but the Marines were established on high ground, and the conquest of Iwo Jima was assured.

Renewed Attack on Tokyo

Tokyo was again attacked on 25 February by Vice Admiral Mitscher's fast carrier task force, which struck the island of Hachijo, off the coast of Honshu, the following day. Weather conditions were extremely adverse, but at least 158 planes were destroyed and 5 small vessels sunk. Numerous ground installations were attacked. The Ota and Koizumi aircraft plants were heavily damaged; radar installations, aircraft hangars, and 2 trains were demolished. Our forces lost 9 fighter planes in combat; the ships of the task force suffered no damage during the attack, but minor damage was inflicted upon two light units during retirement.

On 1 March 1944 our forces were in the Marshall Islands and northeast New Guinea. On 1 March 1945 they were established in Iwo Jima, 750 miles from Tokyo.

CONTINUING OPERATIONS

In addition to the great battles and the major combats, there were many vital continuing operations against the Japanese in the Pacific. Although less spectacular, they were none the less significant in exerting pressure on the enemy at every possible point. These activities, with the exception of those by submarines, took place in areas where campaigns had already been fought and where the fruits of those campaigns were now capitalized on. Favorable positions and bases gained from the enemy became points of attack on his more remote holdings.

Northern Pacific

From bases in the Aleutians our air and surface forces kept up a constant attack on Japanese positions in the northern and central Kurile Islands. In spite of chronically bad weather, Army and Navy planes flew both attack and photographic missions to the Kuriles many times each month. They not only observed Japanese activity, but also destroyed important installations, supply dumps and shipping units. A task force of cruisers and destroyers commanded by the late Rear Admiral E. G. Small bombarded Matsuwa Island in the Kuriles on 13 June and Kurabu Zaki, an important enemy air base on the southeast tip of Paramushiru, on 26 June. Matsuwa Island was again bombarded on 21 November by a task force commanded by Rear Admiral J. L. McCrea. On 5 January 1945, Rear Admiral McCrea's forces bombarded Suribachi Wan, off Paramushiru, returning on 19 February to bombard Kurabu Zaki.

Submarines

The activities of Pacific Fleet and Seventh Fleet submarines grew more extensive and varied after 1 March 1944. As previously, they operated aggressively against enemy combat ships and commerce. No waters of the Pacific were too remote for their operations and their patrols carried them to the interior lines of Japanese sea communication, where they have littered the bottom of the ocean with the sunken wrecks of a large part of Japan's once great merchant fleet, as well as many naval vessels. Their contribution to the success of our advance in the Pacific is noteworthy. Besides their combat patrols, the submarines have rendered invaluable service on reconnaissance missions and have rescued many aviators shot down during strikes against various Japanese bases. Pacific Fleet submarines have been under the command of Vice Admiral C. A. Lockwood, Jr., during the period covered by this report. Seventh Fleet submarines were under the command of Rear Admiral R. W. Christie until 30 December 1944, when he was relieved by Rear Admiral J. Fife, Jr.

The British Pacific Fleet

Recently we have had the pleasure of welcoming the arrival in the Pacific of a strong task force of the Royal Navy, commanded by Admiral Sir Bruce A. Fraser, G.C.B., K.B.E. This potent addition to the Allied naval power in the Far East has been placed under the operational control of the Commander in Chief, United States Fleet, and will work side by side with our armed forces in the common effort against the Japanese. Australian cruisers, destroyers and attack transports—under the command of Rear Admiral V. A. C. Crutchley, V.C., D.S.O., RN, later Commodore J. A. Collins, C.B., RAN, and now Commodore H. B. Farncomb, M.V.O., D.S.O., RAN—have continued to operate as an integral part of our naval task forces, as they have in previous years.

IV

Combat Operations Atlantic-Mediterranean

UNITED STATES ATLANTIC FLEET

DURING the past year the combat operations of the U.S. Atlantic Fleet have been concerned primarily with antisubmarine activities, in coordination with the sea frontier commands. Escort systems in certain transAtlantic convoy routes are also the responsibility of the Commander in Chief, U.S. Atlantic Fleet. As was announced in the monthly statements of the President and the Prime Minister, the antisubmarine war has been on a fairly low scale during the past year. The German submarine force apparently has been engaged in "licking its wounds" after the rough handling it received in 1943. Its operations were badly interfered with by the invasion of the Continent in June, which knocked out the many U-boat bases on the French coast and forced the Germans to use bases less conveniently located in Norway and the Baltic. It is assumed that the long period of relative quiescence has been employed for building more effective types of submarines. The possibility of a renewed outbreak of submarine activity must, therefore, be guarded against. The remarks in my previous report as to the necessity for complete secrecy concerning our antisubmarine methods still hold. I consider it of the greatest importance that the material and technique we have developed for dealing with the submarine menace be kept to ourselves until the conclusion of the war, to the end that the Japanese may not be able to apply our antisubmarine methods against our submarines operating in the Pacific.

An important duty of the U.S. Atlantic Fleet has been the maintenance of what might be called a general reserve of battleships, cruisers and other ships needed to make up a balanced task force. While possibility of a breakout of what was left of the German surface fleet remained, this force was held in readiness to deal with surface raids on Atlantic commerce. From time to time, particularly during the landings in northern and southern France, these ships were assigned first to the invasion of Normandy and then to the Eighth Fleet for the invasion of southern France. With the successful accomplishment of these operations, the need for heavy surface ships in the Atlantic area was reduced, and a large part of this general reserve has been shifted to the Pacific Fleet.

One of the little publicized but valuable tasks of the Atlantic Fleet has been to train for service elsewhere the large number of ships and landing craft built on the Atlantic coast. This has enabled the best use to be made of the facilities on the east coast, and has prevented overcrowding of the congested harbors on the Pacific coast.

The same system is used in training patrol plane squadrons, which insofar as is practicable are fully trained in the Atlantic Fleet before being transferred to combat duty in the Pacific. The fact that during the past year some 3300 ships and craft were "shaken down" in the Atlantic Fleet operational training command indicates the magnitude of these training operations. An important element in this activity is the preparation of new submarines for war, carried on by the Submarine Force of the Atlantic Fleet, and the education of submarine officers and men in the schools at the Submarine Base at New London. The outstanding success of our submarines in the Pacific is in a large measure due to the sound preliminary training they receive in the schools and the school submarines in the Atlantic.

The Atlantic Fleet has worked in close cooperation with the British, Canadian, French, Brazilian and Netherlands Navies. The Brazilians have developed a very efficient antisubmarine force of surface ships and aircraft which, operating as an integrated part of the South Atlantic detachment of the Atlantic Fleet, took its full share of the task of knocking out the German submarine effort directed against the convoy routes off the east coast of South America. Netherlands vessels have continued to serve with distinction in our antisubmarine forces.

UNITED STATES NAVAL FORCES IN EUROPE— THE NORMANDY INVASION

After a long period of careful planning, the assembly of United States Army and Air forces in Great Britain for the invasion of France began early in 1943. The military organization set up for the cross-channel invasion involved ground, naval and air forces of a number of our Allies. The United States naval contingent was assembled and trained under the Commander Twelfth Fleet (Admiral Stark), who at the appropriate time turned it over to the operational control of the Allied Naval Commander in Chief.

The Supreme Commander, Allied Expeditionary Force, General (now General of the Army) Dwight D. Eisenhower, arrived in London and assumed command in January 1944. Meanwhile, his three principal subordinates had already been appointed: Allied Naval Commander in Chief, the late Admiral Sir Bertram H. Ramsay, RN; Commander in Chief Twenty-first Army Group, General (now Field Marshal) Sir Bernard Montgomery, RA; and Air Commander in Chief, the late Air Chief Marshal Sir Trafford Leigh-Mallory, RAF.

The success of our amphibious operations in North Africa, Sicily and Italy had demonstrated that, given air and sea superiority, there would be small doubt of our initial success, even against so strongly fortified a coast as northern France. The critical factor was whether, having seized a beachhead, we would be able to supply and reinforce it sufficiently fast to build an army larger than that which the enemy was certain to concentrate against ours. The operation thus had two phases of almost equal importance—the assault and the build-up. In both, the Navy would play a key part.

The Baie de la Seine beaches in Normandy were selected for the assault because of their proximity to the relatively undamaged ports of southern and western England, and because they were within easy range of fighter plane bases in England. The region was not so heavily fortified as the Pas de Calais area, and could be more easily isolated from other German forces by destruction of the Seine River bridges. The major deficiency of this region was the lack of a good harbor for a quick build-up after the assault. Thus artificial harbors had to be devised to meet the deficiency.

The date of the assault was determined chiefly by weather and tide conditions. The late spring or early summer presented the most favorable weather prospects, and the long days enhanced our air superiority. A spring tide was desirable so that as many as possible of the beach obstacles would be exposed at low water and landing craft could be floated far up the beach at high tide. The time of day was determined so as to allow some daylight for preliminary bombardment before the troops landed, and a half-tide for beaching the first wave, in order to enable the landing craft to pass over rocks which existed at certain of the beaches.

There was little chance of effecting substantial surprise. The final assembly of ships and craft in British ports was so large as to be beyond concealment. All that could be done was to confuse the enemy as to the time and place of the landing.

Joint Army-Navy training began in September 1943. In the spring of 1944 several large scale rehearsals were conducted in order to perfect our technique and to achieve effective coordination between the troops and the vessels of the expeditionary force.

The general scheme of the operation provided for landing United States troops in United States vessels on the western half of the area to be attacked, while the British and Canadians took the eastern half. The naval assault force was consequently divided into the Western [United States] Task Force and the Eastern [British] Task Force. The Western Naval Task Force, under the command of Rear Admiral (now Vice Admiral) A. G. Kirk, transported and landed the First United States Army, commanded by Lieutenant General O. N. Bradley. This task force was comprised of two assault forces: "O," commanded by Rear Admiral J. L. Hall, Jr., and "U," commanded by the late Rear Admiral D. P. Moon, and a follow-up force commanded by Commodore C. D. Edgar. Each assault force in turn contained the necessary transports, bombardment ships, landing craft, escort craft, gunfire support craft, mine sweepers and control craft required to transport and land Army forces. Force "O" was designated to land elements of the V Corps, including the 1st and 29th Infantry Divisions and the 2nd and 5th Ranger Battalions on "Omaha" beach, which was the Vierville-Colleville sector of the Baie de la Seine, extending from Port-en-Bessin to Carentan Estuary. Force "U" landed elements of the 7th Corps on "Utah" beach, near St. Martin-de-Varreville.

The United States Eighth Army Air Force, the United States Ninth Army Air Force and the Royal Air Force were available in the United Kingdom at the time of the invasion. During the final preparatory period (D-minus-90 to D-day) air bombing commitments included industrial, strategic and coast defense targets in northern France, the low countries and western Germany. As D-day approached, attacks were intensified until the maximum effort of planned heavy, medium and fighter bomber missions were executed the night of 5–6 June. A low ceiling on the morning of 6 June hampered the scheduled pre-landing bombing of "Omaha" beach by heavy bombers; to which some of the difficulty later experienced in gaining a foothold on "Omaha" beach may be attributed. The fighter cover throughout the operation limited the

German air force to ineffective sporadic night attacks. The old United States battleships ARKANSAS, TEXAS and NEVADA delivered naval gunfire support, beginning with the preliminary bombardment, and continuing until the troops had advanced beyond range of their major calibre guns. The cruisers TUSCALOOSA and QUINCY and some 30 United States destroyers functioned as fire support ships, together with units of the British, Free French and Dutch Navies. Rear Admiral M. L. Deyo commanded the fire support group of Force "U" and Rear Admiral C. F. Bryant the comparable group in Force "O."

About 124,000 United States naval officers and men participated directly or indirectly in the invasion. Of these, 87,000 were aboard landing craft and small escort vessels, 15,000 were aboard the combatant ships, and 22,000 were attached to the amphibious bases in England.

By 1 June, when the loading of troops began, 2,493 United States Navy ships and craft had been assembled for the operation, and of these only 14 were unable to take part because of material difficulties.

On 3 June all troops had been loaded and briefed, but because of weather conhitions the timing of the operation was still undetermined. At least four days of good weather were needed, commencing with D-day, which was initially set for 5 June. It was apparent on 3 June that unfavorable weather was developing, and early on 4 June the order for a postponement of 24 hours was broadcast. By the evening of 4 June, much improved conditions were forecast for the morning of the 6th, although there were some doubt as to how long the favorable condition would continue. However, because of tide and light considerations, the uncertainty of the weather immediately following D-day was accepted, and on the evening of 4 June, a confirmation of 6 June as D-day was broadcast.

The terrain where the landings were made was of great natural defensive strength, augmented by many strongly protected and cleverly concealed gun emplacements, machine gun nests and pill boxes, together with slit trenches, tank traps, and antitank ditches. In addition, between the high and low water levels on the beaches there were installed several rows of underwater obstacles consisting of hedgehogs, tetrahedrons and pole ramps interconnected by barbed wire and thickly sown with mines. Artillery and machine guns were placed for enfilading fire along the beaches, and in some cases were completely concealed and protected from seaward by concrete walls covered with earth.

The assault plans contemplated overcoming these defenses by the employment of naval gunfire and air bombardment to destroy or neutralize as many of the emplaced installations as possible, to breach the underwater obstacles under cover of an assault by infantry and tanks, and to storm the remaining defenses with succeeding waves of infantry supported by naval gunfire.

The Assault on "Omaha" Beach

Force "O," the larger of the two American assault forces, had as its target the Vierville-Colleville sector of the Normandy beaches, called, for the purpose of these landings, beach "Omaha." On its eastern flank was Port-en-Bessin, which marked the dividing line between the British and American areas. On its western flank was the Carentan estuary, which separated it from Force "U's" beach, "Utah," on the Cherbourg peninsula.

The ships and craft of Force "O" loaded at Portland, Weymouth and Poole on the south coast of England. Cross-channel convoys began moving on 5 June, and were joined by Rear Admiral Bryant's fire support group, which had assembled at Belfast. No enemy action hindered the movement, but a choppy sea with a 20-knot wind from the southwest made landing operations difficult, though possible. Mine sweepers cleared channels, and ARKANSAS, TEXAS and other combat ships opened their scheduled fire on shore batteries. Unfortunately, as previously mentioned, the planned air bombing was badly hampered by weather conditions, and certain LCT(A)'s [landing craft armed with M-4 tanks] and amphibious tanks failed to reach the beach on schedule. In addition, the 352nd Field Division of the German Army happened to be holding exercises in the area, and immediately joined the coastal defense troops in opposing our attack.

The tanks, infantry and demolition parties which landed at H-hour were subjected at once to a heavy cross-fire from artillery, mortars and machine guns, and losses were severe. Troops continued, however, to move in toward the beach, and by 1030 the entire landing force had been committed, though numerous personnel both of the assault waves and the Army-Navy shore party were pinned down on the beach just above high water by enemy fire. Destroyers and gunfire support craft stood in as close to the beach as the depth of water would allow and engaged all enemy guns which they could observe. The first encouraging news came at 1100 when German soldiers began to leave their posts and surrender. At 1300 Colleville was taken, and by 1330 our troops had begun a general advance up the slopes of the beach. At about 1430 Commodore Edgar's follow-up force arrived with the remaining regiments of the 1st and 29th Divisions; by late afternoon, except for sniping and occasional artillery and mortar fire, hostile action against the beach area had ceased, and the work of organizing the beaches for further unloading was progressing in orderly fashion.

Our heavy ships had no trouble in putting the enemy's major shore batteries out of action promptly. Our chief difficulties came from the light artillery and machine guns which the enemy had sited to fire up and down the beach instead of out to sea. These guns, which were very difficult to detect, waited for our troops to land before opening fire. Specially trained Navy Shore Fire Control Parties attached to Army units were put ashore early in the assault to inform our ships by radio of the location of such targets, but many of them were unable to set up their radio equipment because of casualties and enemy fire. At this juncture 8 United States and 3 British destroyers closed the beach and took many enemy positions under fire. This unplanned bombardment, which was directed in part from the ships and in part from those Shore Fire Control Parties which had succeeded in establishing communications, deserves great credit. The battleships and cruisers for the most part fired with air spot at targets designated by Shore Fire Control Parties or by planes which were busily searching for enemy guns inland from the beaches. By 1300 on 6 June the Shore Fire Control Parties had begun to function according to schedule. Acting on their directions, TEXAS and the other ships repeatedly took enemy troops, tanks and vehicles under fire several miles inland. On D-plus-2 day, for example, TEXAS' 14-inch guns demolished the railway station at Isigny and effectively scattered a convoy of German vehicles moving through the town square. It is not surprising that a German Government broadcast on 16 June, recorded by the BBC, expressed admiration of the military value of this naval gunfire. These "floating batteries," it said, "enabled the invaders to achieve overpowering artillery concentrations at any point along the coast." By D-plus-4 day, when the Army's forward line reached the forest of Cerisy, the enemy was beyond the range of our ships.

On the morning of 7 June, the first of the build-up personnel convoys of transports arrived off the beach. Just to seaward of the assault area the transport SUSAN B. ANTHONY struck a mine and eventually sank, though all personnel aboard were taken off During the forenoon, surveys for the establishment of the artificial harbor and the small craft shelters were begun.

The Assault on "Utah" Beach

The mission of Force "U" was to establish tank-supported infantry on the beach area, designated "Utah," near St. Martin-de-Varreville. Consisting of approximately 865 vessels and craft, Force "U" was organized in ports along the English coast between Plymouth and Torquay, although the fire support group of heavier ships assembled at Belfast.

The safety of Force "U's" cross-channel movement lay with three squadrons of United States and three flotillas of British mine sweepers. In general, all waters through which our convoys were to pass were suitable for mining, and the final leg of the course assigned Force "U" lay squarely across a very probable mine field on Cardonnet Bank. The only casualty occurred when the mine sweeper OSPREY was sunk.

The assault on "Utah" beaches progressed substantially as planned. Bombardment by the fire support ships, supplemented by aerial bombing, preceded the landing of waves of amphibious tanks and landing craft carrying troops of the 4th Infantry Division, which were supported by rocket-firing landing craft. Our forward troops encountered no small arms fire, and the little artillery fire directed against the beach from several distant batteries proved inaccurate and ineffectual. Main battery fire from NEVADA and QUINCY had breached the seawall in five places, materially aiding our advance inland. Our amphibious tanks, proceeding through rough waters under their own power, managed to survive the heavy swells, engaged enemy installations on the forward beachhead and pressed on inland.

Following the initial assault against "Utah" beach, the landing of subsequent waves proceeded with but slight deviation from schedule. Nearly all of the beach obstacles were exposed and Army engineers and Navy demolition teams were able to clear lanes for the passage of subsequent waves of troops and vehicles. Although our concentrated air and naval bombardment had temporarily neutralized the enemy's coastal batteries, thus affording the earlier assault waves a reasonably safe landing, the enemy from 1100 onwards brought the beach under accurate artillery fire. Aided by Shore Fire Control Parties, our support ships replied. Some of the enemy batteries were extremely hard to knock out, but by early afternoon all but three had been silenced. These tended to come to life unexpectedly and to fire a few rounds when landing craft offered good targets. Otherwise they caused little hindrance to the work on the beaches. During the first twelve hours we landed 21,328 troops, 1742 vehicles and 1695 tons of supplies.

In the course of the "Utah" landings the destroyers MEREDITH and GLENNON, the destroyer escort RICH, the mine sweeper TIDE, and several landing craft were lost.

During the next few days the batteries of the fire support ships were turned against targets well inland and to the west as the VII Corps fought its way toward Cherbourg, and requests for these support missions continued until the Army had advanced beyond the ships' range. Our troops were now more than half way across the Cotentin peninsula, and were advancing northwest along the coast towards Cherbourg against stubborn opposition.

The Normandy Build-up

Once the Army had been successfully established on the beaches, the Navy's primary responsibility was supply. The enemy had fortified and defensively manned the ports to such an extent as to make the military cost of direct attack upon them extreme. On the other hand, to attempt the assault of a continent over open beaches, affording no protection from the vagaries of the weather, would place the entire operation in jeopardy.

The solution of this problem was one of the most dramatic creations of the war—the artificial harbors, or "Mulberries," and the small boat shelters, or "Gooseberries." There were to be two of the former—"Mulberry A" in the American sector (at St. Laurent in "Omaha" area), and "Mulberry B" in the British sector at Arromanches—and five "Gooseberries," three in the British sector and one on each of the two American beaches.

The "Gooseberries," created by sinking a number of old warships and merchant ships in a line in 2.5 fathoms of water just off the beaches, were to provide a refuge for small craft in rough weather. The blockships were to proceed to the beaches under their own power, and be sunk quickly by internally placed explosives. The "Gooseberries" were a relatively simple undertaking.

The "Mulberries" were much more complicated. Conceived by the British, the tremendous task of manufacturing and assembling the many components had to be carried out with complete secrecy, lest the enemy gain a clue as to our intention to assault a harborless part of the French coast.

It was necessary to tow "Mulberry" units and other essential parts of the invasion armada across the channel. This inconspicuous but important role was carried out by a large pool of British and American tugs. The latter had come across the Atlantic under their own power, many of them manned by civilian masters and crews who had had little experience with naval or military operations. TUG CONTROL operated from Lee Tower, Lee-on-Solent, and was headed by Captain (now Commodore) Edmond J. Moran, USNR.

On 7 June all elements had been towed from England, and Rear Admiral Hall, Commander of Force "O," at "Omaha" beach, gave permission to begin "operation Mulberry." Specially trained Seabees sank hollow concrete caissons, each mounting an AA gun, in designated positions by flooding through built-in valves. Inside the breakwater thus formed were established two Loebnitz floating pierheads. These were connected to the beach by a floating roadway composed of bridgework mounted on pontoons, and two sunken causeways constructed of the same material used in pontoon causeways and Rhino barges. Protecting both the breakwater and the blockships of the nearby "Gooseberry" was a line of steel caissons secured end to end and moored to buoys. The work of installation and construction of "Gooseberries" and "Mulberries" progressed rapidly and smoothly, with all blockships in place by D-plus-4 day.

By this time the delays caused by the unfavorable weather and by the failure of the assault at "Omaha" to proceed as planned had been overcome, and the build-up began to move rapidly and on schedule. At "Utah," in spite of the problems of handling a great number of ferry craft in a small area, often under shell fire, unloading was nearly up to schedule by D-plus-4 day. On the 8th the first pontoon causeway had been successfully established at "Utah," although at the outset it could not be employed because of shell fire. During the first week of occupation we succeeded in landing approximately 74,000 troops, 10,000 vehicles, and 17,000 tons of supplies.

Then came the storm. During the night of 18 June the wind began to freshen, and by mid-afternoon of the 19th it was blowing a moderate gale from the northeast. Ferry service ceased, all craft took shelter inside the "Gooseberry" or "Mulberry," and unloading of almost every type was brought to a halt. It continued to blow steadily for the next three days, with the seas making up to destructive proportions. When the storm ended on the morning of 22 June, the beach was a shambles. More than 300 craft had been washed up high and dry, many of them damaged beyond salvage. The only ferry craft undamaged were the DUKW's, which had remained safely parked ashore during the storm.

The blockships of the "Gooseberry" shelter had held together, although several of them had broken their backs and all had settled, but the storm had been disastrous to the "Mulberry." The concrete caissons had either broken apart or had become submerged in the bottom sands. The roadway to one of the Loebnitz pierheads had been smashed by the impact of LCT's driven against it, and many of its pontoons were flooded. The causeway had held together but was twisted. Many of the steel caissons had carried away from their moorings and had drifted about as a menace to shipping. Others were flooded and half submerged.

The British "Mulberry" suffered less from the storm than the American, which was exposed to heavier seas and had been built on deeper sands, where the scour was far more severe. Consequently, it was decided to abandon the American harbor. The British one was completed, partly with material salvaged from the American.

A major port was absolutely necessary if unloading schedules were to be maintained through the fall and winter. The first to fall to our troops was Cherbourg.

Bombardment of Cherbourg

To assist the VII Corps, which was advancing on the port of Cherbourg from the land side, the fire support group of the Western Naval Task Force, commanded by Rear Admiral Deyo, bombarded the shore batteries which commanded the waters leading to Cherbourg harbor. These enemy coastal defenses consisted of 20 casemated batteries [guns covered by steel and concrete walls and roofs], three of which had 280 mm guns with an estimated range of 40,000 yards [approximately 20 miles].

The force, consisting of the battleships NEVADA, TEXAS and ARKANSAS, United States cruisers TUSCALOOSA and QUINCY, British cruisers GLASGOW and ENTERPRISE, and 11 destroyers, approached the coast shortly before noon on 25 June. The intention was to avoid engaging the enemy batteries as long as possible in order to close the shore and provide the support requested by our troops. The Germans, waiting until our ships arrived well within range, opened fire. The destroyers interposed with smoke, but the enemy fire increased in volume, and shortly afterwards the mine sweepers, which had preceded the force, were obliged to withdraw to the northward.

By 1230 the enemy's fire had become so heavy and accurate that our ships were directed to maneuver independently, and they steamed back and forth in a line ranging from four to eight miles offshore. While the heavy ships fired at targets inland designated by Shore Fire Control Parties and spotting planes, the destroyers endeavored to silence the enemy coastal batteries. The latter were only partly successful, and our ships continued to be under shore fire until, having completed their mission, they retired shortly before 1500. This abnormal exposure of ships to heavy shore guns, without adequate counterfire, was well warranted by the urgent need of supporting our invading troops. The Army later reported that of 21 firings requested on inland targets 19 were successful.

Of the seven heavy ships engaged (battleships and cruisers) all but one were either hit or had fragments on board, and all were closely missed frequently. The destroyer O'BRIEN was considerably damaged, and the destroyers BARTON and LAFFEY slightly damaged. Personnel casualties—14 dead and 28 wounded for the entire force—were remarkably small. The VII Corps occupied Cherbourg two days later, assaulting and capturing the remaining shore batteries from the rear.

Under the command of Commodore W. A. Sullivan, task forces composed of British and American salvage and fire fighting units did phenomenal work repairing ships and craft, and clearing the major ports for dockside unloading of cargo. This important but difficult task was performed with rapidity. Cherbourg's port facilities were in operation early in July. Although we soon secured several minor ports, a second major port was not available until Le Havre surrendered on 12 September. It was opened to small craft in three days, and was in full operation within a month. For some time, however, shipping in the approaches to Le Havre was seriously harrassed by enemy mining. Although organized resistance in Brest ended on 19 September, its facilities were so damaged, and it was then so distant from the battle front, that it did not appear worthwhile to restore the port.

With the approach of winter, it became apparent that only three liberated ports in northern France could be operated on a year round basis. These were Cherbourg, Le Havre, and Rouen, unloading having begun at the last port in mid-October. Antwerp in Belgium, a British commitment, became early in December an important avenue of supplies to our troops. A United States Naval Port Office was opened there, and daily unloadings of up to 22,000 tons of United States stores were handled.

EIGHTH FLEET—ITALY
Support of the Anzio Beachhead

On 22 January 1944 a combined British-American operation secured a beachhead at Anzio on the west coast of Italy, some 60 miles behind the German lines. The landing progressed as scheduled against slight initial opposition; however, the enemy reacted strongly, and rapidly assembled a powerful force around the beachhead. Resistance and counter-attacks were so severe that extraordinary effort was required to maintain and support the Army in this area; the capacity of the small captured port of Anzio and the adjoining beaches was so small that scarcely any part of the Army was free from enemy observation and artillery fire. The beachhead was raided by enemy aircraft 277 times during the first twelve weeks after landing. On 25 May the beachhead forces joined those advancing from the main front; throughout the four months preceding this junction, cruisers and destroyers constantly furnished gunfire support by bombardment of enemy targets on shore. Screening and patrol vessels guarded the anchorage from air-surface attack and amphibious craft transported supplies and fresh troops from the Naples area to Anzio, returning with prisoners and other personnel.

Continuously throughout the year British and U. S. Eighth Fleet motor torpedo boats were on patrol to intercept enemy corvettes, torpedo boats and the barges with which the enemy desperately sought to carry on coast-wise support of his armies in Italy. Destruction of enemy naval strength and coastal commerce in the Ligurian Sea was the prime objective.

Capture of Elba

An amphibious assault resulting in the capture of the island of Elba was carried out on 17 June by a naval task force under the command of Rear Admiral T. H. Troubridge, RN. United States destroyers, mine sweepers, patrol and landing craft formed part of the combined force. One of the immediate objects in securing the island, which is situated only five miles from the coast of Italy, was to set up a heavy battery opposite the mainland to curtail the movement of enemy supply convoys which hugged the coast. The army forces to be landed comprised the French 9th Colonial Division and support elements totaling 11,200 more under the command of General of Army Corps Henri Martin, French Army. Although the attacking forces outnumbered the defenders about five to one, the strongly defended beaches were well alerted and several hours of severe fighting were required to secure the initial beachhead. All organized resistance ended on 19 June.

EIGHTH FLEET—INVASION OF SOUTHERN FRANCE

Landings in southern France were an integral part of the over-all Allied strategy in Western Europe, and as conceived were a logical sequence to the invasion of northern France. By the beginning of 1944, planning was underway and Vice Admiral Hewitt, Commander Eighth Fleet, had been appointed naval commander for the operation with the designation of Commander Western Task Force. Beaches finally selected for landings were east of Toulon, in the Cavalaire-Frejus area, since the necessary forces and supplies required for a quick thrust up the Rhone Valley could be advantageously landed there.

The general situation in the western Mediterranean was favorable for amphibious operations during the summer. The submarine menace was rapidly being brought under control, and enemy naval surface strength was not a serious threat. As a result of losses sustained in the invasion of Normandy, the enemy air force was no longer able to operate in strength in the Mediterranean. The coast to be assaulted had fair beaches with strong enemy defenses; however, these defenses lacked depth, and the enemy had few available reserves for counter-attack.

All forces allocated for the invasion of southern France were included in the Western Task Force under the over-all command of the Supreme Allied Commander, Mediterranean, General (now Field Marshal) Sir Henry Maitland-Wilson. Tactical command was jointly exercised by the Naval Commander, Vice Admiral Hewitt; the Army Commander, Major General (later Lieutenant General) A. M. Patch (now deceased); and the Air Commander, Brigadier General G. P. Saville. Command of the joint Army and Navy forces of the Western Task Force after embarkation was vested in the Naval Commander until the Commanding General landed and assumed command of the Army forces on shore.

Intensive bombing of targets in southern France in support of the invasion commenced on 29 April with a damaging raid on the airport installations of Toulon. Thereafter, according to a plan carefully coordinated with the allied bombing of Europe from England, the assault area was isolated by destruction and damage to bridges, tunnels, viaducts and railroad yards, without definite indication to the enemy of the precise location of the projected landings. This bombing was carried out by the Mediterranean Allied Strategic Air Force and comprised about 5,400 sorties which dropped 6,700 tons of bombs.

On 9 August the first of the assault convoys sailed from Naples, and thereafter further convoys left other ports in order to arrive in the assault area on the morning of the 15th. All convoys arrived on schedule, and 880 ships and craft and 1,370 shipborne landing craft were present. This allied naval force included 515 United States, 283 British, 12 French and 7 Greek ships and craft and 63 merchant ships of various nationalities.

About eight hours before the main landings, French commandos and units of the First Special Service Forces were landed near Cape Negre and on the Hyeres Islands by forces under command of Rear Admiral L. A. Davidson. Rear Admiral T. E. Chandler (subsequently killed in the Philippine Islands in January 1945) commanded a group of gunfire support ships of this force. No resistance was met on the islands and only inaccurate machinegun and small arms fire on the mainland.

In the meantime, diversionary groups were operating to the eastward in the Nice-Cannes area and to the westward between Toulon and Marseille, where a mock landing and repulse were staged at LaCiotat, producing considerable enemy reaction.

The bombing in tactical support of the landings commenced before daylight on D-day. This was followed at dawn with heavy and medium bombing for one hour and twenty minutes by more than 1,300 aircraft along a 40 miles front. The execution of this plan, in conjunction with naval gunfire and barrages of rockets, appeared to paralyze the enemy defenses on all the initial assault beaches.

Preceded by this coordinated neutralizing attack of 1,300 aircraft and 53 gunfire support ships, the assault took place at 0800, about two hours after daylight, on 15 August. The main amphibious landings were carried out in three principal sectors. The attack in the Freius-St. Raphael sector was made by forces under the command of Rear Admiral S. S. Lewis; the St. Maxime-St. Tropez area under the command of Rear Admiral B. J. Rodgers; and the attack on the beaches in Pampelonne and Cavalaire Bays under the command of Rear Admiral F. J. Lowry. Gunfire support groups for these main landing forces were commanded by Rear Admiral Deyo, Rear Admiral Bryant and Rear Admiral R. M. Mansfield, RN, respectively. Two escort carrier groups operating off the coast furnished airplane spotters for the shore bombardment, provided protection for our assault forces against air attack, and assisted the Army Air Force in its attack upon the enemy. This naval air force was under command of Rear Admiral Troubridge, RN, with Rear Admiral Durgin commanding one of the groups.

The amphibious assaults of 15 August established a firm beachhead. Eleven army divisions were used in the operation. The United States Army 3rd, 36th and 45th Infantry Divisions and the French 1st Armored Division comprised the assault forces. The remaining divisions, landed during the follow-up and build-up periods, were entirely French. With strong air support, the Army continued vigorous and rapid thrusts inland and successfully kept the enemy from making a concerted stand. The weakened German defense was stunned by the power and effectiveness of coordinated blows from sea and air.

On the morning of 17 August an operation by a light diversion force was carried out in the Ciotat area. Returning from this operation the destroyer ENDICOTT and two small British gunboats encountered two German corvettes, which were engaged and sunk about 13 miles from Cape Croisette Light; 211 survivors were taken prisoner.

On 18 August, rapid progress by the Army continued, and sustained naval effort was required to speed up unloading to meet the requirements of our rapidly advancing forces.

In the days that followed, United States ships engaged German coast defense batteries along the coast and repulsed attacks by light enemy forces. By 29 August the last defenders of Toulon and Marseilles had surrendered. With the capture of these ports, naval emphasis was shifted to mine sweeping and port clearance. Ships and craft were released from duty in the assault area as rapidly as their services could be spared. On 1 September U. S. Naval Detachment Marseille was established. While Army engineers were clearing the land side of the port of Marseille with full Navy cooperation, additional Seabee personnel were engaged in the rehabilitation of part of the port of Toulon. On 25 September, with the closing of the last beaches used for maintenance, the amphibious phase of the campaign was considered ended. During this phase, naval vessels carried out 850 separate shore bombardment missions, with more than 54,000 rounds fired, and mine sweeping forces swept 550 mines. The invasion of southern France achieved highly satisfactory results with comparatively small losses. As no further large scale amphibious operation appeared in prospect in the Mediterranean, forces were returned as rapidly as practicable to the United States for use in other war areas.

* *

V

Fighting Strength

SHIPS, PLANES AND ORDNANCE

NAVAL accomplishments in this mechanized age are dependent upon production. The best officers and men can do little without an adequate supply of the highly specialized machinery of warfare. Our guiding policy is to achieve not mere adequacy, but overwhelming superiority of material, thereby insuring not only victory, but early victory with the least possible loss of American lives. The excellence of our material is unquestioned. The genius of American research and industry has put us a long step ahead of our naval enemies in effectiveness of ships, planes and weapons. As regards quantity of ships, planes and weapons, the balance of power is, also, decisively on our side. The magnificent productive capacity of the United States has given us the greatest navy in all history.

The Navy is deeply grateful to industry for its accomplishments, which have enabled the Navy to play a large and effective part in the landings of the Allied armies in Europe, as well as to prosecute the Pacific war with a vigor evidenced by the rapid advance towards Japan in recent months. We have gone ahead rapidly because we have been able to keep steady pressure on the enemy. It is of the utmost importance that we not only maintain this pressure but intensify it. There must be no relaxation of the fighting effort, nor of the industrial effort that makes the fighting effort possible. I make a special point of this because of recent indications that industry is having difficulty in meeting the needs of the armed services. This is cause for concern, since, if the industrial output falls off, the effect will be to prolong the war at great cost in American lives as well as money.

Ship Production Program

As the war develops, the changing nature of operations results in shifting of production emphasis from vessels of one type to another. For example, during the first five months of 1944, the need for landing craft was paramount. After the landings in France and the capture of Saipan and Guam, large assault transports had the right-of-way in preparation for operations in the far reaches of the Pacific. Some of the small ship programs have come to completion during the past year, while the construction of the larger vessels goes on with undiminished intensity.

The ship construction program is under constant review. The effect of building too many vessels of any particular type would be as serious as building too few, since the construction of unnecessary craft would involve waste of manpower and critical materials urgently needed for other parts of the war effort. It is not easy to keep the shipbuilding program in balance. It has been necessary to cut back certain programs and to expand others with little warning. This has been embarrassing to industry,

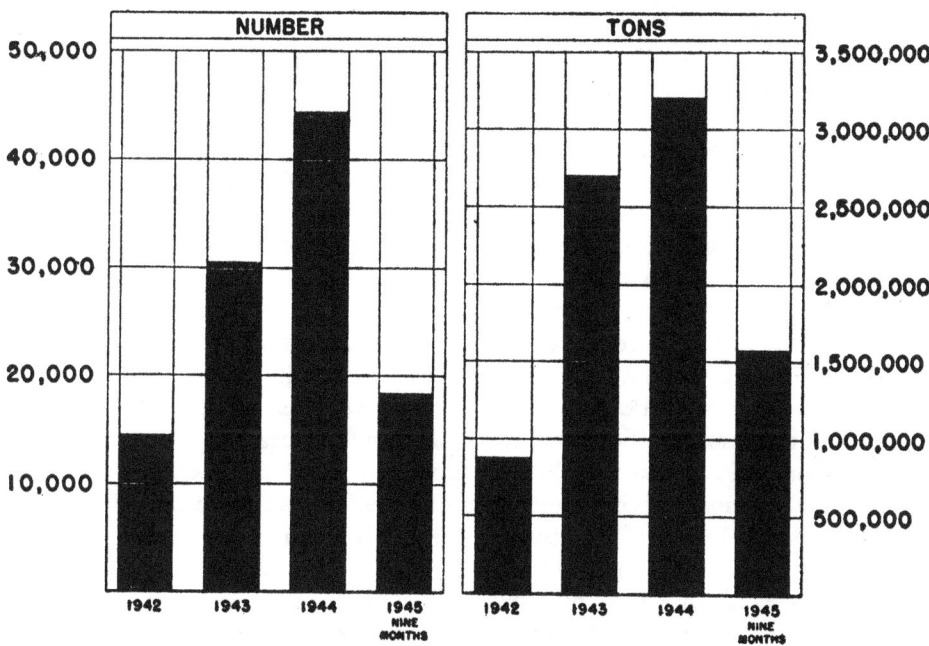

Plate 10.

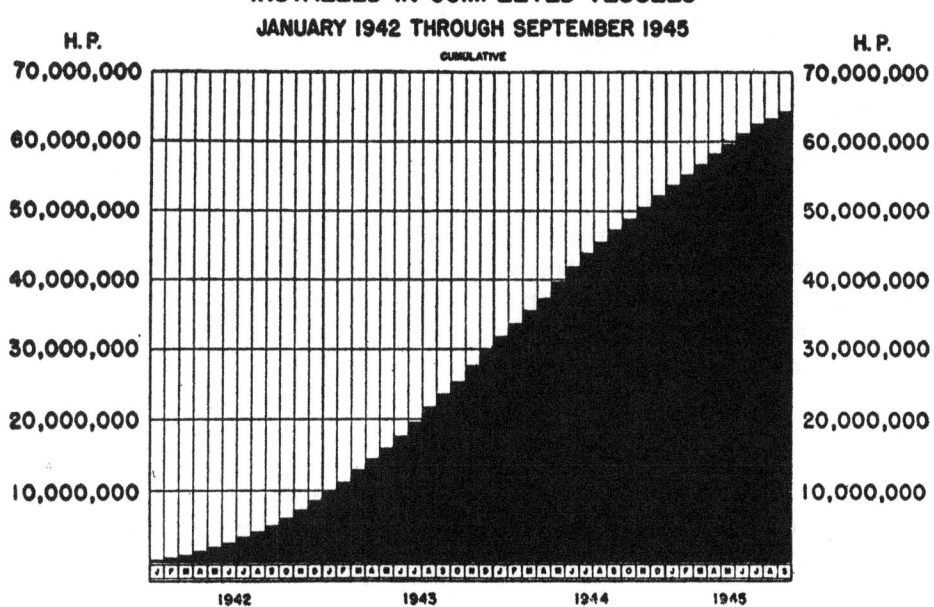

Plate 11.

but I am convinced that the over-all result has been good. Within reasonable limits, we have obtained what we needed without drawing on the productive capacity of the country for things that we do not need.

Since last March, two new IOWA Class battleships—MISSOURI and WISCONSIN—have joined the Fleet. Aircraft carriers have come into service with a steady flow. The small escort carriers, built for the Navy by the Maritime Commission, have been tested in battle and found to be effective fighting units within the expected limitations imposed by their relatively small size, power and speed. The first two 12-inch large cruisers—ALASKA and GUAM—were commissioned during 1944. Heavy cruisers of the BALTIMORE Class, as well as many light cruisers, have been added to the fleet. Destroyers have come into service in large numbers. Auxiliary vessels have been built and acquired in quantity, so that the ever increasing huge demands for transports, supply ships, repair ships, tenders, tankers, tugs, and floating hospitals have almost been met. Many of these auxiliary vessels have been built by the Maritime Commission through designs developed by the Navy Department. The success of our widespread operations in the Pacific is due in no small measure to our good fortune in having an increasing supply of well designed and well built auxiliary vessels.

Among the smaller types, landing craft have been all important. During the past 12 months, the Navy has acquired 6,000 of these, ranging in size from tank lighters to the 457-foot landing ship (dock). In addition, more than 29,000 smaller landing boats of all types have been produced. The effectiveness of our landing craft has been demonstrated from the shores of Normandy to the beaches of Iwo Jima.

Our landing craft, initially conceived merely as carriers of troops and cargo, have been found capable of considerable combat value of their own, due to recent developments in rocket armament and light-weight rapid-fire guns.

The so-called amphibious vehicles, craft that are equally at home on water and on land, have proved their value and are under constant improvement.

As new ships are added daily to the fleet, the maintenance problem grows more difficult. The skilled crews of our vessels do much to keep their ships in repair. Fully equipped repair units follow the fleet as one advanced base after another is captured. The huge machine shops in our repair ships are always near at hand when a man-of-war needs help. By these means, much is done in forward areas to effect battle repairs and normal upkeep.

However, really serious repair problems must be dealt with in our navy yards. Here, manpower shortage has begun to present a critical problem. Battle damage repair has kept some of our combatant ships out of the fighting line for far too long a time. Plate numbers 10 and 11 graphically illustrate the vast increase in hulls and machinery to be maintained. Plate number 12 shows the fall in shipyard employment. The possibility that the situation may get worse is cause for concern.

Aircraft

At the beginning of the current year, most of our fighters were either *Hellcats* or *Corsairs*, while a greatly improved version of the *Wildcat* was operative from escort carriers. In production are still newer fighters, including those which are jet-propelled.

One of the most important innovations of the year has been the employment in combat of night fighters armed with machine guns, cannon and rockets.

The *Sea Hawk* is now replacing the *Seagull* as our standard scout observation plane. The *Seagull* had previously replaced in part the *Kingfisher*.

The *Helldiver*, which as proved its worth time and again in the Pacific campaigns, is now our dive-bomber. It carries, over considerably longer ranges and at much higher speeds, twice the bomb load of the older *Dauntless*. Experimentation is being vigorously pushed to produce dive-bombers with even better performance.

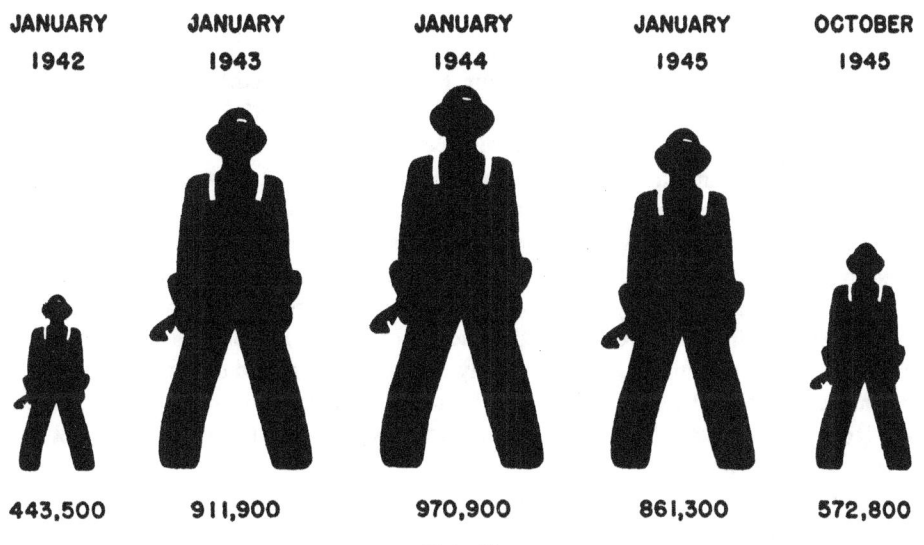

Plate 12.

The *Avenger*, a torpedo-bomber, has replaced the *Devastator*, and is in turn about to be supplanted by new models now in production. All are designed to increase the load, range and rates of climb of the present torpedo-plane. A new night torpedo-bomber has already come into use.

The *Catalina*, a long range twin-engine patrol plane, still in great demand for air-sea rescue work, has been generally supplanted for patrol work by the larger *Mariner* and the *Liberator*. Its bombing work has been taken over in part also by the *Ventura* and the *Privateer*. Experimental patrol planes now envisaged will carry greater loads of fuel or bombs at considerably higher speeds than those of the present day.

The *Mars*, which entered regular service this past year, has proved to be a most efficient cargo carrier in terms of cost per ton-mile. Plans for the experimental transport program now contemplate pressurized cabin planes for high-speed, high-altitude transports.

Amphibious gliders, rotary wing devices, and target aircraft for the improvement of antiaircraft fire, are also under intensive development.

Ordnance

The present technique of amphibious operations has imposed upon the fleet the role of acting as support artillery for our ground forces. Today this artillery support is of major importance, as landings are normally preceded by terrific naval bombardments. After landings have been effected, naval gunfire is often called upon for the destruction of specific targets, to assist the advance of our troops.

Engagements with other sea-going targets are usually relatively brief. Shore bombardment, however, is a tremendously heavy consumer of ammunition, and has increased enormously the volume requirements for firepower. For example, our bombardments from 7 December 1941 to July 1944 (not including the shelling of Saipan) used approximately 40,000 tons of projectiles. During the one-month bombardment of Saipan, from 13 June to 12 July, the ships of the attacking task force fired 11,000 tons of shells. In many cases in the Pacific it has been found possible to neutralize enemy installations before our troops have landed. For example, in an official report of the Guam action it was stated that "coastal defense guns, heavy and light AA guns, dual-purpose guns and all types of defense installations were rendered impotent prior to the landing of troops . . . It is believed that not one fixed gun was left in commission on the west coast that was of greater size than a machine gun."

These shore bombardments have changed ordnance requirements and standards affecting high-capacity shells, rockets, bombs, and fuses. At the time of the attack on Pearl Harbor, the Navy had virtually no high-capacity ammunition [so-called because it contains an extremely high amount of explosive]. Since then, production of this type of projectile has risen rapidly, and currently accounts for 75 per cent of the output of shells from six to sixteen inches in calibre. Monthly naval production of all types of major calibre ammunition now exceeds the total quantity delivered during World War I.

The multiplicity of tasks which must be performed in rendering impotent an enemy-held shore involves far more than volume of fire, however. There are many different types of projectiles and many different types of fuses, but the nature of the objective is the major factor in determining their employment. For example, armor-piercing shells (the only type effective against armored ships) are relatively ineffective against personnel or light structures ashore.

During the year the rocket has become a major weapon. Beach barrage rockets, first used by the Navy in the invasion of North Africa in the fall of 1942, have assisted our landing craft, as well as our heavier ships, to act as support artillery for ground forces. Their great usefulness begins when the barrage and bombing by big guns and planes cease. At this time, when landing troops are most exposed to enemy mortars and machine guns, rockets provide effective fire support. Seven main types of rockets, ranging from 2.25 inches to 5 inches and larger, are now being produced in quantity. Production in 1944 was approximately ten times that of 1943.

Approximately nine hundred ordnance research projects are currently in progress. Although combat experience has proved the efficiency of our ordnance, it has

FIGHTING STRENGTH

ENLISTED PERSONNEL U.S. NAVY
1941-1944
FIGURES AS OF 31 DECEMBER

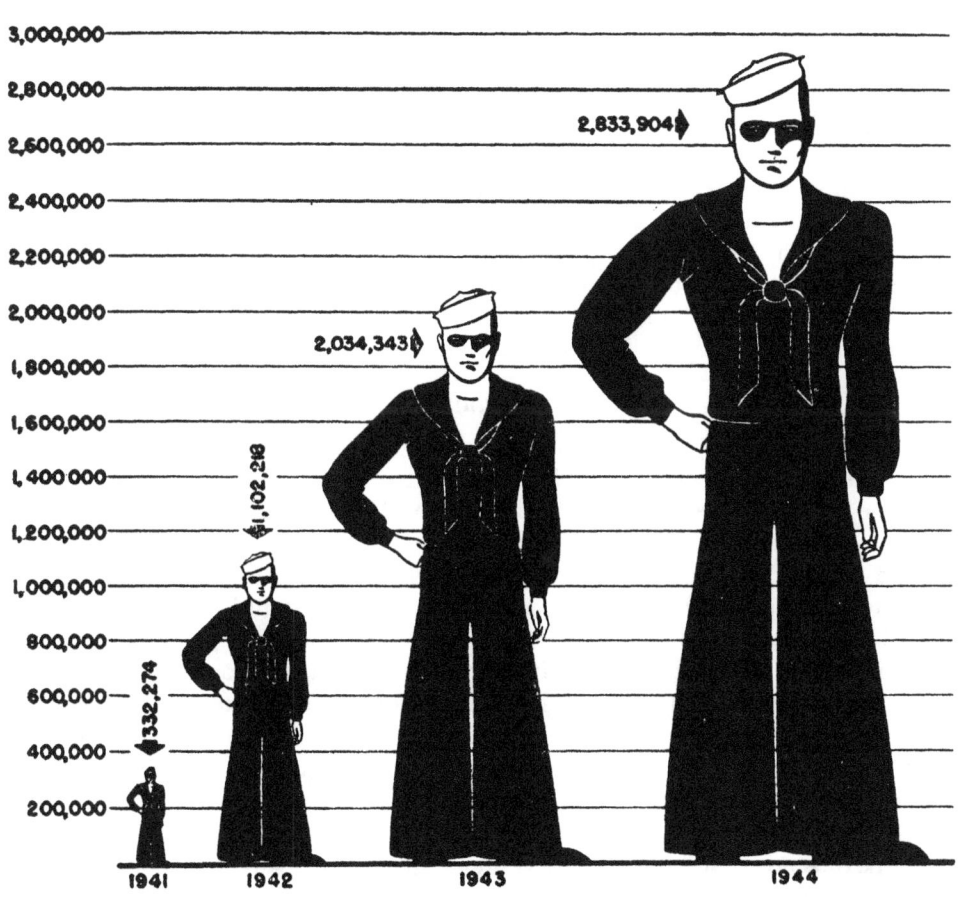

Plate 13.

also emphasized the necessity for the greatest possible concentration on research and development.

The weekly procurement of ordnance equipment during 1944 equalled the total yearly production during 1938. In addition to equipping our naval vessels, we have armed approximately 5500 merchant ships. Although a number of construction programs are due for completion shortly, heavy demand for such expendable items as high-capacity ammunition and rockets will continue until final victory is won.

PERSONNEL

On 19 July 1944, the President authorized the Navy to base its plans upon a total strength of 3,389,000 by 30 June 1945. On 31 December 1944, the personnel strength of the Navy consisted of 300,101 officers, 2,833,904 enlisted men and women, 84,627 officer candidates, and 8,893 nurses. The growth of all branches of the naval service has been as follows:

	7 Dec. 1941	31 Dec. 1942	31 Dec. 1943	31 Dec. 1944
Navy	337,349	1,259,167	2,381,116	3,227,525
Marine Corps	66,048	238,423	405,169	472,682
Coast Guard	25,336	141,769	171,941	169,832

The enormous increase in enlisted personnel is graphically indicated in Plate 13.

Within the past twelve months the Navy has gained by the experience of its personnel from flag officers to gun pointers. A large number of senior commanders have been tried and tested in combat, as have many of the Reserve officers, whose continued professional improvement and excellent performance of duty have made them not only an indispensable but an integral part of the Navy team.

Training

Of the personnel on active duty on the last day of February 1945, only about 10 per cent were in service before Pearl Harbor. It is not surprising, therefore, that in June 1944 we were conducting no less than 947 training schools with a daily average attendance of 303,000. Because the peak of recruitment was reached and passed during the year under consideration, it has been possible to eliminate, consolidate, or adapt to other purposes, a few of the training facilities.

In the early months of the war, when the need was most urgent for large numbers of trained personnel, it was frequently impossible to provide the degree of specialization desired. To some extent this has been remedied by the institution of operational and precommissioning training ashore; this development has become invaluable in molding crews into integrated combat units. The time required to reach petty officer rank varies according to rating, branch, length of specialized training, and vacancies in the complement of the ship or activity to which the man is assigned. The trend is in the direction of still more training ashore, starting with a recruit training period of at least 10 weeks.

One of the most important aspects of our training program is the urgent need for turning over to the fleet men who are familiar not only with the fundamental skills, but with the very latest practices required in the jobs they are to fill. This means that there must be accurate and up-to-date information on the duties and responsibilities of men in fleet assignments. Job analysis specialists are serving aboard combatant vessels to observe and tabulate the operations performed in various billets, the skills required, and the equipment used. This information is used in writing the qualifications for the various rates; in establishing curricula for schools training men for particular rates; and in preparing self-study training courses.

As the war has progressed, many new ratings and subdivisions have been added. There are now more than 450 petty officer ratings and enlisted specialties. To overcome the lack of opportunity for training while at sea and to utilize to best advantage time spent ashore while ships undergo repairs, a program of refresher training has recently been organized at special training centers. These courses serve to bring personnel up to date with the latest advances in tactics and equipment, and thereby promote the efficiency of operating units.

Of officers commissioned since Pearl Harbor, approximately 131,000 were appointed directly from civilian life, 97,000 from officer candidate programs, and 58,000 from enlisted sources. By direct commissioning it was generally possible from 1942 to mid-1944, the period of greatest expansion, to meet the immediate requirements of the service.

Procurement of officers from civilian life for general sea duty was closed on 17 August 1944; since then our principal source of young sea-going officers has been the six Reserve Midshipmen's Schools. Towards the end of 1944, a General Line School at Hollywood, Florida, was opened to provide already commissioned officers with an eight weeks' course of training of sufficient scope to qualify them as junior division officers. The procurement of chaplains, doctors and electrical engineers from civilian life still continues, in order to meet urgent needs.

It is anticipated that we will be able to meet most of our developing needs for new officers through the officer candidate programs—aviation cadet (v-5), reserve midshipmen (v-7), college (v-12)—and by commissioning enlisted personnel of the Regular Navy and Naval Reserve. These appointments to commissioned rank from within the service have steadily increased.

At the end of February 1945 approximately 12,500 aviation cadets were under instruction. During the year ending 28 February 1945, approximately 20,000 officers were commissioned after completing four months' deck and engineering training at the Reserve Midshipmen's Schools: 91 per cent of these were products of the Navy college program (v-12). At the end of February 1945, reserve midshipmen numbered 8,600; the v-12 program was operating 269 units at 185 colleges and universities, with an attendance of 52,000. Through the active assistance and guidance of university authorities, v-12 curricula have been designed to meet our operating needs; the methods used in selecting candidates have enabled us to obtain the most promising material available. Recent congressional authorization has made possible the institution of a plan of transition from the v-12 to an expanded NROTC program.

The Seabees [Construction Battalions] now number approximately 235,000 men and 8,500 Civil Engineering Corps officers. Of these more than three-fourths are serving overseas, not only building the shore facilities required for offensive operations but also providing logistic support for combat forces. Landing with the first waves of assault troops, Seabees have participated in almost every amphibious operation yet undertaken.

During the past year the Women's Reserve has grown to a total of more than 83,000 officers and enlisted women, who are serving in nearly every type of shore activity. At 500 shore stations throughout the United States and more recently in Hawaii, permission having been given them to volunteer for overseas duty at certain non-combat bases in the American area, WAVES have been assigned as direct replacements for men or to fill expanding complements. At the peak of the WAVES training program there were approximately 40 schools preparing them for duty. Beginning on 1 December 1944, however, the Navy established revised recruiting quotas, reducing monthly enlistments to 500. This number, it is believed, will cover current requirements, although it will be increased if future needs show that additional women can be used.

During the latter part of 1944, a new system of classifying Reserve officers was established; symbols were devised to designate as accurately as possible the qualifications necessary for specific types of duty at sea and ashore.

Needs of Personnel

Faced with a war of uncertain length requiring prolonged service, it has been our responsibility to see that military spirit and efficiency are maintained at the highest possible level. In 1944 this involved increasingly close attention not only to material requirements but to the needs and aspirations of personnel. Continuing emphasis was placed upon the effective administration and extension of insurance, dependents' benefits, and family allowance programs, which support the morale of the individual by providing for his long-range welfare and for that of his dependents.

During the year the voluntary off-duty education program was also greatly expanded. It is in operation at overseas and continental bases and stations, is being extended to the fleet, and is an integral part of the rehabilitation program in naval hospitals. During 1944 about 100,000 personnel were enrolled in correspondence courses, 250,000 in courses involving class-room instruction, and self-study materials and reprints of standard texts were supplied for an additional 750,000.

Plans for Demobilization

Since there still exists a critical need for combat and seagoing officers and enlisted personnel, no demobilization of personnel can take place until the defeat of Japan is at hand. When Germany is defeated, we will be confronted with the enormous task of transporting men and material from the European theater to the Pacific. The end of the war in Europe will therefore result in a redistribution rather than a reduction of naval strength.

However, for more than a year, we have worked on demobilization methods and have completed tentative plans. We are considering priority for severance, and intend, when the time comes, to give due consideration to length of service, service outside the continental limits, combat service, and parenthood.

Postwar Navy

Because the postwar size of the Navy is yet to be determined, no precise estimate of the number of naval personnel that will be required is possible. The deciding factor will be the needs of the Navy in order to carry out the strategic commitments of the nation. It is assumed in all the plans now under consideration that many more officers and men will be needed than can be provided by personnel now in the Regular Navy. These comprise but 16 per cent of the wartime Navy. Accordingly, serious attention is being given to regulations under which Reserve officers may transfer to the Regular Navy, and to the organization of the Naval Reserve in the postwar period. In December 1944 a board was appointed to consider these problems and make recommendations concerning the means by which an effective and realistic Naval Reserve may be maintained, and by which Reserve officers of the highest quality and of appropriate age and rank may be attracted towards a naval career, in which they will receive the same training as and compete on an equal basis with Regular officers.

SUPPLY

The supply of combatant forces is a major problem of vital importance at sea, as it is on land. The Navy has two distinct phases of this problem with which to deal: the moving of supplies into advanced shore bases, and the supply of ships while they are at sea.

The United States Navy has for years given great attention to developing means for replenishing fuel, food and ammunition at sea. Before the war began (even as far back as 1916) we had the so-called "Fleet Train" composed of tankers and other auxiliary vessels specially designed for this purpose. Since the war began, we have developed improved types of ships and better technique in using them, with the result that our fleet in the Pacific has been able to keep at sea for long periods of time. This has given us a decided advantage over the Japanese Navy, which is largely dependent on bases as sources of supply, and therefore has much less mobility.

The question of how to supply a fleet must be settled largely on geographical grounds. If the ocean combat area is small, as is the case in European waters, and if it is possible to set up shore-based establishments at strategic points, there is little need for a Fleet Train. However, the problem that we have had to solve in the Pacific is how to project a fleet throughout a vast ocean area initially dominated by the enemy. We are solving this problem by rapidly establishing repair and supply bases in enemy islands as we capture them, and by pushing our supplies forward in ships of the Train, now referred to as the Service Force, to supply our task forces at sea. To paraphrase Napoleon, a fleet swims on its stomach. It has to swim long distances to get at the Japanese. The success of this scheme is a tribute to the far-sighted planning of those who, with clarity of vision concerning the problem of naval logistics in the vast reaches of the Pacific, directed naval affairs during the past 30 years.

The Navy has, I think, the right to be proud of its floating supply system. It has performed its functions successfully since the beginning of the war, largely because of actual experience doing this sort of thing in peacetime exercises. The other part of the problem—the moving of supplies to advance bases—has been less successful, largely because in peacetime we had less opportunity to obtain such actual experience. Performance has, however, improved, and during the past twelve months in the advance across the Pacific the handling of the supply problem has been good. It is being further improved.

Logistic operations in the Pacific require that great quantities of material be landed with and immediately following the first wave of the assault troops. Not only must we supply the ammunition and provisions needed for the assault troops, but we must also commence to build at once the airfields necessary to secure local control of the air without carrier assistance. Immediately following, there must be moved in repair facilities for ships and depots for supplying stores for base activities, ships of the fleet, and vessels of the Fleet Train. Docks and other harbor facilities must be improvised rapidly. The amount of material that is involved is enormous. Air squadrons require living quarters, supply depots, and repair shops on a large scale. Extensive facilities are necessary for ship repairs, to the end that minor battle damage may be remedied without the necessity of returning the ships to the mainland. Large quantities of spare parts must be kept on hand and given careful and specialized handling, so that no ship may be immobilized for want of something necessary to put a vital mechanism into operating condition. Quantities of ordinary stores and ammunition must be handled and protected from the weather.

All necessary material must be provided long before an operation commences and must be stored initially in the continental United States. In consequence the naval supply system for the Pacific Ocean consists of a "pipe line," beginning hundreds of miles inland from the western coast of the United States and extending across the Pacific to the Philippines, with branches to our many ocean bases. The management of this "pipe line" is a difficult problem. The capacity of the "pipe line" is limited, and it requires careful control to insure that the most necessary things get through and that the line be not clogged by the shipment of unessential items. Care must be taken that there is an adequate reserve at the start of the "pipe line," and at intermediate points, but this reserve must not be allowed to reach undue size, since the hoarding of material in storehouses would be a very real handicap to the war effort. The loading of cargo ships must be painstakingly planned, in order to give high priority to the most important cargo. Cargo ship schedules must be carefully worked out so that ships may unload promptly when they reach their destinations; we cannot afford to waste shipping by having vessels lie idle while waiting their turn to unload at their destinations.

The Navy's trans-ocean service of supply is in many respects like any commercial trans-ocean freight business, but it is complicated by the lack of organized ports at the distant termini, and by the fact that the urgency of certain types of cargo is constantly shifting with changes in the military situation. The problem has been attacked by taking into the Navy men of experience in the shipping world, who are bracketed together with naval officers to form teams conversant with all its phases. For the most part shipments to advanced bases are carried in commercial vessels, supplied by the War Shipping Administration, and loaded and unloaded under the direction of the Navy. Assault ships [transports and cargo ships specially fitted to support the first wave of a landing], tankers and other vessels that serve the fleet in combat areas are, as a rule, naval vessels.

On shore, in the western United States, where the flow of supplies largely originates, the problem has become more and more difficult as the scope of the Pacific operations increases. So important has this task become that recently one of the most senior officers in the Navy, Admiral R. E. Ingersoll, was shifted from the assignment of Commander in Chief, United States Atlantic Fleet, in which he had served with distinction since the early days of the war, to the command of the Western Sea Frontier to handle the vital and complex operating and logistic tasks in that area. Recognition of the magnitude of the logistic problem was again emphasized in the promotion of Vice Admiral F. J. Horne, Vice Chief of Naval Operations, to the rank of Admiral on 29 January 1945.

It should be added that supply operations in the Pacific are not solely naval. The Army has a task of at least equal magnitude in supplying its air and ground forces. The supply systems of the two services have been merged together, as much as possible, under Fleet Admiral Nimitz in the Central Pacific and under General of the Army MacArthur in the Southwest Pacific. In some cases, in which only one service uses an item, that item is handled entirely by the service concerned. For example, the supply of spare parts peculiar to the Super-Fortress bombers is handled entirely by the Army, while battleship ammunition, being used only by the Navy, is handled only by the Navy. Certain items in common use are pooled for handling by joint Army-Navy agencies. In other instances, it has been found convenient to have one service look out for the needs of both; fuel in the Pacific is handled entirely by the Navy, while rations for all personnel on shore are handled by the Army.

In the foregoing discussion I have stressed the problems in the Pacific, because they are the most difficult with which to deal from the naval logistic point of view, due mainly to the absence of port facilities in the island bases we have captured, and to the distances involved. In the Atlantic the problem has been easier, because of the more highly developed nature of the ports we have occupied, but the over-all volume of material to be moved and handled has required the maximum service from every ship that could be made available. Extensive logistic operations were also carried out in the Mediterranean. The most spectacular of these efforts was the creation of artificial harbors during the landings in Normandy, previously described. Here United States naval personnel installed and operated the unique breakwater caissons and flexible pier-heads (of British design and fabrication) at the beaches where United States troops landed. The Normandy operation was a striking example of close logistic support of masses of troops during the landing attack.

HEALTH

Despite the great increase in combat operations and the extremely unhealthful conditions in many occupied areas, the health record of the Navy compares favorably with past experience. In terms of total naval strength, recent tabulations indicate an estimated rate for casualty deaths of 3.3 per thousand in 1944 as compared with the final rate of 3.0 per thousand for the previous year. Again, on the basis of preliminary calculations, the total death rate from all causes is estimated at 5.8 per thousand for the year 1944 against the final figure of 5.4 per thousand in 1943.

Experience in this war indicates that of the wounded men who live until they receive medical attention, 98 out of every 100 survive. We are sparing no effort, therefore, to bring medical assistance as close to the battle lines as possible. Accordingly, battle casualties among our medical personnel have been substantial, as in many assaults they have landed simultaneously with the attacking forces. Moreover, it has been found practicable, when there are no off-shore obstacles, to beach landing craft fully equipped surgically. The use of new jeep ambulances is further keeping the handling of wounded men to a minimum. Amphibious tractors, together with newly designed elevators or davits, are being successfully employed to carry wounded promptly, despite difficult terrain conditions, to hospital ships anchored outside reef formations. The extensive use of whole blood, penicillin, plasma, new types of bandages, and serum albumen is proving effective in saving many lives.

The administrative problems which arise during a large-scale landing are considerable. Lately it has been found practicable to divide surgical landing craft in two groups—one to care for the slightly wounded, the other to care for the more serious cases. Medical personnel are correspondingly divided into specialized teams, and liaison units are formed to locate and cooperate with the beach dressing stations. Resuscitation teams are organized to appraise and diagnose injuries and treat casualties suffering from shock. Surgical teams, specializing in certain types of wounds, provide operating rooms, procure and prepare supplies, administer anaesthetics, and perform necessary operations. During several landings last year psychiatrists were assigned to medical divisions to handle cases of combat fatigue. In order to manipulate this complex organization, it has been found desirable to station a medical officer aboard the control ship where he can receive reports and transmit quickly the necessary orders. Systems have been worked out which enable ships to interchange medical equipment efficiently during combat.

On many Pacific islands disease and unsanitary conditions provide serious obstacles to the maintenance of good health. Sanitary measures must be applied as soon as territory is won. The introduction of new insect control methods during the year has brought excellent results. The incidence of dysentery and other epidemic diseases that were troublesome during earlier operations lowered markedly. Hundreds of cases of pulmonary tuberculosis, broncho pneumonia, bacillary dysentery and malnutrition among the natives were treated. Volunteer native nurses, who were recruited in large numbers, were of considerable assistance in caring for both civilian and military patients.

The Navy has provided for the health of thousands of men aboard ships, submarines and planes, and has maintained and operated a system of fleet, advance base, base and naval hospitals, hospital ships and dispensaries. During the year a number of new hospitals and hospital ships were commissioned; several large hotel properties and estates were acquired and converted into convalescent hospitals; and numerous new fleet, advance base and base hospitals, as well as other field units, were established. Also, many new dispensaries were set up to serve the various continental shore activities.

Naval medical research during the year fell into four large divisions; that relating to naval service in general, to naval aviation, to the submarine service, and to the Marine Corps. Among the new developments were personnel selection tests and techniques, protection equipment and devices (relating to such matters as chemical warfare, flash burns, sunburn, sound, immersion and armor), aids to survivors at sea, insecticides and fungistatic agents, training devices, field equipment, and various preventive medicine and surgery techniques.

THE MARINE CORPS

In 1939 the Marine Corps comprised 19,500 officers and men, little more than the equivalent of one division. It is now composed of 478,000 men and women. There are now six full divisions of combat troops in the field, and 118,086 officers and men in Marine Corps aviation.

The greater part of this strength is devoted to the combat divisions and supporting troops, who have so notably furthered our progress in the Pacific by their participation in the amphibious operations described earlier in this report. Twelve thousand Marines are assigned to combatant naval vessels as integral parts of the crews. Others are on duty guarding naval establishments within the United States and at advanced bases.

Marine Corps Schools, Quantico, Virginia, have carried out an intensive officer training program, including advanced studies at its new Command and Staff School, set up to train officers for staff duties in Marine battalions, regiments and divisions. Some 400 officers have been graduated from the Command and Staff School; since 1 March 1944, the Reserve Officers' School has graduated 2,939 officers; and the Officer Candidates' School, as of 1 January 1945, has graduated 3,237 commissioned officers. The Aviation Ground Officers' School, organized in January 1944, has turned out 650 trained specialists to relieve pilots for operational duties. The elementary and specialist training of enlisted men is conducted in recruit depots, sea schools, training centers and other schools, including those of the Army and Navy, when available. In general, the policy has been to transfer basic training activities to the East Coast.

The expansion of the Corps and the altered circumstances of recent operations have necessitated several changes in organization. During March and April of 1944 defense battalions were converted into antiaircraft artillery battalions and field artillery battalions; all Marine raider units were merged into the 4th Marine Regiment. On 15 April the 1st Marine Amphibious Corps was redesignated the 3rd Amphibious Corps. On 5 June Lieutenant General Holland M. Smith was designated type commander of ground forces attached to the Fleet Marine Force in the Pacific Ocean Areas.

The Marine Corps Women's Reserve, now completing its second year of service, reached its total authorized strength of 18,000 in June 1944. Approximately 1700 of their number have been requested for duty in Hawaii.

THE COAST GUARD

The Coast Guard, which is a part of the Navy in time of war, has performed a great variety of duties, both within the United States and abroad, as part of the naval combatant forces, as well as in furtherance of normal Coast Guard functions. As of 31 December 1944 Coast Guard personnel totaled 169,832.

Coast Guard personnel man nearly 300 vessels of the fleet—transports, cargo vessels, fuel ships, destroyer escorts and landing craft of various types—which have participated in numerous amphibious operations in both the Atlantic and Pacific—as well as 600 Coast Guard cutters and 3,000 small craft employed in escort service and harbor security duty. Two hundred and twenty-one cargo vessels under Army control are manned by Coast Guard crews.

Acting as volunteer port security forces, Coast Guard personnel have been assigned to safeguard the nation's ports, with their 5,000,000 linear feet of wharfage.

The Coast Guard has continued to improve aids to navigation along our inland and coastal waterways. The safe movement to the seaboard of landing craft built in the upper Mississippi River basin and on the Great Lakes has been accomplished by Coast Guard pilots, utilizing well marked channels. Intracoastal waterways, recently extended in the Gulf area, have been marked to permit safer movement of vital war materials.

A major function of the Coast Guard has been the inspection of merchant vessels and safety appliances thereon. The efforts of Coast Guard inspectors to ensure that merchant vessels carry adequate safety equipment, and that their crews attain greater efficiency in operation, has contributed to the decline of casualties among our merchant seamen. In home ports, lifeboat drills and safety instruction have been given by the Coast Guard. Marine inspectors detailed to ports in the United States and abroad have examined merchant officers and seamen for upgrading, and have administered discipline.

In carrying out its function of life saving, the Coast Guard, under direction of the Joint Chiefs of Staff, has undertaken the task of developing improved methods and devices for rendering emergency assistance to aircraft and surface vessels in distress and to rescue survivors thereof. In connection with the recovery of these survivors, the use of helicopters from shore and surface craft is being thoroughly evaluated.

SPARS [Women's Reserve of the Coast Guard] are performing practically every type of non-combatant duty, thus releasing men for service at sea. Their enlistment, except for replacements, was terminated in November 1944; the SPAR officer training program was completed in December. As of 31 December 1944, there were 9,829 SPARS.

VI
Conclusion

AT the conclusion of my previous report, I commented upon the successful teamwork between the Army and Navy, which has so effectively furthered the progress of the war. Within the past twelve months the character of our operations has increasingly necessitated a free and rapid interchange of forces of the several services, so that the greatest possible strength can be brought to bear against the enemy at the place and the time that will do the most good. It is a matter of basic policy to freeze the smallest possible number of forces in permanent assignment to any single area, and to leave the major portion of the fleet as a mobile unit which is ready for service where it is most vitally needed. As an example, during the past year Admirals Halsey and Spruance, in turn commanding major units of the Pacific Fleet, have been moving back and forth between the Central and Southwest Pacific in support of the westward advances of Fleet Admiral Nimitz in the Pacific Ocean Areas and of General of the Army MacArthur in the Southwest Pacific Area. As a general principle, all naval forces are placed under a naval commander of the nation which has the primary naval responsibility in the area of operations. During the invasion of Normandy and in the Mediterranean, United States naval forces operated under British naval commanders, while British and Australian naval forces are under our operational control in the Pacific.

The harmonious integration within and between the services has been particularly essential in amphibious operations, where personnel of one service have served under the command of another. In any amphibious operation, command of all forces engaged rests in the hands of the naval commander until the troops have been put ashore and have established their command organization. At this point the landing force commander advises the naval commander that he has assumed command of his troops ashore.

The function of the Navy in an amphibious operation falls into four main phases. During the "approach" phase, the Navy commands passage to the area of landings for the invasion forces, bombards shore batteries, landing beaches and supporting areas, conducts mine sweeping operations and removes beach obstacles. Frequently the bombing of landing beaches and shore defenses is a joint function of Army and Navy aircraft. In the "landing" phase, the Navy, by employment of special landing craft, puts the invasion forces and all their equipment ashore, under cover of ships' guns and carrier aircraft. In the "support" phase, after the consolidation of the beachhead, the Navy continues to provide artillery and air support to the forces ashore for as long a time as they remain within range of ships' guns, and until shore based aviation can relieve our carriers of the task of air support. In the "supply" phase, the Navy guarantees the security of the supply lines of the invasion forces and obstructs the enemy's efforts to reinforce his troops by sea.

The extent and varied character of naval participation in amphibious operations have required vast quantities of ships, men and material. Consider, for example, the Lingayen Gulf landings on 9 January 1945. The naval attack and covering forces for this operation consisted of 1,033 ships, ranging in size from battleships and carriers on down through landing craft. The naval personnel in this force numbered upwards of 273,000. The Army forces put ashore on D-day and during the following four days were slightly more than two-thirds of this number. Similarly, in the landings on Iwo Jima, approximately 800 naval vessels were involved, with a total personnel of over 220,000. Approximately 60,000 Marines were landed in the first three days of the operation, a ratio of ships' personnel to troops landed of slightly less than 4 to 1.

The experience of more than three years of war has demonstrated the soundness of our concept of a "balanced fleet," in which aircraft and ships work together as a coordinated team. There has been no dispute as to "carriers versus battleships." Aircraft can do some things which ships cannot do. Ships can do some things which aircraft cannot do. Working together, surface ships, submarines and aircraft supplement each other so that the strength of the unified team is greater than the sum of the parts.

Given the conditions under which naval war is now fought, it is impossible for a fleet to operate effectively without air power of its own. Our superiority in carrier strength has enabled us to take giant's strides across the Pacific in spite of the enemy's island network of air bases. The fast carrier task forces of the Pacific Fleet, consisting of carriers, battleships, cruisers and destroyers, have repeatedly made bold offensive thrusts into distant waters, inflicting significant damage on the enemy's shipping and installations. They have supported amphibious operations, controlling the air both before and after landings and until air strips could be completed. They have equally proved their worth in the two major actions with the Japanese fleet which have taken place during the past year. The clearest evidence of their effectiveness is seen in the box score of damage inflicted upon the enemy by Admiral Halsey's Third Fleet between 24 August 1944 and 26 January 1945. During these five months, while the Third Fleet was engaged in supporting the Western Carolines and Philippine Island operations, 4,370 enemy aircraft were destroyed, 82 enemy combatant ships sunk and 372 enemy auxiliaries and merchant ships sunk (excluding small craft), against a loss in combat by the Third Fleet of only 449 of our own planes and the light carrier PRINCETON.

The amphibious landings of the past twelve months have repeatedly shown the value of naval gunfire in gaining victory and in saving the lives of our assault troops. Shore bombardments in preparation for landings, during the landings, and for as long after as troops are within range of ships' guns, have been carried out on a scale not contemplated in the past. New methods, joint procedures, and new materials have been developed. A sufficient volume of fire is laid down to knock out the shore and beach defenses and to drive off the beach defense personnel. Initially fire is carried out by heavy ships and support aircraft. Battleship fire provides the only gun (or weapon for that matter) which is sufficiently powerful and accurate to knock out reinforced concrete pillboxes eight to ten feet thick, and other similarly strong land gun emplacements. Just prior to landing, destroyers, gunboats, and rocket ships lay down heavy barrages of fire; ships and aircraft continue to give support as the troops move in. Although ships are designed primarily to fight other ships, their effectiveness against heavy shore batteries has been well proven in this war, as in the past. The risk of so exposing ships is justifiable if the object sought is sufficiently important, more especially when command of the sea is not in jeopardy. The Normandy landing was an especially convincing demonstration of the value of naval gunfire in support of troops, not only as they land but also as they move inland off the beaches. The new applications of naval gunfire in amphibious operations, as well as in fleet actions, have demonstrated that the battleship is a versatile and essential vessel, far from obsolete.

We have heard much of things being ahead of schedule in the Pacific. Actually we have had no schedule, except to go as far and as fast as the means in hand would permit. It can be said that the war today is ahead of our expectations of last year. This should stimulate rather than sap our determination to carry on with every means we can muster. I have said before, and I repeat—a quick and easy Pacific victory cannot be taken for granted, even after the European war is over. While we rejoice in the reoccupation of Guam and of the Philippines, from which our forces were driven three years ago, we must constantly realize that we are only now gaining a position from which we can assault the heart of the Japanese strength. That is our goal, and the enemy is welcome to know that we shall continue to press him with every means at our command. But the very speed of our advance has created new production problems. Our accelerated operations are placing a heavy strain upon reserves of certain vital items, while production of certain necessities is falling behind mounting requirements. It is only by unrelenting support and effort on the home front that our advance can continue.

While we contemplate with pride the accomplishments of the past twelve months—accomplishments without precedent in naval history—we must never forget that there is a long, tough and laborious road ahead.

Third and Final Report

TO THE
SECRETARY OF THE NAVY

*Covering the period 1 March 1945
to 1 October 1945*

BY

FLEET ADMIRAL ERNEST J. KING
COMMANDER IN CHIEF, UNITED STATES FLEET,
AND CHIEF OF NAVAL OPERATIONS

(*Issued 8 December 1945*)

UNITED STATES FLEET

HEADQUARTERS OF THE COMMANDER IN CHIEF
NAVY DEPARTMENT
WASHINGTON 25, D. C.

Dear Mr. Secretary:

On 1 March of this year I presented to you my second annual report of the progress of our naval operations and the expansion of our naval establishment during the preceding year.

Since the terminal date of my second report major hostilities on all fronts have terminated victoriously for the nations allied against the Axis powers, and I transmit to you herewith my third and final report of operations of the United States Navy in World War II. This report covers the period 1 March 1945 to 1 October 1945.

The Navy built and manned by the united efforts of this country continued to carry the action to the enemy, engaged him by sea and air, maintained control of the essential lanes of sea communication and transported men and supplies over all oceans to all theaters. The significant role of amphibious operations in this war was strikingly portrayed in the capture of Iwo Jima and Okinawa, which were the outstanding operations of this type during the last months of the war. They exemplify the teamwork of all services which brought victory on both the European and Pacific fronts.

For the officers and men of the Navy, Marine Corps, and Coast Guard, I am happy to report, at the end of the war, that the missions and tasks assigned all of them, singly and collectively, have been successfully accomplished.

Ernest J. King

Fleet Admiral, U. S. Navy,
Commander in Chief, United States Fleet
and Chief of Naval Operations

The Honorable James Forrestal,
   Secretary of the Navy,
      Washington, D.C.

* *

I
Introduction

MY two previous reports carried to 1 March 1945 the account of the development of our naval strength and the participation of the United States Navy in combat operations. The present report is intended primarily to cover the period of the succeeding seven months, during which Germany surrendered and the war with Japan came to an end. This being my last report, however, I am including herein my considered general comment and observations on the war as a whole.

The major strategic decision of the war provided first for the defeat of Germany and then for the defeat of Japan. Both of these tasks have now been accomplished and we can view in clearer perspective the two major compaigns which led to victory. The contrast between them is at once apparent. The war in Europe was primarily a ground and air war with naval support, while the war in the Pacific was primarily a naval war with ground and air support.

In the European war, sea power was an essential factor because of the necessity of transmitting our entire military effort across the Atlantic and supporting it there. Without command of the sea, this could not have been done. Nevertheless, the surrender of the land, sea and air forces of the German Reich on 8 May 1945 was the direct result of the application of air power over land and the power of the Allied ground forces.

In the Pacific war, the power of our ground and strategic air forces, like sea power in the Atlantic, was an essential factor. By contrast with Germany, however, Japan's armies were intact and undefeated and her air forces only weakened when she surrendered, but her navy had been destroyed and her merchant fleet had been fatally crippled. Dependent upon imported food and raw materials and relying upon sea transport to supply her armies at home and overseas, Japan lost the war because she lost command of the sea, and in doing so lost—to us—the island bases from which her factories and cities could be destroyed by air.

From the earliest days of the war our submarines, operating offensively in the farthest reaches of the Pacific, exacted a heavy toll of Japanese shipping. At a conservative estimate, they sank, in addition to many combatant ships, nearly two thirds of the merchant shipping which Japan lost during the war.

Our surface forces—fast task forces composed of aircraft carriers, fast battleships, cruisers, and destroyers—carried the war to the enemy homeland and destroyed impressive numbers of naval vessels and merchant ships. Our amphibious forces, operating initially behind air offensives and under air cover launched from carriers, seized the island bases which made possible the achievements of land-based aircraft in cutting enemy lines of communications and in carrying devastation to the Japanese home islands.

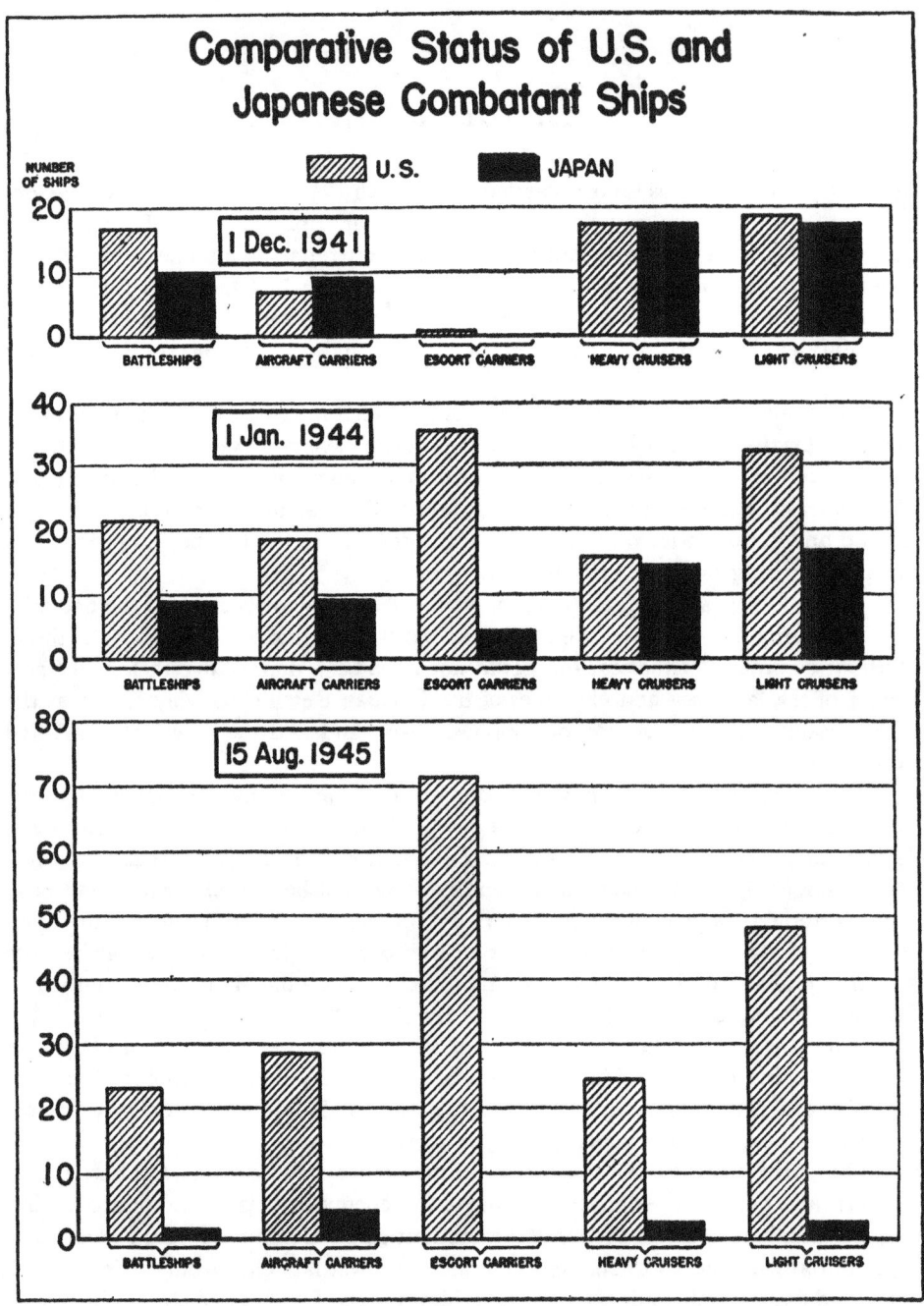

Plate 14.

INTRODUCTION

Thus our sea power separated the enemy from vital resources on the Asiatic mainland and in the islands which he had seized early in the war, and furnished us the bases essential to the operations of shore-based aircraft from which the atomic bombs finally were despatched, and on which troops and supplies were being massed for the invasion of Kyushu and of Honshu. The defeat of Japan was directly due to our overwhelming power at sea.

The destruction of the Japanese Navy followed the Nelsonian doctrine that naval victory should be followed up until the enemy fleet is annihilated. Of 12 battleships, 11 were sunk; of 26 carriers, 20 were sunk; of 43 cruisers, 38 were destroyed; and so on throughout the various types of ships, which collectively constituted a fleet considerably larger than ours was before the war began. The few ships that remained afloat were for the most part so heavily damaged as to be of no military value.

In striking contrast is the record of our ships. (See Plate 14.) Although 2 old battleships were lost at Pearl Harbor, 8 new battleships have since joined the fleet. Against 5 aircraft carriers and 6 escort carriers lost, we completed 27 carriers and 110 escort carriers. While we lost 10 cruisers, 48 new cruisers have been commissioned. We lost 52 submarines and built 203. The capacity of the United States to build warships, auxiliary ships and merchant ships, while supporting our forces and our allies all over the world, exceeded all former records and surpassed our most sanguine hopes. It proved to be a vital component of that sea power which Fleet Admiral Chester W. Nimitz has well defined in the following words:

> "Sea power is not a limited term. It includes many weapons and many techniques. Sea power means more than the combatant ships and aircraft, the amphibious forces and the merchant marine. It includes also the port facilities of New York and California; the bases in Guam and in Kansas; the factories which are the capital plant of war; and the farms which are the producers of supplies. All these are elements of sea power. Furthermore, sea power is not limited to materials and equipment. It includes the functioning organization which has directed its use in the war. In the Pacific we have been able to use our naval power effectively because we have been organized along sound lines. The present organization of our Navy Department has permitted decisions to be made effectively. It has allowed great flexibility. In each operation we were able to apply our force at the time and place where it would be most damaging to the enemy."

In the successful application of our sea power, a prime factor has been the flexibility and balanced character of our naval forces. In the Atlantic the German Navy was virtually limited to the use of submarines, without surface and naval air support. In the Pacific, Japanese sea power was hampered by army control, and Japanese naval officers lacked the freedom of initiative so necessary to gain and exercise command of the seas. On the other hand, while ours was a vast fleet, it was also a highly flexible and well balanced fleet, in which ships, planes, amphibious forces and service forces in due proportion were available for unified action whenever and wherever called upon.

It is of interest to note, in connection with formulation of plans for the future strength of our Navy, that our fleet in World War II was not solely engaged in fighting enemy fleets. On numerous occasions a large part of the fleet effort was devoted to operations against land objectives. A striking example is the capture of Okinawa. During the three months that this operation was in progress our Pacific Fleet—the greatest naval force ever assembled in the history of the world—was engaged in a continuous battle which for sustained intensity has never been equaled in naval history; yet at this time the Japanese Navy had virtually ceased to exist—we were fighting an island, not an enemy fleet.

With the possible exception of amphibious warfare, which covers a field of considerably broader scope, the outstanding development of the war in the field of naval strategy and tactics has been the convincing proof and general acceptance of the fact that, in accord with the basic concept of the United States Navy, a concept established some 25 years ago, naval aviation is and must always be an integral and primary component of the fleet. Naval aviation has proved its worth not only in its basic purpose of destroying hostile air and naval forces, but also in amphibious warfare involving attacks in support of landing operations, in reconnaissance over the sea and in challenging and defeating hostile land-based planes over positions held in force by the enemy. In these fields our naval aviation has won both success and distinction. Because of its mobility and the striking power and long range of its weapons, the aircraft carrier has proved itself a major and vital element of naval strength, whose only weakness—its vulnerability—demands the support of all other types, and thereby places an additional premium on the flexibility and balance of our fleet. The balanced fleet is the effective fleet.

In a balanced fleet the several components must be welded together rather than simply coordinated. For example, submarines normally operate "on their own" and hasty consideration might lead to the false conclusion that it would be advantageous for submarines to constitute a separate independent service. However, careful consideration will disclose the fallacy inherent in reasoning from this premise. Actually, the commanding officer of a submarine, to fight his ship most effectively, must be familiar with all phases of naval tactics and strategy. It is also essential that officers in surface ships understand the capabilities and limitations of submarines. This is accomplished in time of peace by requiring that submarine officers alternate periods of submarine duty with duty in vessels of other types. By this means, the point of view of the officer corps as a whole is broadened and in the higher echelons of command there are always included officers who have had submarine experience.

Aviation, though a specialty, is much more closely interwoven with the rest of the fleet than is the submarine branch of the Navy. It is, in fact, impossible to imagine an efficient modern fleet in which there is not a complete welding of aviation and surface elements. This is accomplished by requiring aviators to rotate in other duties in the same manner as do submarine officers, and by requiring non-aviators to familiarize themselves with aircraft operations—not a difficult matter since not only carriers but also battleships and cruisers are equipped with aircraft. Aviation is part of the ordinary daily life of the officer at sea.

INTRODUCTION

Of course, it is not possible to effect rotation of duties of all submarine and air officers during war. As a matter of fact, this is true of duty in all classes of ships. It is necessary during wartime to train certain officers—especially the Reserves—for one particular type of duty and to keep them at it. However, the long periods of peacetime training, in which an officer obtains the rounded experience to fit him for higher command, have been utilized in the past to give officers experience in varied duties and the practice will be continued in the future. The wisdom of that system was proved during the war by the efficiency of aircraft carriers, commanded by qualified aviators who also were experienced in handling ships, and, particularly, by the efficiency of the high combat commands of the Pacific Fleet. Many of the major units of the Pacific Fleet, composed of carriers and vessels of all other types, were commanded by aviators. The strength of the Navy lies in the complete integration of its submarine, surface and air elements.

The epic advance of our united forces across the vast Pacific, westward from Hawaii and northward from New Guinea, to the Philippines and to the shores of Japan, was spearheaded by naval aviation and closely supported by the power of our fleets. In these advances, some of the steps exceeded 2000 miles and the assaulting troops often had to be transported for much greater distances. The Navy moved them over water, landed them and supported them in great force at the beaches, kept them supplied and, particularly at Okinawa, furnished air cover during weeks of the critical fighting ashore.

The outstanding development of this war, in the field of joint undertakings, was the perfection of amphibious operations, the most difficult of all operations in modern warfare. Our success in all such operations, from Normandy to Okinawa, involved huge quantities of specialized equipment, exhaustive study and planning, and thorough training, as well as complete integration of all forces, under unified command.

Integration and unification characterized every amphibious operation of the war and all were successful. Command was determined chiefly by application of the principle of paramount capability. A naval officer was in over-all command of an amphibious operation while troops were embarked and until they had been landed and were firmly established in their first main objectives ashore. Beyond that point, an officer of the ground forces was in command and directed whatever naval support was considered necessary.

Unity of command at the highest military level, in Washington (as an extension of the principle of unity of command), was never attempted nor, in fact, seriously considered. It is a matter of record that the strategic direction of the war, as conducted collectively by the Joint Chiefs of Staff, was fully as successful as were the operations which they directed. The Joint Chiefs of Staff system proved its worth. There is no over-all "paramount capability" among the Joint Chiefs of Staff to warrant elevating one of their members to a position of military commander of all the armed forces—nor, in my opinion, is there any known system or experience which can be counted upon to produce the man qualified for such a position. This war has produced no such man—for the records of the Joint Chiefs of Staff will show that the proposals or the convictions of no one member were as sound, or as promising of success, as the united judgment and agreed decisions of all of the members.

In connection with the matter of command in the field, there is perhaps a popular misconception that the Army and the Navy were intermingled in a standard form of joint operational organization in every theater throughout the world. Actually, the situation was never the same in any two areas. For example, after General of the Army Dwight D. Eisenhower had completed his landing in Normandy, his operation became purely a land campaign. The Navy was responsible for maintaining the line of communications across the ocean and for certain supply operations in the ports of Europe, and small naval groups became part of the land army for certain special purposes, such as the boat groups which helped in the crossing of the Rhine. But the strategy and tactics of the great battles leading up to the surrender of Germany were primarily army affairs and no naval officer had anything directly to do with the command of this land compaign.

A different situation existed in the Pacific, where, in the process of capturing small atolls, the fighting was almost entirely within range of naval gunfire; that is to say, the whole operation of capturing an atoll was amphibious in nature, with artillery and air support primarily naval. This situation called for a mixed Army-Navy organization which was entrusted to the command of Fleet Admiral Nimitz. A still different situation existed in the early days of the war during the Solomon Islands campaign where Army and Navy became, of necessity, so thoroughly intermingled that they were, to all practical purposes, a single service directed by Admiral William F. Halsey, Jr. Under General of the Army Douglas MacArthur, Army, Army Aviation, and the naval components of his command were separate entities tied together only at the top in the person of General MacArthur himself. In the Mediterranean the scheme of command differed somewhat from all the others.

All these systems of command were successful largely because each was placed in effect to meet a specific condition imposed by the characteristics of the current situation in the theater of operations. I emphasize this fact because it is important to realize that there can be no hard and fast rule for setting up commands in the field. Neither is it possible to anticipate with accuracy the nature of coming wars. Methods adopted in one may require radical alteration for the next, as was true of World Wars I and II. It was fortunate that the War Department and the Navy Department, working together for many years—definitely since World War I—before the war began, had correctly diagnosed what was likely to occur and had instituted, not rigid rules, but a set of principles for joint action in the field which proved sufficiently flexible to meet the varying conditions that were encountered during the war.

We now have before us the essential lessons of the war. It is my earnest conviction that whatever else may have been learned as to the most effective relationship of the ground, naval and air forces, the most definite and most important lesson is that to attempt unity of command in Washington is ill-advised in concept and would be impracticable of realization.

* *

II
Combat Operations: Pacific

THE final phase of the Pacific naval war commenced with the assault on Iwo Jima in February 1945, closely followed by that on Okinawa in April. These two positions were inner defenses of Japan itself; their capture by United States forces meant that the heart of the Empire would from then on be exposed to the full fury of attack, not only by our carrier aircraft but also by land-based planes, the latter in a strength comparable to that which wreaked such devastation against the better protected and less vulnerable cities of Germany. After Okinawa was in our hands, the Japanese were in a desperate situation, which could be alleviated only if they could strike a counterblow, either by damaging our fleet or by driving us from our advanced island positions. The inability of the Japanese to do either was strong evidence of their increasing impotence and indicated that the end could not be long delayed.

THE CAPTURE OF IWO JIMA

The strategic situation prior to the assault on Iwo Jima, the command organization for that operation and the forces involved, the landing on 19 February, and the first ten days of ground fighting, have been included in my previous report and will not be repeated herein. As March opened, fierce ground fighting on Iwo Jima was still in progress. The front line ran roughly parallel to the short axis of the island, the northeastern third of which was still held by the enemy. Our right flank (4th Marine Division) extended inland from the beach just beyond the East Boat Basin and faced the enemy's skillfully prepared defense positions in steep and rough terrain, which made progress difficult; our left flank (5th Marine Division) rested on Hiraiwa Bay directly across the island; in the center the 3rd Marine Division had pushed a salient along the central Motoyama Plateau to occupy Motoyama village and the near end of Airfield No. 3. By nightfall of 2 March this last airfield and the whole of the Motoyama tableland were under our control, leaving the enemy in possession of a diminishing horseshoe-shaped area fringing the northeastern end of the island.

Airfield No. 1 had for some days been in use by light artillery spotting planes, but on 3 March it came into its own when a B-29, after a strike against the Japanese mainland, made a successful forced landing at Iwo Jima. More of such landings followed as the tempo of air strikes against Japan was stepped up. On 6 March the first land-based fighter planes came in, made patrol flights the following day, and relieved carrier aircraft in close support of troops on the third day after arrival. Airfield No. 2 was operational on 16 March.

Progress during the first week of March was slow despite daily artillery preparation, supplemented by naval gunfire and air strikes before each ground attack. On the night of 7-8 March the 4th Marine Division killed about 1000 enemy troops who had organized a major infiltration. Subsequently the resistance to our attacks diminished somewhat, and during the next three days control was secured of all the eastern coastline to a distance of approximately 4000 yards south of Kitano Point at the northeastern extremity of the island. On 16 March the northwest shore had been reached and Kitano Point isolated. Much mopping up remained to be done, particularly of a small stubborn pocket of resistance in one of the rugged gulches running southwest to the beaches from Kitano Point; but on 16 March all organized resistance was declared ended as of 1800, and the 4th Marine Division started re-embarking.

On 14 March the flag was raised officially and the establishment of military government was proclaimed. On 18 March the 5th Marine Division re-embarked. On 20 March the United States Army 147th Infantry Regiment of the garrison force arrived. At 0800 on 26 March, responsibility for the defense and development of Iwo Jima passed to the garrison force and the Commander Forward Area, Central Pacific. The capture of the island had taken 26 days of actual combat; over 20,000 enemy troops were destroyed; and our casualties ashore, as reported on 17 March, were 20,196, of whom 4,305 were killed in action.

The diminutive size of Iwo Jima and its general barrenness, lack of natural facilities and resources should lead no one either to minimize the importance of capturing it or to deprecate as unreasonable and unnecessary our heavy losses in doing so. It was important solely as an air base, but as such its importance was great. Not only was the pressure of air attack by our Marianas-based B-29's materially intensified by the availability of Iwo for topping them off with fuel and for supplying them with fighter cover from there on, but also there was an increase in combat effectiveness of the B-29's due to the heightened morale of personnel, heavier bomb loads, and decrease in abortive flights. There was, moreover, a substantial saving in valuable life in the number of B-29's which would have been shot down over Japan had there been no fighter cover, and in the number which would have been lost at sea had Iwo Jima not been available for emergency landings. It is estimated that the lives saved through this latter factor alone, subsequent to the capture of Iwo Jima, exceeded the lives lost in the capture itself.

This loss of life during the capture resulted inevitably from the strength of Iwo Jima as a defensive position and from the readiness of the enemy. Neither strategic nor tactical surprise was possible in our landing since, with Luzon and the Marianas in our hands, the seizure of some point in the Nanpo Shoto chain was obviously our next move, and Iwo Jima was by its location and the character of its terrain the most profitable objective.

It had no extensive coast line to afford invading troops a choice of landing points where they would meet little opposition, either on the beaches or in subsequent deployments for advance against enemy positions. Landing was feasible on only two beaches of limited extent, and they were so situated that a single defensive organization could oppose an assault against either separately or both simultaneously. The Japanese were, therefore, well prepared to meet us.

The defensive organization of Iwo Jima was the most complete and effective yet encountered. The beaches were flanked by high terrain favorable to the defenders.

Artillery, mortars, and rocket launchers were well concealed, yet could register on both beaches—in fact, on any point on the island. Observation was possible, both from Mount Suribachi at the south end and from a number of commanding hills rising above the northern plateau. The rugged volcanic crags, severe escarpments, and steep defiles sloping to the sea from all sides of the central Motoyama tableland afforded excellent natural cover and concealment, and lent themselves readily to the construction of subterranean positions to which the Japanese are addicted.

Knowing the superiority of the firepower that would be brought against them by air, sea, and land, they had gone underground most effectively, while remaining ready to man their positions with mortars, machine guns, and other portable weapons the instant our troops started to attack. The defenders were dedicated to expending themselves—but expending skillfully and protractedly in order to exact the uttermost toll from the attackers. Small wonder then that every step had to be won slowly by men inching forward with hand weapons, and at heavy costs. There was no other way of doing it.

The skill and gallantry of our Marines in this exceptionally difficult enterprise was worthy of their best traditions and deserving of the highest commendation. This was equally true of the naval units acting in their support, especially those engaged at the hazardous beaches. American history offers no finer example of courage, ardor and efficiency.

As a whole the operation affords a striking illustration of the inherently close relation between land, sea and air power. The fleet with its ships and planes delivered and supported the land forces. The Marines took an air base from which our land-based planes could operate with effectiveness far beyond that possible from our other bases in the rear. The same general pattern marked our long progress all the way across the vast central and western Pacific.

ASSAULT ON OKINAWA AND ITS CAPTURE

Our capture of the Marianas and Philippines had placed us on a strategic line some 1300 miles from the Japanese homeland and across its direct routes of communication to the south. The occupation of Iwo Jima had advanced this line to within 640 miles of Tokyo at the eastern end. The next step directed by the Joint Chiefs of Staff was to secure a position in the Nansei Shoto chain, which extends in a shallow loop from Kyushu, the southernmost of the main Japanese islands, down to Japanese held Formosa. Okinawa, the largest and most populous island in this chain, offered numerous sites for airfields from which almost any type of plane could reach industrial Kyushu, only 350 miles distant, and attack the enemy's communications to Korea, to the Chinese mainland, and to the Indo-China and Singapore areas. Since Okinawa also contained several excellent naval anchorages, it was chosen as the objective; the operations against it followed immediately on those for the capture of Iwo Jima.

From many standpoints the Okinawa operation was the most difficult ever undertaken by our forces in the Pacific. It was defended by about 120,000 men (including native Okinawans serving with the combat forces) with tanks and artillery. As possible reinforcements there were some 60,000 troops in various other positions in the Nansei Shoto chain, plus much larger forces in nearby Formosa, Kyushu, and the

Shanghai area. Also of great importance was the large native population, which afforded the enemy an unlimited supply of labor, and which might easily become a serious problem to us by clogging roads and imposing a burden of relief.

The most serious threat to us, however, lay in the very factor for which we had initiated the operation, namely the short distance from Okinawa to the Japanese homeland, where lay the main reserves of air and naval power. Just as we would be able to strike Japan to better effect after securing Okinawa, the Japanese could strike us while we were attacking that island. Japan's naval strength had been so reduced that it could not hope for success against our own in a decisive action; but hit-and-run raids, or perhaps forlorn-hope, honor-saving attempts, were a possibility. Air attack, particularly of the suicide variety, was the greatest menace, since the Japanese airfields within easy range of Okinawa were too numerous to permit more than their partial and temporary interdiction by our own air strikes against them. Severe damage and losses, therefore, had to be expected and accepted as the price of our success.

The operations for the capture of Okinawa were under the command of Admiral R. A. Spruance, Commander Fifth Fleet. Major forces participating under him were: the Joint Expeditionary Force (all elements engaged directly in the landings), Vice Admiral (now Admiral) R. K. Turner; the Expeditionary Troops (all ground forces engaged), the late Lieutenant General S. B. Buckner, USA; the Fast Carrier Force, Vice Admiral M. A. Mitscher, (including the battleships and other fire support vessels of the late Vice Admiral W. A. Lee's Striking Force); the British Carrier Force, Vice Admiral H. B. Rawlings; the Logistic Supply Group (tankers and cargo vessels which serviced the fleet under way close to the combat areas), Rear Admiral D. B. Beary; Service Squadron Ten (the repair, supply and service vessels of all kinds, based on Leyte Gulf, the Marianas, etc.), Commodore W. R. Carter; the Amphibious Support Force (comprising escort carriers, minesweepers, underwater demolition teams, gun-boats, and the gunnery ships assigned to bombardment missions), Rear Admiral (now Vice Admiral) W. H. P. Blandy; and the Gunfire and Covering Force (the battleships and other gunnery vessels not with the fast carriers), Rear Admiral M. L. Deyo. Numerous other participating task groups and units and their commanders are not mentioned herein. About 548,000 men of the Army, Navy, and Marine Corps took part, with 318 combatant vessels and 1139 auxiliary vessels, exclusive of personnel landing craft of all types.

The greater part of the intelligence information required for the operation was obtained from photographic coverage. Adequate small scale coverage for mapping purposes was first obtained on 29 September 1944 by B-29's of the XXI Bomber Command; from then on until the conclusion of the operation, additional photographing was done at frequent intervals by Army planes and planes of the Fast Carrier Force. The prompt developing, printing, and interpreting of these photos, and the early and wide distribution of the prints and of the information gleaned from them, was an important feature of the operation.

The island of Okinawa, which is about 65 miles long, is roughly divided into almost equal northern and southern parts. The northern area is generally rugged, mountainous, wooded and undeveloped. The southern area, which is generally rolling

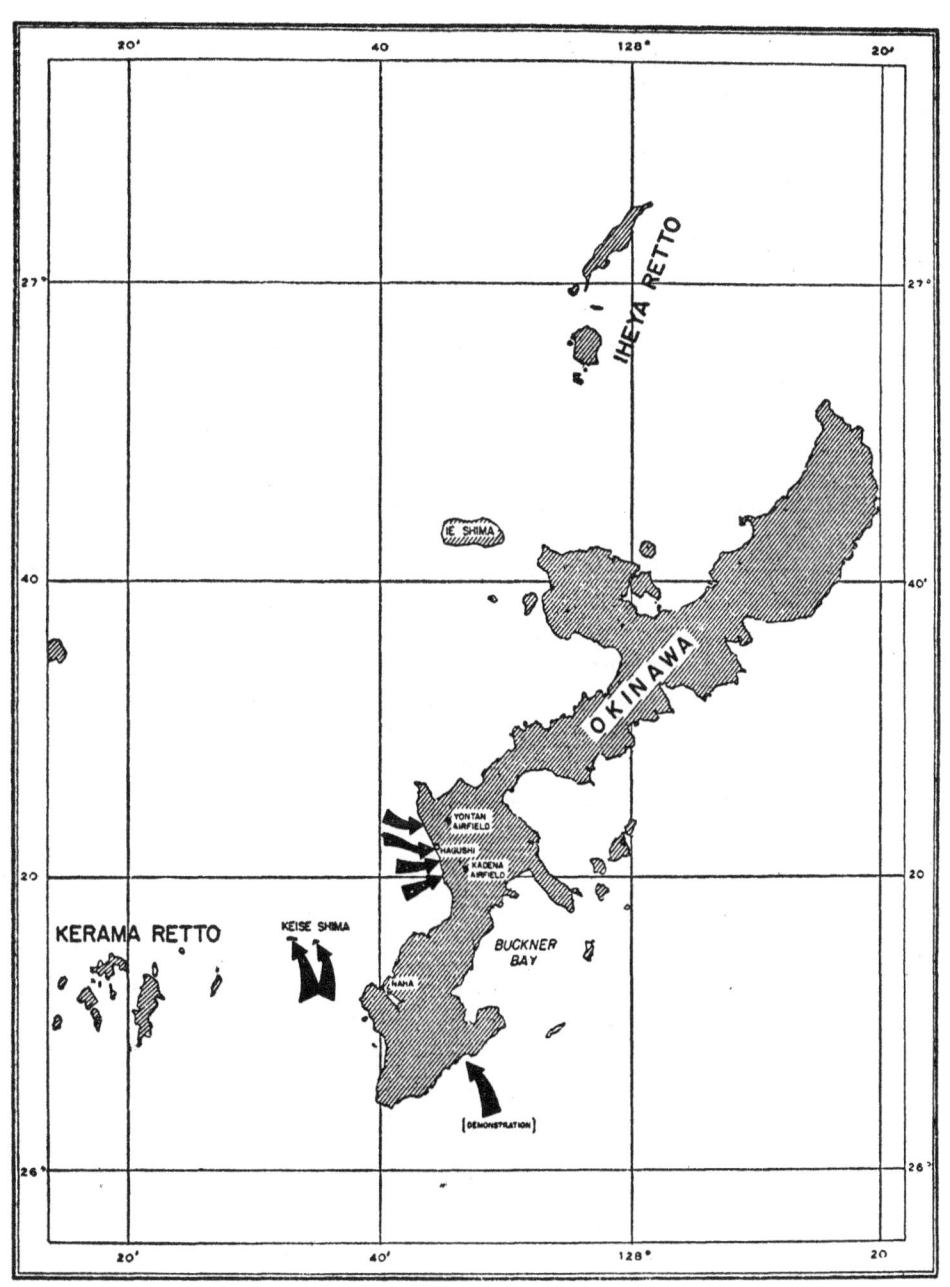

Plate 15.

but frequently broken by deep scarps and ravines, is the developed part of the island, containing the greater number of towns, roads, and cultivated areas, the capital city of Naha, all five of the island's airfields, and the strongest defenses. (See Plate 15.)

The preferred plan called for our ground forces to land on six miles of beach on the southwest shore, protected from the prevailing northeast trade winds and closely bordering the island's Yontan and Kadena airfields. Four divisions were to be landed abreast on these beaches. With the two center divisions advancing directly across the island to the east coast, and with the left and right flank divisions pivoting toward the north and south respectively, the Japanese forces in the southern part of the island would be isolated by these maneuvers, and were then to be overcome by attack from the north. Coincident with the main troop attack, there was planned for the southeast coast a demonstration, and an actual landing, if necessary.

Planned operations preliminary to and in support of the main landings included the following: the seizure of the islands of the Kerama Retto group, 20 miles to the southwest, in order to establish therein a logistics supply and naval repair base and a seaplane base; the seizure of the small island of Keise Shima, about 20,000 yards from the landing beaches and 11,000 yards from Naha city, and landing army artillery there to command the lower end of Okinawa; mine sweeping on a scale greater than in any previous operation; the usual work by underwater demolition teams; and the intensive bombardments by air and naval forces.

Cargo and troops were loaded and embarked on the United States west coast, in the Hawaiian Islands, in the southwestern Pacific, the Marshalls, the Carolines, and Leyte. The various elements proceeded to assemble afloat at Ulithi, Guadalcanal, Saipan, and Leyte. Following rehearsals the several forces departed for the objective in the more than 1200 ships of all kinds which the Joint Expeditionary Force contained. Movement of all forces to the objective was carried out without enemy interference. Operational breakdowns en route were insignificant, a fact which speaks well for the efficiency of our material and our personnel in operation, maintenance, and repair. An indispensable element in the campaign as a whole was the covering operations of the Fast Carrier Force, which are given in some detail in the next section of this report.

The mine sweepers were in the van, and on L-minus-8 day, 24 March, commenced sweeping under cover of gunfire from battleships of the Fast Carrier Force, and continued this work up to L-day, 1 April. There were 75 sweepers; and the entire coastal perimeter of southern Okinawa was cleared of mines during this pre-assault phase, in addition to the sweeping necessary for the capture of Kerama Retto and Ie Shima. Including re-sweeping, over 3000 square miles were swept and declared safe prior to L-day. Some 177 mines were swept and about 80 floaters destroyed. The thoroughness of this task is evidenced by the safety with which bombardment and assault ships in great numbers closed the assault beaches without significant loss from mines.

On L-minus-6 day the assault on Kerama Retto was commenced, and by L-minus-1, 31 March, these islands and also Keise Shima had been occupied against minor resistance. Nets were immediately laid to protect the anchorages, and the seaplane base was established. Tankers, ammunition ships and repair vessels were brought directly to this anchorage, which assumed a progressively more important role as the principal haven for ships damaged by "kamikaze" attacks of suicide planes.

Since L-minus-7, 25 March, Okinawa itself had been under intermittent bombing and gunfire, and on L-day, 1 April, preceded by intense naval and air bombardment, the Tenth Army landed according to schedule over the Hagushi beaches on Okinawa against light enemy resistance. The assault waves, embarked in amphibious vehicles, hit the beach at 0830, moved rapidly inland, and by 1230 had captured both Yontan and Kadena airfields with light losses. Prior to dark the Tenth Army, with approximately 50,000 troops ashore, had gained a beachhead 4000 to 5000 yards in depth. Proceeding rapidly against initially weak resistance, our troops crossed the island to the east shore, and on 4 April the Yontan-Kadena segment of the island was in our hands.

The Japanese had made no serious attempt to stop us at the beaches where we had landed; as the attack progressed from day to day, it was evident that they had withdrawn most of their forces into the southernmost part of the island, and had established their defenses in depth on terrain admirably suited for defense and delaying action tactics. The enemy defenses consisted of blockhouses, pillboxes, and caves, protected by double apron barbed wire and minefields. Here the enemy used his artillery unstintingly, and his defensive tactics were described as "artful and fantastic."

In the north progress was rapid against scattered opposition; on 22 April all organized resistance in the northern two thirds of the island had ceased, though patrolling and mopping up continued. In the south our advance was stubbornly contested. From 4 April to 26 May our lines had advanced only about four miles, and it took from 26 May to 21 June to cover the remaining ten miles to the southern tip of the island. On 21 June, after eighty-two days of bitter fighting, organized resistance was declared to have ended, although mopping up of two small enemy pockets remained to be done.

On 18 June, while observing the attack of the Marine 8th Regimental Combat Team, Lieutenant General Buckner, Commanding General of the Tenth Army and the Ryukyus Forces, was instantly killed by a shell burst. Command of the ground forces was then assumed by Major General Roy S. Geiger, USMC, until after the capture of the island, when he was relieved by General Joseph W. Stilwell, USA, on 23 June.

The general pattern of the operation for the capture of Okinawa was similar to those for the capture of Iwo Jima, the Marianas, the Marshalls, etc.; it differed mainly in the size of the air, naval, and ground forces employed, the length of time required to secure it after the initial landing, and the number of naval vessels damaged or sunk at the scene of operations by air attack, mainly of the suicide variety. Having been experienced in previous operations, this form of attack was not new, but the shorter distance from numerous air bases in Japan, and the desperate situation which would threaten the Japanese if our assault on Okinawa were successful, stimulated them to their greatest and most fanatical effort.

The time element was closely connected with the extent of our ship losses. By its very nature an amphibious invasion implies advancing a huge number of vessels, both combatant and noncombatant, from a zone dominated by one's own land-based air forces into one hitherto dominated by the enemy's. Our vessels are localized by the landing so that the enemy has not the problem of finding them, but only of hitting them. Thus exposed, their protection depends wholly on their own antiaircraft fire, smoke, and on cover from our own carrier-based air forces, which are to that extent diverted from offensive missions. This precarious situation for shipping continues until progress ashore at the objective results in relief: first, by the establishment of our own air forces, air facilities, antiaircraft radars, and fighter-directors ashore in strength sufficient to dominate the area; secondly, and more important, by releasing most of the shipping so that there are fewer vulnerable targets presented to any enemy that gets through. The longer this relief is delayed by the continuance of ground fighting, the higher our shipping casualties mount. The longer the Navy must remain in support of assault troop operations, the more vulnerable it is to attack, and the higher is the proportion of personnel and ship casualties. Slow progress on the ground is directly reflected, therefore, in naval losses.

The first enemy air attack at Okinawa occurred on 24 March when the mine sweepers arrived; the first damage was done on 26 March; and by 21 June, when organized resistance had ceased, about 250 vessels of all classes, from battleships and carriers down to destroyers and landing ships, had been hit by air attack, by far the greatest proportion of them in suicide crashes. Some 34 destroyers or smaller craft were sunk. Early warning of impending attacks proved to be the best countermeasure and for this purpose destroyers and other small vessels were stationed as pickets at appropriate distances from the concentrations of heavier shipping. These pickets took the heaviest losses themselves, but in so doing they undoubtedly saved many bigger and more valuable vessels during a critical three months.

FAST CARRIER FORCE OPERATIONS IN SUPPORT OF OKINAWA INVASION

After the supporting operations for the Iwo Jima campaign were completed, Vice Admiral Mitscher proceeded with his fast carrier task force in support of the forth-coming Okinawa campaign. First he went toward the Nansei Shoto in order to obtain photographic coverage of that area. Planes were launched on 1 March, and excellent photo reconnaissance was obtained for use in planning the Okinawa campaign. While in this area, cruisers of the force bombarded Okino Daito Shima on 2 March, starting numerous fires and providing valuable training for the ships participating. The force then proceeded to Ulithi for a ten-day period of regrouping and logistic replenishment.

On 14 March the task force departed from Ulithi and proceeded toward Japan to carry out its part in the invasion of Okinawa. On 18–19 March, from a position 100 miles southeast of Kyushu, air strikes were launched against airfields on that island in order to eliminate future airborne resistance to our Okinawa invasion forces. Fleet units at Kure and Kobe were also attacked with considerable success.

On the morning of the 19th the carrier FRANKLIN was badly damaged by fires started when she was hit by two bombs from an enemy plane. Outstanding rescue operations saved 850 men from the water, but the dead and missing totalled 772.

During that afternoon the task force retired southward, launching additional sweeps against enemy airfields to forestall an organized attack on the slowly moving damaged ships and escorts. On 21 March 48 enemy planes were intercepted 60 miles from the force by 24 carrier-based planes. In the ensuing battle all the Japanese planes were shot down with a loss of only two of our fighters.

In a four-day period Vice Admiral Mitscher's forces destroyed 528 enemy planes, damaged 16 enemy surface craft, and either destroyed or damaged scores of hangars, factories, and warehouses. Our own plane losses were 116. As a result of this operation, the enemy was unable to mount any strong air attack against our forces on Okinawa for a week after the initial landing.

On 24 March, under the command of Vice Admiral Lee, battleships of the task force bombarded the southeastern coast of Okinawa. This was part of a diversionary move to cover up the actual location of our landing beaches; apparently the ruse was successful.

When the invasion of Okinawa began on 1 April, planes from the fast carriers began a series of almost continuous strikes and combat air patrols in direct support of the operation. For a few days enemy air opposition was almost nonexistent, but on 6 April the Japanese finally struck with fury against our ground and supporting forces. All units of the carrier force performed admirably during the day's attack, knocking down 248 planes, while losing only 2.

The carrier task force then proceeded northward, and on 7 April attacked strong Japanese fleet units which had been located in the East China Sea off Kyushu. Heavy weather handicapped our airmen, but in spite of this they sank the battleship YAMATO, the cruiser YAHAGI, and 4 destroyers. Fires were started on 2 other destroyers, and only 3 destroyers in the entire force escaped without damage.

While our planes were otherwise occupied in striking YAMATO and those ships, the enemy resumed the heavy assaults of the previous day against the carrier force. Combat air patrols destroyed 15 planes over the force, and ships' gunfire knocked down 3 more. One suicide plane penetrated the antiaircraft fire, however, and dropped a bomb on the carrier HANCOCK; it then crashed on her flight deck, killing 28 men, and badly damaging the carrier.

On 11 April the enemy resumed the air attacks on the fast carrier task force. The number of Japanese planes participating was not large, but their pilots were determined to destroy themselves by diving their planes directly on the chosen target. Fortunately there were no direct hits, but 8 near misses caused some damage. During the day our carrier-based planes shot down 17 of these suicide planes, and ships' gunfire destroyed 12 more, but they still constituted a serious threat to our forces.

The next day the enemy shifted the weight of his suicide attacks to the ships anchored at Okinawa, and the combat air patrols from both fast and escort carriers had little difficulty in shooting down 151 enemy planes over the islands.

On 15 April the carriers launched a surprise attack against southern Kyushu airfields, destroying 51 enemy planes on the ground and setting numerous ground installations afire. The Japanese managed to launch some planes in opposition, and 29 of these were shot down before our aircraft returned to the carriers.

Fighter sweeps were again launched against Kyushu on 16 April in an effort to break up an obvious major enemy air attack. They shot down 17 air-borne planes and destroyed 54 on the ground. In spite of this success, however, the enemy launched heavy air attacks during the day against our Okinawa forces and the fast carrier task force. All ground support was cancelled, and every effort was concentrated on a successful defense of the task force. The final score for the day was 210 enemy aircraft shot down, against a loss of 9 of our planes. Heavy damage was caused to the carrier INTREPID when a suicide plane crashed on her flight deck at the height of the battle.

On 19 April Vice Admiral Lee commanded a division of fast battleships in the bombardment of the southeastern coast of Okinawa. This action coincided with the beginning of the Tenth Army's all-out offensive. The bombardment not only destroyed important military installations, but it assisted in making a feint landing at that point appear authentic.

On 29 April suicide planes again attacked the task force in strength, hitting and badly damaging two destroyers. The enemy paid for them, however, with 25 aircraft knocked out of the air by planes and guns of the task force.

After several days of relative calm, enemy aircraft returned in large numbers on 4 May to attack our land and amphibious forces in the Okinawa area. This attack was apparently part of a counter-landing operation to aid their own ground forces. The fast carrier task force was not attacked, however, and its fighters were free to defend the Okinawa area, shooting down 98 enemy aircraft, while losing only 5 planes.

On 11 May another major air battle was fought over Okinawa and the ships of the task force. Carrier-based planes shot down 69 enemy aircraft, ships' gunfire accounted for 3 more, while 2 were destroyed in suicide dives on the carrier BUNKER HILL. This ship was badly damaged, and 373 of her personnel were killed, with 19 missing.

The fast carriers moved northward on 12 May and launched additional air strikes against Kyushu airfields on 13–14 May. Few planes were found and virtually no air opposition was encountered over the fields. On the morning of the 14th, however, the enemy managed to launch a force of 26 planes against the ships of the task force. Of these 6 were shot down by ships' gunfire and 19 by combat air patrol; the remaining plane was destroyed in a damaging suicide crash on ENTERPRISE.

On 24 May the fast carriers launched a clean-up sweep by 98 planes against airfields in southern Kyushu. Except on Kanoya airfield little activity was found, and it was evident that the previous strikes against this area had been very effective. The score for the day was 84 enemy planes destroyed, while our losses were confined to 3 planes lost to antiaircraft fire off Kanoya.

On 28 May the late Vice Admiral J. S. McCain relieved Vice Admiral Mitscher as commander of the fast carrier task forces.

On 2–3 June further long-range sweeps were launched against Kyushu, but bad weather impaired their effectiveness. Only 30 enemy planes were destroyed, while our losses were 16. By 4 June the bad weather had developed into a typhoon, and the ships of the task force spent the next 24 hours in attempting to avoid the storm's center. Serious damage to 3 cruisers, 2 carriers, and 1 destroyer resulted.

Operations were resumed on 8 June when a final attack was made on southern Kyushu. It was well executed, but previous raids had so reduced Japanese air strength in this area that only 29 planes could be destroyed. Only 4 of our carrier planes were lost. On 8 and 9 June, cruisers and battleships from Vice Admiral McCain's task force bombarded Okino Daito and Minami Daito to the east of Okinawa. These attacks terminated the supporting action of the fast carrier task force, and on 10 June course was set for Leyte Gulf, where they anchored on 13 June for a period of replenishment and repair.

For a period of nearly three months, the fast carriers and their escorts had operated in and near the Okinawa area, giving invaluable support to our occupation forces. During this time the task force had destroyed 2336 enemy planes, while losing 557 of its own aircraft. In addition, widespread damage had been inflicted upon shore installations in Japan, the Nansei Shoto, and upon important units of the Japanese fleet. This remarkable record detracted considerably from the ability of the enemy to oppose our landing forces on Okinawa, thereby contributing notably to our final success.

British Carrier Operations

A fast British carrier task force, under the command of Vice Admiral Rawlings, was assigned to Admiral Spruance's Fifth Fleet to assist in the air support operations for the Okinawa assault. From 26 March to 20 April, and again from 4 May to 25 May, planes from this force rendered valuable service in neutralizing the enemy air installations on Sakishima Gunto, southwest of Okinawa. Carriers of the force were subjected to frequent attacks by suicide planes, but none of them was put out of action. Battleships and cruisers of the force bombarded Miyako Jima on 4 May with satisfactory results.

JOINT OPERATIONS IN THE PHILIPPINES AND BORNEO

The situation in the Philippines on 1 March 1945 found United States forces controlling all of Leyte and Mindoro, most of Samar except a small area in the north, the central part of Luzon from Lingayen Gulf to Manila and certain areas to the south. Isolated resistance was still encountered within a few buildings in Manila and islands in the bay. Guerillas controlled substantial areas of the Visayan Islands and Mindanao. Landings had been made on 28 February at Puerto Princesa on the east coast of Palawan with practically no opposition. Control was quickly extended over adjacent territory, providing airfields from which enemy sea traffic in waters to the westward and southward could be observed and attacked. Japanese concentrations still existed in many key cities of the Philippines and along certain of the routes which our ships had to travel to bring up vitally needed supplies and munitions. In addition, though their general air strength in the area had greatly diminished, the Japanese still controlled a number of airfields which permitted harassing attacks.

A series of operations was undertaken to gain control of the important straits leading into central Philippine waters in order to cut off enemy reinforcements and to set the stage for the ultimate reduction of remaining Japanese strongholds in the Philippines. The capture of Palawan provided an effective barrier on the west and gave us a base for naval and air operations which controlled the Balabac Strait entrance from the South China Sea to the Sulu Sea. At the same time we secured the most direct sea lane to Manila with an amphibious assault on Lubang Island, controlling the Verde Island Passage just south of the capital. The islands of Burias and Ticao were siezed on 4 March and Romblon and Simara on 12 March. Possession of these islands afforded protection to our shipping through San Bernardino Strait and obviated the need for the roundabout route through Surigao Strait which was still subject to air attacks from the Visayas.

The campaign to complete the reoccupation of the Philippines resolved itself naturally into a series of amphibious landings to seize control of coastal cities and other strongly held Japanese positions. In March three such landings were made by forces of Admiral Thomas C. Kinkaid's Seventh Fleet. (See Plate 9.)

The first of these landings was made on 10 March at Zamboanga, at the southwest tip of Mindanao, in order to obtain control of the passage from the Sulu to the Celebes Sea, secure naval and air facilities with which to compress the Japanese remaining in the central Philippines, and provide a further steppingstone down the Sulu Archipelago for future operations towards Borneo. The attack group was under command of the late Rear Admiral F. B. Royal. Light cruisers and destroyers bombarded enemy positions there for two days while mine sweepers made sure the approaches were clear. On 10 March the 41st Division was put ashore under moderate enemy artillery and mortar fire. The troops quickly overran Zamboanga City and the two airfields nearby, driving the Japanese back into the hills. A further landing was made on Basilan Island on 16 March without enemy opposition.

On 18 March a similar assault force landed at Iloilo on the island of Panay. To clear this island and establish radar and air facilities as well as motor torpedo boat bases, the 40th Division was staged from Lingayen Gulf. Only token opposition to the landings was offered, and naval gunfire preparation was withheld to save the lives of natives. The assault group was commanded by Rear Admiral A. D. Struble. Iloilo City was secured on the 20th; the docks and harbor area were found practically undamaged. Subsequent minor operations had by the end of March virtually cleared Panay and nearby smaller islands.

Troops of the Americal Division were used for the landing at Cebu on 26 March. Captain A. T. Sprague, Jr., commanded the attack group, which was supported by a covering group of cruisers and destroyers under the command of Rear Admiral R. S. Berkey. Although the beaches were well organized for defense, the enemy positions there were found abandoned. Cebu City was captured on the next day, but considerable opposition to the advance of the troops inland developed, requiring extensive ground operations to clear the island.

On 17 April, after naval bombardment and air strikes, the X Corps with two divisions landed at Malabang (on Moro Gulf in southern Mindanao) and moved overland toward Davao Gulf against light opposition. Rear Admiral A. G. Noble commanded the naval task group and Rear Admiral R. S. Riggs the cruiser force which covered the landing. Cotobato and its airfield were secured on the next day. A novel feature of this campaign was the successful use of light landing craft on rivers lead ng inland. Davao Gulf was reached late in April and Davao City was captured on 4 May, followed by further extension of control along the shores of the Gulf. In the meantime, troops also advanced northward and effected a junction on 23 May with a regimental combat team which had been landed at Macajalar on the north

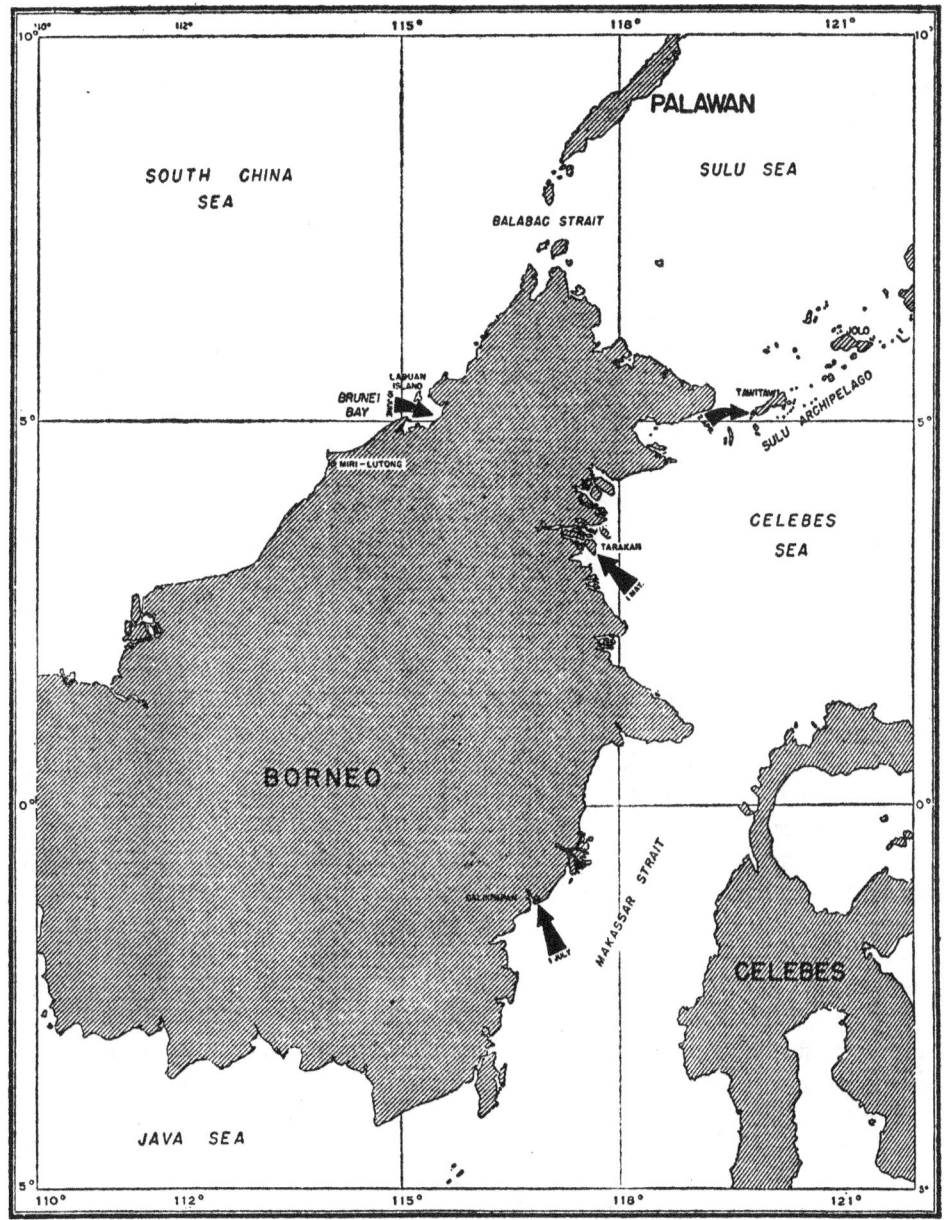

Plate 16.

coast on 9 May. These operations effectively sealed off enemy garrisons in the interior of the island where they could be mopped up at leisure.

The landing at Malabang was the last large amphibious assault necessary for the reoccupation of the Philippines, but a number of minor landings on the small islands were required in order to eliminate their garrisons. The most important of these were: the crossing of a regimental combat team from Iloilo to Pulupandan Point on northern Negros on 29 March, to assist in clearing that island of the enemy; the landing of another at Legaspi, Luzon, on 1 April to facilitate the clearing of the Bicol Peninsula; and landings by a third such unit at Sanga Sanga in the Tawi Tawi group on 2 April and at Jolo on 8 April. Such landings were generally supported by naval gunfire, as well as by air strikes. Landings were also made at Masbate on 3 April; on Busuanga Island, lying between Mindoro and Palawan, on 9 April; and at Tagbiliran, Bohol Island, on 11 April. Bohol was the only major island in the Philippines on which we had not yet established a firm hold. From this time until the close of hostilities, most naval operations in the Philippines involved small groups transporting and covering American troops and guerillas in shore-to-shore movements. The major units of the Seventh Fleet were occupied with the invasion of Borneo to the south.

The operations against Borneo, which began in May, were designed to deny the enemy the fruits of his conquests in the Netherlands East Indies and his use of the approaches to those areas. These included the capture of Tarakan to obtain its petroleum resources and to provide an airfield for support of the Balikpapan operation; the seizure of Brunei Bay to establish an advance fleet base and protect resources in that area; and the occupation of Balikpapan to establish naval air and logistic facilities and to conserve petroleum installations there. (See Plate 16.) Vice Admiral D. E. Barbey was designated the commander of the Borneo attack force.

The first Borneo operation was directed against the island of Tarakan, approximately 185 miles southwest of Tawi Tawi, to overcome some 3000 Japanese that were estimated to be on the island, and to develop facilities for future operations. Australian and American cruisers and destroyers began shelling the island on 27 April and continued through 1 May. At the same time the mine-sweeping group cleared the necessary approaches. Numerous neutralizing air raids had been made on airfields in the area. On 1 May the attack group under Rear Admiral Royal moved in. Units of the 9th Australian Division were landed on schedule with only small arms opposition.

In the second Borneo operation the 9th Australian Division, reinforced, was transported from Morotai to the Brunei Bay area of northern Borneo. Three separate landings were made at Labuan Island and on the mainland at Bintang and Cape Polompong. Air support was furnished by the United States Thirteenth Air Force and the Australian First Tactical Air Force. For ten days preceding the target date air strikes neutralized enemy airfields and harassed troop movements and shipping in Borneo, with emphasis on Brunei Bay targets the last three days. Mine sweeping began on 7 June under the protection of Rear Admiral Berkey's covering force of cruisers and destroyers. The mine sweeper SALUTE struck a mine and sank with many casualties.

Beginning on 9 June a distant covering group of cruisers and destroyers under Rear Admiral Riggs patrolled 50 miles west of Brunei Bay to prevent enemy surface interference.

The attack group commander was again Rear Admiral Royal. On 10 June, after an hour of heavy bombardment which caused the enemy to retreat from the beaches, the assault waves landed without opposition and moved inland against slight resistance.

When the landings had been successfully executed and one of the two Japanese cruisers in the area had been sunk off the Malay coast by a British submarine, the distant cover group was withdrawn on 11 June. Throughout the operation motor torpedo boats rendered valuable assistance strafing shore targets and patrolling the area. One hundred twenty miles to the south at Miri-Lutong a supplementary landing was made by combined forces after a week of mine sweeping in which 458 mines were swept.

The operations against Balikpapan were carried out under Rear Admiral Noble as commander of the attack group, and Rear Admiral Riggs as commander of the cruiser covering group. In preparation for the attack heavy air strikes had been made for a month using the Army, Navy and Australian air forces with as many as 100 sorties a day. The target date was set for 1 July. Sixteen days prior to this, mine sweeping and underwater demolition activities began with covering fire from cruisers and destroyers. This was met with intense reaction from enemy coastal guns. Three mine sweepers were damaged by enemy fire and three were sunk and one damaged by exploding mines. There was some doubt as to whether the target date could be met, but finally on 24 June destroyers were able to get close enough inshore to smother the enemy guns before the landing. An escort carrier group under the late Rear Admiral W. D. Sample provided day and night air cover, since land planes were based too far distant to assure their presence in the case of bad weather.

The attack force consisted of the largest number of ships used in the Southwest Pacific area since the Lingayen landings. In the cover and carrier groups were 9 cruisers (including 2 Australian and 1 Dutch), 3 escort carriers and destroyer escorts. The attack group was of comparable scale. After an intense two-hour bombardment on 1 July, the assault waves moved ashore. In spite of enemy artillery, mortar and small arms fire, seventeen assault waves landed without a single casualty. Stiffening resistance was met as the troops progressed inland and fire support was rendered by cruisers both day and night. This support continued through 7 July. A further landing at Cape Penajam was made without casualties on 5 July. There was no surface or subsurface interference with the attacking forces, and only four light harassing attacks were made by enemy planes with no damage to our ships or personnel.

While the period covered by this report witnessed no single naval operation of the size and scope of the Leyte or Lingayen landings, the numerous amphibious operations in which the Seventh Fleet participated contributed materially to the consolidation of our positions in the Philippines and the wresting of vital resources from the enemy in Borneo.

These numerous amphibious landings were conducted on short notice and in many instances were so closely spaced that for all practical purposes they were concurrent operations. Their successful completion on schedule reflects great credit on the commanders responsible for their planning and execution. In addition to the landing operations, unremitting and constantly mounting pressure was maintained on the enemy by Seventh Fleet submarines, aircraft, and motor torpedo boats, which by June had brought to a virtual standstill all enemy sea-borne and coastal transport in the Southwest Pacific area.

Of equal importance with the offensive operations mentioned above were the large movements of men and supplies into the Philippines, and the extensive redeployment of men and equipment within the area in preparation for the staging of the projected landings on the Japanese home islands. The control and protection of the large number of ships employed for this task were successfully accomplished without loss from enemy action, although a considerable strain was placed on the available facilities and forces.

With the cessation of hostilities, the Commander Seventh Fleet was relieved of all responsibilities as senior naval officer in the Southwest Pacific area and with a reconstituted Seventh Fleet assigned the tasks of occupying and controlling the waters of the Yellow Sea, Gulf of Pohai, the coastal waters of China south to twenty degrees north and the navigable portion of the Yangtze River; the landing and establishing of United States Army troops in Korea, and United States Marines in North China; the evacuation of ex-prisoners of war and internees; the support of operations of United States forces in the China Theater; the clearance of mine fields and opening of ports in the Seventh Fleet area; and the routing and protection of friendly shipping. The planning for and execution of these tasks in the initial stages were necessarily accomplished in great haste and with certain improvisations. However, the new organization has been perfected rapidly with attendant uniformly satisfactory progress.

FAST CARRIER FORCE PRE-INVASION OPERATIONS AGAINST JAPAN

After nearly three weeks of replenishment in Leyte Gulf, subsequent to their support of the Okinawa operation, the fast carrier forces of Admiral Halsey's Third Fleet, comprising the greatest mass of sea power ever assembled, proceeded northward on 1 July toward Japan. This huge armada was to complete the destruction of the Japanese fleet, conduct a preinvasion campaign of destruction against every industry and resource contributing to Japan's ability to wage war, and maintain maximum pressure on the Japanese in order to lower their will to fight.

On 10 July the force arrived in the launching area, 170 miles southeast of Tokyo. On that day strikes were made against airfields and industrial plants in the Tokyo area; 72 planes were destroyed on the ground and extensive damage inflicted on other targets. No attempt was made to conceal the location of the fleet but, in spite of this, little enemy air opposition was encountered.

Admiral Halsey then moved north to attack northern Honshu and southern Hokkaido on 14–15 July. Aerial strikes dealt a severe blow to critical water transportation facilities between Hokkaido and Honshu, when 5 railroad ferries were sunk and 4 others damaged. Again, little air opposition was encountered by our planes. Simultaneously with these air strikes heavy units of the force shelled Kamaishi and Muroran, causing damage to the steel mills and oil installations in those cities.

On 17 July the Third Fleet moved south and was joined by units of the British Pacific Fleet under the command of Vice Admiral Rawlings. Admiral Halsey was in over-all command and, on that day, ordered the first combined American-British bombardment of the Japanese homeland. Battleships fired 2000 tons of shells into the coastal area northeast of Tokyo and encountered no enemy opposition during the operation.

On the following day American and British carrier-based planes struck at enemy fleet units concealed at the Yokosuka naval base in Tokyo Bay. NAGATO, one of two remaining Japanese battleships, was badly damaged. Numerous shore installations and transportation facilities were also hit.

On 24 and 25 July the combined British and American naval forces launched extensive air strikes against targets in the Inland Sea area. The planes concentrated on the major fleet units still afloat at the Kure naval base. Six major ships were badly damaged and, in all, 22 naval units totalling 258,000 tons were either sunk or put out of action, sounding the death knell of Japanese sea power. Intensive antiaircraft fire was met, and for the first time the enemy mounted aggressive, air-borne opposition. A total of 113 enemy aircraft were destroyed during the two-day attack, while only 12 British and American planes were lost.

A follow-up attack was made on Kure and the Inland Sea area by the carrier-based planes on 28 July. Reconnaissance indicated that the enemy fleet units had been effectively reduced by the previous strikes, but additional bombs were dropped for good measure. Extensive damage was also done to merchant shipping and to vital shore installations, particularly railroad facilities. Strong air opposition was encountered once more, but our aircraft knocked down 21 Japanese planes air-borne and destroyed 123 on the ground for a total of 144 for the day, while our forces lost 36.

On 30 July the Tokyo area was harassed for the third time in three weeks by aircraft from the fast carriers, our airmen destroying 121 enemy planes during the day and inflicting severe damage on lighter enemy fleet units found in the region. Meanwhile, the fast battleships were shelling the port of Hamamatsu on the east coast of central Honshu, spreading havoc in that area.

For the first eight days of August the harassed Japanese homeland was given a temporary respite while Admiral Halsey's fleet was riding out a heavy typhoon. On 9 and 10 August, however, the offensive was renewed with another air attack on northern Honshu. It was known that the enemy had withdrawn a large part of his air force to fields in this area, and the strikes were designed to destroy as many of them as possible. The plan was partially successful, for during the two days 397 enemy planes were destroyed and 320 others damaged. Almost no air-borne opposition was encountered, and all but 10 of the destroyed planes were caught on the ground. The British and Americans lost only 34 planes. While these air strikes were in progress, battleships from the Third Fleet bombarded the coastal city of Kamaishi for a second time, inflicting further heavy damage on the steel mills in the area.

Admiral Halsey's final blow was delivered against Tokyo on 13 August. Airfields and other military installations were the primary targets, with 46 planes being destroyed on the ground. The Japanese tried to get through to the surface ships, but 21 planes were shot down in the futile attempt. The strong protective screen around the fleet was too much for the fading enemy air strength.

On 15 August the order of Fleet Admiral Nimitz to "cease fire" was received too late to stop the first of the day's air strikes planned for Tokyo. It knocked 30 enemy planes out of the air and destroyed 10 more on the ground. The second strike had also been launched, but it was recalled in time; its pilots were ordered to jettison their bombs and return to their carriers.

Since 10 July the forces under Admiral Halsey's command had destroyed or damaged 2804 enemy planes, sunk or damaged 148 Japanese combat ships, sunk or damaged 1598 enemy merchant ships, destroyed 195 locomotives, and damaged 109 more. In addition, heavy blows had been struck at industrial targets and war industries, effectively supplementing the bombing by B-29's. This impressive record speaks for itself and helps to explain the sudden collapse of Japan's will to resist. Naval air power, acting in close conjunction with naval surface power and Army bombers, had beaten enemy land-based air power besides inflicting critical losses on naval ships and seriously damaging many shore targets.

CONTRIBUTORY OPERATIONS

Although somewhat obscured by the more spectacular amphibious assaults and carrier force operations which marked our major advances toward the Japanese homeland, there were many other vital and necessary activities which by their nature had more the form of a continuous pressure than of major individual operations against the enemy. Outstanding parts were played by the submarines (whose achievements are summarized in a later chapter), by the land-based air forces, and, to a lesser extent, by the Northern Pacific forces.

Northern Pacific Forces

Although usually hampered by foul weather, which ran the gamut of fogs, rain, gales, snow, and floating ice fields, naval and air forces of the Northern Pacific continued to exert pressure against the Japanese-held northern Kurile Islands, posing a constant threat to the enemy's northern flank.

Army and Navy aircraft flew such searches as weather permitted, bombed and rocketed Japanese shipping and bases in the Kuriles several times each month, and maintained photographic coverage to detect any increase in enemy installations. Light naval task forces, usually consisting of 3 of the older cruisers and from 5 to 7 destroyers, bombarded coastal positions in the Kuriles once in March, once in May, twice in June, and once in July, and even penetrated the Okhotsk Sea in search of enemy shipping. On 11–12 August cruisers and destroyers commanded by Rear Admiral J. H. Brown, Jr., combining a high-speed antishipping sweep on both sides of the central and northern Kuriles with bombardments of enemy shore installations, intercepted two enemy convoys and destroyed 10 trawlers and a subchaser.

Land-Based Air Forces

With the exception of the B-29's of the Twentieth Air Force, the principal missions of land-based air forces of the Pacific Ocean Areas were support of the Iwo Jima and Okinawa operations, attacks on Japanese shipping, and continued neutralization of by-passed enemy bases.

During the period of this report, the greatest expansion of land-based air forces took place in the Army's Twentieth Air Force. Airfields in the Marianas were constantly increased to accommodate greater numbers of B-29's. When Iwo Jima became available for emergency landings, greater bomb loads were carried safely, and fighter support became possible. From that time until the end of hostilities, strategic bombing against vital Japanese industries and cities was constantly stepped up, coordinating with bombing by fleet planes, and many thousands of mines were dropped in Japan's harbors and sea lanes. Destruction resulting from these raids, and the final blows dealt with two powerful atomic bombs, undoubtedly were a major factor in forcing Japanese capitulation.

Of less spectacular nature, yet also important in their effect on the war, were the operations of other land-based air forces against enemy shipping and by-passed islands in the Pacific. With the capture and development of airfields on Okinawa, Army and Marine Corps bombers and fighters of the Tactical Air Force and Fleet Air Wings One and Eighteen were brought within easy range of the China coast, Korea, Shikoku, Kyushu, and even Honshu, and were enabled to bring Japanese shipping in these waters to a virtual standstill. Okinawa, as did Iwo Jima, returned rich dividends for the investment involved in its capture by hastening the war's end.

Support of the Iwo Jima and Okinawa campaigns, routine searches, and constant neutralizing attacks against the many islands of the Pacific still in the hands of enemy garrisons, were tasks which absorbed much of the time and effort of Army, Navy, and Marine land-based aviators throughout the Pacific, and were well coordinated with the air operations of the fast carrier task forces in the advance toward Japan.

The last night of the war saw the first and only offensive mission carried out from Okinawa against Japan by the B-29's of the recently deployed Eighth Air Force, with their target the industrial city of Kumagaya in northern Honshu.

Antisubmarine Warfare in the Pacific

By 1 March Japanese submarines had been nearly driven out of the central Pacific by our countermeasures. Only an occasional supply or reconnaissance submarine ventured into this area. Near the beginning of March Japanese submarines were encountered near Iwo Jima, and during the Okinawa campaign the Japanese made their main submarine effort around that island. After the fall of Okinawa, most of the Japanese submarines were drawn back to the homeland to aid in the defense against our expected invasion. In addition to these anti-invasion employments, the enemy was building and using a number of cargo submarines in an attempt to supply by-passed positions. A considerable number of his submarines were also employed for antisubmarine work. Our submarines made many reports of sighting hostile periscopes and torpedo wakes. A number of German U-boats continued to operate out of Penang, even after the surrender of Germany.

In the main the Japanese submarines were ineffective, and our antisubmarine measures, bolstered by the advanced techniques used in the Atlantic, took heavy toll. In return we suffered very light losses, with the exception of the sinking—with heavy loss of life—of the heavy cruiser INDIANAPOLIS, probably by an enemy submarine, on 30 July. In March and April antisubmarine measures executed by screening vessels, by planes from land bases and carriers, and by regular hunter-killer groups, effectively checked the Japanese submarines and accounted for several kills. It is interesting to note that several of these kills were made by our own submarines. Through May, June, July, and August the Japanese put an increased underwater fleet around Okinawa and managed to cause some damage, including the sinking of a destroyer escort in July. For these operations the Japanese were building and operating large numbers of midget submarines and human torpedoes. It is believed that the destroyer escort mentioned above was sunk by ramming a human torpedo. The Japanese submarine effort was rapidly descending to the suicide level; but by the end of the war it was well under control, as the Japanese shipyards were taking heavy damage from the air and more escorts were being released from the Atlantic after the surrender of Germany.

THE SURRENDER AND OCCUPATION OF JAPAN

With the reduction of Okinawa in June 1945, the campaign against the Japanese Empire was concentrated on the home islands, with intensified bombing by the Army Strategic Air Force from the Marianas, a rapid acceleration of attacks by the Okinawa-based Tactical Air Force, and far-ranging air attacks and bombardments by the Third Fleet. These operations were climaxed by the employment of the atomic bomb against Hiroshima and Nagasaki and, almost simultaneously, Russia's entry into the war to open a strong three-pronged attack on Japanese forces in Manchuria and Korea.

On 14 August Japan declared her acceptance of the terms of the Potsdam Proclamation, which involved complete disarmament and surrender of all military forces and equipment as set forth by the heads of the states of Great Britain, the United States, and China. The instrument of surrender was presented to Japanese representatives by General of the Army MacArthur at Manila on 19 August 1945. This instrument provided that Commander in Chief, Army Forces, Pacific should receive the surrender of the Imperial General Headquarters, its senior commanders, and all ground, sea, air, and auxiliary forces in the main islands of Japan, minor islands adjacent thereto, Korea south of 38° North latitude, and the Philippines; whereas the Commander in Chief, U.S. Pacific Fleet was designated to receive the surrender of the senior Japanese commanders and of all ground, sea, air and auxiliary forces in the Japanese mandated islands, Ryukyus, Bonins, and other Pacific islands.

For this purpose the Third and Fifth Fleets, which had heretofore been alternative organizational titles for much the same assemblage of ships, were now each assigned approximately equal forces and became separate entities. Correlating the fleet assignments with the various zones of responsibility assigned the various Army commands, Commander in Chief, U.S. Pacific Fleet assigned naval responsibility to the Third Fleet for the zone of the Eighth Army (to the northward and eastward of a line crossing Honshu west of Yokohama and Tokyo); to the Fifth Fleet for the zone of the Sixth Army (the remainder of the Japanese home islands to the southward and westward of that line); to the Seventh Fleet for that of the XXIV Corps (Korea south of 38° North latitude), as well as any operations which might be carried out in Chinese waters; and to the Commander, North Pacific, local responsibility for northern Honshu and for Hokkaido.

Similarly, the three amphibious forces were coordinated with the respective fleets and armies; the Third Amphibious Force under the Commander Third Fleet for operations of the Eighth Army; the Fifth under the Commander Fifth Fleet for operations of the Sixth Army; and the Seventh under the Commander Seventh Fleet

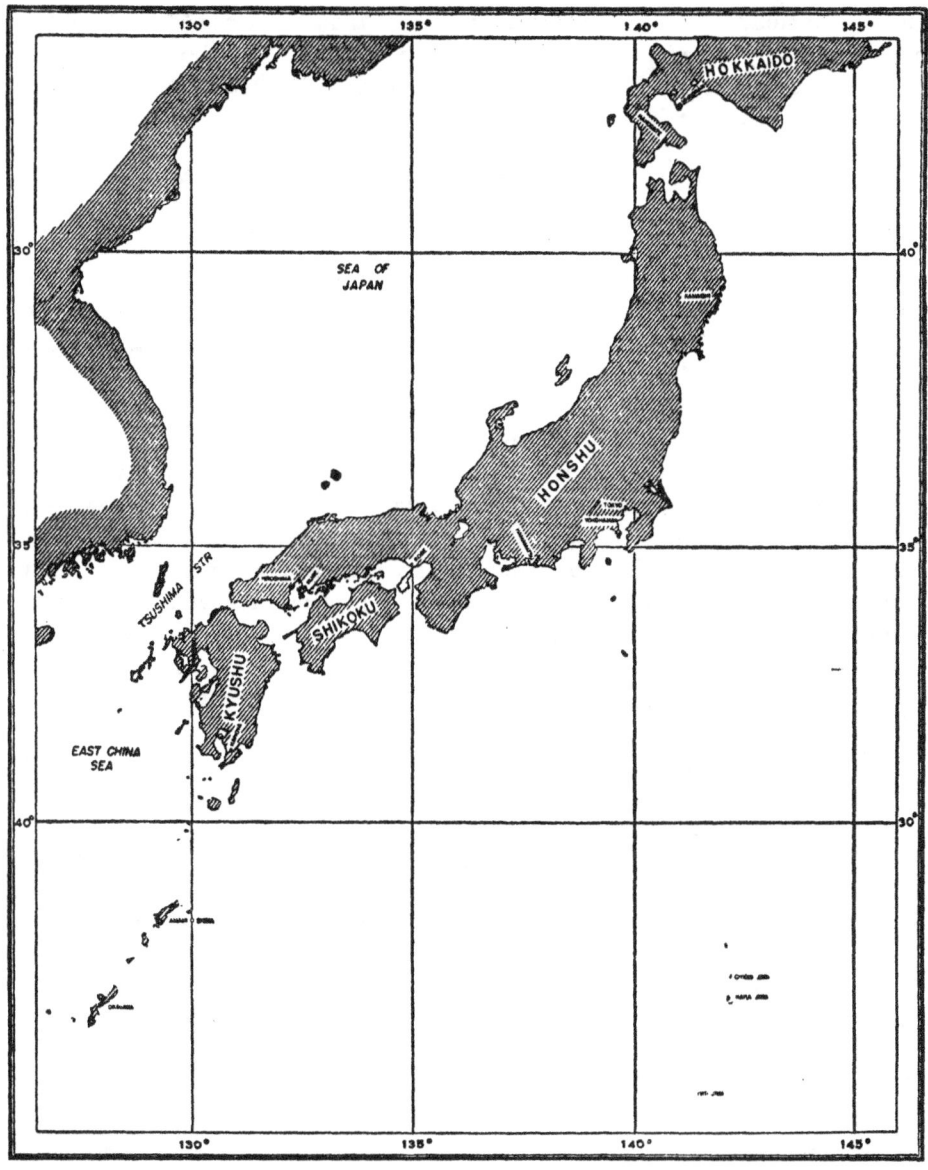

Plate 17.

for operations of the XXIV Corps and of any troops which might require transportation to China. B-day (the date designated by Commander in Chief, Army Forces, Pacific for the initiation of operations) was proclaimed as 15 August 1945. At that time orders were issued to the U.S. Pacific Fleet and to other forces under the command of Fleet Admiral Nimitz to cease offensive operations against the Japanese.

On 28 August a small force of our Army Air Force technicians landed at Atsugi Airfield, 14 miles southwest of Tokyo, to prepare the way for a subsequent large-scale air-borne landing and for the landing at the Yokosuka naval base of Marine and Navy units. Originally it had been planned that this preliminary air-borne force should land at Atsugi on the 26th, and that General of the Army MacArthur should land there personally on the 28th to discuss occupation arrangements with members of the Imperial General Staff; simultaneously, Marine and Navy units should land at the Yokosuka naval base below Tokyo, as well as at points in Sagami Bay.

The beginning of the occupation, however, was delayed 48 hours by a typhoon, which also caused postponement from 31 August until 2 September of signing of the formal instrument of surrender, a copy of which Japanese emissaries had brought back from Manila. Nevertheless, on the morning of 27 August an advanced unit of the Third Fleet, guided by a group of Japanese naval officers, harbor pilots, and interpreters, and provided with maps and charts, moved into Sagami Bay, which is just southwest of Tokyo Bay.

On 29 August Fleet Admiral Nimitz arrived from Guam to break his flag in the battleship SOUTH DAKOTA. Aboard MISSOURI, Admiral Halsey, Commander Third Fleet, entered Tokyo Bay and anchored off Yokosuka naval base. The following day General of the Army MacArthur arrived at Atsugi Airfield to set up General Headquarters at Yokohama. With him came an aerial armada of troop-carrying planes. At the same time about 10,000 Marines and naval personnel landed and took possession of the Yokosuka base and neighboring fortress islands. Working toward a junction, the two forces deployed. The last day of August many American prisoners of war were freed and the area of occupation was expanded; new forces came ashore from transports, some groups reaching the outskirts of Tokyo.

The Japanese naval base of Tateyama, across the bay from Yokosuka, was occupied by Marines on 1 September, as American control spread smoothly and swiftly throughout the whole area south of the capital.

The formal surrender of the Japanese Imperial Government, the Japanese Imperial General Headquarters, and all Japanese and Japanese-controlled armed forces wherever located, was signed on board the battleship MISSOURI in Tokyo Bay at 0908 on 2 September 1945. General of the Army MacArthur signed as Supreme Commander for the Allied Powers, and Fleet Admiral Nimitz signed as representative for the United States.

Even before the formal surrender of the Japanese government, the Japanese commander of Mille Atoll in the Marshall Islands had surrendered on 22 August aboard the destroyer escort LEVY, Mille being the first of the many Japanese island possessions to capitulate as a result of the Emperor's acceptance of the Potsdam Proclamation. Nine days later, on 31 August, on board the destroyer BAGLEY, Rear Admiral F. E. M. Whiting received the surrender of Marcus Island.

The largest-scale island surrender, however, came shortly after the senior Japanese Army and Navy officers at Truk Atoll had received word of the capitulation of the Imperial government. By the act of signing the terms of the surrender, the Commander of the 31st Imperial Japanese Army committed the following islands under his control to laying down their arms and awaiting United States occupation: Truk, Wake, the Palaus, Mortlock, Mille, Ponape, Kusaie, Jaluit, Maloelap, Wotje, Enderby, Mereyon, Rota and Pagan. The affixing of the signature of the Commander of the Imperial Japanese Fourth Fleet further entailed the surrender of the Japanese Navy-controlled bases of Namorik, Nauru, and Ocean. In the case of both Army and Navy surrenders, the actual capitulation by individual islands was effected over a period of several days following; however, their submission became only a matter of time after the Truk ceremony.

It was estimated that a total of 130,000 Japanese military personnel were involved in the Truk surrender—on Truk itself a total of 49,000 military and 9,000 civilians; on Babelthuap in the Palaus, 27,000 military and 12,000 civilians; on Ponape 8,900; and additional large groups on Rota and Yap, with the remainder spread thinly throughout the Caroline and Marianas Islands. On 3 September the surrender of the Bonin Islands was received, and four days later the capitulation of 105,000 Japanese Army and Navy forces in some 60 islands of the Ryukyu group was signed at General Stilwell's Tenth Army Headquarters on Okinawa.

Five days after the formal Japanese surrender, General of the Army MacArthur entered Tokyo, and his troops raised the United States flag over the American Embassy. It was the same flag which had flown over Washington, D.C., on 7 December 1941; which had been hoisted over Rome and Berlin; and which had been flown on the battleship MISSOURI while the Japanese signed their surrender there.

Our access to the Japanese homeland gave opportunity at last for securing reliable information as to conditions there, both by our own observation and by conversation with Japanese officials who no longer had the incentive or the ability to deceive either their enemies or their own people. It was at once apparent that while the damage to their cities and production centers by strategic bombing was fully as great as photographic reconnaissance had indicated, the strangulation from our less obvious but relentlessly effective surface and submarine blockade and from our carrier-based air attacks had been a decisive factor in the enemy's collapse. Their merchant marine had been reduced to a fraction of its former size; of the few remaining ships, mostly small ones, only half were still operable. Their food situation was critical, and their remaining resources in fuel and all strategic materials were not less so. It had been known that their few remaining carriers and heavy naval vessels had been damaged, but it appeared that the fury of our carrier strikes had forced them to withdraw all but a handful of men from these ships, practically abandoning them.

Never before in the history of war had there been a more convincing example of the effectiveness of sea power than when a well-armed, highly efficient and undefeated army of over a million men surrendered their homeland unconditionally to the invader without even token resistance.

True, the devastation already wrought by past bombings, as well as the terrible demonstration of power by the first atomic bombs, augured nothing less for the Japanese than total extinction; yet without sea power there would have been no possession of Saipan, Iwo Jima and Okinawa from which to launch these bombings. True, the Japanese homeland might have been taken by assault in one final amphibious operation of tremendous magnitude, yet without sea power such an assault could not have been attempted.

III
Logistics and Bases—Pacific

BEFORE the conclusion of the war, plans were maturing for the invasion and occupation of the main Japanese islands. Two major operations were projected: the first, with the code name of "Olympic," against southern Kyushu; after consolidation there, the next—"Coronet"—into the Tokyo plain area which is the industrial heart of Japan. The amphibious parts of these operations—involving the preparation of landing beaches by mine sweeping, underwater demolition teams, bombardment and bombing; the transportation of the assault troops; and the initial landing for the establishment of firmly held beachheads—were to have been the responsibility of Fleet Admiral Nimitz.

The large-scale bombardments and bombings of the Third Fleet that began on 10 July were actually in preparation for operation "Olympic." In mid-August, as the war ended, the United States Navy had in the Pacific 90 per cent of its combatant vessels of submarine size or larger and 42 per cent of its combatant aircraft. These ships, aircraft, support auxiliaries and landing craft included:

Battleships	23
Aircraft carriers	26
Escort carriers	64
Cruisers	52
Destroyers	323
Escort vessels	298
Submarines	181
Mine craft	160
Auxiliary vessels	1,060
Large landing craft	2,783
Combat aircraft	14,847
Transport, training and utility aircraft	1,286

All six Marine divisions, or 100 per cent of the Marine Corps combat strength, were also available for Pacific operations. The "Olympic" and "Coronet" operations as planned would have been the largest amphibious operations in history. While the Third Fleet provided strategic cover and support for the amphibious forces making the invasion, the Fifth Fleet was to have executed the amphibious phases of the invasions of Kyushu and Honshu by transporting their troops and equipment to the attack position on shore. By the application of naval force they would have established the necessary ground troops in positions favorable for further maneuvers to complete the destruction of Japanese ground forces.

In discharging its responsibilities for the amphibious phase of the Kyushu or "Olympic" operation the United States Navy would have employed 3033 combatant and noncombatant vessels of a size larger than personnel landing boats. Although the application of our sea power in its various forms proved sufficient to bring Japan to terms without the necessity of invading her home islands, the possibility of invasion on the scale contemplated indicates the amazing progress in matters of supply and support that had been made in less than four years of war.

In this evolution advance bases have played a vital role. The 1940 Navy had no properly equipped advance bases other than Pearl Harbor. More than 400 have since been established in the Atlantic and Pacific areas in order to maintain the fleet and air forces in the forward areas where there was fighting to be done. As we progressed across the Pacific, islands captured in one amphibious operation were converted into bases which became spring boards for the next advance. These bases were set up for various purposes depending upon the next operation. At first they were mainly air bases for the support of bombers and for the use of protective fighters. This gradually changed to the establishment of staging bases for the anchoring, fueling and refitting of armadas of transports and cargo ships, and for replenishing mobile support squadrons which actually accompanied the combat forces and serviced them at sea. Further advances made necessary the development of repair and refitting bases for large amphibious forces. As we progressed further and further across the Pacific, it became necessary to set up main repair bases for the maintenance, repair and servicing of larger fleet units. The first of such large bases was set up at Espiritu Santo in the New Hebrides and was followed by a main repair base at Manus in the Admiralty Islands. It was then determined that so long as ships were in condition to function in the battle line, minor battle damage and derangements should be rectified in the forward area, thus eliminating the necessity of returning ships to continental bases or even to the Hawaiian Islands.

These conditions were recognized and steps were taken to support the entire fleet in the Marianas, Philippines and Okinawa areas. A very large base, capable of supporting one third of the Pacific Fleet, was set up at Guam; another large base was established at Leyte-Samar; a third was in process of construction at Okinawa when the war ended. Each of these bases was designed to dock ships of various sizes, some being able to take ships of the heaviest tonnage. All of the bases could repair major battle damage to hull and equipment. Facilities were established ashore with piers, roads and machine shops, in large measure duplicating the type of facilities found at any of our navy yards. There was also provided the replenishment storage necessary to restock every type of vessel with fuel, ammunition and consumable supplies as well as food. The stocks currently on hand at Guam would have filled a train 120 miles long. The magnitude of the fuel supply alone is indicated by the total of 25,026,000 barrels of bulk fuel which was shipped to the Pacific in June 1945 for military purposes. At Guam alone one million gallons of aviation gas were used daily. As these bases were gradually pushed forward, assault forces were brought two to five days' steaming nearer the enemy. By proper selection of the strategic points necessary to accomplish the advance, we were able to by-pass and ignore many bases established by the Japanese which they could no longer use because of their loss of command of the sea.

But for this chain of advance bases the fleet could not have operated in the western reaches of the Pacific without the necessity for many more ships and planes than it actually had. A base to supply or repair a fleet 5000 miles closer to the enemy multiplies the power which can be maintained constantly against him and greatly lessens the problems of supply and repair. The scope of the advance base program is indicated by the fact that the personnel assigned directly to it aggregated almost one fifth of the entire personnel of the Navy—over half a million men, including almost 200,000 Seabees. In the concluding months of the war 82 per cent of the Seabees were in the Pacific, the vast majority of them at work on bases. In the Naval Supply Depot at Guam there were 93 miles of road. At Okinawa alone there were more than fifty naval construction battalions building roads, supply areas, airfields and fleet facilities for what would have been one of the gigantic staging areas for the final invasion of Japan.

In the period covered by this report almost two million measurement tons of materiel were shipped in connection with the advance base program.

An essential element in the facilities of our advance bases were floating drydocks, which were capable of receiving vessels ranging from small craft to the battleship MISSOURI. One hundred fifty two of these docks were produced. They proved their special value in the speed with which damaged ships could be returned to combat.

As our advance came nearer to the Japanese islands, the rear areas which had been the scene of combat operations in earlier months were utilized for logistic support. In the South Pacific, for example, more than 400 ships were staged for the Okinawa operation. They received varied replenishment services, including routine and emergency overhaul as required. Approximately 100,000 officers and men were staged from this area alone for the Okinawa campaign, including four Army and Marine combat divisions plus certain headquarters and corps troops and various Army and Navy service units. Concurrently with the movement of troops large quantities of combat equipment and necessary material were transferred forward, thus contributing automatically to the roll-up of the South Pacific area. Similarly in the Southwest Pacific area Army service troops were moved with their equipment from the New Guinea area to the Philippines in order to prepare staging facilities for troops deployed from the European Theater. The roll-up was similarly continued and progress made in reducing our installations in Australia and New Guinea.

This vast deployment of our forces throughout the Pacific required careful planning not only at the front but also in the United States. During the last six months of the war the problem of materiel distribution became of primary importance, and throughout this period our system of logistic support had to be constantly modified to meet the rapidly changing tactical conditions. War production had shifted the emphasis from procurement to distribution; that is, while production was still of high importance, a still greater problem was that of getting well balanced materiel support to designated positions at certain fixed times. Put another way, motion, not size, had become the important factor. It was, nevertheless, essential in insuring the uninterrupted flow of material through the pipe-line of supply to our forces overseas that the reservoir within the United States which kept these pipelines full did not become too large. On 1 June 1945 a set of standards for Navy inventory control was promulgated which stressed a balance between procurement and inventory. The attainment of these standards was of primary importance to efficient distribution of materiel within the United States, and particularly on the west coast, which was our major base for the logistic support of the Pacific Fleet.

It has always been a cardinal principle of our Pacific logistic support policy that the west coast be utilized to its maximum capacity. There are two reasons for this: the source of supply must be as close to the point of requirement as possible so that inventories at advance bases may be kept to a minimum; secondly, greater utilization of shipping can be achieved by the shortest haul possible. The integration of these two elements, supply and shipping, was a major task in 1945.

When the collapse of Germany was imminent, a review in conjunction with the Army of our policy of maximum west coast utilization was necessary. It was concluded that approximately 68 per cent of the Navy's predicted logistic requirements would have to be moved from the west coast to bases in the Marianas, Philippines and Okinawa, as well as to the mobile logistic support forces—Service Squadrons Six and Ten. Bases in the Admiralties, New Guinea, and the Hawaiian Sea Frontier, since they were in nonoperational areas, could be supported from the east and Gulf coasts. In May, after a joint Army-Navy study, a ceiling was set on the amount of materiel which could be shipped to the Pacific from the west coast by the Army and Navy; this ceiling was based on the estimated capacity of the six major west coast ports. By detailed study of the capacities of port facilities and supply activities, as well as a complete analysis of the types of commodities shipped by the Navy since the first of the year, Commander, Western Sea Frontier (who coordinated naval logistic matters on the west coast) reallocated the Navy's share of west coast capacity among the various ports. Estimated tonnages were set for each port, both by types of commodity and by overseas destination to be served.

In the establishment and execution of this planned employment of west coast facilities, Commander, Western Sea Frontier provided one of the major links between the distribution systems of the continental United States and Pacific Theater. Since the flow of materiel and the ships to carry it are immobilized when more ships have sailed to a destination than that destination can receive, the planned employment of west coast ports was a matter of vital concern.

This was facilitated by the expansion of the functions of the Western Sea Frontier which had taken place in November 1944 when the necessity for coastal defense had assumed relatively minor proportions. The expansion of function included placing every major activity of the three west coast naval districts under a single command, with a view to coordinating all essential matters of materiel and personnel and to eliminating activities within the Western Sea Frontier which did not contribute to the major effort.

While defensive operations became secondary, the responsibility of the Western Sea Frontier to regulate the movement of ships and aircraft through frontier waters was greatly increased. The eastern Pacific had become a network of channels for the passage of traffic to the forward areas. These channels were the most heavily traveled military highways on and above the sea. In the period covered by this report there were over 17,000 sailings of vessels large and small through the six million square miles of Western Sea Frontier waters. In the same period an average of one aircraft arrived on or departed from the west coast each fifteen minutes on the longest overwater flight lane in the world.

The substantial increase in the level of Navy materiel movement which occurred between March and July 1945 fully justified the planning for an increased west coast load which had been undertaken. Total exports, excluding aircraft, from May through July showed a 25 per cent increase over March and April shipments. Items used in the construction of new bases doubled during May and July as compared with March and April. Ammunition shipments doubled, because of the considerable expenditures during the Okinawa campaign (where 50,000 tons of 5-inch to 16-inch projectiles were fired by surface ships) and the necessity for building up a reserve for the assault upon Japan.

By the vast system thus developed the great concluding operations in the Pacific were supported. Each month in the immediate past we shipped out 600,000 long tons a month into the Pacific Ocean areas. The momentum generated by this materiel operation can be imagined. The problem presented by the deceleration of this great tide of supply after V-J day can also be imagined.

The following steps taken in the days immediately after the surrender of Japan indicate the effort the Navy has made to reduce its logistic energy as rapidly as possible without damage either to the domestic economy or to the support of fleet elements still at sea. All shipments of ammunition and of advance base components were stopped except those required for occupational purposes and those specifically requested by the fleet commanders as necessary for further operations. Maintenance materiel movements overseas were subjected to careful review and reduction. Stock levels at overseas bases of provisions, clothing, equipment, medical needs, aviation requirements and spare parts items were reduced to a thirty-day minimum and a sixty-day maximum. Orders prepared in advance cancelling procurement of materials were mailed in tremendous volume from the Navy Department on the night of 14 August. All continental public works construction projects, including those actually under construction and those on which it was possible to begin construction, were carefully reviewed—projects which were not required for demobilization purposes or postwar purposes were cancelled.

IV
Submarine Operations

SUBMARINE warfare was an important factor in the defeat of the Japanese. With the end of hostilities, it is now possible to reveal in greater detail the splendid accomplishments of the submarines of the Pacific Fleet and the Seventh Fleet. Our submarines are credited with almost two thirds of the total tonnage of Japanese merchant marine losses, or a greater part than all other forces, surface and air, Army and Navy combined. (See Plate 18.) Of the total number of Japanese naval vessels sunk, our submarines are credited with almost one third.

ATTACKS ON MERCHANT SHIPPING

Our submarines, operating thousands of miles from their bases and deep within enemy-controlled waters, began their campaign of attrition on Japanese shipping immediately following the attack on Pearl Harbor, and continued to fight with telling effectiveness until the Japanese capitulated. During the early part of 1942, while our surface forces were still weakened by the Japanese initial attack of 7 December 1941, submarines were virtually the only United States naval forces which could be risked in offensive operations. Although the number of submarines available at the start was so small that the 1500 ton fleet-type class was augmented by older types, submarine attacks produced immediate and damaging results, which were greatly needed at the time. They made it more difficult for the enemy to consolidate his forward positions, to reinforce his threatened areas, and to pile up in Japan an adequate reserve of fuel oil, rubber, and other loot from his newly conquered territory. Their operations thus hastened our ultimate victory and resulted in the saving of American lives.

Sinking of enemy merchant ships rose from 134 ships totalling 580,390 tons in 1942 to 284 ships totalling 1,341,968 tons in 1943. Then in 1944, when submarine coordinated attack groups reached the peak of their effectiveness, the merchant fleet of Japan suffered its worst and most crippling blow—492 ships of 2,387,780 tons were sunk or destroyed in submarine torpedo and gun attacks. The figures given above, which are based on evaluated estimates, include only ships of 1000 tons and larger. It should be borne in mind that our submarines sank or destroyed, chiefly by gunfire, large numbers of smaller vessels, particularly during the latter part of the war, when few large enemy ships still remained afloat.

In 1945, because of the tremendous attrition on Japanese shipping by our earlier submarine operations and the destructive sweeps by our fleets and carrier air forces, enemy merchantmen sunk by submarines dropped to 132 ships totalling 469,872 tons. The advance of our forces had further driven Japanese ships back to the coast lines and shallow waters of Japan and the Asiatic mainland. Our submarines followed the enemy shipping into these dangerous waters and made many skillful and daring attacks, such as the one in April when TIRANTE entered a patrolled anchorage in Quelpart Island to blow up a 10,000 ton tanker and two 1,500 ton escort vessels, which were peacefully lying at anchor. Further south, persistent submarine patrolling plus air sweeps had, by the end of March, stopped almost all enemy traffic along the sea lanes of the East Indies and the coast of Indo-China.

Plate 18.

For a time, Japanese shipping continued to ply in the East China and Yellow Seas, but the invasion of Okinawa in April soon made the East China Sea untenable to the Japanese. Causing heavy damage, our submarines were very active during April and May in the Yellow Sea and along the east and south coasts of the main Japanese islands. In June the landlocked Sea of Japan was penetrated in force. The submarines had excellent hunting, and in a series of coordinated attacks did tremendous damage to the remnants of the Japanese merchant fleet. One of the intruders, BARB, even landed a party on the coast of Honshu, and successfully blew up a bridge and the speeding train that was crossing it. By the end of the war, the Japanese merchant fleet was virtually nonexistent.

ATTACKS ON NAVAL VESSELS

While United States submarines were effectively eliminating the Japanese merchant fleet, they were also carrying out damaging attacks on Japanese naval units. During the course of the war, the following principal Japanese combatant types were sent to the bottom as a result of these attacks:

Battleship	1
Carriers	4
Escort carriers	4
Heavy cruisers	3
Light cruisers	9
Destroyers	43
Submarines	23
Minor combatant vessels and naval auxiliaries (including 60 escort vessels)	189

Details of these sinkings will be found in Appendix A. While the loss of the heavier naval units was critical to the Japanese, especially as the strength of our surface fleet increased, the surprisingly high losses of enemy destroyers and escort vessels to submarine attack are particularly noteworthy. Our submarines, refusing to accept the role of the hunted, even after their presence was known, frequently attacked their arch-enemies under circumstances of such great risk that the failure of their attack on the enemy antisubmarine vessel placed the submarine in extreme danger of loss. So successful, however, were these attacks that the Japanese developed a dangerous deficiency of destroyer screening units in their naval task forces, and their merchant shipping was often inadequately escorted.

SPECIAL MISSIONS

Among the special missions performed by submarines were reconnaissance, rescue, supply and lifeguard duties. An outstanding result of effective submarine reconnaissance was the vital advance information furnished our surface and air forces prior to the Battle for Leyte Gulf, information which contributed materially to that victory. Our submarines in a number of instances rescued stranded personnel and performed personnel evacuation duties, notably from Corregidor. The supplies and equipment delivered by submarines to friendly guerilla forces in the Philippines did much to keep alive the spirit of resistance in those islands.

When our air forces came into positions from which they could intensify their attacks on Japanese-held territory, United States submarines were called upon to carry out lifeguard operations to rescue aviators forced down at sea in enemy waters. Sometimes assisted by friendly aircraft, which provided fighter cover and assisted in locating survivors, and sometimes operating alone, our submarines rescued more than 500 aviators during the course of the war.

Fifty-two United States submarines were lost from all causes during the war, forty-six due to enemy action, six due to accidents and stranding. These losses were due to continued penetration deep within the enemy zone of defense, far from our bases, and, until the last phase of the war, far beyond the areas where our surface ships and aircraft could operate. Because of the nature of submarine operations and the general necessity of submarines operating alone, the personnel loss in most instances was the entire ship's company. As heavy as were the losses in submarine personnel and equipment, submarine training and building programs supplied replacements so effectively that our submarine force at the end of the war far exceeded its pre-Pearl Harbor strength—and was the most powerful and effective in the world. The Japanese capitulation found our submarines on station searching for the remnants of the Japanese Navy and merchant marine, and on the alert to rescue downed aviators off the coast of Japan.

Submarines of the Pacific Fleet have been commanded by Vice Admiral C. A. Lockwood, Jr., since February 1943. Rear Admiral James Fife, Jr., has commanded the Seventh Fleet submarines, including a number of British and Dutch submarines, since December 1944.

No account of submarine warfare in the Pacific would be complete without mention of the splendid contribution of the submarines of our Allies. These craft, operating in the southwest Pacific, contributed materially to the destruction of Japanese naval and merchant shipping, and inflicted losses over and above those previously listed.

V
Atlantic Operations

THE operations of the United States Navy in the Atlantic and Mediterranean Theaters culminated in the victory of the Allied nations in Europe. The success of the joint antisubmarine campaign and the tremendous achievements in shipbuilding were essential preludes to the landings in Normandy and southern France and the great land offensive, which in three months carried the Allied Expeditionary Forces to the German frontier and brought total victory on German soil six months later. This victory was possible because ships were available and their protection by the Navy effective.

ANTISUBMARINE OPERATIONS

In the antisubmarine campaign our Atlantic Fleet had responsibility for Atlantic areas under United States operational command, and the British Admiralty was responsible for North Atlantic and European operations in which United States naval task forces participated. In the British control areas Commander U.S. Naval Forces in Europe assured proper liaison between the Admiralty and the Tenth Fleet organization in my Headquarters, which was responsible for convoy and routing of United States shipping and the development of plans, weapons, and tactics to be employed in antisubmarine operations.

In the final month of the European war, German submarines made a last determined effort, in great strength, to reach the eastern coast of the United States. That attempt was thwarted by a powerful task force of the U.S. Atlantic Fleet, which, during an engagement lasting several days, destroyed five U-boats. The United States Navy's final successful action against German submarines occurred on 6 May, only two days before V-E day, when a U-boat was sunk off Block Island by the destroyer escort ATHERTON with the frigate MOBERLY assisting. The development of new techniques, the intensive training of antisubmarine crews, and the persistence with which the U-boats were hunted offensively all played vital parts in the surrender campaign. German submarines began to surface and surrender shortly after V-E day, and U.S. Atlantic Fleet escort vessels brought several of them to the United States east coast ports.

A review of antisubmarine and convoy operations since 1939 illustrates clearly these major naval contributions to victory in Europe. The summarized statistics on the Battle of the Atlantic are as follows:

Year	German Submarines Sunk	Allied Shipping Sunk	New Construction			Net Gains or Losses
			U.S.	British	Total	
	(Number)	(In thousands of tons)				
1939 (4 months)	9	810	101	231	332	−478
1940	22	4,407	439	780	1,219	−3,188
1941	35	4,398	1,169	815	1,984	−2,414
1942	85	8,245	5,339	1,843	7,182	−1,063
1943	237	3,611	12,384	2,201	14,585	+10,974
1944	241	1,422	11,639	1,710	13,349	+11,927
1945 (4 months)	153	458	3,551	283	3,834	+3,376
Totals	782	23,351	34,622	7,863	42,485	+19,134

From the foregoing statistical summary the chief features of the Battle of the Atlantic are clear:

(a) Until the closing months of 1942 the German submarines were continuing to reduce the available total of Allied tonnage;

(b) Antisubmarine operations resulted in the sinking of an average of 12 German submarines per month after 1 January 1943, or a total of 480 in the two years 1943–44;

(c) American shipyards alone produced an average of a million tons per month of new merchant ships after 1 January 1943, or a total of 24,000,000 tons in two years.

In the 12 months from 1 June 1944, 135 convoys arrived in United Kingdom ports from overseas with a total of 7157 merchant ships totalling more than 50,000,000 gross tonnage. The escort of this shipping and the provision of trained naval armed guard crews aboard the merchant vessels were among the primary tasks performed by the United States Navy in the prosecution of the war in Europe. The Navy's antisubmarine campaign with the British-United States integrated convoy system was in great part responsible for the vital shipping necessary for the Allied land offensive which broke into the Fortress of Europe in 1944 and overwhelmed the Germans ashore in 1945.

TENTH FLEET

On 15 June 1945 the Tenth Fleet was dissolved. This effective organization was established 20 May 1943 under my direct command, with Headquarters in the Navy Department, to exercise unity of control over United States antisubmarine operations in that part of the Atlantic Ocean under United States strategic control. The first Chief of Staff of the Tenth Fleet was Rear Admiral Francis S. Low, who was relieved in January 1945 by Rear Admiral A. R. McCann.

To the Tenth Fleet were assigned the following tasks:

(a) Destruction of enemy submarines.

(b) Protection of Allied shipping in the Eastern, Gulf, and Caribbean Sea Frontiers.

(c) Support of other antisubmarine forces of our own and of the other Allied nations operating in the Atlantic areas.

(d) Exercise of control of convoys and shipping that were United States responsibilities.

(e) Correlation of United States antisubmarine training and materiel development.

To accomplish these tasks the Tenth Fleet was organized into four principal divisions: Operations; Antisubmarine Measures (materiel, training, analysis and statistics, and operational research); Convoy and Routing; and a Scientific Council composed of distinguished civilian scientists.

The Tenth was a fleet without a ship. However, this highly specialized command coordinated and directed our naval forces in the Battle of the Atlantic, making available the latest intelligence to the Commander in Chief, U.S. Atlantic Fleet and to other fleet and sea frontier commanders who directed the actual operations at sea, and supplying antisubmarine training and operating procedures to our forces afloat. The Tenth Fleet correlated the antisubmarine developments of the various technical bureaus of the Navy Department and the fleet training schools concerned with antisubmarine activities. In addition, it worked closely with the General Staff of the United States Army and with the British Admiralty and Canadian Naval Headquarters to avoid duplication and confusion, and to insure that maximum effort would be directed against the German underseas fleet. The effective work of the Tenth Fleet contributed outstandingly to the success of the United States naval operations in the Battle of the Atlantic.

U.S. NAVAL FORCES IN EUROPE

During the spring and summer of 1945 the United States Naval Forces in Europe were faced with a series of varied responsibilities. Until the surrender of Germany the Navy was actively engaged in coastal offensive operations and in supporting afloat the United States Army's build-up of men and supplies, which included assistance in areas as far inland as the Rhine; with the capitulation of the enemy came the establishment of United States naval commands in Germany to aid in the military occupation and government of that country and in the enforcement of the surrender terms. United States naval components also assumed duties with the Allied Military Missions to Denmark and Norway similar to those already established in France, Belgium and Holland. With the end of the war in Europe, the Navy speeded up the process of closing out the multitude of bases and other facilities which had been established earlier in the war in the United Kingdom, on the Continent, and in the Mediterranean Theater of Operations.

Rhine River Crossing

The crossing of the Rhine River in March 1945 will be remembered as one of the spectacular achievements of the American forces during the closing months of the European war. In this operation the United States Navy had the honor of taking part as a floating segment of General of the Army Eisenhower's forces. LCVP's and

LCM's, which had been used with great success in the coastal Normandy invasion, were again employed to carry our troops on rivers. The naval crews assigned to the operation began training in England in October 1944 and held their final practice maneuvers on the Continent later in the winter. Considerable ingenuity and improvisation were necessary to overcome technical difficulties, the craft employed having been constructed for salt water use and not as river craft in the fresh water of the swift-flowing Rhine. Five LCVP units of 24 craft each were formed in England and later moved to the Continent and placed under the operational control of United States Army commanders and administrative control of Vice Admiral Alan G. Kirk, Commander, U.S. Naval Forces France; of these, three actually participated in the crossings.

The first LCVP unit went into action with the United States First Army at the Remagen bridgehead on 11 March 1945, assisting, under heavy gunfire, in the erection of treadway and heavy pontoon bridges, in ferrying troops, and in patrolling the river. At Oppenheim on 23 March another LCVP unit carried portions of General Patton's Third Army across the Rhine, and the following day made a second crossing under heavy enemy fire at Boppard. Another crossing had been planned at St. Goar, but because of enemy resistance the operation was staged instead at Oberwesel, where, on 26 March, other units of the Third Army were ferried across. Still another crossing was made at Mainz. The LCVP units also served with the United States Ninth Army in its crossing of the Rhine south of Wesel, which occurred almost simultaneously with the Third Army's advance.

U.S. Naval Forces France

A second major operation in which the United States Navy played an important part during the last days of Nazi resistance was that directed against the German-held pockets in western France. Vice Admiral Kirk was placed in operational command of the French naval task force which was assembled for the attack. The United States Navy supplied fuel, training facilities, a repair unit, aircraft, and 24 LCVP's. The operation, which was directed against the enemy forces in the Ile d'Oleron and at the mouth of the Gironde River, began with a general naval bombardment at 0750 on 15 April. For five days the naval task force assisted the French ground forces with naval bombardment and aerial reconnaissance in the assault on Royan and the Point de Grave area at the mouth of the Gironde. By 20 April this section was cleared of the enemy and the assault on the Ile d'Oleron began the following day. Twenty-four United States LCVP's manned by French crews were used and supported by extensive naval bombardment. The actual landings on Ile d'Oleron took place on 30 April and all enemy resistance ceased there on 2 May. With the general capitulation of the enemy on 8 May, the remaining German pockets at La Rochelle, Lorient, St. Nazaire, etc., were occupied by French forces accompanied by American naval observers.

While the Rhine crossings and the attacks on the German pockets were going on, the Navy was continuing its less publicized but equally important task of assisting the Army's build-up of troops and materiel through its port operations, both along the English Channel and in the southern French ports. Men and munitions poured onto the Continent through Marseilles, Toulon, Cherbourg, Le Havre and Rouen. At the great port of Antwerp alone almost 20,000 tons of supplies were unloaded daily.

From the United States Navy's airfield at Dunkeswell in Devon, patrol planes of Fleet Air Wing Seven maintained a constant search of shipping lanes for enemy submarines. When the surrender of Germany came on 8 May, the German High Command was ordered to instruct its U-boats at sea to surface, radio their position, jettison their ammunition, fly a black flag and proceed by fixed routes to prescribed ports. The first U-boat to comply with this order surrendered on 9 May to a PB4Y-1 plane of Fleet Air Wing Seven on patrol off Lands End, England.

U.S. Naval Forces Germany

With the disintegration of the enemy armies and the movement of Allied forces deeper into Germany, the organization of the United States naval command for Germany was put into effect. Vice Admiral Robert L. Ghormley, as Commander, U.S. Naval Forces Germany, became responsible for all United States naval forces operating in Germany. As head of the Naval Division of the United States Group of the Allied Control Council, Vice Admiral Ghormley acted as General of the Army Eisenhower's adviser in all naval matters and conferred with the other Allied naval commanders in Germany on such questions as repairs of shipping and disposition of enemy naval vessels. In June Vice Admiral Ghormley established his headquarters in Frankfurt. On 1 July he assumed operational control of all naval forces on the Continent assigned to occupation duties or to the support of the Army in the European Theater of Operations. These included, in addition to the forces in Germany, the United States Naval Components of the Military Missions to Norway, Denmark, Holland and Belgium, the United States Naval Group France, and the Naval Division of the Allied Control Commission for Austria.

Under Vice Admiral Ghormley's command in Germany was Rear Admiral A. G. Robinson, who, as Commander of U.S. Ports and Bases Germany, was charged with the operation of the ports of Bremen and Bremerhaven in the American-controlled Weser River Enclave. Rear Admiral Robinson's headquarters were established in Bremen on 15 May. This task force began operating at once, supervising the disposition of captured and surrendered naval personnel, clearing the port areas for incoming shipping, and seizing prize merchant ships which had been captured there. Of these the liner EUROPA was by far the most important. A modern ship in relatively good condition, she was converted into a troop transport almost immediately; although somewhat hampered by lack of facilities and skilled labor, EUROPA was commissioned as United States Navy AP-177 and manned by naval personnel. She sailed from Bremerhaven on 11 September to Southampton to embark her first load of almost 5000 returning American troops.

Bremen and Bremerhaven, as the two United States naval controlled ports in Germany, had an important role to play in the occupation of the country. They served as important supply and evacuation ports for the United States occupation forces; their shipyards and repair facilities, under United States naval control, were used for the repair of German and Allied ships in the area.

Another United States naval command whose work was accelerated by the surrender of Germany was the U.S. Naval Technical Mission Europe, under Commodore H. A. Schade. This organization, which is under the operational control of the Chief of Naval Operations, is the agency for the collection of intelligence information from the surrendered nations for the use of the United States Navy. Working closely with the Army G-2 Staff Division and with Allied Intelligence Services, the U.S. Naval Technical Mission Europe has uncovered a vast amount of data concerning German wartime industrial and scientific developments, the status of experiments on secret weapons, etc.

U.S. Naval Forces Northwest African Waters

In March 1945 the U.S. Eighth Fleet, which had been under the command of Admiral H. Kent Hewitt since March 1943, was dissolved; in April the naval forces and bases in the Mediterranean Theater were placed under the administrative control of Commander, U.S. Naval Forces in Europe. These forces, commanded by Vice Admiral W. A. Glassford as Commander, U.S. Naval Forces Northwest African Waters, thereby became a task force of the Twelfth Fleet.

Although the over-all strength was reduced, small naval detachments were maintained in Italy to support the United States Army there, to assist United States merchant shipping, and to continue United States naval representation on the Allied Commission for Italy.

Changes in Command

In the Azores United States naval forces were engaged chiefly in patrolling routes used for Army aircraft being returned to the United States. Commander, U.S. Naval Forces in Europe assumed administrative control of the Azores forces in July 1945.

A little over two months after the signing of the German surrender at Rheims, the Supreme Allied Military command under General of the Army Eisenhower was dissolved. On 14 July control of the American, British and French military and naval forces reverted to their respective national commands. For the American forces General of the Army Eisenhower remained the Supreme Commander with a composite United States Army-Navy-Air European Theater Staff. Commander, U.S. Naval Forces in Europe in London retained administrative control of all remaining United States naval forces in the theater. On 16 August Admiral Hewitt relieved Admiral Harold R. Stark as Commander, Twelfth Fleet and Commander, U.S. Naval Forces in Europe.

Redeployment

When the fighting in Europe ceased, the United States Army was faced with the gigantic task of redeploying millions of its forces. Some of its men were to be sent home for discharge; others were to be ordered to the Far East. During the summer of 1945, through its various port parties and naval detachments, the Navy cooperated closely with the Army in speeding troop movement. Over 53,000 men were embarked from northern French ports in May, and in June more than 210,000. The July figures approached 350,000. The southern French ports of Marseilles and Toulon were also used for this work. From Le Havre and Antwerp many shipments of war materiel no longer needed in this theater were sent back to the United States.

Similarly the United States Navy developed its own redeployment program, transferring to the United States or to the Pacific forces and materiel no longer required for naval activities in Europe. Hundreds of amphibious ships and craft which had been used for assault operations and for the support of the Army build-up were no longer needed and were returned to the United States. Nearly all United States naval advanced bases, supply and repair facilities, etc., in Britain and the Mediterranean were now unnecessary and their closing proceeded at a rapid rate.

In Great Britain the summer months of 1945 saw the closing of the amphibious bases at Falmouth, Plymouth, Dartmouth, Portland-Weymouth and Southampton. With the end of the submarine menace the planes of Fleet Air Wing Seven, based at Dunkeswell, Devon, were returned to the United States. In France, Italy and in North Africa the operation of most of the liberated ports was rapidly returned to the national authorities. Port detachments were maintained at Le Havre, Marseilles and Naples to aid in the Army's redeployment program. When the command of U.S. Naval Forces France was abolished as a separate task force on 1 July, a naval task group, under Commander, U.S. Naval Forces Germany, was substituted therefor. In the Mediterranean, United States naval activities were likewise reduced. Naval Operating Base Oran was closed out and a naval detachment took its place in July. During the same month the office of Commander, Moroccan Sea Frontier was abolished. The naval facilities at Port Lyautey, Casablanca, Dakar and Agadir were organized as a naval task group. The naval advanced base at Bizerte was decommissioned and reductions were effected at Palermo and Naples.

U. S. ATLANTIC FLEET

During the entire war combat vessels, auxiliaries, and landing craft were built and trained in large numbers on the east coast of the United States for duty in the Pacific. With the capitulation of Germany, the U.S. Atlantic Fleet was able to increase and intensify the redeployment of ships, men, and supplies to the Pacific. By 1 June Atlantic convoys were stopped, and all available escort ships and tankers thus released were made ready for operations against the Japanese. Large numbers of landing craft were returned from Europe and overhauled for Pacific duty. The further necessity of providing refresher training for the crews of these ships and craft devolved upon the Atlantic Fleet Operational Training Command. The Battle of the Atlantic had been chiefly a war against submarines; now all training was concentrated upon meeting the requirements of the Pacific war for accurate antiaircraft firing and shore bombardment. During the period covered by this report the Operational Training Command, Atlantic Fleet, trained some 995 ships for duty in the Pacific, of which 358 were new ships receiving the normal shakedown and 637 were ships which had been engaged in some phase of the European war.

Similarly, the Air Force Atlantic Fleet turned with increased intensity to the training of carrier air units and shore-based patrol squadrons for the Pacific Fleet.

Typical of the changing nature of the carrier training program was the decommissioning of all composite squadrons, which had produced such effective results against the U-boats, and the commissioning of air groups for the large new carriers of the MIDWAY class. These new air groups are approximately one and one-half times the size of a normal carrier air group.

The surrender of Japan, occurring when the Atlantic Fleet redeployment program was at its height, necessitated rapid readjustments. Many ships, which were on their way to the Pacific or had just reached the forward areas, were ordered to return to the east coast ports. Instructions were promulgated indicating the status of vessels in the postwar Atlantic Fleet, and an appraisal of berthing areas for the Atlantic Fleet Reserve ships was pressed to completion. Similarly the program for revising, absorbing or decommissioning shore-based Atlantic Fleet activities was accelerated. In the South Atlantic a similar process had long since begun. In March 1945 the Rio-Trinidad convoys were discontinued. Then on 15 April the Fourth Fleet became a task force of the U.S. Atlantic Fleet, with Vice Admiral W. R. Munroe as task force commander and Commander, South Atlantic Force. The roll-up of forces continued, and on 13 August Vice Admiral Munroe hauled down his flag; the remaining naval activities in the South Atlantic were placed under the Commandant, Naval Operating Base Rio de Janeiro.

* *

VI
Ships, Aircraft and Personnel

FIGHTING men are not effective, individually or collectively, unless they are imbued with high morale. Morale may be defined as a state of mind wherein there is confidence, courage and zeal among men united together in a common effort—a "conviction of excellence." One factor largely responsible for the extremely high morale of the men of the naval services has been their confidence in the excellence of the ships and planes provided them.

SHIPBUILDING PROGRAM

During the period 1 March to 1 October 1945 the following combatant ships were completed: 4 aircraft carriers (one of which was MIDWAY, the first of the three 45,000 ton carriers under construction), 8 escort carriers, 3 light cruisers, 6 heavy cruisers, 53 destroyers, 2 destroyer escorts and 24 submarines. During this same period over 300 auxiliary ships were completed by the Navy and the Maritime Commission, among them six of the most modern air-conditioned hospital ships in existence. The landing craft and district craft construction programs were continued, with the delivery of large numbers of each type. Twenty-nine mine-sweeping vessels were delivered. It was necessary to place particular emphasis upon the production of repair ships of all types. The large numbers of these delivered during this period, together with existing ships of the type, performed indispensable services in the forward areas in returning quickly to service many of the ships damaged in the Okinawa operation.

To meet changing conditions of war during this period, it was necessary to undertake a number of conversions of ships from one type to another. Notable among these was the conversion of certain patrol craft to control vessels for amphibious operations; frigates and certain patrol craft to weather station ships; a large number of personnel landing ships to gunboats for close inshore support of amphibious operations; a number of destroyer escorts to fast transports; certain destroyers and destroyer escorts to radar picket ships; and a number of destroyers to high-speed mine sweepers.

During the later phases of the war, as Japanese sea power waned, a review was made of the Navy's shipbuilding program to bring it in line with estimated operational requirements. On 10 August 1945 the Secretary of the Navy approved the termination of contracts for the construction of 56 combatant ships and 39 vessels of other types. Following the surrender of Japan, a complete review was made of the status of the construction and conversion program of auxiliaries, landing craft, district craft and small boats, in consequence of which the total number of cancellations was raised to the following:

Combatant Ships	56
Auxiliaries	94
Landing Ships	2
Patrol Craft	44
District Craft	121
Small Landing Craft	over 8,000

The effect of these cancellations is shown graphically in Plate 19.

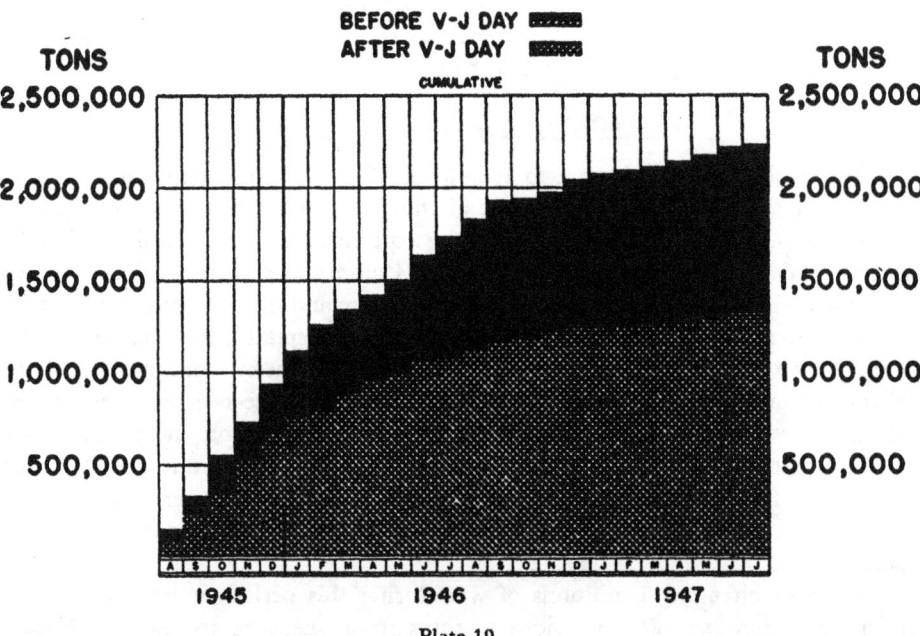

Plate 19.

Every effort has been made to keep the ships of the fleet fitted with the latest available equipment to meet rapidly changing combat conditions. Improved radar sets, aircraft and antiaircraft weapons, fire-control systems for guns, and fire-fighting equipment have been installed. The improvement of the offensive and defensive qualities of our ships by such alterations had been going on since the beginning of the war; as the war drew to a close, most ships of the fleet had reached a point at which no additional weights could be added without compensatory weight removals. The problem of applying the latest technological developments to our ships has thus become more difficult; nevertheless such application has been accomplished on an extensive scale by the cooperation of all concerned, both afloat and ashore.

AIRCRAFT

Comparisons between standard Navy aircraft types at the beginning of the war and the end vividly illustrate the outstanding technical advances accomplished in less than four years of fighting. At the war's end we had the best airplanes of every kind, both ashore and afloat, but newer and better planes were on the production lines and would soon have taken their place against the enemy. Among these were the Grumman *Tigercat*, a twin-engine, single-seat fighter plane with heavy firepower and bomb-carrying characteristics. Although this plane had arrived in the Pacific, it never got into actual combat. Three other fighter planes, faster and possessing higher tactical performance than standard existing types, had satisfactorily passed the long period of experiments and flight tests and were in production. These included the Ryan *Fireball*, the Navy's first fighter plane to use jet propulsion. The others were Grumman's *Bearcat* and Goodyear's F2G (to which no popular name has yet been given), both high-speed, highly maneuverable and fast climbing planes. The latter was the first naval fighter to use the new Pratt and Whitney 3000 horsepower engine.

The Grumman *Wildcat*, which was a new fighter at the time of Pearl Harbor, had an approximate speed of 300 miles an hour and mounted four .50-caliber machine guns. The *Hellcats* and *Corsairs*, which were both carrier and shore-based on V-J day, have speeds of more than 400 and 425 miles an hour, respectively, and mount six .50-caliber machine guns, or proportionate numbers of 20-millimeter cannon, in addition to rockets. Bombs weighing up to 2000 pounds could also be carried by these planes when they were assigned fighter-bomber missions. These planes played the leading role in our tactical development of fighter-bombing, a World War II innovation. Other technical developments, primarily air-borne radar, helped to bring into existence the Navy's night-fighting force. The *Wildcat*, greatly improved by various modifications by General Motors to give it greater speed and climb, continued to be used on the escort carrier.

Our dive-bomber, the *Helldiver*, has a speed of more than 250 miles an hour, can carry 2000 pounds of bombs, and is equipped with eight rocket launchers, two 20-millimeter cannon and two .30-caliber machine guns. These characteristics were developed through five modifications. The Douglas *Dauntless* was the standard dive-bomber when the war began, and delivered heavy blows against the enemy before it was retired as a first line plane. Its top speed was 230 miles an hour; it carried 1000 pounds of bombs, and mounted two .30-caliber and two .50-caliber machine guns.

Our torpedo bomber at the start of the war was the Douglas *Devastator*, a plane which had a speed of about 150 miles an hour and was very lightly armed. The Grumman *Avenger*, and later modifications of this plane by General Motors, gave us a plane with a speed of more than 250 miles an hour, capable of carrying 2000 pounds of bombs or a torpedo, four machine guns and rockets. One modification of the *Avenger* was a carrier-based night bomber to operate with night fighters.

Development and research in the dive-bomber and torpedo bomber field during the war yielded designs by Consolidated, Douglas and Martin. A few production models had been turned out by Consolidated and Douglas and several experimental models by Martin when V-J day came.

The standard scout-observation plane based aboard battleships and cruisers became the Curtiss *Seahawk*, replacing the Chance Vought *Kingfisher* and Curtiss *Seagull*. The *Seahawk* and *Kingfisher* played no small part in air-sea rescues.

The Consolidated *Catalina*, the veteran twin-engine patrol plane, was in operation at the start of the war and has proved to be one of the most valuable all-purpose planes. Planes of the sixth modification—or sixth major change—giving it greater range and speed are now with the fleet. The Martin *Mariner*, a larger, heavier plane, has taken over many of the patrol duties formerly handled by the *Catalinas*. Both of these planes also have performed outstanding service in air-sea rescue work.

For our four-engine, land-based search plane, we have replaced the Consolidated *Liberator* with the Consolidated *Privateer*, a plane with a range of well over 3000 miles, heavy armament and a wealth of new navigational, radio and radar equipment, enabling it to fly long hours of reconnaissance over trackless oceans. These planes, which carry bombs and depth charges, have made impressive records against isolated Japanese ships, small convoys, submarines and enemy-held islands in their search areas. Our newest twin-engine search plane is the Lockheed *Harpoon*, which took over the duties of the Lockheed *Ventura*. It carries bombs and rockets and has ten .50-caliber machine guns with which to protect itself. The range of the *Harpoon* is in excess of 2000 miles and its speed is more than 300 miles an hour.

The Naval Air Transport Service utilizes as its standard transport planes the Martin *Mars*, Douglas *Skymasters* (R5D) and *Skytrains* (R4D), and Consolidated *Coronado* flying boats, while Marine Corps air transport groups use the Curtiss *Commandos* in large numbers. Established on 1 December 1943, the Naval Air Transport Service routes extend over approximately 80,000 miles, covering three quarters of the globe. In addition to carrying freight and passengers, the Service flew whole blood daily from the west coast to combat areas in the Pacific and evacuated wounded during the Okinawa campaign.

Improved cooling and other changes have increased the horsepower of standard combat engines 10 per cent with little or no increase in weight. Thus it has been possible to translate added power into increased climb and speed. New superchargers made it possible to hold high take-off horsepower to higher altitudes than was possible before. The adoption of water injection for engines to give pilots greater speed in emergencies also became general for all combat types.

Our requirement for the utmost in reliability and our long-held conviction that an air cooled power plant installation was less vulnerable to damage than a liquid cooled, has caused us to devote primary attention to the development of air cooled engines, and hence, has contributed substantially to the aircraft program of the country. It can be claimed without exaggeration that the air cooled aircraft engine of today would not have been developed effectively had it not been for the Navy continued interest.

Other technological advances in naval aircraft have included the development of jet assisted take off (which made it possible for seaplanes to carry much heavier loads), the largest helicopter yet flying, and radio-controlled antiaircraft target drones and missiles.

PERSONNEL

The personnel strength of the United States Navy on 2 September 1945 was as follows:

SHIPS, AIRCRAFT AND PERSONNEL

Navy only	Male	Female	Total
Officers (including warrants)	316,675	8,399	325,074[1]
Nurses	....	10,968	10,968
Officer Candidates	62,913	12	62,925[2]
Enlisted	2,935,695	73,685	3,009,380
Total	3,315,283	93,064	3,408,347

Data concerning the number of personnel on board and the deployment of personnel overseas throughout the war is presented in graphic form in Plates 20 and 21.

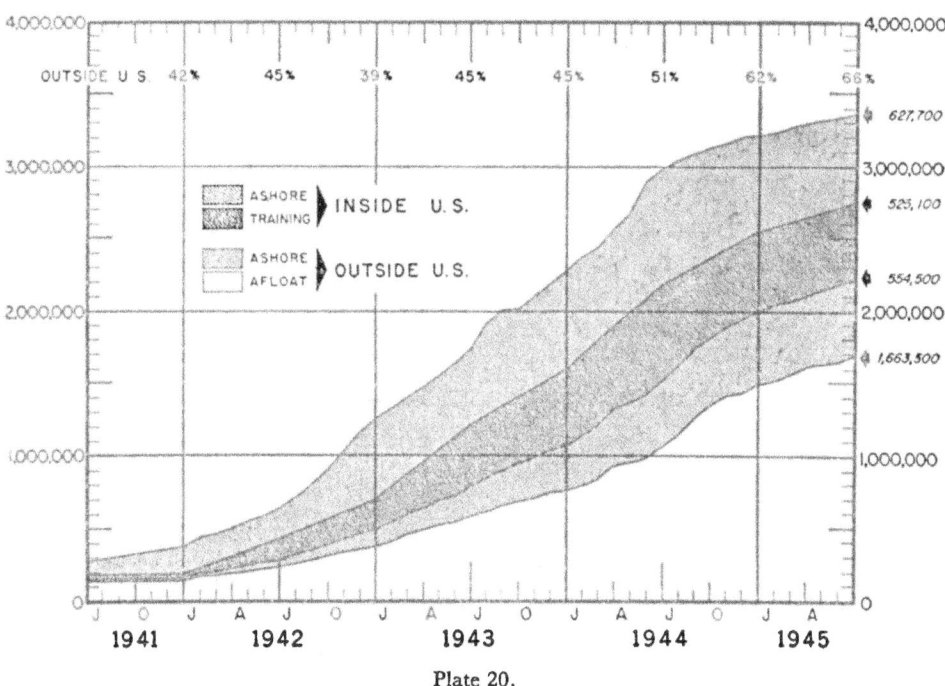

Plate 20.

After nearly four years of procuring personnel, the Navy is now faced with the task of ensuring the orderly return to civilian life of three million men and women. By January of 1946 one of every three persons in the war-time Navy will have been separated. By the end of January half the total personnel, and by the end of March two thirds, will have been demobilized. It is expected that the rest of the temporary personnel will be discharged by 1 September 1946.

Guided by national policy, as determined by the Congress, careful consideration is being given to the size of the Navy that will be required when demobilization is completed. Roughly the current estimate provides for an active Navy which will be 30 per cent of our present war strength.

[1] Includes 4,038 male officers and 196 female officers whose separations are pending.

[2] Includes 5,129 personnel in enlisted ratings who are taking officer candiate training.

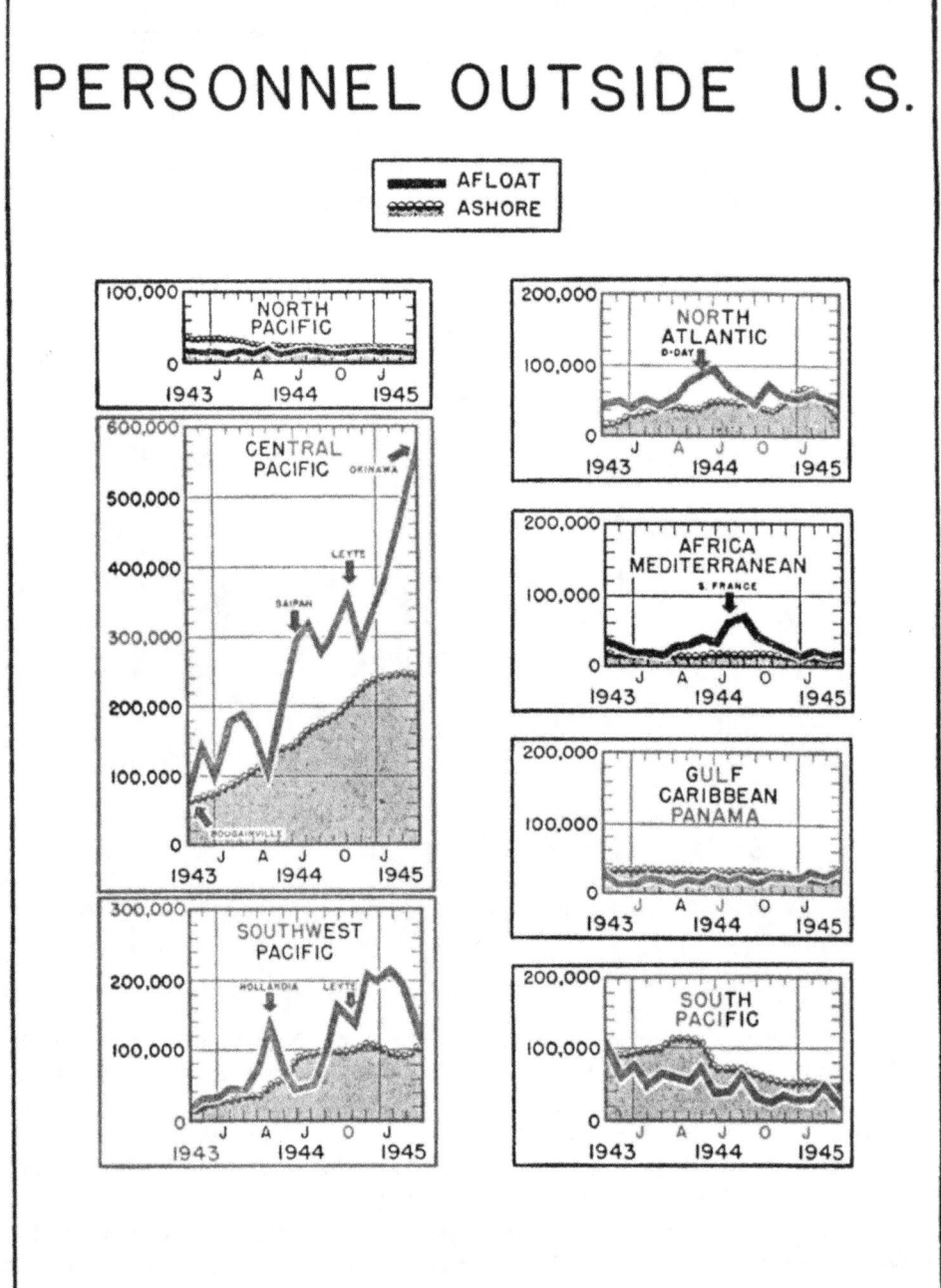

Plate 21.

The Navy's need for officers after the war is governed by the size of the fleet which the Congress determines is necessary to defend the United States and Western Hemisphere, and to discharge our international agreements and obligations. We know that the Navy will need more officers and men than it now has in the Regular Navy—approximately 30,000 more officers and a total of about 500,000 men. One of the best sources of the additional officers required is the Reserve and Temporary officers now on duty. The program for their selection and transfer is well under way. On 16 August 1945 the Secretary of the Navy addressed a message to the service requesting that Reserve and Temporary USN officers desiring to transfer to the Regular Navy submit their applications. The legislation upon which the program is dependent has been introduced in Congress.

The Navy is extremely proud of the work done by the Women's Reserve. It is our plan to keep a WAVES component in the Naval Reserve. Further, if Congress approves, we will seek to retain on active duty a reasonable number of WAVES who wish to remain and who may be needed in certain specialties. We know from experience that they can be useful after the war in such specialties as communications, the Medical Corps, and certain types of naval aviation duty.

HEALTH

During the spring and summer of 1945 the Medical Department applied the medical experience of earlier operations in its support of the Navy's assault upon the inner defenses of Japan. Improvements in medical care of naval personnel included a more effective chain of evacuation, of which large-scale use of aircraft formed an important part, the provision for a smoother and more rapid flow of medical supplies to the fighting fronts, and the development of an intensive program of preventive medicine, which kept illnesses throughout the Navy and Marine Corps at a low level.

In past wars, disease and infection have caused more deaths and disability in armed forces than actual combat itself. World War I significantly checked this tendency, but the real advantages of modern medical procedures, techniques, and knowledges were experienced during World War II. Navy medical statistics show that of the wounded who survived until they could receive medical care, about 98 out of 100 lived. The most recent tabulations indicate an estimated rate for casualty deaths of 8.7 for the first six months in 1945 in terms of total naval strength as against 4.3 per thousand in 1944. This is primarily a reflection of Iwo Jima, Okinawa, and the attacks of the Japanese "kamikaze" pilots. The total death rate from all causes was 6.7 per thousand for 1944 in terms of total naval strength as against 6.0 per thousand in 1943. According to preliminary data the total death rate from all causes for the first six months of 1945 was estimated at 11.9 per thousand. Over-all cases of sickness and injuries, exclusive of battle injuries, were at the rate of 495.4 per thousand average strength in 1944 as against a corresponding figure of 602.8 in 1943. Two statistical trends in naval morbidity are worthy of note as indicative of the effect of combat. The first is the average per cent of total strength in hospitals, which increased from 1.7 per thousand in 1941 to 2.1 per thousand in 1944 and 2.5 per thousand for the first six months of 1945. Among other things this shows the effect of the longer convalescent periods required for recovery and rehabilitation of war casualties from such injuries as penetrating wounds and fractured bones. Thus, even though the over-all casualty rate has been maintained at a relatively low figure, the total hospital population has been gradually increasing because of the trend toward a longer average number of sick days per patient. The second significant trend was that of mental disease case incidence, which increased from 9.5 per thousand of total naval strength in 1941 to 11.8 per thousand in 1943 and 14.2 per thousand in 1944. These statistics demonstrate clearly the increase in tempo of modern war with its grueling, unfamiliar horrors. This was the motivating factor which has caused the Medical Department of the Navy consistently to emphasize its neuropsychiatric services.

Statistically the wartime rates indicated above compare favorably with past experience in the Navy, even though the war years have necessitated the maintenance of a large number of naval personnel in foreign waters or on foreign shores where they are subjected to many endemic diseases and infections which are rarely encountered in times of peace. When final statistics are computed on medical care during the war years, there is every indication, upon the basis of preliminary figures, that medical science will be shown to have assumed an importance in the preservation of the health and lives of our fighting men never before equalled in the history of the United States Navy.

While the Navy Medical Department was actively engaged throughout the year in giving medical support to amphibious operations in the Pacific, it was also providing medical care for thousands of Navy men aboard the ships, submarines, and planes which were daily carrying the war into enemy skies and enemy waters. Good organization, careful training, and judicious dispersal of medical personnel and supplies made it possible for the Medical Department to meet all demands made upon it in spite of heavy casualties aboard some vessels. These activities included careful classification of the wounded in terms of the urgency of their cases; the use of voluntary crewmen as stretcher bearers, thus releasing hospital corpsmen to assist in caring for the wounded; and the existence of the blood banks aboard many of the vessels making available whole blood for the more serious cases.

The Medical Department's second line of defense after the support given in actual battle areas has been its system of fleet, advance base, base and naval hospitals, its dispensaries, and its hospital ships. Scattered throughout the world, they have provided many thousands of beds and the other medical facilities to give patients complete and definitive care.

In order to give adequate support to the operational portion of the Medical Department, numerous technical and administrative services have been required. Medical research has been one of these. New drugs, new applications of earlier discoveries, and new techniques have been developed through untiring research and observation. Perhaps the most advertised of these is penicillin, which has been found capable of stopping infection, even where the sulfa drugs are powerless. Prevention and care of burns, use of blood plasma, transportation of whole blood by air to battle areas, and proper methods for healing fractures are some of the problems receiving attention to the end that the Navy Medical Department will not only stay abreast of the developments in medical science but may maintain its position as a leader.

Rehabilitation programs for casualties are being conducted at a number of hospital centers scattered throughout the United States. The essential purpose of the program is to develop a clear-cut integrated procedure for the rehabilitation of men for return to duty or to civilian life. This part of the program, involving as it does the best possible medical, surgical, and neuropsychiatric care, may be regarded as a policy of the Navy. Special facilities in various naval hospitals are made available to those casualties requiring them. A second part of the program provides for the close cooperation of the Medical Department with specialized rehabilitation agencies which are designed to assist men to make the necessary adjustments and receive the proper training to fit them for useful employment in civilian life. Considerable emphasis has been placed upon the development of a neuropsychiatric program, and efforts are made by the psychiatrists to reach casualties needing their services as quickly as possible after they are affected, so that permanent injuries are avoided. Moreover, psychiatrists assist naval offenders, who have been imprisoned, in making readjustments. As a result, many men who were formerly serious disciplinary problems are now returned to full active duty.

With the coming of peace, the previously prepared plans of the Medical Department for handling the medical aspects of demobilization have been put into effect. Every precaution is being taken to see that the men returned to civilian life are in sound physical condition, particularly in regard to infectious diseases and defects of a serious nature. Those requiring hospitalization, medical or dental attention, are cared for until fit for release, if desired by the individual, or until arrangements have been made for continued treatment outside of the Navy.

THE MARINE CORPS

Prior to 1 March 1945 the Marine Corps had organized and deployed as planned all combat units within the authorized strength of 478,000. In addition to the six divisions, four air wings and supporting units of the Fleet Marine Force, there were 11,000 Marines serving in detachments included within the complements of combatant naval vessels, and another 28,000 providing security for naval shore establishments both within and outside of the United States and at advance bases. The remainder of the Corps was employed in logistic establishments and in training activities necessary for the continuous support of field units.

Since practically all of the Marine Corps' efforts during the war were directed toward the Pacific Theater, the victory in Europe resulted in a negligible change in commitments. Consequently it was not possible to effect a reduction of the size of the Corps at that time.

When it became apparent that the authorized strength was inadequate to provide for the increasing numbers who were hospitalized or convalescent, and to maintain the desired rehabilitation program, the President, on 29 May 1945, raised the troop ceiling of the Corps to 503,000. Although the rate of procurement was increased to provide this new strength, the surrender of Japan occurred as the Corps attained a strength of 484,631, and plans for partial demobilization were put into effect at once.

In order to provide immediate replacements for Marines serving overseas who were entitled to early release from the service, training activities, other than recruit depots, sea-schools, and certain specialist schools, were suspended as soon as demobilization was directed. Upon completion of their recruit tra ning, enlisted men now receive their advanced training in the organizations to which they are assigned. This is in accordance with former peacetime practices within the Corps. Training overhead was further reduced by initiating a program of restricting future officer training to candidates who appear to be postwar Regular officer material.

Demobilization of personnel is being effected at the maximum rate consistent with the availability of facilities and with the immediate commitments of the Corps, particularly the Fleet Marine Force. Concurrent with this demobilization is the reorganization of the regular component of the Corps to meet planned postwar requirements. Preparation is being made for the transfer of qualified Reserve and Temporary officers to the Regular service in such numbers as may be authorized. When Japan surrendered there were 71,460 Marines serving under current four-year regular enlistments. Recruiting of Regulars for four-year enlistments has been resumed, with the priority in opportunity to enlist in the Regular service being afforded to those who served in the war.

On v-j day there were 1000 Women's Reserves serving in or en route to Hawaii, and at that time their further assignments to overseas duty were cancelled. Women's Reserves are being demobilized as expeditiously as possible, and essentially in accordance with the same policies that apply to the men, but with lower critical scores.

THE COAST GUARD

On 1 September 1945 Coast Guard personnel totalled 170,480, including 9,624 in the SPARS. Since its total postwar military strength is planned at 34,500, the Coast Guard has taken prompt action looking toward the ultimate demobilization of its wartime forces. All enlistments in the Reserve and Women's Reserve (SPARS) have been discontinued and future enlistments will be in the Regular Coast Guard only and limited to 17-year olds. Legislation is being requested to permit the acceptance of a limited number of Reserve officers and enlisted men in the Regular Coast Guard.

In addition to the 1677 Coast Guard craft in active service at the end of the 1945 fiscal year, Coast Guard personnel on 1 August 1945 were manning 326 Navy craft and 254 Army vessels, about 50,000 Coastguardmen serving on Navy and 6,000 on Army craft. Only 84 Reserve vessels remained in service out of a total of 2,089 which had been taken over early in the war, principally to combat the submarine menace along the coasts. There had also been 908 other vessels acquired during the war through purchase, charter or gift, and all but 252 of these had been disposed of.

Following the defeat of Germany, port security measures on the Atlantic and Gulf coasts were relaxed. The examination of vessels leaving and entering ports was discontinued, as were identification card requirements and licenses for individual vessel movements. Certain restricted areas on these coasts were abolished along with anti-sabotage water patrols and guards on cargo vessels and waterfront facilities. By the end of the 1945 fiscal year, only 34 ports had Coast Guard port protection as against 117 ports a year earlier; the total personnel engaged in such activities had declined from 23,817 to 16,304.

After v-e day, three port protective programs were intensified—fire fighting, supervision over explosive handling, and anti-oil pollution. The training of personnel in fire prevention and fire fighting techniques was followed by a program coordinated with the Army to improve and strengthen fire protection measures at ports of embarkation. Thirty Navy fireboats, Coast Guard manned, were assigned to forward areas in the Pacific. Supervisory activities over the proper handling and stowage of explosives were extended to naval ammunition depots having port facilities, as well as to naval bases in the Pacific and to European ports handling explosives and ammunition then being deployed to the Pacific. Finally, an intensive educational campaign against oil pollution in American ports was begun. With the surrender of Japan the size of the Coast Guard's munition handling details in the Pacific was considerably increased and their task of supervising the handling and loading of explosives for return to the United States was expected to extend over a period of several months.

While the activities of Temporary Reservists, who serve without pay and are principally engaged in port security work, were being discontinued along the Atlantic and Gulf coasts and the inland waterways systems after v-e day, enrollments on the west coast did not relax with the heavy movements to the Pacific of personnel and supplies which continued up to the surrender of Japan. By 1 September 1945, however, there were less than 12,000 Temporary Reservists assigned to active duty out of a onetime total of 52,333. Some of these were pilots, who, under limited control exercised by the Coast Guard, had handled 120,000 pilotage assignments in 39 ports during the 1945 fiscal year.

In July 1945, 64 fixed and 17 mobile LORAN (Long Range Navigation) stations were being operated by the Coast Guard. This advanced method of establishing navigational positions by electronics had been installed promptly on Iwo Jima and Okinawa and provided LORAN lines of position over the Japanese mainland, making for successful bombing missions. Forty-five RACON (Radar Beacon) stations which give, within 120 miles of the station, the distance and bearing of an airplane or ship, had been installed and were being operated by the Coast Guard on the Atlantic and Pacific coasts and in Alaska. While certain aids to navigation in the Atlantic area used primarily for war purposes, such as swept channel markings, were being removed, there was an accelerated demand for aids to navigation throughout the Pacific area to facilitate the forward movement of our armed forces. Meanwhile studies are being made of the possibility of designing lightships which could be operated without regular crews on board.

Some 1627 new vessels, aggregating 9,009,216 gross tons, which had been constructed during the fiscal year 1945, had been certificated by the Coast Guard under the marine inspection laws. Annual inspections on 9720 vessels were completed during the year. The passing of the peak of the emergency ship construction relieved a number of field inspectors who were transferred from the east coast and Great Lakes to Pacific ports for temporary duty.

Merchant Marine Hearing Units continued to operate in all important United States ports while others functioned in Europe, Suez, Ceylon, the south and southwest Pacific and the Canal Zone. They promptly investigated marine casualties and acted as government liaison officers in merchant marine affairs.

The Coast Guard maintained nine air stations along the coasts of the United States, under the operational control of the various sea frontiers, with a total of 165 planes. These have served as task units in the conduct of air-sea rescue. Assistance was rendered in 686 plane crashes and 786 lives were saved during the fiscal year; 5357 emergency medical cases were transported and 149 obstructions to navigation and derelicts were sighted for removal.

VII
Naval Research and Development during World War II

IN December 1941 the United States faced seasoned enemies, who not only had long been preparing for war but who had actually been waging it for several years. Within the limited facilities and means available throughout the years of peace, the United States Navy had, however, equipped itself with weapons the equal of, or superior to, those of other navies and had laid the groundwork for still further development. During the war the science and industry of this country and our allies were mobilized to apply existing scientific knowledge to the perfection of these weapons and the development of new and more deadly means of waging war. As a result the United States Navy was able to maintain the technical advantage over the navies of our enemies, which contributed so materially to the outcome of World War II.

The means of accomplishing this were not so much directed towards making new discoveries, as towards the exploitation of the skills and techniques which civilian scientists had already cultivated in years of peace. When war appeared imminent, the War and Navy Departments and the National Academy of Sciences gave close attention to the most profitable manner of utilizing the strength of American science in military and naval research. It was decided to attempt a solution involving the maximum flexibility and initiative, in which the fundamental principle would be cooperation between science and the armed forces, rather than to bring the scientists into military and naval laboratories, as was done in England. The principle proved thoroughly sound. The arrangement adopted was the establishment by executive order of the Office of Scientific Research and Development, which had as its scientific and technical working bodies the National Defense Research Council, the Medical Research Council, and later the Office of Field Service. To assure full integration of the potentialities of these organizations with the Navy's own research and development program and the needs of the service, the late Secretary Knox, in July 1941, established the office of Coordinator of Research and Development. Throughout the war, the development of new weapons and devices has been accelerated by the teamwork between the users, the scientists, the engineer-designers and the producers.

The devices and weapons resulting from the research and development program have been put to use in every phase of naval warfare. Particular examples, cited because of their complexity and diversification, are amphibious warfare, carrier warfare, submarine and antisubmarine warfare. In each of these cases, our combat effectiveness has been materially increased by improvements in communications, navigational devices, fire control, detection equipment, firepower, aircraft performance (range, speed, armament, handling characteristics) and by advanced training methods and equipment.

Perhaps the greatest technological advances of the entire war have been made in the field of electronics, both within the naval laboratories and in collaboration with the Office of Scientific Research and Development. Pre-existing radar sets were developed and new models created for ship and air-borne search, fire control, and for accurate long-range navigation. Identification and recognition equipment were developed for use in conjunction with radar systems. New and highly efficient short-range radio telephones were used for tactical communication. In the successful antisubmarine campaign in the Atlantic, small radio-sono-buoys were used; these, when dropped from aircraft, listened for the noise made by a submarine and automatically relayed the information to the searching plane. Great strides have been made in electronic antisubmarine detection equipment. Underwater echo-ranging gear and listening equipment have been improved in quality and extended in function since the outbreak of the war. Countermeasures have been developed for jamming enemy radar and communication systems, disrupting the control signals for his guided missiles, and counteracting his measures to jam our own equipment.

The foundation for our shipboard radar systems had been laid before the war. The earliest observations of radio phenomena of the kind that are exploited by radar were made at the Naval Research Laboratory by groups working with Dr. A. H. Taylor and Dr. R. N. Page, and the military possibilities were immediately grasped by these scientists and by Rear Admiral H. G. Bowen, then Director of the Laboratory. Because of this, at the outset of the war, our Navy alone had on its ships a search radar specifically designed for shipboard use. We had already incorporated in these radars the technical development of using a single antenna for transmission and reception. Radar of this type contributed to the victories of the Coral Sea, Midway, and Guadalcanal. Over 26,000 sets of air-borne radar equipment were produced from the Naval Research Laboratory's redesign of British air-borne equipment. Ours was the first navy to install radar in submarines. Similarly, a highly efficient supersonic echo-ranging gear for submarine and antisubmarine warfare had been completely developed, and was installed before the war began. The success of all these electronic devices can be traced back to intensive early development of new types of vacuum tubes.

Initially, from want of experience against an enemy attacking with the persistence demonstrated by the Japanese, our antiaircraft batteries were inadequate. Particularly was this true in the case of automatic weapon batteries, consisting at that time of the .50-caliber and 1.1-inch machine guns. The main antiaircraft batteries in the fleet, consisting of 5-inch and 3-inch main batteries were controlled by directors employing optical range information. Although antiaircraft fire-control radar was under development, no installations were operative in the fleet.

By the time Japan surrendered, our defenses had been revolutionized. The fleet was equipped with accurate antiaircraft fire-control radar. Our antiaircraft gun defenses consisted of multiple power-driven 40-millimeter mounts, 20-millimeter mounts, and 5-inch twin and single mounts, many of which were controlled by small intermediate range radar-fed gun directors. The VT, or proximity influence fuse, initially sponsored by the Navy and by the Office of Scientific Research and Development, marked a radical change from previous methods of detonating a projectile and vastly increased the effectiveness of antiaircraft defenses.

At the end of the war, the 8-inch rapid-fire turret had been developed and was ready for introduction to the fleet. Completely automatic in action, it can be used against ship, aircraft, or land targets. The guns are loaded from the handling rooms automatically and are automatically laid.

When the threat of the German magnetic mines became known in 1939, the Navy immediately mobilized scientific talent and industrial capacity to produce a countermeasure. Several methods of demagnetizing our ships were developed. These were applied before Pearl Harbor to all combatant vessels, and later to all other vessels, and were of material assistance in maintaining the safety of our vital shipping lanes. At the same time, acoustic and magnetic firing devices were developed and produced in quantity for our mines and depth charges. Electric torpedoes were developed to supplement the air-steam torpedo, which at the outbreak of war was our weapon of underwater attack.

Rockets and rocket launchers were developed, with the assistance of California Institute of Technology and other agencies, for use on board ships and aircraft. Appropriate types of rockets were developed for use against submarines, for the support of amphibious landings, and for aircraft. These allowed heavy firepower to be concentrated in light craft.

Fighter-plane speed was greatly increased during the war. At the end an experimental model ready for combat use had a speed of over 550 miles per hour. This plane was powered with turbo-jet engines, little known before 1941. Development of the conventional aircraft engine had also progressed; whereas initially the maximum size was 1000 horsepower, improved types of 3000 horsepower are now in use. Torpedo bombers, scout bombers, patrol bombers, and scout observation planes have all been rapidly developed during the period. Carrier-borne aircraft with increased speed, range, and armament carried the battle to the Japanese homeland, and patrol aircraft with high speed, long range, and greater offensive power aided in supplying the information necessary to the success of those operations. Development of the arresting gear, launching catapults, and handling equipment of our surface ships kept pace with the increasing weights of planes, and allowed more planes per ship to be carried than had been possible in peacetime.

Our aircraft were a focus for developments in many fields. Radar opened new possibilities for search, night combat, and operations under poor visibility conditions. Aircraft guns were increased in size from the .30-caliber World War I weapon to 20-millimeter, 37-millimeter, and 75-millimeter guns. Air-borne rockets up to 11.75 inches in diameter radically increased the striking power of conventional aircraft, with little penalty on performance. Rocket power was also used on seaplanes for assistance in take-off with heavy loads and in high seas, making possible the rescue of many downed aviators and thereby reducing our combat losses. Development of the "fire bomb" further extended the tactical versatility of aircraft.

Training was enormously expedited by the introduction of a great variety of synthetic training devices. These endeavored to offer trainees an approximation of battle experience and to develop the reactions of a veteran before actual combat. As an example, it is now possible for the entire crew of a submarine to rehearse approaches and torpedo attacks against enemy task forces in trainers on dry land, which provide simulated visual observation of the enemy, simulated radar and sonar information, and in which all of the complex battle gear and fire-control mechanisms operate as they do in a real submarine.

Certain developments, whose progress was most promising, were not completed in time for extensive combat use. These are primarily guided missiles and pilotless aircraft, utilizing remote control by electronic apparatus. These new developments will play a major role in warfare of the future, carrying new explosives over greatly increased ranges.

In the early days of research leading towards the application of atomic energy for military purposes, the Naval Research Laboratory was the only government facility engaged in this type of work. At the Laboratory there was developed a liquid thermal diffusion process for separation of uranium isotopes. Enriched chemicals, as well as basic designs and operating practices, were later supplied to the Army and used in one of the Oak Ridge plants manufacturing the atomic bomb.

The complexity of modern warfare in both methods and means demands exacting analysis of the measures and countermeasures introduced at every stage by ourselves and the enemy. Scientific research can not only speed the invention and production of weapons, but also assist in insuring their correct use. The application, by qualified scientists, of the scientific method to the improvement of naval operating techniques and material, has come to be called operations research. Scientists engaged in operations research are experts who advise that part of the Navy which is using the weapons and craft—the fleets themselves. To function effectively they must work under the direction of, and have close personal contact with, the officers who plan and carry on the operations of war.

During the war we succeeded in enlisting the services of a group of competent scientists to carry out operations research. This group was set up as a flexible organization able to reassign personnel quickly when new critical problems arose. Fiscal and administrative control of the group was originally vested in the Office of Scientific Research and Development. The group as a whole was assigned to the Navy for functional control, and in the course of time was attached to my Headquarters.

The initial impulse toward the formation of such a group arose in April 1942, during the early days of the antisubmarine war. With the cooperation of the Antisubmarine Division of the National Defense Research Committee, seven scientists were recruited by Columbia University and assigned to the Antisubmarine Warfare Unit, Atlantic Fleet.

During the year 1942 the group was considerably increased in size, and in July 1943, at a strength of approximately forty members, it was incorporated into the staff of the Tenth Fleet as the Antisubmarine Warfare Operations Research Group. Subsequently the administrative responsibility for the group was transferred from Columbia University to the Office of Field Service, without alteration in relationships with the Navy. In October 1944, with the decline of the submarine menace, the group was transferred to the Readiness Division of my Headquarters and renamed the Operations Research Group. At the close of the war it consisted of seventy-three scientists, drawn from a wide variety of backgrounds. Many of the members were attached, as the need arose, to the staffs of fleet and type commanders overseas, and at operating bases in war theaters. So far as possible they were afforded the opportunity of observing combat operations at first hand.

Operations research, as it developed, fell into two main categories: theoretical analysis of tactics, strategy and the equipment of war on the one hand; and statistical analysis of operations on the other. Each type of naval operation had to be analyzed theoretically to determine the maximum potentialities of the equipment involved, the probable reactions of the personnel, and the nature of the tactics which would combine equipment and personnel in an optimum manner. Action reports, giving the actual results obtained in this type of operation, were studied in a quantitative manner in order to amplify, correct, and correlate closely the theoretical analysis with what was actually happening on the field of battle. The knowledge resulting from this continued cross-check of theory with practice made it possible to work out improvements in tactics which sometimes increased the effectiveness of weapons by factors of three or five, to detect changes in the enemy's tactics in time to counter them before they became dangerous, and to calculate force requirements for future operations.

The late war, more than any other, involved the interplay of new technical measures and opposing countermeasures. For example, the German u-boats had to revise their tactics and equipment when we began to use radar on our antisubmarine aircraft; and we, in turn had to modify our tactics and radar equipment to counter their changes. In this see-saw of techniques the side which countered quickly, before the opponent had time to perfect the new tactics and weapons, had a decided advantage. Operations research, bringing scientists in to analyze the technical import of the fluctuations between measure and countermeasure, made it possible to speed up our reaction rate in several critical cases.

Likewise, in their struggle to counteract our improved convoy escort tactics, the u-boats introduced the acoustic torpedo, which steers for a ship by listening to the sound it makes under water. Our development of countermeasures was based on studies by the Operations Research Group into the pattern of sound produced in the sea by ships' propellers and on the probable reaction of the torpedo to various decoy devices. In this and other cases, information derived from intelligence sources was interpreted by the members of the group in the light of their own scientific knowledge and utilized to devise improved countermeasures.

Submarine and antisubmarine operations are closely complementary. Methods developed for attack have as a counterpart methods for defense based on the principles underlying both. In the subgroup devoted to submarine warfare, theoretical and operational studies were carried out on coordination of attack by groups of submarines; torpedo fire control; effectiveness of rescue of downed aviators; causes of loss of United States submarines; the relative merits of various types of torpedoes under differing circumstances; and enemy countermeasures to our radar search equipment.

Research on air problems has been devoted in the main to perfection of tactics designed to minimize flak hazard to naval aircraft attacking gun-defended targets, and to analysis of accuracy and effectiveness of aerial weapons, primarily against seaborne targets. Bombs, rockets, and torpedoes are designed for distinct uses, conditioned by the accuracy of launching and by their lethal effectiveness. Studies of the peculiarities of these weapons have led to recommendations for tactics and training procedures.

Studies were carried out by other subgroups on defense of task forces against suicide attacks, on the effectiveness of antiaircraft fire, and on problems of naval gunfire as a support for amphibious landings.

The Operations Research Group, to be renamed the Operations Evaluation Group as more closely descriptive of its function, will be continued as part of the naval organization at an appropriate peacetime strength.

The assistance and cooperation of industry and science have been indispensable. Without this assistance, many of the weapons which have come into being as the result of intensive wartime research and development otherwise never would have been completed and introduced into the fleet.

It had often been predicted that in a national emergency the totalitarian countries would have a great technical advantage over the democracies because of their ability to regiment scientific facilities and manpower at will. The results achieved by Germany, Italy and Japan do not bear out this contention. Studies made since the close of the war indicate that in none of these countries was the scientific effort as effectively handled as in the United States. The rapid, effective and original results obtained in bringing science into our effort are proof of the responsiveness of our form of government to meeting emergencies, the technical competence of American scientists, and the productive genius of American industry.

It would be unfair to others to single out by name individual scientists who made important scientific and technical contributions to the improvement of old or the development of new weapons. There were thousands of such contributions. It is generally conceded that with respect to originality of ideas and individual resourcefulness the scientists in the axis countries were as competent as our own. Where American science outdistanced the axis powers was in the superior administration of the over-all effort so that the available scientific manpower of the country could function with the maximum effectiveness. The leadership for what may be broadly termed the civilian emergency scientific effort was provided by the same individuals during the entire war period. These individuals deserve special mention among those responsible for the superb administrative efficiency which characterized the American conduct of the war throughout. Dr. Vannevar Bush as the Director of the Office of Scientific Research and Development carried the over-all administrative and technical responsibility for that organization. Under him Dr. James B. Conant as Chairman of the National Defense Research Committee; Dr. Alfred N. Richards as Chairman of the Committee on Medical Research, and Dr. Karl T. Compton as the head of the Office of Field Services administered the scientific and technical activities of the Office of Scientific Research and Development. Dr. Frank B. Jewett as the President of the National Academy of Sciences and of its working body the National Research Council, and Dr. Jerome C. Hunsaker as the Chairman of the National Advisory Committee for Aeronautics directed the activities of these organizations during this period. The coordination of the work of these groups with the Navy was handled by the Office of the Coordinator of Research and Development headed by Rear Admiral J. A. Furer.

I wish to pay particular tribute to the group of scientists, industrialists and officers of the Army and Navy who, under the direction of Major General L. R. Groves, USA, achieved the final outstanding technical success of the war—the development of a practical atomic bomb and the method of using it from aircraft.

Sufficient progress in the technical development and use of improved weapons and associated equipment has been made during the war to emphasize the necessity for continued progress. Working under the stress of an emergency, the factor of primary importance was immediate effectiveness against the enemy. This resulted in "crash designs" and production that required considerably more personnel, weight and space, than the more seasoned designs that might have been produced had time been available. Thus, the rapid expansion and development of new weapons and devices during the war was often at the cost of factors of major importance, such as the reserve buoyancy and stability of the ships in which they were installed. Those wartime designs, while they have well served their purpose against the enemy, have nevertheless created problems of refinement and improvement in the ultimate design of equipment, which must be so resolved that a minimum of personnel, weight and space will be required to attain the desired effect. These problems must be energetically attacked in the coming years of peace. Only by continuing vigorous research and development can this country hope to be protected from any potential enemies and maintain the position which it now enjoys in possessing the greatest effective naval fighting force in history.

* *

VIII
Conclusion

IN my previous reports, I have touched upon the effective cooperation between our Allies which has been of such fundamental and signal importance in accounting for the success of our combined undertakings. This cooperation has continued and been extended in the period since my last report.

I have spoken before of the full measure of cooperation and support rendered by the ground, air and service forces of the Army in a partnership of accomplishment, which neither Navy nor Army could have carried out singly. For that cooperation, undiminished throughout the war, and to the wholehearted support from the great body of citizens who performed the countless and varied tasks which made up our war effort, I reaffirm my appreciation.

Just as the Navy depended upon its sister services and upon the multitude of activities which produced the implements of war, so also did the Navy rely for success upon the Reserves and the Regulars, the men and women who constituted its mutually supporting elements—the Fleet, the Shore Establishment, the Marine Corps, the Coast Guard and the Seabees—each of which contributed its full share to victory.

The end of the war came before we had dared to expect it. As late as August 1943 strategic studies drawn up by the British and United States planners contemplated the war against Japan continuing far into 1947. Even the latest plans were based upon the Japanese war lasting a year after the fall of Germany. Actually Japan's defeat came within three months of Germany's collapse. The nation can be thankful that the unrelenting acceleration of our power in the Pacific ended the war in 1945.

The price of victory has been high. Beginning with the dark days of December 1941 and continuing until September 1945, when ships of the Pacific Fleet steamed triumphant into Tokyo Bay, the Navy's losses were severe. The casualties of the United States Navy, Marine Corps and Coast Guard reached the totals of 56,206 dead, 80,259 wounded, and 8,967 missing. Many of these gallant men fell in battle; many were lost in strenuous and hazardous operations convoying our shipping or patrolling the seas and skies; others were killed in training for the duties that Fate would not permit them to carry out. All honor to these heroic men. To their families and to those who have suffered the physical and mental anguish of wounds, the Navy includes its sympathy in that of the country they served so well.

It is my sincere hope—and expectation—that the United States will hereafter remain ever ready to support and maintain the peace of the world by being ever ready to back up its words with deeds.

Appendix A

Status of major combatant ships of Japanese Navy at the conclusion of hostilities

Name	Date Commissioned (Prior to 7 December 1941 unless otherwise indicated)	Final Disposition

BATTLESHIPS

Name	Date Commissioned	Final Disposition
FUSO		SUNK 25 October 1944 in Surigao Straits, P.I., by U.S. destroyers
HARUNA		SUNK 28 July 1945 at Kure by U.S. carrier planes
HIYEI		SUNK 13–14 November 1942 off Savo Is., Solomons, by U.S. fleet units and aircraft
HYUGA		SUNK 28 July 1945 at Kure by U.S. carrier planes
ISE		SUNK 28 July 1945 at Kure by U.S. carrier planes
KIRISHIMA		SUNK 15 November 1942 off Savo Is., Solomons, by U.S. fleet units
KONGO		SUNK 21 November 1944 off Foochow, China, by U.S. submarine
MUSASHI	August 1942	SUNK 25 October 1944 in Sibuyan Sea, P.I., by U.S. carrier planes
MUTSU		SUNK 8 June 1943 in Hiroshima Bay by accidental explosion
NAGATO		HEAVILY DAMAGED 18 July 1945 at Yokosuka by U.S. carrier planes
YAMASHIRO		SUNK 25 October 1944 in Surigao Straits, P.I., by U.S. fleet units
YAMATO	December 1941	SUNK 7 April 1945 off Kyushu by U.S. carrier planes

AIRCRAFT CARRIERS

Name	Date Commissioned	Final Disposition
AKAGI		SUNK 4 June 1942 off Midway by U.S. carrier planes
AMAGI	August 1944	HEAVILY DAMAGED 24–28 July 1945 at Kure by U.S. carrier planes

Name	Date Commissioned	Final Disposition
CHITOSE	January 1944	SUNK 25 October 1944 N.E. of Luzon by U.S. carrier planes
CHIYODA	October 1943	SUNK 25 October 1944 N.E. of Luzon by U.S. carrier planes and fleet units
HAYATAKA (JUNYO)	May 1942	HEAVILY DAMAGED 9 December 1944 off Nagasaki; out of action at Sasebo
HIRYU		SUNK 5 June 1942 off Midway by U.S. carrier planes
HITAKA (HIYO)	July 1942	SUNK 20 June 1944 in Philippine Sea by U.S. carrier planes
HOSHO		OUT OF ACTION, lightly damaged, in Japan area
KAGA		SUNK 4 June 1942 off Midway by U.S. carrier planes
KASAGI	Not commissioned	Under camouflage at Sasebo; fitting out discontinued
KATSURAGI	October 1944	HEAVILY DAMAGED 24–28 July 1945 at Kure by U.S. carrier planes
RYUHO	November 1942	HEAVILY DAMAGED 19 March 1945 at Kure by U.S. carrier planes
RYUJO		SUNK 24 August 1942 off Malaita Is., Solomons, by U.S. carrier planes
SHINANO	November 1944	SUNK 29 November 1944 S. of Honshu by U.S. submarine
SHOHO	December 1941	SUNK 7 May 1942 in Coral Sea by U.S. carrier planes
SHOKAKU		SUNK 19 June 1944 off Yap by U.S. submarine
SORYU		SUNK 4 June 1942 off Midway by U.S. carrier planes and submarine
TAIHO	March 1944	SUNK 19 June 1944 off Yap by U.S. submarine
UNRYU	1944	SUNK 19 December 1944 in E. China Sea by U.S. submarine
ZUIHO		SUNK 25 October 1944 N.E. of Luzon by U.S. carrier planes
ZUIKAKU		SUNK 25 October 1944 N.E. of Luzon by U.S. carrier planes

ESCORT AIRCRAFT CARRIERS

Name	Date Commissioned	Final Disposition
CHUYO	November 1942	SUNK 4 December 1943 S.E. of Honshu by U.S. submarine
KAIYO	November 1943	SUNK 24 July 1945 in Beppu Bay, Japan, by U.S. carrier planes
JINYO	December 1943	SUNK 17 November 1944 in S. Yellow Sea by U.S. submarine

Name	Date Commissioned	Final Disposition
OTAKA	1942	SUNK 18 August 1944 N.W. of Luzon by U.S. submarine
UNYO	1942	SUNK 16 September 1944 in S. China Sea by U.S. submarine

HEAVY CRUISERS

Name	Final Disposition
AOBA	SUNK 28 July 1945 at Kure by U.S. carrier planes
ASHIGARA	SUNK 8 June 1945 S.E. of Singapore by British submarine
ATAGO	SUNK 23 October 1944 off Palawan, P.I., by U.S. submarine
CHIKUMA	SUNK 25 October 1944 E. of Samar, P.I., by U.S. carrier planes and fleet units
CHOKAI	SUNK 24 October 1944 E. of Samar, P.I., by U.S. carrier planes
FURUTAKA	SUNK 11 October 1942 off Savo Is., Solomons, by U.S. fleet units
HAGURO	SUNK 16 May 1945 off Penang by British carrier planes and destroyers
KAKO	SUNK 10 August 1942 off New Ireland by U.S. submarine
KINUGASA	SUNK 14 November 1942 off Savo Is., Solomons, by U.S. carrier planes
KUMANO	SUNK 25 November 1944 off W. Luzon by U.S. carrier planes
MAYA	SUNK 23 October 1944 off Palawan, P.I., by U.S. submarine
MIKUMA	SUNK 6 June 1942 off Midway Is., by U.S. carrier planes
MOGAMI	SUNK 25 October 1944 in Mindanao Sea, P.I., by U.S. fleet units and aircraft
MYOKO	OUT OF ACTION at Singapore; heavily damaged 13 December 1944 S.W. of Saigon by U.S. submarine
NACHI	SUNK 5 November 1944 in Manila Bay by U.S. carrier planes
SUZUYA	SUNK 25 October 1944 E. of Samar, P.I., by U.S. carrier planes
TAKAO	OUT OF ACTION at Singapore; heavily damaged 23 October 1944 off Palawan, P.I., by U.S. submarine
TONE	SUNK 28 July 1945 at Kure by U.S. carrier aircraft

Name	Date Commissioned	Final Disposition
\	\	**LIGHT CRUISERS**
ABUKUMA		SUNK 26 October 1944 off Negros, P.I., by B-24's and fleet units
AGANO	October 1942	SUNK 16 February 1944 N. of Truk by U.S. submarine
ISUZU		SUNK 7 April 1945 N. of Soembawa, N.E.I., by U.S. submarines
JINTSU		SUNK 13 July 1943 N. of Kolombangara, Solomons, by U.S. fleet units
KINU		SUNK 26 October 1944 S.W. of Masbate, P.I., by U.S. carrier planes
KISO		SUNK 13 November 1944 in Manila Bay by U.S. carrier planes
KITAGAMI		HEAVILY DAMAGED 24–28 July 1945 off Kure by U.S. carrier planes
KUMA		SUNK 11 January 1944 off Penang by British submarine
NAGARA		SUNK 7 August 1944 W. of Kyushu by U.S. submarine
NAKA		SUNK 17 February 1944 S.W. of Truk by U.S. carrier planes
NATORI		SUNK 18 August 1944 E. of Samar, P.I., by U.S. submarine
NOSHIRO		SUNK 26 October 1944 N.W. of Panay, P.I., by U.S. carrier planes
OI		SUNK 19 July 1944 in S. China Sea by U.S. submarine
OYODO	February 1943	SUNK 28 July 1945 at Kure by U.S. carrier planes
SAKAWA	November 1944	In Japan
SENDAI		SUNK 2 November 1943 W. of Bougainville, Solomons by U.S. fleet units
TAMA		SUNK 25 October 1944 N.E. of Luzon by U.S. submarine
TATSUTA		SUNK 14 March 1944 S. of Yokohama by U.S. submarine
TENRYU		SUNK 18 December 1942 in Bismarck Sea by U.S. submarine
YAHAGI	December 1943	SUNK 7 April 1945 off Kyushu by U.S. carrier planes
YUBARI		SUNK 27 April 1944 S. of Palau by U.S. submarine
YURA		SUNK 25 October 1942 off Santa Isabel, Solomons by U.S. planes

APPENDIX A

Name	Date Commissioned	Final Disposition

TRAINING CRUISERS

KASHII		SUNK 12 January 1945 in S. China Sea by U.S. carrier planes
KASHIMA		In Japan
KATORI		SUNK 17 February 1944 at Truk by U.S. fleet units and carrier planes

DESTROYERS

AKATSUKI		SUNK 13 November 1942 off Savo Is., Solomons, by U.S. cruiser
AKEBONO		SUNK 13 November 1944 in Manila Bay by U.S. carrier planes
AKIGUMO	1942	SUNK 11 April 1944 off Zamboanga, Mindanao, by U.S. submarine
AKIKAZE		SUNK 3 November 1944 in S. China Sea by U.S. submarine
AKISHIMO	1944	SUNK 13 November 1944 in Manila Bay by U.S. carrier planes
AKITSUKI	1942	SUNK 22 December 1944 off Omai Saki, Honshu, by U.S. submarine
AMAGIRI		SUNK 23 April 1944 in Makassar Strait by mine
AMATSUKAZE		DESTROYED 6 April 1945 off Amoy by B-25's
ARARE		SUNK 5 July 1942 off Kiska by U.S. submarine
ARASHI		SUNK 6 August 1943 in Vella Gulf, New Georgia, by U.S. destroyers
ARASHIO		SUNK 3 March 1943 in Huon Gulf, New Guinea, by U.S. Army bombers
ARIAKE		SUNK 28 July 1943 off Cape Gloucester, New Britain, by B-25's
ASAGAO		HEAVILY DAMAGED 22 August 1945 near Moji; in Japan
ASAGIRI		SUNK 28 August 1942 off Santa Isabel, Solomons, by Marine bombers
ASAGUMO		SUNK 25 October 1944 in Surigao Strait by U.S. fleet units
ASAKAZE		SUNK 23 August 1944 off Cape Bolinao, Luzon, by U.S. submarine
ASANAGI		SUNK 22 May 1944 N.W. of Bonin Is., by U.S. submarine
ASASHIMO	1943	SUNK 7 April 1945 off Kyushu by U.S. carrier planes
ASASHIO		SUNK 3 March 1943 in Huon Gulf, New Guinea by U.S. Army bombers

Name	Date Commissioned	Final Disposition
AYANAMI		SUNK 15 November 1942 off Savo Is., Solomons, by U.S. fleet units
ENOKI	1945	HEAVILY DAMAGED 24 July 1945 near Maizuru; in Japan
FUBUKI		SUNK 11 October 1942 off Savo Is., Solomons, by U.S. fleet units
FUJINAMI	1943	SUNK 27 October 1944 S. of Mindoro, P.I., by U.S. carrier planes
FUMITSUKI		SUNK 17 February 1944 at Truk by U.S. carrier planes
FUYO		SUNK 20 December 1943 off Manila by U.S. submarine
FUYUTSUKI	1944	HEAVILY DAMAGED at Moji by mine; decommissioned
HAGI		DAMAGED; in Japan
HAGIKAZE		SUNK 6 August 1943 in Vella Gulf, New Georgia, by U.S. destroyers
HAKAZE		SUNK 23 January 1943 off Steffen Strait, Bismarcks, by U.S. submarine
HAMAKAZE		SUNK 7 April 1945 off Kyushu by U.S. carrier planes
HAMANAMI	1944	SUNK 11 November 1944 in Ormoc Bay by U.S. carrier planes
HANATZUKI	1945	LIGHTLY DAMAGED; in Japan
HARUKAZE		HEAVILY DAMAGED 21 January 1945 at Bako; in Japan
HARUSAME		SUNK 8 June 1944 N.W. of Manokwari, New Guinea, by B-25's
HARUTSUKI	1945	In Japan
HASU		HEAVILY DAMAGED 16 January 1945 off Hongkong; at Tsingtao
HATAKAZE		SUNK 15 January 1945 in Takao Harbor
HATSUHARU		SUNK 13 November 1944 in Manila Bay by U.S. carrier planes
HATSUKAZE		SUNK 2 November 1943 W. of Bougainville Is., by U.S. fleet units
HATSUME	1945	Not manned; in Japan
HATSUSHIMO		SUNK 30 July 1945 in Miyazu Bay
HATSUYUKI		SUNK 17 July 1943 off Kahili, Bougainville, by U.S. Naval and Marine planes
HATSUZAKURA	1945	In Japan
HATSUZUKI	1942	SUNK 25 November 1944 S.W. of Manila by U.S. submarine
HAYANAMI	1943	SUNK 7 June 1944 S.E. of Sibutu passage, P.I., by U.S. submarine

APPENDIX A

Name	Date Commissioned	Final Disposition
HAYASHIMO	1944	SUNK 26 October 1944 S.E. of Mindoro, P.I., by U.S. carrier planes
HAYASHIO		SUNK 24 November 1942 in Huon Gulf, New Guinea by B-17's
HAYATE		SUNK 11 December 1941 off Wake Is. by shore batteries
HIBIKI		HEAVILY DAMAGED 29 March 1945 at Himejima; in Japan
HINOKI	1944	HEAVILY DAMAGED 5 January 1945 off Manila; in Japan
HOKAZE		SUNK 6 July 1944 in S. Celebes Sea by U.S. submarine
IKAZUCHI		SUNK 13 April 1944 S.W. of Guam by U.S. submarine
INAZUMA		SUNK 14 May 1944 off Tawi Tawi, P.I., by U.S. submarine
ISOKAZE		SUNK 7 April 1945 off Kyushu by U.S. carrier planes
ISONAMI		SUNK 9 April 1943 in Buton passage, Celebes, by U.S. submarine
IWANAMI	1944	SUNK 4 December 1944 in S. China Sea by U.S. submarine
KABA	1944	HEAVILY DAMAGED 24 July 1945 in Inland Sea; in Japan
KAEDE	1944	HEAVILY DAMAGED 31 January 1945 S. of Formosa; in Japan
KAGERO		SUNK 8 May 1943 in Blackett Strait, New Georgia, by mines and aircraft
KAKI	1944	Not manned; in Japan
KAMIKAZE		Operational; at Singapore
KARUKAYA		SUNK 10 May 1944 off Manila Bay by U.S. submarine
KASHI	1944	HEAVILY DAMAGED 21 January 1945 at Takao; in Japan
KASHIWA	Not commissioned	In Japan
KASUMI		SUNK 7 April 1945 off Kyushu by U.S. carrier planes
KAWAKAZE		SUNK 6 August 1943 in Vella Gulf, New Georgia, by U.S. destroyers
KAYA	1944	HEAVILY DAMAGED 27 December 1944 off Mindoro; in Japan
KAZEGUMO	1942	SUNK 8 June 1944 off Davao, Mindanao, P.I., by U.S. submarine
KEYAKI	1945	Not manned; in Japan

Name	Date Commissioned	Final Disposition
KIKUTSUKI		SUNK 4 May 1942 off Tulagi, Solomons, by U.S. carrier planes
KIRI	1944	HEAVILY DAMAGED 12 December 1944 near Leyte; in Japan
KISARAGI		SUNK 11 December 1941 off Wake Is. by shore batteries
KISHINAMI	1943	SUNK 20 November 1944 in Luzon Strait by U.S. submarine (?)
KIYONAMI	1943	SUNK 20 July 1943 in Vella Gulf, New Georgia, by U.S. Army and Navy planes
KIYOSHIMO	1944	SUNK 26 December 1944 off Mindoro, P.I., by U.S. PT's and Army planes
KURETAKE		SUNK 30 December 1944 in Luzon Strait by U.S. submarine
KURI		At Tsingtao
KUROSHIO		SUNK 8 May 1943 in Blackett Strait, New Georgia, by mines
KUSUNOKI	1945	At Maizuru; not manned
KUWA	1944	SUNK 3 December 1944 in Ormoc Bay by U.S. destroyers
MAIKAZE		SUNK 17 February 1944 N.W. of Truk by U.S. fleet units and carrier planes
MAKI	1944	HEAVILY DAMAGED 9 December 1944 off Mejima Is.; in Japan
MAKIGUMO	1942	SUNK 1 February 1943 off Guadalcanal Is. by mine, PT boat, or aircraft
MAKINAMI	1942	SUNK 25 November 1943 N.W. of Buka Is., Solomons, by U.S. destroyers
MATSU	1944	SUNK 4 August 1944 N.W. of Bonin Is. by U.S. fleet units
MATSUKAZE		SUNK 9 June 1944 E. of Bonin Is. by U.S. submarine
MICHISHIO		SUNK 25 October 1944 in Surigao Strait by U.S. destroyers
MIKATSUKI		SUNK 28 July 1943 off Cape Gloucester, New Britain, by B-25's
MINAZUKI		SUNK 6 June 1944 S. of Sibutu passage, P.I., by U.S. submarine
MINEGUMO		SUNK 6 March 1943 in Kula Gulf, New Georgia by U.S. fleet units
MINEKAZE		SUNK 10 February 1944 E. of Formosa by U.S. submarine
MOCHIZUKI		SUNK 24 October 1943 E. of New Britain by U.S. Navy patrol bomber

APPENDIX A

Name	Date Commissioned	Final Disposition
MOMI	1944	SUNK 5 January 1945 S.W. of Manila Bay by U.S. carrier planes
MOMO	1944	SUNK 15 December 1944 W. of Luzon from unknown cause
MURAKUMO		SUNK 12 October 1942 off New Georgia Is. by U.S. carrier planes
MURASAME		SUNK 6 March 1943 in Kula Gulf, New Georgia, by U.S. fleet units
MUTSUKI		SUNK 25 August 1942 off Santa Isabel, Solomons, by B-17's
NAGANAMI	1942	SUNK 11 November 1944 in Ormoc Bay by U.S. carrier planes
NAGATSUKI		SUNK 6 July 1943 in Kula Gulf, New Georgia, by U.S. fleet units
NAMIKAZE		HEAVILY DAMAGED 8 September 1944 in Kuriles; in Japan
NARA	1945	HEAVILY DAMAGED 30 June 1945 in Shimonoseki Strait; in Japan
NASHI	1945	SUNK 28 July 1945 at Kure
NATSUGUMO		SUNK 11 October 1942 off Savo Is., Solomons, by U.S. fleet units
NATSUSHIO		SUNK 8 February 1942 off Makassar, Celebes, by U.S. submarine
NATSUZUKI	1945	HEAVILY DAMAGED 16 June 1945 near Matsure; in Japan
NENOHI		SUNK 4 July 1942 off Agattu, Aleutians, by U.S. submarine
NIRE	1945	HEAVILY DAMAGED 22 June 1945 at Kure; in Japan
NIIZUKI	1943	SUNK 6 July 1943 in Kula Gulf, New Georgia, by U.S. fleet units
NOKAZE		SUNK 20 February 1945 N.E. of Saigon by U.S. submarines
NOWAKE		SUNK 25 October 1944 in Surigao Strait by U.S. fleet units
NUMAKAZE		SUNK 18 December 1943 in E. China Sea by U.S. submarine
OBORO		SUNK 12 August 1942 S. of Honshu by U.S. submarine
OINAMI	Not commissioned	
OITE		SUNK 18 February 1944 at Truk by U.S. carrier planes
OKIKAZE		SUNK 10 January 1943 off Honshu by U.S. submarine

Name	Date Commissioned	Final Disposition
OKINAMI	1944	SUNK 13 November 1944 in Manila Bay by U.S. carrier planes
ONAMI	1943	SUNK 25 November 1943 N.W. of Buka Is., Solomons, by U.S. destroyers
OSHIO		SUNK 20 February 1943 N. of Admiralty Is. by U.S. submarine
OTAKE	1945	At Maizuru; not manned
OYASHIO		SUNK 8 May 1943 in Blackett Strait, New Georgia, by mines and aircraft
SAGIRI		SUNK 24 December 1941 off Kuching, Borneo, by Dutch submarine
SAKURA	1945	SUNK 11 July 1945 near Osaka
SAMIDARE		SUNK 26 August 1944 off Palau by U.S. carrier planes and submarine
SANAE		SUNK 18 November 1943 in Celebes Sea by U.S. submarine
SATSUKI		SUNK 21 September 1944 in Manila Bay by U.S. carrier planes
SAWAKAZE		DECOMMISSIONED; in Japan
SAZANAMI		SUNK 14 January 1944 S.E. of Yap Is. by U.S. submarine
SHII	1945	Operational; in Japan area
SHIGEZAKURA	1945	SUNK 18 July 1945 Yokosuka by U.S. carrier planes
SHIGURE		SUNK 24 January 1945 N.W. of Borneo by U.S. submarine
SHIKINAMI		SUNK 12 September 1944 S. China Sea by U.S. submarine
SHIMAKAZE	1943	SUNK 11 November 1944 in Ormoc Bay by U.S. carrier planes
SHIMOTSUKI	1944	SUNK 25 November 1944 W. of Borneo by U.S. submarine
SHINONOME		SUNK 18 December 1941 off Miri, Borneo, by mine
SHIOKAZE		HEAVILY DAMAGED 31 January 1945 S. of Formosa; in Japan
SHIRAKUMO		SUNK 16 March 1944 S.E. of Hokkaido by U.S. submarine
SHIRANUHI		SUNK 27 October 1944 in P.I. by U.S. carrier planes
SHIRATSUYU		SUNK 20 June 1944 in Philippine Sea by U.S. carrier planes
SHIRAYUKI		SUNK 3 March 1943 Huon Gulf, New Guinea, by U.S. Army bombers

Name	Date Commissioned	Final Disposition
SUGI		HEAVILY DAMAGED 21 January 1945 at Takao; in Japan
SUMIRE	1945	At Maizuru; not manned
SUZUKAZE		SUNK 26 January 1944 N.W. of Ponape by U.S. submarine
SUZUNAMI	1943	SUNK 11 November 1943 at Rabaul by U.S. carrier planes
SUZUTSUKI	1942	HEAVILY DAMAGED 7 April 1945 S. of Kyushu; decommissioned; in Japan
TACHIBANA	1945	SUNK 15 July 1945 at Ominato by U.S. fleet units
TACHIKAZE		SUNK 17 February 1944 at Truk by U.S. carrier planes
TAKANAMI	1942	SUNK 30 November 1942 off Savo Is., Solomons, by U.S. fleet units
TAKE	1944	In Inland Sea
TAMANAMI	1943	SUNK 7 July 1944 S.W. of Manila by U.S. submarine
TANIKAZE		SUNK 9 June 1944 in Sibutu passage, P.I., by U.S. submarine
TERUTSUKI	1942	SUNK 12 December 1942 off Guadalcanal Is. by U.S. PT boats
TOKITSUKAZE		SUNK 3 March 1943 in Huon Gulf, New Guinea, by U.S. Army bombers
TSUBAKI	1945	HEAVILY DAMAGED 24 July 1945 near Okayama; in Japan
TSUGA		SUNK 15 January 1945 off Pescadores Is. by U.S. carrier planes
TSUTA	1945	In Inland Sea
UME	1944	SUNK 31 January 1945 S.W. of Takao by B-25's
UMIKAZE		SUNK 1 February 1944 S.E. of Truk by U.S. submarine
URAKAZE		SUNK 9 June 1944 in Sibutu passage, P.I., by U.S. submarine
URANAMI		SUNK 26 October 1944 S.W. of Masbate, P.I., by U.S. carrier planes
USHIO		HEAVILY DAMAGED 14 November 1944 at Manila; in Japan
USUGUMO		SUNK 7 July 1944 in Sea of Okhotsk by U.S. submarine
UZUKI		SUNK 11 December 1944 off Leyte by U.S. PT boats
WAKABA		SUNK 24 October 1944 S. of Mindoro by U.S. carrier planes

Name	Date Commissioned	Final Disposition
WAKATAKE		SUNK 30 March 1944 at Palau by U.S. carrier planes
WAKATSUKI	1943	SUNK 11 November 1944 in Ormoc Bay by U.S. carrier planes
YAKAZE		Converted to target ship; in Japan area
YAMAGUMO		SUNK 25 October 1944 in Surigao Strait by U.S. destroyers
YAMAKAZE		SUNK 25 June 1942 off Yokohama by U.S. submarine
YANAGI	1945	HEAVILY DAMAGED 15 July 1945 at Ominato by U.S. fleet units
YAYOI		SUNK 11 September 1942 off Normanby Is. by B-17's
YOITSUKI	1945	HEAVILY DAMAGED 2 June 1945 N. of Hime-jima; in Japan
YUDACHI		SUNK 13 November 1942 off Savo Is., Solomons, by U.S. fleet units
YUGIRI		SUNK 25 November 1943 N.W. of Buka Is., Solomons, by U.S. destroyers
YUGUMO		SUNK 6 October 1943 N.W. of Vella Lavella, Solomons, by U.S. destroyers
YUGURE		SUNK 20 July 1943 in Vella Gulf, New Georgia, by U.S. Navy bombers
YUKAZE		Converted to target ship; in Japan
YUKIKAZE		HEAVILY DAMAGED 30 July 1945 at Miyazu; in Japan
YUNAGI		SUNK 25 August 1944 off N.W. Luzon by U.S. submarine
YUZUKI		SUNK 13 December 1944 in Leyte area by U.S. carrier planes

SUBMARINES

Submarine losses indicated in this list have been confirmed. Dates and locations of losses in some cases are estimates based upon the best available information.

I-1		SUNK 29 January 1943 off Guadalcanal by New Zealand corvettes
I-2		SUNK 7 April 1944 E. of Admiralty Is. by U.S. destroyer
I-3		SUNK 9 December 1942 off Guadalcanal by U.S. PT boat
I-4		SUNK 21 December 1942 S. of Rabaul by U.S. submarine

APPENDIX A

Name	Date Commissioned	Final Disposition
I-5		SUNK 10 June 1944 N.W. of Bismarck Is. by U.S. destroyer
I-6		SUNK 4 July 1944 E. of Saipan by U.S. fleet units
I-7		SUNK 22 June 1943 off Kiska by U.S. destroyer
I-8		SUNK 31 March 1945 S.W. of Okinawa by U.S. destroyers
I-9		SUNK 10 June 1943 N.E. of Attu by U.S. patrol craft
I-10		SUNK 18 July 1944 N. of Truk by U.S. destroyer escort
I-11	May 1942	SUNK 17 February 1944 E. of Marshall Is. by U.S. destroyer
I-12	May 1944	SUNK May 1945 in South Pacific
I-13	December 1944	SUNK 16 July 1945 E. of Honshu by U.S. carrier aircraft
I-14	March 1945	Captured at sea 27 August 1945; in Japan; decommissioned
I-15		SUNK October/November 1942 in South Pacific
I-16		SUNK 19 May 1944 N.E. of Solomons by U.S. destroyer escort
I-17		SUNK 19 August 1943 off New Caledonia by Allied surface craft and planes
I-18		SUNK 25 December 1942 off Kumusi R., New Guinea, by U.S. PT boat
I-19		SUNK 26 November 1943 W. of Makin Is. by U.S. destroyers
I-20		SUNK 1 October 1943 N. of Kolombangara Is. by U.S. destroyer
I-21		SUNK 5 February 1944 in S. Marshalls by U.S. destroyer escorts
I-22		SUNK 19 November 1942 off San Cristobal Is. by U.S. destroyer
I-23		SUNK 26 April 1942 off Johnston Is. by U.S. submarine
I-24		SUNK 27 July 1943 S.W. of New Hanover by U.S. submarine
I-25		SUNK October/November 1943 in Central Pacific
I-26		SUNK 25 October 1944 in Leyte Gulf by U.S. destroyer escort
I-27	February 1942	SUNK 12 February 1944 S.W. of Maldive Is. by British destroyers
I-28	February 1942	SUNK 17 May 1942 S. of Truk by U.S. submarine

Name	Date Commissioned	Final Disposition
I-29	February 1942	SUNK 26 July 1944 in Luzon Strait by U.S. submarine
I-30	March 1942	SUNK May/June 1942 in Western Pacific
I-31	May 1942	SUNK 13 June 1943 N. of Kiska by U.S. destroyer
I-32	April 1942	SUNK 24 March 1944 E. of Marshall Is. by U.S. fleet units
I-33	June 1942	SUNK June 1942 in Western Pacific by accident
I-34	August 1942	SUNK 13 November 1943 in Malacca Straits by British submarine
I-35	August 1942	SUNK 23 November 1943 off Tarawa by U.S. destroyers
I-36	September 1942	In Japan
I-37	March 1943	SUNK 18 November 1944 E. of Samar by U.S. destroyer and carrier planes
I-38	January 1943	SUNK 13 November 1944 N.E. of Oahu by U.S. fleet units
I-39	April 1943	SUNK 24 December 1943 off Guadalcanal by U.S. destroyer
I-40	July 1943	SUNK March/April 1944 in Central Pacific
I-41	September 1943	SUNK 16 September 1944 E. of Honshu by U.S. submarine
I-42	November 1943	SUNK 23 March 1944 S.W. of Palau by U.S. submarine
I-43	November 1943	SUNK 15 February 1944 N.W. of Truk by U.S. submarine
I-44	1944	SUNK 18 April 1945 E. of Okinawa by U.S. destroyers
I-45	December 1943	SUNK 29 October 1944 E. of Dinegat Is. by U.S. destroyer escort
I-46	February 1944	SUNK December 1944 in Western Pacific
I-47	July 1944	Operational; in Japan area
I-48	September 1944	SUNK 23 January 1945 off Ulithi by U.S. destroyer escorts
I-49	May 1944	In Japan
I-52	December 1943	SUNK 24 June 1944 in Atlantic Ocean by U.S. carrier planes
I-53	February 1944	HEAVILY DAMAGED 30 March 1945; in Japan
I-54	March 1944	SUNK 28 October 1944 E. of Leyte Gulf by U.S. destroyer
I-55	April 1944	SUNK 27 July 1944 E. of Saipan by U.S. destroyer escort
I-56	June 1944	SUNK 5 April 1945 W. of Okinawa by U.S. destroyer

APPENDIX A

Name	Date Commissioned	Final Disposition
I-58	September 1944	Operational; in Japan
I-121		Operational; in Japan
I-122		SUNK 10 June 1945 in Japan Sea by U.S. submarine
I-123		SUNK 29 August 1942 E. of Guadalcanal Is. by U.S. destroyer
I-124		SUNK 20 January 1942 off Port Darwin by Allied surface craft
I-153		DECOMMISSIONED; in Japan
I-154		DECOMMISSIONED; in Japan
I-155		DECOMMISSIONED; in Japan
I-156		In Japan
I-157		In Japan
I-158		Operational; in Japan
I-159		Operational; in Japan
I-160(60)		SUNK 17 January 1942 in Sunda Straits by British destroyer
I-162		In Japan
I-164		SUNK 17 May 1942 S. of Kyushu by U.S. submarine
I-165		SUNK 27 June 1945 E. of Marianas Is. by naval aircraft
I-166		SUNK 17 July 1944 off Penang by British submarine
I-168		SUNK 3 September 1943 off New Hebrides by U.S. destroyer
I-169		SUNK 4 April 1944 at Truk
I-170(70)		SUNK 10 December 1941 off Pearl Harbor by U.S. carrier plane
I-171		SUNK 1 February 1944 W. of Buka by U.S. destroyer
I-172		SUNK October/November 1942 in South Pacific
I-173(73)		SUNK 27 January 1942 off Midway by U.S. submarine
I-174		SUNK 12 April 1944 N. of Truk by U.S. Navy bomber
I-175		SUNK 30 April 1944 S. of Truk by U.S. destroyers
I-176	July 1942	SUNK 17 May 1944 N.E. of Buka by U.S. destroyers
I-177	December 1942	SUNK November 1944 in South Pacific
I-178	December 1942	SUNK June 1943 in Central Pacific
I-179	June 1943	SUNK February 1944 in South Pacific

Name	Date Commissioned	Final Disposition
I-180	June 1943	SUNK 26 April 1944 off Kodiak, Alaska, by U.S. destroyer
I-181	May 1943	SUNK 16 January 1944 off St. George Channel, Bismarcks, by U.S. Navy planes
I-182	May 1943	SUNK 9 September 1943 in Surigao Strait by U.S. submarine
I-183	October 1943	SUNK 29 April 1944 off Bungo Channel, Japan, by U.S. submarine
I-184	October 1943	SUNK 21 June 1944 E. of Saipan by U.S. fleet units
I-185	September 1943	SUNK 17 June 1944 N.W. of Guam by U.S. destroyers
I-201	February 1945	In Japan
I-202	February 1945	In Japan
I-203	June 1945	In Japan
I-351	January 1945	SUNK 15 July 1945 N.W. of Borneo by U.S. submarine
I-361	May 1944	SUNK 30 May 1945 in Japanese waters
I-362	May 1944	SUNK 27 November 1944 in Camotes Sea by U.S. destroyers
I-363	July 1944	Operational; in Japan
I-364	June 1944	SUNK October 1944 in South Pacific
I-365	August 1944	SUNK 29 November 1944 S.E. of Tokyo Bay by U.S. submarine
I-366	August 1944	Operational; in Japan
I-367	August 1944	Operational; in Japan
I-368	August 1944	SUNK 26 February 1945 S. of Iwo Jima by U.S. destroyer escort
I-369	October 1944	DECOMMISSIONED September 1945; in Japan
I-370	September 1944	SUNK 26 February 1945 N.W. of Iwo Jima by U.S. carrier planes
I-371	October 1944	SUNK January 1945 in Truk area
I-372	November 1944	SUNK 18 July 1945 at Yokosuka by carrier planes
I-373	April 1945	SUNK 14 August 1945 in E. China Sea by U.S. submarine
I-400	December 1944	Captured at sea 27 August 1945; in Japan; decommissioned
I-401	January 1945	Captured at sea 29 August 1945; in Japan; decommissioned
I-402	July 1945	DECOMMISSIONED September 1945; in Japan
I-501	July 1945	At Singapore
I-502	July 1945	At Singapore
I-503	July 1945	In Japan
I-504	July 1945	In Japan

APPENDIX A

Name	Date Commissioned	Final Disposition
I-505	July 1945	At Batavia
I-506	July 1945	At Surabaya
RO-30		SUNK April 1942 in Western Pacific
RO-31		DECOMMISSIONED during 1944; in Japan
RO-32		SUNK April 1942 in Western Pacific
RO-33		SUNK 29 August 1942 S.E. of New Guinea by Australian destroyer
RO-34		SUNK 7 April 1943 N.W. of San Cristobal Is. by U.S. destroyer
RO-35	March 1943	SUNK October 1943 in Solomons
RO-36	May 1943	SUNK 13 June 1944 E. of Saipan by U.S. destroyer
RO-37	June 1943	SUNK 22 January 1944 E. of Solomons by U.S. destroyer
RO-38	July 1943	SUNK February/March 1944 in Central Pacific
RO-39	September 1943	SUNK 3 February 1944 off Wotje, Marshalls, by U.S. destroyer
RO-40	June 1943	SUNK February/March 1944 in Central Pacific
RO-41	November 1943	SUNK 31 March 1945 E. of Okinawa by U.S. destroyer
RO-42	August 1943	SUNK 10 June 1944 N.E. of Kwajalein by U.S. destroyer escort
RO-43	December 1943	SUNK 14 February 1945 N.E. of Luzon by U.S. submarine
RO-44	September 1943	SUNK 16 June 1944 E. of Eniwetok by U.S. destroyer escort
RO-45	January 1944	SUNK 20 April 1944 W. of Saipan by U.S. submarine
RO-46	February 1944	SUNK 9 April 1945 S.E. of Okinawa by U.S. destroyers
RO-47	January 1944	SUNK 23 March 1945 in Philippine Sea by U.S. destroyer
RO-48	March 1944	SUNK 14 July 1944 W. of Saipan by U.S. fleet units
RO-49	1944	SUNK 24 February 1945 off Bungo Channel, Japan by U.S. submarine
RO-50	July 1944	Operational; in Japan
RO-55	September 1944	SUNK 14 February 1945 N.E. of Luzon by U.S. submarine
RO-56	November 1944	SUNK May 1945 in Kuriles
RO-57		DECOMMISSIONED (?)
RO-58		DECOMMISSIONED (?)
RO-59		DECOMMISSIONED (?)
RO-60		SUNK 29 December 1941 at Kwajalein by grounding

Name	Date Commissioned	Final Disposition
RO-61		SUNK 31 August 1942 in Aleutians by U.S. destroyer and plane
RO-62		DECOMMISSIONED September 1945; in Japan area
RO-63		DECOMMISSIONED September 1945; in Japan area
RO-64		SUNK May 1945 in Hiroshima Bay
RO-65		SUNK 28 September 1942 at Kiska by B-24's
RO-66		SUNK 17 December 1941 W. of Wake Is. by collision
RO-67		SUNK 4 April 1945 in Inland Sea by mine
RO-68		DECOMMISSIONED September 1945; in Japan
RO-100	September 1942	SUNK 25 November 1943 off Bougainville Is. by U.S. fleet units
RO-101	October 1942	SUNK 1 July 1943 E. of Rendova Is., Solomons, by U.S. destroyer
RO-102	November 1942	SUNK 4 April 1943 S. of Santa Isabel Is. by U.S. destroyer
RO-103	October 1942	SUNK 29 May 1943 off New Hebrides by U.S. patrol craft
RO-104	February 1943	SUNK 23 May 1944 N. of Bismarck Is. by U.S. destroyer escort
RO-105	March 1943	SUNK 31 May 1944 N. of Bismarck Is. by U.S. fleet units
RO-106	December 1942	SUNK 22 May 1944 N. of Bismarck Is. by U.S. destroyer escort
RO-107	December 1942	SUNK May/June 1943 in South Pacific
RO-108	April 1943	SUNK 26 May 1944 N. of Bismarck Is. by U.S. destroyer escort
RO-109	April 1943	SUNK 29 April 1945 S.E. of Okinawa by U.S. fleet units
RO-110	July 1943	SUNK 11 February 1944 off Vizagapatam, India, by Allied sloops
RO-111	July 1943	SUNK 16 June 1944 off Truk by U.S. Navy PBY
RO-112	September 1943	SUNK 11 February 1945 N. of Luzon by U.S. submarine
RO-113	October 1943	SUNK 13 February 1945 N. of Luzon by U.S. submarine
RO-114	November 1943	SUNK 16 June 1944 W. of Guam by U.S. destroyers
RO-115	November 1943	SUNK 10 February 1945 N. of Luzon by U.S. submarine
RO-116	January 1944	SUNK 24 May 1944 N. of Bismarck Is. by U.S. destroyer escort
RO-117	January 1944	SUNK 17 June 1944 N.W. of Truk by U.S. Navy PBY

APPENDIX A

Name	Date Commissioned	Final Disposition
RO-500	September 1943	DECOMMISSIONED September 1945; in Japan
RO-501	February 1944	SUNK 13 May 1944 in Atlantic Ocean by U.S. destroyer
HA-101	November 1944	DECOMMISSIONED September 1945
HA-102	December 1944	DECOMMISSIONED September 1945
HA-103	February 1945	In Japan
HA-104	December 1944	DECOMMISSIONED September 1945
HA-105	February 1945	In Japan
HA-106	December 1944	DECOMMISSIONED September 1945
HA-107	February 1945	In Japan
HA-108	May 1945	In Japan
HA-109	March 1945	In Japan
HA-111	July 1945	In Japan
HA-201	May 1945	In Japan
HA-202	May 1945	In Japan
HA-203	June 1945	DECOMMISSIONED September 1945
HA-204	June 1945	DECOMMISSIONED September 1945
HA-205	July 1945	In Japan
HA-207	August 1945	In Japan
HA-208	August 1945	In Japan
HA-209	August 1945	In Japan
HA-210	August 1945	In Japan
HA-215	Not commissioned	In Japan
HA-216	August 1945	In Japan
HA-217	June 1945	In Japan
HA-218	July 1945	In Japan

Appendix B

Major combatant ships added to United States Fleet 7 December 1941–1 October 1945

Type & No.	Name	Comm. Date	Total	Remarks

BATTLESHIPS

BB 57	SOUTH DAKOTA	20 Mar. 1942		
58	INDIANA	30 Apr. 1942		
59	MASSACHUSETTS	12 May 1942		
60	ALABAMA	16 Aug. 1942		
61	IOWA	22 Feb. 1943		
62	NEW JERSEY	23 May 1943		
63	MISSOURI	11 June 1944		
64	WISCONSIN	16 Apr. 1944	8	

HEAVY CRUISERS

CA 68	BALTIMORE	15 Apr. 1943		
69	BOSTON	30 June 1943		
70	CANBERRA	14 Oct. 1943		
71	QUINCY	15 Dec. 1943		
72	PITTSBURG	10 Oct. 1944		
73	SAINT PAUL	17 Feb. 1945		
74	COLUMBUS	8 June 1945		
75	HELENA	4 Sept. 1945		
130	BREMERTON	29 Apr. 1945		
131	FALL RIVER	1 July 1945		
132	MACON	26 Aug. 1945		
135	LOS ANGELES	22 July 1945		
136	CHICAGO	10 Jan. 1945	13	

LARGE CRUISERS

CB 1	ALASKA	17 June 1944		
2	GUAM	17 Sept. 1944	2	

Type & No.		Name	Comm. Date	Total	Remarks

LIGHT CRUISERS

CL	51	ATLANTA	24 Dec. 1941		SUNK
	52	JUNEAU	14 Feb. 1942		SUNK
	53	SAN DIEGO	10 Jan. 1942		
	54	SAN JUAN	28 Feb. 1942		
	55	CLEVELAND	15 June 1942		
	56	COLUMBIA	29 July 1942		
	57	MONTPELIER	9 Sept. 1942		
	58	DENVER	15 Oct. 1942		
	60	SANTA FE	24 Nov. 1942		
	62	BIRMINGHAM	29 Jan. 1943		
	63	MOBILE	24 Mar. 1943		
	64	VINCENNES	21 Jan. 1944		
	65	PASADENA	8 June 1944		
	66	SPRINGFIELD	9 Sept. 1944		
	67	TOPEKA	23 Dec. 1944		
	80	BILOXI	31 Aug. 1943		
	81	HOUSTON	20 Dec. 1943		
	82	PROVIDENCE	15 May 1945		
	86	VICKSBURG	12 June 1944		
	87	DULUTH	18 Sept. 1944		
	89	MIAMI	28 Dec. 1943		
	90	ASTORIA	17 May 1944		
	91	OKLAHOMA CITY	22 Dec. 1944		
	92	LITTLE ROCK	17 June 1945		
	95	OAKLAND	17 July 1943		
	96	RENO	28 Dec. 1943		
	97	FLINT	31 Aug. 1944		
	98	TUCSON	3 Feb. 1945		
	101	AMSTERDAM	8 Jan. 1945		
	102	PORTSMOUTH	25 June 1945		
	103	WILKES-BARRE	1 July 1944		
	104	ATLANTA	2 Dec. 1944		
	105	DAYTON	7 Jan. 1945	33	

AIRCRAFT CARRIERS

CV	9	ESSEX	31 Dec. 1942		
	10	YORKTOWN	15 Apr. 1943		
	11	INTREPID	16 Aug. 1943		
	12	HORNET	29 Nov. 1943		
	13	FRANKLIN	31 Jan. 1944		

Type & No.		Name	Comm. Date	Total	Remarks
CV	14	TICONDEROGA	8 May 1944		
	15	RANDOLPH	9 Oct. 1944		
	16	LEXINGTON	17 Feb. 1943		
	17	BUNKER HILL	25 May 1943		
	18	WASP	24 Nov. 1943		
	19	HANCOCK	15 Apr. 1944		
	20	BENNINGTON	6 Aug. 1944		
	21	BOXER	16 Apr. 1945		
	31	BON HOMME RICHARD	26 Nov. 1944		
	36	ANTIETAM	28 Jan. 1945		
	38	SHANGRI-LA	15 Sept. 1944		
	39	LAKE CHAMPLAIN	3 June 1945	17	

LARGE AIRCRAFT CARRIERS

Type & No.		Name	Comm. Date	Total	Remarks
CVB	41	MIDWAY	10 Sept. 1945	1	

LIGHT AIRCRAFT CARRIERS

Type & No.		Name	Comm. Date	Total	Remarks
CVL	22	INDEPENDENCE	14 Jan. 1943		
	23	PRINCETON	25 Feb. 1943		SUNK
	24	BELLEAU WOOD	31 Mar. 1943		
	25	COWPENS	28 May 1943		
	26	MONTEREY	17 June 1943		
	27	LANGLEY	31 Aug. 1943		
	28	CABOT	24 July 1943		
	29	BATAAN	17 Nov. 1943		
	30	SAN JACINTO	15 Dec. 1943	9	

ESCORT AIRCRAFT CARRIERS

Type & No.		Name	Comm. Date	Total	Remarks
CVE	6	BATTLER			To U.K. 10-31-42
	7	ATTACKER			To U.K. 9-30-42
	8	HUNTER			To U.K. 1-9-43
	9	BOGUE	26 Sept. 1942		
	10	CHASER			To U.K. 4-9-43
	11	CARD	8 Nov. 1942		
	12	COPAHEE	15 June 1942		
	13	CORE	10 Dec. 1942		
	14	FENCER			To U.K. 3-1-43
	15	STALKER			To U.K. 12-21-42
	16	NASSAU	20 Aug. 1942		
	17	PURSUER			To U.K. 6-14-43

APPENDIX B

Type & No.		Name	Comm. Date	Total	Remarks
CVE	18	ALTAMAHA	15 Sept. 1942		
	19	STRIKER			To U.K. 4-28-43
	20	BARNES	20 Feb. 1943		
	21	BLOCK ISLAND	8 Mar. 1943		SUNK
	22	SEARCHER			To U.K. 4-7-43
	23	BRETON	12 Apr. 1943		
	24	RAVAGER			To U.K. 4-25-43
	25	CROATAN	28 Apr. 1943		
	26	SANGAMON	25 Aug. 1942		ex-AO 28
	27	SUWANNEE	24 Sept. 1942		ex-AO 33
	28	CHENANGO	19 Sept. 1942		ex-AO 31
	29	SANTEE	24 Aug. 1942		ex-AO 29
	30	CHARGER	3 Mar. 1942		ex-BAVG 4
	31	PRINCE WILLIAM	9 Apr. 1943		
	32	SLINGER			To U.K. 8-11-43
	33	ATHELING			To U.K. 7-31-43
	34	EMPEROR			To U.K. 8-6-43
	35	AMEER			To U.K. 7-19-43
	36	BEGUM			To U.K. 8-2-43
	37	TRUMPETER			To U.K. 8-4-43
	38	EMPRESS			To U.K. 8-13-43
	39	KHEDIVE			To U.K. 8-25-43
	40	SPEAKER			To U.K. 11-20-43
	41	NABOB			To U.K. 9-7-43
	42	PREMIER			To U.K. 11-3-43
	43	SHAH			To U.K. 9-27-43
	44	PATROLLER			To U.K. 10-22-43
	45	RAJAH			To U.K. 1-17-44
	46	RANEE			To U.K. 11-8-43
	47	TROUNCER			To U.K. 1-31-44
	48	THANE			To U.K. 11-19-43
	49	QUEEN			To U.K. 12-7-43
	50	RULER			To U.K. 12-22-43
	51	ARBITER			To U.K. 12-31-43
	52	SMITER			To U.K. 1-20-44
	53	PUNCHER			To U.K. 2-5-44
	54	REAPER			To U.K. 2-18-44
	55	CASABLANCA	8 July 1943		
	56	LISCOME BAY	7 Aug. 1943		SUNK
	57	ANZIO	27 Aug. 1943		
	58	CORREGIDOR	31 Aug. 1943		
	59	MISSION BAY	13 Sept. 1943		
	60	GUADALCANAL	25 Sept. 1943		

Type & No.		Name	Comm. Date	Total	Remarks
CVE	61	MANILA BAY	5 Oct. 1943		
	62	NATOMA BAY	14 Oct. 1943		
	63	ST. LO	23 Oct. 1943		SUNK
	64	TRIPOLI	31 Oct. 1943		
	65	WAKE ISLAND	7 Nov. 1943		
	66	WHITE PLAINS	15 Nov. 1943		
	67	SOLOMONS	21 Nov. 1943		
	68	KALININ BAY	27 Nov. 1943		
	69	KASAAN BAY	4 Dec. 1943		
	70	FANSHAW BAY	9 Dec. 1943		
	71	KITKUN BAY	15 Dec. 1943		
	72	TULAGI	21 Dec. 1943		
	73	GAMBIER BAY	28 Dec. 1943		SUNK
	74	NEHENTA BAY	3 Jan. 1944		
	75	HOGGATT BAY	11 Jan. 1944		
	76	KADASHAN BAY	18 Jan. 1944		
	77	MARCUS ISLAND	26 Jan. 1944		
	78	SAVO ISLAND	3 Feb. 1944		
	79	OMMANEY BAY	11 Feb. 1944		SUNK
	80	PETROF BAY	18 Feb. 1944		
	81	RUDYERD BAY	25 Feb. 1944		
	82	SAGINAW BAY	2 Mar. 1944		
	83	SARGENT BAY	9 Mar. 1944		
	84	SHAMROCK BAY	15 Mar. 1944		
	85	SHIPLEY BAY	21 Mar. 1944		
	86	SITKOH BAY	28 Mar. 1944		
	87	STEAMER BAY	4 Apr. 1944		
	88	CAPE ESPERANCE	9 Apr. 1944		
	89	TAKANIS BAY	15 Apr. 1944		
	90	THETIS BAY	21 Apr. 1944		
	91	MAKASSAR STRAIT	27 Apr. 1944		
	92	WINDHAM BAY	3 May 1944		
	93	MAKIN ISLAND	9 May 1944		
	94	LUNGA POINT	14 May 1944		
	95	BISMARCK SEA	20 May 1944		SUNK
	96	SALAMAUA	26 May 1944		
	97	HOLLANDIA	1 June 1944		
	98	KWAJALEIN	7 June 1944		
	99	ADMIRALTY ISLANDS	13 June 1944		
	100	BOUGAINVILLE	18 June 1944		
	101	MATANIKAU	24 June 1944		
	102	ATTU	30 June 1944		
	103	ROI	6 July 1944		

APPENDIX B

Type & No.	Name	Comm. Date	Total	Remarks
CVE 104	MUNDA	8 July 1944		
105	COMMENCEMENT BAY	27 Nov. 1944		
106	BLOCK ISLAND	30 Dec. 1944		
107	GILBERT ISLANDS	5 Feb. 1945		
108	KULA GULF	12 May 1945		
109	CAPE GLOUCESTER	5 Mar. 1945		
110	SALERNO BAY	19 May 1945		
111	VELLA GULF	9 Apr. 1945		
112	SIBONEY	14 May 1945		
113	PUGET SOUND	18 June 1945		
115	BAIROKO	16 July 1945		
117	SAIDOR	4 Sept. 1945		
			110	(33 Leased)
BAVG 2	AVENGER			To U.K. 3-2-42
3	BITER			To U.K. 5-6-42
5	DASHER			To U.K. 7-2-42
6	TRACKER			To U.K. 1-31-43
			4	(4 Leased)

DESTROYERS

Type & No.	Name	Comm. Date	Remarks
DD 445	FLETCHER	30 June 1942	
446	RADFORD	22 July 1942	
447	JENKINS	31 July 1942	
448	LA VALLETTE	12 Aug. 1942	
449	NICHOLAS	4 June 1942	
450	O'BANNON	26 June 1942	
451	CHEVALIER	20 July 1942	SUNK
455	HAMBLETON	22 Dec. 1941	Now DMS 20
456	RODMAN	27 Jan. 1942	Now DMS 21
458	MACOMB	26 Jan. 1942	Now DMS 23
459	LAFFEY	31 Mar. 1942	SUNK
460	WOODWORTH	30 Apr. 1942	
461	FORREST	13 Jan. 1942	Now DMS 24
462	FITCH	3 Feb. 1942	Now DMS 25
463	CORRY	18 Dec. 1941	SUNK
464	HOBSON	22 Jan. 1942	Now DMS 26
465	SAUFLEY	29 Aug. 1942	
466	WALLER	1 Oct. 1942	
467	STRONG	7 Aug. 1942	SUNK
468	TAYLOR	28 Aug. 1942	
469	DE HAVEN	21 Sept. 1942	SUNK
470	BACHE	14 Nov. 1942	
471	BEALE	23 Dec. 1942	

Type & No.	Name	Comm. Date	Total	Remarks
DD 472	GUEST	15 Dec. 1942		
473	BENNETT	9 Feb. 1943		
474	FULLAM	2 Mar. 1943		
475	HUDSON	13 Apr. 1943		
476	HUTCHINS	17 Nov. 1942		
477	PRINGLE	15 Sept. 1942		SUNK
478	STANLY	15 Oct. 1942		
479	STEVENS	1 Feb. 1943		
480	HALFORD	10 Apr. 1943		
481	LEUTZE	4 Mar. 1944		
483	AARON WARD	4 Mar. 1942		SUNK
484	BUCHANAN	21 Mar. 1942		
485	DUNCAN	16 Apr. 1942		SUNK
486	LANSDOWNE	29 Apr. 1942		
487	LARDNER	13 May 1942		
488	MC CALLA	27 May 1942		
489	MERVINE	17 June 1942		Now DMS 31
490	QUICK	3 July 1942		Now DMS 32
491	FARENHOLT	2 Apr. 1942		
492	BAILEY	11 May 1942		
493	CARMICK	28 Dec. 1942		Now DMS 33
494	DOYLE	27 Jan. 1943		Now DMS 34
495	ENDICOTT	25 Feb. 1943		Now DMS 35
496	MC COOK	15 Mar. 1943		Now DMS 36
497	FRANKFORD	31 Mar. 1943		
498	PHILIP	21 Nov. 1942		
499	RENSHAW	5 Dec. 1942		
500	RINGGOLD	24 Dec. 1942		
501	SCHROEDER	1 Jan. 1943		
502	SIGSBEE	23 Jan. 1943		
507	CONWAY	9 Oct. 1942		
508	CONY	30 Oct. 1942		
509	CONVERSE	20 Nov. 1942		
510	EATON	4 Dec. 1942		
511	FOOTE	22 Dec. 1942		
512	SPENCE	8 Jan. 1943		SUNK
513	TERRY	26 Jan. 1943		
514	THATCHER	10 Feb. 1943		
515	ANTHONY	26 Feb. 1943		
516	WADSWORTH	16 Mar. 1943		
517	WALKER	3 Apr. 1943		
518	BROWNSON	3 Feb. 1943		SUNK
519	DALY	10 Mar. 1943		

APPENDIX B

Type & No.	Name	Comm. Date	Total	Remarks
DD 520	ISHERWOOD	12 Apr. 1943		
521	KIMBERLY	24 May 1943		
522	LUCE	21 June 1943		SUNK
526	ABNER READ	5 Feb. 1943		SUNK
527	AMMEN	12 Mar. 1943		
528	MULLANY	23 Apr. 1943		
529	BUSH	10 May 1943		SUNK
530	TRATHEN	28 May 1943		
531	HAZELWOOD	18 June 1943		
532	HEERMAN	6 July 1943		
533	HOEL	29 July 1943		SUNK
534	MC CORD	19 Aug. 1943		
535	MILLER	31 Aug. 1943		
536	OWEN	20 Sept. 1943		
537	THE SULLIVANS	30 Sept. 1943		
538	STEPHEN POTTER	21 Oct. 1943		
539	TINGEY	25 Nov. 1943		
540	TWINING	1 Dec. 1943		
541	YARNALL	30 Dec. 1943		
544	BOYD	8 May 1943		
545	BRADFORD	12 June 1943		
546	BROWN	10 July 1943		
547	COWELL	23 Aug. 1943		
550	CAPPS	23 June 1943		
551	DAVID W. TAYLOR	18 Sept. 1943		
552	EVANS	11 Dec. 1943		
553	JOHN D. HENLEY	2 Feb. 1944		
554	FRANKS	30 July 1943		
555	HAGGARD	31 Aug. 1943	-	
556	HAILEY	30 Sept. 1943		
557	JOHNSTON	27 Oct. 1943		SUNK
558	LAWS	18 Nov. 1943		
559	LONGSHAW	4 Dec. 1943		SUNK
560	MORRISON	18 Dec. 1943		SUNK
561	PRICHETT	15 Jan. 1944		
562	ROBINSON	31 Jan. 1944		
563	ROSS	21 Feb. 1944		
564	ROWE	13 Mar. 1944		
565	SMALLEY	31 Mar. 1944		
566	STODDARD	15 Apr. 1944		
567	WATTS	29 Apr. 1944		
568	WREN	20 May 1944		
569	AULICK	27 Oct. 1942		

Type & No.	Name	Comm. Date	Total	Remarks
DD 570	CHARLES AUSBURNE	24 Nov. 1942		
571	CLAXTON	8 Dec. 1942		
572	DYSON	30 Dec. 1942		
573	HARRISON	25 Jan. 1943		
574	JOHN RODGERS	9 Feb. 1943		
575	MC KEE	31 Mar. 1943		
576	MURRAY	20 Apr. 1943		
577	SPROSTON	19 May 1943		
578	WICKES	16 June 1943		
579	WILLIAM D. PORTER	6 July 1943		SUNK
580	YOUNG	31 July 1943		
581	CHARRETTE	18 May 1943		
582	CONNER	8 June 1943		
583	HALL	6 July 1943		
584	HALLIGAN	19 Aug. 1943		SUNK
585	HARADEN	16 Sept. 1943		
586	NEWCOMB	10 Nov. 1943		
587	BELL	4 Mar. 1943		
588	BURNS	3 Apr. 1943		
589	IZARD	15 May 1943		
590	PAUL HAMILTON	25 Oct. 1943		
591	TWIGGS	4 Nov. 1943		SUNK
592	HOWORTH	3 Apr. 1944		
593	KILLEN	4 May 1944		
594	HART	4 Nov. 1944		
595	METCALF	18 Nov. 1944		
596	SHIELDS	8 Feb. 1945		
597	WILEY	22 Feb. 1945		
598	BANCROFT	30 Apr. 1942		
599	BARTON	29 May 1942		SUNK
600	BOYLE	15 Aug. 1942		
601	CHAMPLIN	12 Sept. 1942		
602	MEADE	22 June 1942		
603	MURPHY	27 July 1942		
604	PARKER	31 Aug. 1942		
605	CALDWELL	10 June 1942		
606	COGHLAN	10 July 1942		
607	FRAZIER	30 July 1942		
608	GANSEVOORT	25 Aug. 1942		
609	GILLESPIE	18 Sept. 1942		
610	HOBBY	18 Nov. 1942		
611	KALK	17 Oct. 1942		
612	KENDRICK	12 Sept. 1942		

APPENDIX B

Type & No.	Name	Comm. Date	Total	Remarks
DD 613	LAUB	24 Oct. 1942		
614	MAC KENZIE	21 Nov. 1942		
615	MC LANAHAN	19 Dec. 1942		
616	NIELDS	15 Jan. 1943		
617	ORDRONAUX	13 Feb. 1943		
618	DAVISON	11 Sept. 1942		Now DMS 37
619	EDWARDS	18 Sept. 1942		
620	GLENNON	8 Oct. 1942		SUNK
621	JEFFERS	5 Nov. 1942		Now DMS 24
622	MADDOX	31 Oct. 1942		SUNK
623	NELSON	26 Nov. 1942		
624	BALDWIN	30 Apr. 1943		
625	HARDING	25 May 1943		Now DMS 28
626	SATTERLEE	1 July 1943		
627	THOMPSON	10 July 1943		Now DMS 38
628	WELLES	16 Aug. 1943		
629	ABBOT	23 Apr. 1943		
630	BRAINE	11 May 1943		
631	ERBEN	28 May 1943		
632	COWIE	1 June 1942		Now DMS 39
633	KNIGHT	23 June 1942		Now DMS 40
634	DORAN	4 Aug. 1942		Now DMS 41
635	EARLE	1 Sept. 1942		Now DMS 42
636	BUTLER	15 Aug. 1942		Now DMS 29
637	GHERARDI	15 Sept. 1942		Now DMS 30
638	HERNDON	20 Dec. 1942		
639	SHUBRICK	7 Feb. 1943		
640	BEATTY	7 May 1942		SUNK
641	TILLMAN	4 June 1942		
642	HALE	15 June 1943		
643	SIGOURNEY	29 June 1943		
644	STEMBEL	16 July 1943		
645	STEVENSON	15 Dec. 1942		
646	STOCKTON	11 Jan. 1943		
647	THORN	1 Apr. 1943		
648	TURNER	15 Apr. 1943		SUNK
649	ALBERT W. GRANT	24 Nov. 1943		
650	CAPERTON	30 July 1943		
651	COGSWELL	17 Aug. 1943		
652	INGERSOLL	31 Aug. 1943		
653	KNAPP	16 Sept. 1943		
654	BEARSS	12 Apr. 1944		
655	JOHN HOOD	7 June 1944		

Type & No.	Name	Comm. Date	Total	Remarks
DD 656	VAN VALKENBURGH	2 Aug. 1944		
657	CHARLES J. BADGER	23 July 1943		
658	COLAHAN	23 Aug. 1943		
659	DASHIELL	20 Mar. 1943		
660	BULLARD	9 Apr. 1943		
661	KIDD	23 Apr. 1943		
662	BENNION	14 Dec. 1943		
663	HEYWOOD L. EDWARDS	26 Jan. 1944		
664	RICHARD P. LEARY	23 Feb. 1944		
665	BRYANT	4 Dec. 1943		
666	BLACK	21 May 1943		
667	CHAUNCEY	31 May 1943		
668	CLARENCE K. BRONSON	11 June 1943		
669	COTTEN	24 July 1943		
670	DORTCH	7 Aug. 1943		
671	GATLING	19 Aug. 1943		
672	HEALY	3 Sept. 1943		
673	HICKOX	10 Sept. 1943		
674	HUNT	22 Sept. 1943		
675	LEWIS HANCOCK	29 Sept. 1943		
676	MARSHALL	16 Oct. 1943		
677	MC DERMUT	19 Nov. 1943		
678	MC GOWAN	20 Dec. 1943		
679	MC NAIR	30 Dec. 1943		
680	MELVIN	24 Nov. 1943		
681	HOPEWELL	30 Sept. 1943		
682	PORTERFIELD	30 Oct. 1943		
683	STOCKHAM	11 Feb. 1944		
684	WEDDERBURN	9 Mar. 1944		
685	PICKING	21 Sept. 1943		
686	HALSEY POWELL	25 Oct. 1943		
687	UHLMANN	22 Nov. 1943		
688	REMEY	30 Sept. 1943		
689	WADLEIGH	19 Oct. 1943		
690	NORMAN SCOTT	5 Nov. 1943		
691	MERTZ	19 Nov. 1943		
692	ALLEN M. SUMNER	26 Jan. 1944		
693	MOALE	28 Feb. 1944		
694	INGRAHAM	10 Mar. 1944		
695	COOPER	27 Mar. 1944		SUNK
696	ENGLISH	4 May 1944		
697	CHARLES S. SPERRY	17 May 1944		
698	AULT	31 May 1944		

APPENDIX B

Type & No.	Name	Comm. Date	Total	Remarks
DD 699	WALDRON	8 June 1944		
700	HAYNSWORTH	22 June 1944		
701	JOHN W. WEEKS	21 July 1944		
702	HANK	28 Aug. 1944		
703	WALLACE L. LIND	8 Sept. 1944		
704	BORIE	21 Sept. 1944		
705	COMPTON	4 Nov. 1944		
706	GAINARD	23 Nov. 1944		
707	SOLEY	7 Dec. 1944		
708	HARLAN R. DICKSON	17 Feb. 1945		
709	HUGH PURVIS	1 Mar. 1945		
710	GEARING	3 May 1945		
711	EUGENE A. GREENE	8 June 1945		
712	GYATT	2 July 1945		
713	KENNETH D. BAILEY	31 July 1945		
714	WILLIAM R. RUSH	21 Sept. 1945		
722	BARTON	30 Dec. 1943		
723	WALKE	21 Jan. 1944		
724	LAFFEY	8 Feb. 1944		
725	O'BRIEN	25 Feb. 1944		
726	MEREDITH	14 Mar. 1944		SUNK
727	DE HAVEN	31 Mar. 1944		
728	MANSFIELD	14 Apr. 1944		
729	LYMAN K. SWENSON	2 May 1944		
730	COLLETT	16 May 1944		
731	MADDOX	2 June 1944		
732	HYMAN	16 June 1944		
733	MANNERT L. ABELE	4 July 1944		SUNK
734	PURDY	18 July 1944		
741	DREXLER	14 Nov. 1944		SUNK
742	FRANK KNOX	11 Dec. 1944		
743	SOUTHERLAND	22 Dec. 1944		
744	BLUE	20 Mar. 1944		
745	BRUSH	17 Apr. 1944		
746	TAUSSIG	20 May 1944		
747	SAMUEL N. MOORE	24 June 1944		
748	HARRY E. HUBBARD	22 July 1944		
752	ALFRED A. CUNNINGHAM	23 Nov. 1944		
753	JOHN R. PIERCE	30 Dec. 1944		
754	FRANK E. EVANS	3 Feb. 1945		
755	JOHN A. BOLE	3 Mar. 1945		
756	BEATTY	31 Mar. 1945		
757	PUTNAM	12 Oct. 1944		

Type & No.	Name	Comm. Date	Total	Remarks
DD 758	STRONG	8 Mar. 1945		
759	LOFBERG	26 Apr. 1945		
770	LOWRY	23 July 1944		
774	HUGH W. HADLEY	25 Nov. 1944		
775	WILLARD KEITH	27 Dec. 1944		
776	JAMES C. OWENS	17 Feb. 1945		
777	ZELLARS	25 Oct. 1944		
778	MASSEY	24 Nov. 1944		
779	DOUGLAS H. FOX	26 Dec. 1944		
780	STORMES	27 Jan. 1945		
781	ROBERT K. HUNTINGTON	3 Mar. 1945		
782	ROWAN	31 Mar. 1945		
783	GURKE	12 May 1945		
784	MC KEAN	9 June 1945		
785	HENDERSON	4 Aug. 1945		
792	CALLAGHAN	27 Nov. 1943		SUNK
793	CASSIN YOUNG	31 Dec. 1943		
794	IRWIN	14 Feb. 1944		
795	PRESTON	20 Mar. 1944		
796	BENHAM	20 Dec. 1943		
797	CUSHING	17 Jan. 1944		
798	MONSSEN	12 Feb. 1944		
799	JARVIS	3 June 1944		
800	PORTER	24 June 1944		
801	COLHOUN	8 July 1944		SUNK
802	GREGORY	29 July 1944		
803	LITTLE	19 Aug. 1944		SUNK
804	ROOKS	2 Sept. 1944		
805	CHEVALIER	9 Jan. 1945		
806	HIGBEE	27 Jan. 1945		
807	BENNER	13 Feb. 1945		
808	DENNIS J. BUCKLEY	2 Mar. 1945		
829	MYLES C. FOX	20 Mar. 1945		
830	EVERETT F. LARSON	6 Apr. 1945		
831	GOODRICH	24 Apr. 1945		
832	HANSON	11 May 1945		
833	HERBERT J. THOMAS	29 May 1945		
834	TURNER	12 June 1945		
835	CHARLES P. CECIL	29 June 1945		
836	GEORGE K. MAC KENZIE	13 July 1945		
837	SARSFIELD	31 July 1945		
838	ERNEST G. SMALL	21 Aug. 1945		

APPENDIX B

Type & No.	Name	Comm. Date	Total	Remarks
DD 839	POWER	13 Sept. 1945		
857	BRISTOL	17 Mar. 1945		
858	FRED T. BERRY	12 May 1945		
859	NORRIS	9 June 1945		
860	MC CAFFERY	26 July 1945		
861	HARWOOD	28 Sept. 1945		
862	VOGELGESANG	28 Apr. 1945		
863	STEINAKER	26 May 1945		
864	HAROLD J. ELLISON	23 June 1945		
865	CHARLES R. WARE	21 July 1945		
866	CONE	17 Aug. 1945		
867	STRIBLING	29 Sept. 1945		
873	HAWKINS	10 Feb. 1945		
874	DUNCAN	25 Feb. 1945		
875	HENRY W. TUCKER	12 Mar. 1945		
876	ROGERS	26 Mar. 1945		
877	PERKINS	5 Apr. 1945		
878	VESOLE	23 Apr. 1945		
879	LEARY	7 May 1945		
880	DYESS	21 May 1945		
881	BORDELON	5 June 1945		
882	FURSE	10 July 1945		
883	NEWMAN K. PERRY	26 July 1945		
884	FLOYD B. PARKS	31 July 1945		
885	JOHN R. CRAIG	20 Aug. 1945		
886	ORLECK	15 Sept. 1945	349	

LIGHT MINE LAYERS

Type & No.	Name	Comm. Date	Remarks
DM 23	ROBERT H. SMITH	4 Aug. 1944	ex-DD 735
24	THOMAS E. FRASER	22 Aug. 1944	ex-DD 736
25	SHANNON	8 Sept. 1944	ex-DD 737
26	HARRY F. BAUER	22 Sept. 1944	ex-DD 738
27	ADAMS	10 Oct. 1944	ex-DD 739
28	TOLMAN	27 Oct. 1944	ex-DD 740
29	HENRY A. WILEY	31 Aug. 1944	ex-DD 749
30	SHEA	30 Sept. 1944	ex-DD 750
31	J. WILLIAM DITTER	28 Oct. 1944	ex-DD 751
32	LINDSEY	20 Aug. 1944	ex-DD 771
33	GWIN	30 Sept. 1944	ex-DD 772
34	AARON WARD	28 Oct. 1944	ex-DD 773

Type & No.	Name	Comm. Date	Total	Remarks

DESTROYER ESCORTS

Type & No.		Name	Comm. Date	Total	Remarks
BDE	1	BAYNTUN			To U.K. 2-13-43
	2	BAZELY			To U.K. 2-18-43
	3	BERRY			To U.K. 3-15-43
	4	BLACKWOOD			To U.K. 3-27-43
	12	BURGES			To U.K. 6-2-43
	46	DRURY			To U.K. 4-12-43
				6	(6 Leased)
DE	5	EVARTS	15 Apr. 1943		
	6	WYFFELS	21 Apr. 1943		
	7	GRISWOLD	28 Apr. 1943		
	8	STEELE	4 May 1943		
	9	CARLSON	10 May 1943		
	10	BEBAS	15 May 1943		
	11	CROUTER	25 May 1943		
	13	BRENNAN	20 Jan. 1943		
	14	DOHERTY	6 Feb. 1943		
	15	AUSTIN	13 Feb. 1943		
	16	EDGAR G. CHASE	20 Mar. 1943		
	17	EDWARD C. DALY	3 Apr. 1943		
	18	GILMORE	17 Apr. 1943		
	19	BURDEN R. HASTINGS	1 May 1943		
	20	LE HARDY	15 May 1943		
	21	HAROLD C. THOMAS	31 May 1943		
	22	WILEMAN	11 June 1943		
	23	CHARLES R. GREER	25 June 1943		
	24	WHITMAN	3 July 1943		
	25	WINTLE	10 July 1943		
	26	DEMPSEY	24 July 1943		
	27	DUFFY	5 Aug. 1943		
	28	EMERY	14 Aug. 1943		
	29	STADTFELD	26 Aug. 1943		
	30	MARTIN	4 Sept. 1943		
	31	SEDERSTROM	11 Sept. 1943		
	32	FLEMING	18 Sept. 1943		
	33	TISDALE	11 Oct. 1943		
	34	EISELE	18 Oct. 1943		
	35	FAIR	23 Oct. 1943		
	36	MANLOVE	8 Nov. 1943		
	37	GREINER	18 Aug. 1943		
	38	WYMAN	1 Sept. 1943		
	39	LOVERING	17 Sept. 1943		

APPENDIX B

Type & No.	Name	Comm. Date	Total	Remarks
DE 40	SANDERS	1 Oct. 1943		
41	BRACKETT	18 Oct. 1943		
42	REYNOLDS	1 Nov. 1943		
43	MITCHELL	17 Nov. 1943		
44	DONALDSON	1 Dec. 1943		
45	ANDRES	15 Mar. 1943		
47	DECKER	3 May 1943		
48	DOBLER	17 May 1943		
49	DONEFF	10 June 1943		
50	ENGSTROM	21 June 1943		
51	BUCKLEY	30 Apr. 1943		
52	BENTINCK			To U.K. 5-19-43
53	CHARLES LAWRENCE	31 May 1943		Now APD 37
54	DANIEL T. GRIFFIN	9 June 1943		Now APD 38
55	BYARD			To U.K. 6-18-43
56	DONNELL	26 June 1943		Now IX 182
57	FOGG	7 July 1943		
58	CALDER			To U.K. 7-15-43
59	FOSS	23 July 1943		
60	GANTNER	29 July 1943		Now APD 42
61	DUCKWORTH			To U.K. 8-4-43
62	GEORGE W. INGRAM	11 Aug. 1943		Now APD 43
63	IRA JEFFERY	15 Aug. 1943		Now APD 44
64	DUFF			To U.K. 8-23-43
65	LEE FOX	30 Aug. 1943		Now APD 45
66	AMESBURY	31 Aug. 1943		Now APD 46
67	ESSINGTON			To U.K. 9-7-43
68	BATES	12 Sept. 1943		Now APD 47
69	BLESSMAN	19 Sept. 1943		Now APD 48
70	JOSEPH E. CAMPBELL	23 Sept. 1943		Now APD 49
71	AFFLECK			To U.K. 9-29-43
72	AYLMER			To U.K. 9-30-43
73	BALFOUR			To U.K. 10-7-43
74	BENTLEY			To U.K. 10-13-43
75	BRICKERTON			To U.K. 10-17-43
76	BLIGH			To U.K. 10-22-43
77	BRAITHWAITE			To U.K. 11-13-43
78	BULLEN			To U.K. 10-25-43
79	BYRON			To U.K. 10-30-43
80	CONN			To U.K. 10-31-43
81	COTTON			To U.K. 11-8-43
82	CRANSTOUN			To U.K. 11-13-43
83	CUBITT			To U.K. 11-17-43

Type & No.	Name	Comm. Date	Total	Remarks
DE 84	CURZON			To U.K. 11-20-43
85	DAKINS			To U.K. 11-23-43
86	DEANE			To U.K. 11-26-43
87	EKINS			To U.K. 11-29-43
88	FITZROY			To U.K. 10-16-43
89	REDMILL			To U.K. 11-30-43
90	RETALICK			To U.K. 12-8-43
91	HALSTEAD			To U.K. 11-3-43
92	RIOU			To U.K. 12-14-43
93	RUTHERFORD			To U.K. 12-16-43
94	COSBY			To U.K. 12-20-43
95	ROWLEY			To U.K. 12-22-43
96	RUPERT			To U.K. 12-24-43
97	STOCKHAM			To U.K. 12-28-43
98	SEYMOUR			To U.K. 12-23-43
99	CANNON	26 Sept. 1943		To Brazil 12-19-44
100	CHRISTOPHER	23 Oct. 1943		To Brazil 12-19-44
101	ALGER	12 Nov. 1943		To Brazil 3-10-45
102	THOMAS	21 Nov. 1943		
103	BOSTWICK	1 Dec. 1943		
104	BREEMAN	12 Dec. 1943		
105	BURROWS	19 Dec. 1943		
106	SENEGALAIS			To French 1-2-44
107	ALGERIEN			To French 1-23-44
108	TUNISIEN			To French 2-11-44
109	MAROCAIN			To French 2-29-44
110	HOVA			To French 3-18-44
111	SOMALI			To French 4-9-44
112	CARTER	2 May 1944		
113	CLARENCE L. EVANS	25 June 1944		
129	EDSALL	10 Apr. 1943		
130	JACOB JONES	29 Apr. 1943		
131	HAMMANN	17 May 1943		
132	ROBERT E. PEARY	31 May 1943		
133	PILLSBURY	7 June 1943		
134	POPE	25 June 1943		
135	FLAHERTY	26 June 1943		
136	FREDERICK C. DAVIS	14 July 1943		SUNK
137	HERBERT C. JONES	21 July 1943		
138	DOUGLAS L. HOWARD	29 July 1943		
139	FARQUHAR	5 Aug. 1943		
140	J. R. Y. BLAKELY	16 Aug. 1943		
141	HILL	16 Aug. 1943		

APPENDIX B

Type & No.	Name	Comm. Date	Total	Remarks
DE 142	FESSENDEN	25 Aug. 1943		
143	FISKE	25 Aug. 1943		SUNK
144	FROST	30 Aug. 1943		
145	HUSE	30 Aug. 1943		
146	INCH	8 Sept. 1943		
147	BLAIR	13 Sept. 1943		
148	BROUGH	18 Sept. 1943		
149	CHATELAIN	22 Sept. 1943		
150	NEUNZER	27 Sept. 1943		
151	POOLE	29 Sept. 1943		
152	PETERSON	29 Sept. 1943		
153	REUBEN JAMES	1 Apr. 1943		
154	SIMS	24 Apr. 1943		Now APD 50
155	HOPPING	21 May 1943		Now APD 51
156	REEVES	9 June 1943		Now APD 52
157	FECHTELER	1 July 1943		SUNK
158	CHASE	18 July 1943		Now APD 54
159	LANING	1 Aug. 1943		Now APD 55
160	LOY	12 Sept. 1943		Now APD 56
161	BARBER	10 Oct. 1943		Now APD 57
162	LEVY	13 May 1943		
163	MCCONNELL	28 May 1943		
164	OSTERHAUS	12 June 1943		
165	PARKS	22 June 1943		
166	BARON	5 July 1943		
167	ACREE	19 July 1943		
168	AMICK	26 July 1943		
169	ATHERTON	29 Aug. 1943		
170	BOOTH	19 Sept. 1943		
171	CARROLL	24 Oct. 1943		
172	COONER	21 Aug. 1943		
173	ELDRIDGE	27 Aug. 1943		
174	MARTS	3 Sept. 1943		To Brazil 3-20-45
175	PENNEWILL	15 Sept. 1943		To Brazil 8-1-44
176	MICKA	23 Sept. 1943		
177	REYBOLD	29 Sept. 1943		To Brazil 8-15-44
178	HERZOG	6 Oct. 1943		To Brazil 8-1-44
179	MCANN	11 Oct. 1943		To Brazil 8-15-44
180	TRUMPETER	16 Oct. 1943		
181	STRAUB	25 Oct. 1943		
182	GUSTAFSON	1 Nov. 1943		
183	SAMUEL S. MILES	4 Nov. 1943		
184	WESSON	11 Nov. 1943		

Type & No.	Name	Comm. Date	Total	Remarks
DE 185	RIDDLE	17 Nov. 1943		
186	SWEARER	24 Nov. 1943		
187	STERN	1 Dec. 1943		
188	O'NEILL	6 Dec. 1943		
189	BRONSTEIN	13 Dec. 1943		
190	BAKER	23 Dec. 1943		
191	COFFMAN	27 Dec. 1943		
192	EISNER	1 Jan. 1944		
193	GARFIELD THOMAS	24 Jan. 1944		
194	WINGFIELD	28 Jan. 1944		
195	THORNHILL	1 Feb. 1944		
196	RINEHART	12 Feb. 1944		
197	ROCHE	21 Feb. 1944		
198	LOVELACE	7 Nov. 1943		
199	MANNING	1 Oct. 1943		
200	NEUENDORF	18 Oct. 1943		
201	JAMES E. CRAIG	1 Nov. 1943		
202	EICHENBERGER	17 Nov. 1943		
203	THOMASON	10 Dec. 1943		
204	JORDAN	17 Dec. 1943		
205	NEWMAN	26 Nov. 1943		Now APD 59
206	LIDDLE	6 Dec. 1943		Now APD 60
207	KEPHART	7 Jan. 1944		Now APD 61
208	COFER	19 Jan. 1944		Now APD 62
209	LLOYD	11 Feb. 1944		Now APD 63
210	OTTER	21 Feb. 1944		
211	HUBBARD	6 Mar. 1944		Now APD 53
212	HAYTER	16 Mar. 1944		Now APD 80
213	WILLIAM T. POWELL	28 Mar. 1944		
214	SCOTT	20 July 1943		
215	BURKE	20 Aug. 1943		Now APD 65
216	ENRIGHT	21 Sept. 1943		Now APD 66
217	COOLBAUGH	15 Oct. 1943		
218	DARBY	15 Nov. 1943		
219	J. DOUGLAS BLACKWOOD	15 Jan. 1943		
220	FRANCIS M. ROBINSON	15 Jan. 1944		
221	SOLAR	15 Feb. 1944		
222	FOWLER	15 Mar. 1944		
223	SPANGENBERG	15 Apr. 1944		
224	RUDDEROW	15 May 1944		
225	DAY	10 June 1944		
230	CHAFFEE	9 May 1944		
231	HODGES	27 May 1944		

APPENDIX B

Type & No.	Name	Comm. Date	Total	Remarks
DE 238	STEWART	31 May 1943		
239	STURTEVANT	16 June 1943		
240	MOORE	1 July 1943		
241	KEITH	19 July 1943		
242	TOMICH	26 July 1943		
243	J. RICHARD WARD	5 July 1943		
244	OTTERSTETTER	6 Aug. 1943		
245	SLOAT	16 Aug. 1943		
246	SNOWDEN	23 Aug. 1943		
247	STANTON	7 Aug. 1943		
248	SWASEY	31 Aug. 1943		
249	MARCHAND	8 Sept. 1943		
250	HURST	30 Aug. 1943		
251	CAMP	16 Sept. 1943		
252	HOWARD D. CROW	27 Sept. 1943		
253	PETTIT	23 Sept. 1943		
254	RICKETTS	5 Oct. 1943		
255	SELLSTROM	12 Oct. 1943		
256	SEID	11 June 1943		
257	SMARTT	18 June 1943		
258	WALTER S. BROWN	25 June 1943		
259	WILLIAM C. MILLER	2 July 1943		
260	CABANA	9 July 1943		
261	DIONNE	16 July 1943		
262	CANFIELD	22 July 1943		
263	DEEDE	29 July 1943		
264	ELDEN	5 Aug. 1943		
265	CLOUES	10 Aug. 1943		
266	CAPEL			To U.K. 8-24-43
267	COOKE			To U.K. 8-30-43
268	DACRES			To U.K. 8-31-43
269	DOMETT			To U.K. 9-10-43
270	FOLEY			To U.K. 9-16-43
271	GARLIES			To U.K. 9-20-43
272	GOULD			To U.K. 9-25-43
273	GRINDALL			To U.K. 9-30-43
274	GARDINER			To U.K. 9-30-43
275	GOODALL			To U.K. 10-11-43
276	GOODSON			To U.K. 10-16-43
277	GORE			To U.K. 10-22-43
278	KEATS			To U.K. 10-28-43
279	KEMPTHORNE			To U.K. 10-31-43
280	KINGSMILL			To U.K. 11-6-43

Type & No.	Name	Comm. Date	Total	Remarks
DE 301	LAKE	5 Feb. 1944		
302	LYMAN	19 Feb. 1944		
303	CROWLEY	25 Mar. 1944		
304	RALL	8 Apr. 1944		
305	HALLORAN	27 May 1944		
306	CONNOLLY	8 July 1944		
307	FINNEGAN	19 Aug. 1944		
316	HARVESON	12 Oct. 1943		
317	JOYCE	30 Sept. 1943		
318	KIRKPATRICK	23 Oct. 1943		
319	LEOPOLD	18 Oct. 1943		SUNK
320	MENGES	26 Oct. 1943		
321	MOSLEY	30 Oct. 1943		
322	NEWELL	30 Oct. 1943		
323	PRIDE	13 Nov. 1943		
324	FALGOUT	15 Nov. 1943		
325	LOWE	22 Nov. 1943		
326	THOMAS J. GARY	27 Nov. 1943		
327	BRISTER	30 Nov. 1943		
328	FINCH	13 Dec. 1943		
329	KRETCHMER	13 Dec. 1943		
330	O'REILLY	28 Dec. 1943		
331	KOINER	27 Dec. 1943		
332	PRICE	12 Jan. 1944		
333	STRICKLAND	10 Jan. 1944		
334	FORSTER	25 Jan. 1944		
335	DANIEL	24 Jan. 1944		
336	ROY O. HALE	3 Feb. 1944		
337	DALE W. PETERSON	17 Feb. 1944		
338	MARTIN H. RAY	28 Feb. 1944		
339	JOHN C. BUTLER	31 Mar. 1944		
340	O'FLAHERTY	8 Apr. 1944		
341	RAYMOND	15 Apr. 1944		
342	RICHARD W. SUESENS	26 Apr. 1944		
343	ABERCROMBIE	1 May 1944		
344	OBERRENDER	11 May 1944		STRICKEN
345	ROBERT BRAZIER	18 May 1944		
346	EDWIN A. HOWARD	25 May 1944		
347	JESSE RUTHERFORD	31 May 1944		
348	KEY	5 June 1944		
349	GENTRY	14 June 1944		
350	TRAW	20 June 1944		
351	MAURICE J. MANUEL	30 June 1944		

APPENDIX B

Type & No.	Name	Comm. Date	Total	Remarks
DE 352	NAIFEH	4 July 1944		
353	DOYLE C. BARNES	13 July 1944		
354	KENNETH M. WILLETT	19 July 1944		
355	JACCARD	26 July 1944		
356	LLOYD E. ACREE	1 Aug. 1944		
357	GEORGE E. DAVIS	11 Aug. 1944		
358	MACK	16 Aug. 1944		
359	WOODSON	24 Aug. 1944		
360	JOHNNIE HUTCHINS	28 Aug. 1944		
361	WALTON	4 Sept. 1944		
362	ROLF	7 Sept. 1944		
363	PRATT	18 Sept. 1944		
364	ROMBACH	20 Sept. 1944		
365	MCGINTY	25 Sept. 1944		
366	ALVIN C. COCKRELL	7 Oct. 1944		
367	FRENCH	9 Oct. 1944		
368	CECIL J. DOYLE	16 Oct. 1944		
369	THADDEUS PARKER	25 Oct. 1944		
370	JOHN L. WILLIAMSON	31 Oct. 1944		
371	PRESLEY	7 Nov. 1944		
372	WILLIAMS	11 Nov. 1944		
382	RAMSDEN	19 Oct. 1943		
383	MILLS	12 Oct. 1943		
384	RHODES	25 Oct. 1943		
385	RICHEY	30 Oct. 1943		
386	SAVAGE	29 Oct. 1943		
387	VANCE	1 Nov. 1943		
388	LANSING	10 Nov. 1943		
389	DURANT	16 Nov. 1943		
390	CALCATERRA	17 Nov. 1943		
391	CHAMBERS	22 Nov. 1943		
392	MERRILL	27 Nov. 1943		
393	HAVERFIELD	29 Nov. 1943		
394	SWENNING	1 Dec. 1943		
395	WILLIS	10 Dec. 1943		
396	JANSSEN	18 Dec. 1943		
397	WILHOITE	16 Dec. 1943		
398	COCKRILL	24 Dec. 1943		
399	STOCKDALE	31 Dec. 1943		
400	HISSEM	13 Jan. 1944		
401	HOLDER	18 Jan. 1944		SCRAPPED
402	RICHARD S. BULL	26 Feb. 1944		
403	RICHARD M. ROWELL	9 Mar. 1944		

Type & No.	Name	Comm. Date	Total	Remarks
DE 404	EVERSOLE	21 Mar. 1944		SUNK
405	DENNIS	20 Mar. 1944		
406	EDMONDS	3 Apr. 1944		
407	SHELTON	4 Apr. 1944		SUNK
408	STRAUS	6 Apr. 1944		
409	LA PRADE	20 Apr. 1944		
410	JACK MILLER	13 Apr. 1944		
411	STAFFORD	19 Apr. 1944		
412	WALTER C. WANN	2 May 1944		
413	SAMUEL B. ROBERTS	28 Apr. 1944		SUNK
414	LE RAY WILSON	10 May 1944		
415	LAWRENCE C. TAYLOR	13 May 1944		
416	MELVIN R. NAWMAN	16 May 1944		
417	OLIVER MITCHELL	14 June 1944		
418	TABBERER	23 May 1944		
419	ROBERT F. KELLER	17 June 1944		
420	LELAND E. THOMAS	19 June 1944		
421	CHESTER T. O'BRIEN	3 July 1944		
422	DOUGLAS A. MUNRO	11 July 1945		
423	DUFILHO	21 July 1944		
424	HAAS	2 Aug. 1944		
438	CORBESIER	31 Mar. 1944		
439	CONKLIN	21 Apr. 1944		
440	MCCOY REYNOLDS	2 May 1944		
441	WILLIAM SEIVERLING	1 June 1944		
442	ULVERT M. MOORE	18 July 1944		
443	KENDALL C. CAMPBELL	31 July 1944		
444	GOSS	26 Aug. 1944		
445	GRADY	11 Sept. 1944		
446	CHARLES E. BRANNON	1 Nov. 1944		
447	ALBERT T. HARRIS	29 Nov. 1944		
448	CROSS	8 Jan. 1945		
449	HANNA	27 Jan. 1945		
450	JOSEPH E. CONNOLLY	28 Feb. 1945		
508	GILLIGAN	12 May 1944		
509	FORMOE	5 Oct. 1944		
510	HEYLIGER	24 Mar. 1945		
516	LAWFORD			To U.K. 11-3-43
517	LOUIS			To U.K. 11-18-43
518	LAWSON			To U.K. 11-25-43
519	PAISLEY			To U.K. 11-29-43
520	LORING			To U.K. 12-5-43
521	HOSTE			To U.K. 12-14-43

APPENDIX B

Type & No.	Name	Comm. Date	Total	Remarks
DE 522	MOORSOM			To U.K. 12-20-43
523	MANNERS			To U.K. 12-27-43
524	MOUNSEY			To U.K. 12-31-43
525	INGLIS			To U.K. 1-12-44
526	INMAN			To U.K. 1-24-44
527	O'TOOLE	22 Jan. 1944		
528	JOHN J. POWERS	29 Feb. 1944		
529	MASON	20 Mar. 1944		
530	JOHN M. BERMINGHAM	8 Apr. 1944		
531	EDWARD H. ALLEN	16 Dec. 1943		
532	TWEEDY	12 Feb. 1944		
533	HOWARD F. CLARK	25 May 1944		
534	SILVERSTEIN	14 July 1944		
535	LEWIS	5 Sept. 1944		
536	BIVIN	31 Oct. 1944		
537	RIZZI	26 June 1945		
563	SPRAGGE			To U.K. 1-14-44
564	STAYNER			To U.K. 12-30-43
565	THORNBOROUGH			To U.K. 12-31-43
566	TROLLOPE			To U.K. 1-10-44
567	TYLER			To U.K. 1-14-44
568	TORRINGTON			To U.K. 1-18-44
569•	NARBROUGH			To U.K. 1-21-44
570	WALDEGRAVE			To U.K. 1-25-44
571	WHITAKER			To U.K. 1-28-44
572	HOLMES			To U.K. 1-31-44
573	HARGOOD			To U.K. 2-7-44
574	HOTHAM			To U.K. 2-8-44
575	AHRENS	12 Feb. 1944		
576	BARR	15 Feb. 1944		Now APD 39
577	ALEXANDER J. LUKE	19 Feb. 1944		
578	ROBERT I. PAINE	28 Feb. 1944		
579	RILEY	13 Mar. 1944		
580	LESLIE L. B. KNOX	22 Mar. 1944		
581	MCNULTY	31 Mar. 1944		
582	METIVIER	7 Apr. 1944		
583	GEORGE A. JOHNSON	15 Apr. 1944		
584	CHARLES J. KIMMEL	20 Apr. 1944		
585	DANIEL A. JOY	28 Apr. 1944		
586	LOUGH	2 May 1944		
587	THOMAS F. NICKEL	9 June 1944		
588	PEIFFER	15 June 1944		
589	TINSMAN	26 June 1944		

Type & No.	Name	Comm. Date	Total	Remarks
DE 633	FOREMAN	22 Oct. 1943		
634	WHITEHURST	19 Nov. 1943		
635	ENGLAND	10 Dec. 1943		Now APD 41
636	WITTER	29 Dec. 1943		Now APD 58
637	BOWERS	27 Jan. 1944		Now APD 40
638	WILLMARTH	13 Mar. 1944		
639	GENDREAU	17 Mar. 1944		
640	FIEBERLING	11 Apr. 1944		
641	WILLIAM C. COLE	12 May 1944		
642	PAUL G. BAKER	25 May 1944		
643	DAMON M. CUMMINGS	29 June 1944		
644	VAMMEN	27 July 1944		
665	JENKS	19 Jan. 1944		
666	DURIK	24 Mar. 1944		
667	WISEMAN	4 Apr. 1944		
675	WEBER	30 June 1943		Now APD 75
676	SCHMITT	24 July 1943		Now APD 76
677	FRAMENT	15 Aug. 1943		Now APD 77
678	HARMON	31 Aug. 1943		
679	GREENWOOD	25 Sept. 1943		
680	LOESER	10 Oct. 1943		
681	GILLETTE	27 Oct. 1943		
682	UNDERHILL	15 Nov. 1943		SUNK
683	HENRY R. KENYON	30 Nov. 1943		
684	DE LONG	31 Dec. 1943		
685	COATES	24 Jan. 1944		
686	EUGENE E. ELMORE	4 Feb. 1944		
693	BULL	12 Aug. 1943		Now APD 78
694	BUNCH	21 Aug. 1943		Now APD 79
695	RICH	1 Oct. 1943		SUNK
696	SPANGLER	31 Oct. 1943		
697	GEORGE	20 Nov. 1943		
698	RABY	7 Dec. 1943		
699	MARSH	12 Jan. 1944		
700	CURRIER	1 Feb. 1944		
701	OSMUS	23 Feb. 1944		
702	EARL V. JOHNSON	18 Mar. 1944		
703	HOLTON	1 May 1944		
704	CRONIN	5 May 1944		
705	FRYBARGER	18 May 1944		
706	HOLT	9 June 1944		
707	JOBB	4 July 1944		
708	PARLE	29 July 1944		

APPENDIX B

Type & No.	Name	Comm. Date	Total	Remarks
DE 709	BRAY	4 Sept. 1944		Now APD 139
739	BANGUST	30 Oct. 1943		
740	WATERMAN	30 Nov. 1943		
741	WEAVER	31 Dec. 1943		
742	HILBERT	4 Feb. 1944		
743	LAMONS	29 Feb. 1944		
744	KYNE	4 Apr. 1944		
745	SNYDER	5 May 1944		
746	HEMMINGER	30 May 1944		
747	BRIGHT	30 June 1944		
748	TILLS	8 Aug. 1944		
749	ROBERTS	2 Sept. 1944		
750	MC CLELLAND	19 Sept. 1944		
763	CATES	15 Dec. 1943		
764	GANDY	7 Feb. 1944		
765	EARL K. OLSEN	10 Apr. 1944		
766	SLATER	1 May 1944		
767	OSWALD	12 June 1944		
768	EBERT	12 July 1944		
769	NEAL A. SCOTT	31 July 1944		
770	MUIR	30 Aug. 1944		
771	SUTTON	22 Dec. 1944		
789	TATUM	22 Nov. 1943		Now APD 81
790	BORUM	30 Nov. 1943		
791	MALOY	13 Dec. 1943		
792	HAINES	27 Dec. 1943		Now APD 84
793	RUNELS	3 Jan. 1944		Now APD 85
794	HOLLIS	24 Jan. 1944		Now APD 86
795	GUNASON	1 Feb. 1944		
796	MAJOR	12 Feb. 1944		
797	WEEDEN	19 Feb. 1944		
798	VARIAN	29 Feb. 1944		
799	SCROGGINS	30 Mar. 1944		
800	JACK W. WILKE	7 Mar. 1944		
			498	(86 Leased)

HIGH SPEED TRANSPORTS

Type & No.	Name	Comm. Date	Remarks
APD 69	YOKES	18 Dec. 1944	ex-DE 668
70	PAVLIC	29 Dec. 1944	ex-DE 669
71	ODUM	12 Jan. 1945	ex-DE 670
72	JACK C. ROBINSON	2 Feb. 1945	ex-DE 671
73	BASSETT	23 Feb. 1945	ex-DE 672
74	JOHN P. GRAY	15 Mar. 1945	ex-DE 673

Type & No.	Name	Comm. Date	Total	Remarks
APD 87	CROSLEY	22 Oct. 1944		ex-DE 226
88	CREAD	29 July 1945		ex-DE 227
89	RUCHAMKIN	16 Sept. 1945		ex-DE 228
91	KINZER	1 Nov. 1944		ex-DE 232
92	REGISTER	11 Jan. 1945		ex-DE 233
93	BROCK	9 Feb. 1945		ex-DE 234
94	JOHN Q. ROBERTS	8 Mar. 1945		ex-DE 235
95	WILLIAM M. HOBBY	4 Apr. 1945		ex-DE 236
96	RAY K. EDWARDS	11 June 1945		ex-DE 237
97	ARTHUR L. BRISTOL	25 June 1945		ex-DE 281
98	TRUXTUN	9 July 1945		ex-DE 282
99	UPHAM	23 July 1945		ex-DE 283
100	RINGNESS	25 Oct. 1944		ex-DE 590
101	KNUDSON	25 Nov. 1944		ex-DE 591
102	REDNOUR	30 Dec. 1944		ex-DE 592
103	TOLLBERG	31 Jan. 1945		ex-DE 593
104	WILLIAM J. PATTISON	27 Feb. 1945		ex-DE 594
105	MYERS	26 Mar. 1945		ex-DE 595
106	WALTER B. COBB	25 Apr. 1945		ex-DE 596
107	EARLE B. HALL	15 May 1945		ex-DE 597
108	HARRY L. CORL	5 June 1945		ex-DE 598
109	BELET	15 June 1945		ex-DE 599
110	JULIUS A. RAVEN	28 June 1945		ex-DE 600
111	WALSH	11 July 1945		ex-DE 601
112	HUNTER MARSHALL	17 July 1945		ex-DE 602
113	EARHEART	26 July 1945		ex-DE 603
114	WALTER S. GORKA	7 Aug. 1945		ex-DE 604
115	ROGERS BLOOD	22 Aug. 1945		ex-DE 605
116	FRANCOVICH	6 Sept. 1945		ex-DE 606
117	JOSEPH M. AUMAN	25 Apr. 1945		ex-DE 674
118	DON O. WOOD	28 May 1945		ex-DE 721
119	BEVERLY W. REID	25 June 1945		ex-DE 722
120	KLINE	18 Oct. 1944		ex-DE 687
121	RAYMOND W. HERNDON	3 Nov. 1944		ex-DE 688
122	SCRIBNER	20 Nov. 1944		ex-DE 689
123	DIACHENKO	8 Dec. 1944		ex-DE 690
124	HORACE A. BASS	21 Dec. 1944		ex-DE 691
125	WANTUCK	30 Dec. 1944		ex-DE 692
126	GOSSELIN	31 Dec. 1944		ex-DE 710
127	BEGOR	14 Mar. 1945		ex-DE 711
128	CAVALLARO	13 Mar. 1945		ex-DE 712
129	DONALD W. WOLF	14 Apr. 1945		ex-DE 713
130	COOK	25 Apr. 1945		ex-DE 714

APPENDIX B

Type & No.	Name	Comm. Date	Total	Remarks
APD 131	WALTER X. YOUNG	1 May 1945		ex-DE 715
132	BALDUCK	7 May 1945		ex-DE 716
133	BURDO	2 June 1945		ex-DE 717
134	KLEINSMITH	12 June 1945		ex-DE 718
135	WEISS	7 July 1945		ex-DE 719
136	CARPELLOTTI	30 July 1945		ex-DE 720
			55	

SUBMARINES

Type & No.	Name	Comm. Date	Remarks
SS 212	GATO	31 Dec. 1941	
213	GREENLING	21 Jan. 1942	
214	GROUPER	12 Feb. 1942	
215	GROWLER	20 Mar. 1942	SUNK
216	GRUNION	11 Apr. 1942	SUNK
217	GUARDFISH	8 May 1942	
218	ALBACORE	1 June 1942	SUNK
219	AMBERJACK	19 June 1942	SUNK
220	BARB	8 July 1942	
221	BLACKFISH	22 July 1942	
222	BLUEFISH	24 May 1943	
223	BONEFISH	31 May 1943	SUNK
224	COD	21 June 1943	
225	CERO	4 July 1943	
226	CORVINA	6 Aug. 1943	SUNK
227	DARTER	7 Sept. 1943	SUNK
229	FLYING FISH	10 Dec. 1941	
230	FINBACK	31 Jan. 1942	
231	HADDOCK	14 Mar. 1942	
232	HALIBUT	10 Apr. 1942	
233	HERRING	4 May 1942	SUNK
234	KINGFISH	20 May 1942	
235	SHAD	12 June 1942	
236	SILVERSIDES	15 Dec. 1942	
237	TRIGGER	31 Jan. 1942	SUNK
238	WAHOO	15 May 1942	SUNK
239	WHALE	1 June 1942	
240	ANGLER	1 Oct. 1943	
241	BASHAW	25 Oct. 1943	
242	BLUEGILL	11 Nov. 1943	
243	BREAM	24 Jan. 1944	
244	CAVALLA	29 Feb. 1944	
245	COBIA	29 Mar. 1944	
246	CROAKER	21 Apr. 1944	

Type & No.	Name	Comm. Date	Total	Remarks
SS 247	DACE	23 July 1943		
248	DORADO	28 Aug. 1943		SUNK
249	FLASHER	25 Sept. 1943		
250	FLIER	18 Oct. 1943		SUNK
251	FLOUNDER	29 Nov. 1943		
252	GABILAN	28 Dec. 1943		
253	GUNNEL	20 Aug. 1942		
254	GURNARD	18 Sept. 1942		
255	HADDO	9 Oct. 1942		
256	HAKE	30 Oct. 1942		
257	HARDER	2 Dec. 1942		SUNK
258	HOE	16 Dec. 1942		
259	JACK	6 Jan. 1943		
260	LAPON	23 Jan. 1943		
261	MINGO	12 Feb. 1943		
262	MUSKALLUNGE	15 Mar. 1943		
263	PADDLE	29 Mar. 1943		
264	PARGO	26 Apr. 1943		
265	PETO	21 Nov. 1942		
266	POGY	10 Jan. 1943		
267	POMPON	17 Mar. 1943		
268	PUFFER	27 Apr. 1943		
269	RASHER	8 June 1943		
270	RATON	13 July 1943		
271	RAY	27 July 1943		
272	REDFIN	31 Aug. 1943		
273	ROBALO	28 Sept. 1943		SUNK
274	ROCK	26 Oct. 1943		
275	RUNNER	30 July 1942		SUNK
276	SAWFISH	26 Aug. 1942		
277	SCAMP	18 Sept. 1942		SUNK
278	SCORPION	1 Oct. 1942		SUNK
279	SNOOK	24 Oct. 1942		SUNK
280	STEELHEAD	7 Dec. 1942		
281	SUNFISH	15 July 1942		
282	TUNNY	1 Sept. 1942		
283	TINOSA	15 Jan. 1943		
284	TULLIBEE	15 Feb. 1943		SUNK
285	BALAO	4 Feb. 1943		
286	BILLFISH	20 Apr. 1943		
287	BOWFIN	1 May 1943		
288	CABRILLA	24 May 1943		
289	CAPELIN	4 June 1943		SUNK

APPENDIX B

Type & No.	Name	Comm. Date	Total	Remarks
SS 290	CISCO	10 May 1943		SUNK
291	CREVALLE	24 June 1943		
292	DEVILFISH	1 Sept. 1944		
293	DRAGONET	6 Mar. 1944		
294	ESCOLAR	2 June 1944		SUNK
295	HACKLEBACK	7 Nov. 1944		
297	LING	8 June 1945		
298	LIONFISH	1 Nov. 1944		
299	MANTA	18 Dec. 1944		
300	MORAY	26 Jan. 1945		
301	RONCADOR	27 Mar. 1945		
302	SABALO	19 June 1945		
304	SEAHORSE	31 Mar. 1943		
305	SKATE	15 Apr. 1943		
306	TANG	15 Oct. 1943		SUNK
307	TILEFISH	28 Dec. 1943		
308	APOGON	16 July 1943		
309	ASPRO	31 July 1943		
310	BATFISH	21 Aug. 1943		
311	ARCHERFISH	4 Sept. 1943		
312	BURRFISH	14 Sept. 1943		
313	PERCH	7 Jan. 1944		
314	SHARK	14 Feb. 1944		SUNK
315	SEALION	8 Mar. 1944		
316	BARBEL	3 Apr. 1944		SUNK
317	BARBERO	29 Apr. 1944		
318	BAYA	20 May 1944		
319	BECUNA	27 May 1944		
320	BERGALL	12 June 1944		
321	BESUGO	19 June 1944		
322	BLACKFIN	4 July 1944		
323	CAIMAN	17 July 1944		
324	BLENNY	27 July 1944		
325	BLOWER	10 Aug. 1944		
326	BLUEBACK	28 Aug. 1944		
327	BOARFISH	23 Sept. 1944		
328	CHARR	23 Sept. 1944		
329	CHUB	21 Oct. 1944		
330	BRILL	26 Oct. 1944		
331	BUGARA	15 Nov. 1944		
332	BULLHEAD	4 Dec. 1944		
333	BUMPER	9 Dec. 1944		
334	CABEZON	30 Dec. 1944		

Type & No.	Name	Comm. Date	Total	Remarks
SS 335	DENTUDA	30 Dec. 1944		
336	CAPITAINE	26 Jan. 1945		
337	CARBONERO	7 Feb. 1945		
338	CARP	28 Feb. 1945		
339	CATFISH	19 Mar. 1945		
340	ENTEMEDOR	6 Apr. 1945		
341	CHIVO	28 Apr. 1945		
342	CHOPPER	25 May 1945		
343	CLAMAGORE	28 June 1945		
344	COBBLER	8 Aug. 1945		
345	COCHINO	25 Aug. 1945		
361	GOLET	30 Nov. 1943		SUNK
362	GUAVINA	23 Dec. 1943		
363	GUITARRO	26 Jan. 1944		
364	HAMMERHEAD	1 Mar. 1944		
365	HARDHEAD	18 Apr. 1944		
366	HAWKBILL	17 May 1944		
367	ICEFISH	10 June 1944		
368	JALLAO	8 July 1944		
369	KETE	31 July 1944		SUNK
370	KRAKEN	8 Sept. 1944		
371	LAGARTO	14 Oct. 1944		SUNK
372	LAMPREY	17 Nov. 1944		
373	LIZARDFISH	30 Dec. 1944		
374	LOGGERHEAD	9 Feb. 1945		
375	MACABI	29 Mar. 1945		
376	MAPIRO	30 Apr. 1945		
377	MENHADEN	22 June 1945		
378	MERO	17 Aug. 1945		
381	SAND LANCE	9 Oct. 1943		
382	PICUDA	16 Oct. 1943		
383	PAMPANITO	6 Nov. 1943		
384	PARCHE	20 Nov. 1943		
385	BANG	4 Dec. 1943		
386	PILOTFISH	16 Dec. 1943		
387	PINTADO	1 Jan. 1944		
388	PIPEFISH	22 Jan. 1944		
389	PIRANHA	5 Feb. 1944		
390	PLAICE	12 Feb. 1944		
391	POMFRET	19 Feb. 1944		
392	STERLET	4 Mar. 1944		
393	QUEENFISH	11 Mar. 1944		
394	RAZORBACK	3 Apr. 1944		

APPENDIX B

Type & No.	Name	Comm. Date	Total	Remarks
ss 395	REDFISH	12 Apr. 1944		
396	RONQUIL	22 Apr. 1944		
397	SCABBARDFISH	29 Apr. 1944		
398	SEGUNDO	9 May 1944		
399	SEA CAT	16 May 1944		
400	SEA DEVIL	24 May 1944		
401	SEA DOG	3 June 1944		
402	SEA FOX	13 June 1944		
403	ATULE	21 June 1944		
404	SPIKEFISH	30 June 1944		
405	SEA OWL	17 July 1944		
406	SEA POACHER	31 July 1944		
407	SEA ROBIN	7 Aug. 1944		
408	SENNET	22 Aug. 1944		
409	PIPER	23 Aug. 1944		
410	THREADFIN	30 Aug. 1944		
411	SPADEFISH	9 Mar. 1944		
412	TREPANG	22 May 1944		
413	SPOT	3 Aug. 1944		
414	SPRINGER	18 Oct. 1944		
415	STICKLEBACK	29 Mar. 1945		
417	TENCH	6 Oct. 1944		
418	THORNBACK	13 Oct. 1944		
419	TIGRONE	25 Oct. 1944		
420	TIRANTE	6 Nov. 1944		
421	TRUTTA	16 Nov. 1944		
422	TORO	8 Dec. 1944		
423	TORSK	16 Dec. 1944		
424	QUILLBACK	29 Dec. 1944		
475	ARGONAUT	15 Jan. 1945		
476	RUNNER	6 Feb. 1945		
477	CONGER	14 Feb. 1945		
478	CUTLASS	17 Mar. 1945		
479	DIABLO	31 Mar. 1945		
480	MEDREGAL	14 Apr. 1945		
481	REQUIN	28 Apr. 1945		
482	IREX	14 May 1945		
483	SEA LEOPARD	11 June 1945		
484	ODAX	11 July 1945		
485	SIRAGO	13 Aug. 1945		

ALL OTHER CLASSES OF VESSELS COMPLETED
7 DECEMBER 1941–1 OCTOBER 1945
SUMMARY

Class	Number of Vessels
MINE CRAFT	874
PATROL CRAFT	1,824
AUXILIARIES	1,531
DISTRICT CRAFT (Self Propelled)	1,355
DISTRICT CRAFT (Non Self Propelled)	1,431
LARGE LANDING CRAFT	4,094
SMALL LANDING CRAFT	79,418
SMALL BOATS	19,259
Total	109,786

Note: Figures include New Construction Vessels built; Vessels Converted; and Vessels Acquired, no conversion required. Lend Lease Vessels included.

Type	Number of Vessels	Total	Type	Number of Vessels	Total
MINE CRAFT			AF	30	
			AG	40	
ACM	8		AGC	13	
AM	218		AGP	15	
AMb	21		AGS	3	
AMc	50		AH	9	
BAM	20		AK	143	
CM	3		AKA	94	
YMS	474		AKN	3	
BYMS	80		AKS	12	
		874	AN	45	
PATROL CRAFT			AO	63	
			AOG	63	
PC	315		AP	101	
PCE	51		APA	200	
PCE(R)	13		APB	6	
PCS	59		APc	100	
PF	96		APH	3	
PG	41		APL	42	
PGM	23		AR	8	
PT	690		ARB	12	
BPT	58		ARG	12	
PY	10		ARH	1	
PYc	24		ARL	33	
SC	444		ARS	35	
		1824	ARS(T)	3	
AUXILIARIES			ARV	2	
AD	7		ARV(A)	2	
AE	14		ARV(E)	2	

APPENDIX B

Type	Number of Vessels	Total
AS	10	
ASR	6	
AT	11	
ATA	45	
ATF	53	
ATR	100	
AV	8	
AVP	27	
AW	4	
BAK	4	
BARS	6	
BAT	11	
IX	130	
		1531

DISTRICT CRAFT (SP)

Type	Number of Vessels	Total
YAG	27	
YCF	2	
YDG	9	
YDT	2	
YF	80	
YFB	33	
YG	13	
YH	2	
YHB	16	
YHT	1	
YMT	11	
YN	11	
YNT	1	
YO	106	
YOG	42	
YP	497	
YSD	53	
YSR	1	
YT	4	
BYT	3	
PYT	2	
YTB	169	
YTL	200	
YTM	32	
YW	38	
		1355

DISTRICT CRAFT (NSP)

Type	Number of Vessels	Total
YC	398	
YCF	89	
YCK	51	
YCV	14	
YF	609	
YFT	4	
YG	10	
YHB	5	
YNg	17	
YO	52	
YOG	38	
YOS	12	
YR	41	
YRD(H)	8	
YRD(M)	8	
YS	17	
YSP	6	
YSR	26	
YTT	3	
YW	23	
		1431

LARGE LANDING CRAFT

Type	Number of Vessels	Total
LCI(L)	921	
LCS(L)(3)	130	
LCT(5)	470	
LCT(6)	965	
LSD	22	
LSM	481	
LSM(R)	58	
LST	1041	
LSV	6	
		4094

SMALL LANDING CRAFT

Type	Number of Vessels	Total
LCC(1)	54	
LCC(2)	45	
LCM(6)	2730	
LCM(3)	8631	
LCM(2)	31	
LCS(S)(1)	150	
LCS(S)(2)	408	
LCP(L)	1755	

Type	Number of Vessels	Total	Type	Number of Vessels	Total
LCP(R)	2635		LCP(N)	12	
LCVP	23398		LCR(L)	9981	
LCV	2279		LCR(S)	8150	
LVT(1)	1174		45' Artillery Lighters	6	
LVT(A)(1)	510		26' Outboard Landing Craft	4	
LVT(2)	2962				
LVT(A)(2)	450		Army Storm Boats	6	
LVT(3)	2964		Army Assault Boats	226	
LVT(4)	8351		Landing Craft Electric	344	
LVT(A)(4)	1890		Amphibian Truck	3	
LVT(A)(5)	269				79,418

Appendix C

Losses of United States Naval Vessels from all causes 7 December 1941–1 October 1945

Name	Location	Date
BATTLESHIPS		
ARIZONA	Pearl Harbor	7 December 1941
OKLAHOMA	Pearl Harbor	7 December 1941
AIRCRAFT CARRIERS		
HORNET	08 38 S, 166 43 E	26 October 1942
LEXINGTON	15 12 S, 155 27 E	8 May 1942
PRINCETON	15 21 N, 123 31 E	24 October 1944
WASP	12 25 S, 164 08 E	15 September 1942
YORKTOWN	30 36 N, 176 34 W	7 June 1942
ESCORT AIRCRAFT CARRIERS		
BISMARCK SEA	Off Iwo Jima	21 February 1945
BLOCK ISLAND	31 13 N, 23 03 W	29 May 1944
GAMBIER BAY	11 31 N, 126 12 E	25 October 1944
LISCOME BAY	02 54 N, 172 30 E	24 November 1943
OMMANEY BAY	Off Panay I., P.I.	4 January 1945
SAINT LO	11 13 N, 126 05 E	25 October 1944
HEAVY CRUISERS		
ASTORIA	Off Savo I., Solomons	9 August 1942
CHICAGO	11 25 S, 160 56 E	30 January 1943
HOUSTON	Off Java, N.E.I.	1 March 1942
INDIANAPOLIS	NE of Leyte I., P.I.	29 July 1945
NORTHAMPTON	Off Savo I., Solomons	30 November 1942
QUINCY	Off Savo I., Solomons	9 August 1942
VINCENNES	Off Savo I., Solomons	9 August 1942
LIGHT CRUISERS		
ATLANTA	Off Lunga Point, Guadalcanal	13 November 1942
HELENA	Kula Gulf, Solomons	6 July 1943
JUNEAU	10 34 S, 161 04 E	13 November 1942
DESTROYERS		
AARON WARD	9 10 S, 160 12 E	7 April 1943
ABNER READ	10 47 N, 125 22 E	1 November 1944

Name	Location	Date
BARTON	Off Guadalcanal I., Solomons	13 November 1942
BEATTY	37 10 N, 6 00 E	6 November 1943
BENHAM	Off Savo I., Solomons	15 November 1942
BLUE	9 17 S, 160 02 E	22 August 1942
BORIE	North of Azores	1 November 1943
BRISTOL	37 19 N, 6 19 E	13 October 1943
BROWNSON	Off New Britain	26 December 1943
BUCK	40 00 N, 14 30 E	9 October 1943
BUSH	27 16 N, 127 48 E	6 April 1945
CALLAGHAN	25 43 N, 126 55 E	29 July 1945
CHEVALIER	Off Vella Lavella, Solomons	6 October 1943
COLHOUN	Off Okinawa, Ryukyus	6 April 1945
COOPER	Ormoc Bay, P.I.	3 December 1944
CORRY	49 31 N, 1 11 W	6 June 1944
CUSHING	Off Savo I., Solomons	13 November 1942
DE HAVEN	9 09 S, 159 52 E	1 February 1943
DREXLER	Off Okinawa, Ryukyus	28 May 1945
DUNCAN	Off Savo I., Solomons	12 October 1942
EDSALL	S of Java, N.E.I.	1 March 1942
GLENNON	50 32 N, 1 12 W	8 June 1944
GWIN	7 41 S, 157 27 E	13 July 1943
HALLIGAN	26 10 N, 127 30 E	26 March 1945
HAMMANN	30 36 N, 176 34 W	6 June 1942
HENLEY	7 40 S, 148 06 E	3 October 1943
HOEL	11 46 S, 126 33 E	25 October 1944
HULL	14 57 N, 127 58 E	18 December 1944
INGRAHAM	42 34 N, 60 05 W	22 August 1942
JACOB JONES	38 42 N, 74 39 W	28 February 1942
JARVIS	Off Guadalcanal I., Solomons	9 August 1942
JOHNSTON	11 46 N, 126 09 E	25 October 1944
LAFFEY	Off Savo I., Solomons	13 November 1942
LANSDALE	37 03 N, 3 51 E	20 April 1944
LEARY	45 00 N, 22 00 W	24 December 1943
LITTLE	26 24 N, 126 15 E	3 May 1945
LONGSHAW	26 11 N, 127 37 E	18 May 1945
LUCE	26 35 N, 127 10 E	4 May 1945
MADDOX	Off Sicily	10 July 1943
MAHAN	Ormoc Bay, P.I.	7 December 1944
MANNERT L. ABELE	27 25 N, 126 59 E	12 April 1945
MEREDITH (DD 434)	Off San Cristobal I., Solomons	15 October 1942
MEREDITH (DD 726)	49 33 N, 1 06 W	8 June 1944
MONAGHAN	14 57 N, 127 58 E	18 December 1944
MONSSEN	9 04 S, 159 54 E	13 November 1942
MORRISON	27 10 N, 127 58 E	4 May 1945

Name	Location	Date
O'BRIEN	12 28 S, 164 08 E	15 September 1942
PARROTT	Norfolk, Virginia	2 May 1944
PEARY	Port Darwin, Australia	19 February 1942
PERKINS	Off New Guinea	29 November 1943
PILLSBURY	Bali Strait, N.E.I.	1 March 1942
POPE	Java Sea	1 March 1942
PORTER	8 32 S, 167 17 E	26 October 1942
PRESTON	Off Savo I., Solomons	15 November 1942
PRINGLE	27 25 N, 126 59 E	16 April 1945
REID	9 50 N, 124 55 E	11 December 1944
REUBEN JAMES	51 59 N, 27 05 W	31 October 1941
ROWAN	40 07 N, 14 18 E	11 September 1943
SIMS	Coral Sea	7 May 1942
SPENCE	14 57 N, 127 58 E	18 December 1944
STEWART	Off Surabaya, Java, N.E.I.	19 February 1942
STRONG	Kula Gulf, Solomons	5 July 1943
STURTEVANT	Off Key West, Fla.	26 April 1942
TRUXTUN	Placentia Bay, Newfoundland	18 February 1942
TUCKER	Off Espiritu Santo I., New Hebrides	4 August 1942
TURNER	Off Ambrose Light, New York	3 January 1944
TWIGGS	26 08 N, 127 35 E	16 June 1945
WALKE	Off Savo I., Solomons	15 November 1942
WARRINGTON	27 00 N, 73 00 W	13 September 1944
WILLIAM D. PORTER	27 06 N, 127 38 E	10 June 1945
WORDEN	Amchitka I., Aleutians	12 January 1943

DESTROYER ESCORT VESSELS

Name	Location	Date
EVERSOLE	10 10 N, 127 28 E	28 October 1944
FECHTELER	36 07 N, 02 40 W	5 May 1944
FISKE	47 11 N, 33 29 W	2 August 1944
FREDERICK C. DAVIS	43 52 N, 40 15 W	24 April 1945
HOLDER	Mediterranean Sea	11 April 1944
LEOPOLD	58 44 N, 25 50 W	9 March 1944
OBERRENDER	Off Okinawa, Ryukyus	9 May 1945
RICH	49 31 N, 1 10 W	8 June 1944
SAMUEL B. ROBERTS	Off Samar I., P.I.	25 October 1944
SHELTON	2 32 N, 129 13 E	3 October 1944
UNDERHILL	19 20 N, 126 42 E	24 July 1945

SUBMARINES

Name	Location	Date
ALBACORE	Japanese home waters	November 1944
AMBERJACK	Off New Britain	February 1943
ARGONAUT	Off New Britain	10 January 1943
BARBEL	Off Borneo	February 1945

Name	Location	Date
BONEFISH	Japanese home waters	May 1945
BULLHEAD	Java Sea	August 1945
CAPELIN	Celebes Sea	December 1943
CISCO	South Pacific Ocean	October 1943
CORVINA	Marshall Islands	November 1943
DARTER	Palawan Passage, P.I.	24 October 1944
DORADO	Canal Zone, Panama	October 1943
ESCOLAR	Japanese home waters	October 1944
FLIER	Off Borneo	August 1944
GOLET	Japanese home waters	June 1944
GRAMPUS	Off New Britain	February 1943
GRAYBACK	Ryukyu Islands	February 1944
GRAYLING	Philippine waters	August 1943
GRENADIER	Malayan waters	21 April 1943
GROWLER	Philippine waters	November 1944
GRUNION	Aleutian waters	July 1942
GUDGEON	Marianas Islands	May 1944
HARDER	Philippine waters	August 1944
HERRING	Kurile Islands	May 1944
KETE	Ryukyu Islands	March 1945
LAGARTO	South China Sea	June 1945
PERCH	Java Sea	3 March 1942
PICKEREL	Japanese home waters	May 1943
POMPANO	Japanese home waters	September 1943
R-12	Off Key West, Fla.	12 June 1943
ROBALO	Off Borneo	26 July 1944
RUNNER	Japanese home waters	June 1943
S-26	Gulf of Panama	24 January 1942
S-27	Amchitka I., Aleutians	19 June 1942
S-28	Off Oahu, T. H.	4 July 1944
S-36	Straits of Makassar, N.E.I.	20 January 1942
S-39	Off Rossell I., SW Pacific	14 August 1942
S-44	Kurile Islands	7 October 1943
SCAMP	Japanese home waters	November 1944
SCORPION	East China Sea	January 1944
SCULPIN	Gilbert Islands	19 November 1943
SEALION	Cavite, P. I.	10 December 1941
SEAWOLF	Off Morotai I., N.E.I.	October 1944
SHARK (SS 174)	Molucca Sea	February 1942
SHARK (SS 314)	Off Hong Kong, China	October 1944
SNOOK	Off Hainan I., S. China Sea	April 1945
SWORDFISH	Ryukyu Islands	January 1945
TANG	Formosa Strait	25 October 1944
TRIGGER	Ryukyu Islands	March 1945

APPENDIX C

Name	Location	Date
TRITON	Admiralty Islands	March 1943
TROUT	Ryukyu Islands	February 1944
TULLIBEE	Off Palau I.	26 March 1944
WAHOO	Japanese home waters	October 1943

MINELAYERS

GAMBLE	Off Iwo Jima	18 February 1945
MIANTONOMAH	Off Le Havre, France	25 September 1944
MONTGOMERY	Ngulu Lagoon, South Pacific	17 October 1944

MINESWEEPERS

BITTERN	At Cavite, P. I.	10 December 1941
BUNTING	San Francisco Bay	3 June 1942
CROW	Puget Sound	23 August 1943
EMMONS	Off Okinawa, Ryukyus	6 April 1945
FINCH	At Corregidor, P. I.	10 April 1942
HORNBILL	San Francisco Bay	30 June 1942
HOVEY	Lingayen Gulf, P. I.	6 January 1945
LONG	16 12 N, 120 11 E	6 January 1945
OSPREY	50 12 N, 1 20 W	5 June 1944
PALMER	Lingayen Gulf, P. I.	7 January 1945
PENGUIN	At Guam	8 December 1941
PERRY	Off Palau I.	13 September 1944
PORTENT	41 23 N, 12 43 E	22 January 1944
QUAIL	Corregidor, P. I.	5 May 1942
SALUTE	5 07 N, 115 04 E	8 June 1945
SENTINEL	Off Licata, Sicily	11 July 1943
SKILL	40 20 N, 14 35 E	25 September 1943
SKYLARK	26 20 N, 127 41 E	28 March 1945
SWALLOW	Off Okinawa, Ryukyus	22 April 1945
SWERVE	41 31 N, 12 28 E	9 July 1944
TANAGER	At Corregidor, P. I.	4 May 1942
TIDE	49 37 N, 1 05 W	7 June 1944
VALOR	41 28 N, 70 57 W	29 June 1944
WASMUTH	Aleutian Islands	29 December 1942

SUBMARINE CHASERS

PC 496	37 23 N, 9 52 W	4 June 1943
PC 558	38 41 N, 13 43 E	9 May 1944
PC 815	Off San Diego	11 September 1945
PC 1129	Off Luzon, P. I.	31 January 1945
PC 1261	Off France	6 June 1944
PC 1603	26 25 N, 127 56 E	26 May 1945
SC 521	11 03 S, 164 50 E	10 July 1945

Name	Location	Date
SC 632	Off Okinawa, Ryukyus	16 September 1945
SC 636	Off Okinawa, Ryukyus	16 September 1945
SC 694	Off Palermo, Sicily	23 August 1943
SC 696	Off Palermo, Sicily	23 August 1943
SC 700	Vella Lavella, Solomons	10 March 1944
SC 709	Cape Breton, Nova Scotia	21 January 1943
SC 740	15 32 S, 147 06 E	17 June 1943
SC 744	Tacloban Bay, P. I.	27 November 1944
SC 751	21 56 S, 113 53 E	22 June 1943
SC 984	In New Hebrides	9 April 1944
SC 1019	22 28 N, 84 30 W	22 April 1945
SC 1024	35 12 N, 74 57 W	2 March 1943
SC 1059	In Bahama Islands	11 December 1944
SC 1067	Off Attu, Aleutians	19 November 1943

GUNBOATS

Name	Location	Date
PGM 7	Bismarck Sea	18 July 1944
PGM 17	Off Okinawa	4 May 1945
PGM 18	26 13 N, 127 54 E	8 April 1945
ASHEVILLE	South of Java, N.E.I.	3 March 1942
ERIE	12 03 N, 68 58 W	12 November 1942
LUZON	At Corregidor, P. I.	5 May 1942
MINDANAO	Off Corregidor, P. I.	2 May 1942
OAHU	At Corregidor, P. I.	4 May 1942
PLYMOUTH	36 17 N, 74 29 W	5 August 1943
ST AUGUSTINE	38 00 N, 74 05 W	6 January 1944
WAKE	At Shanghai, China	8 December 1941
PE 56	Portland, Maine	23 April 1945

COAST GUARD VESSELS

Name	Location	Date
CG 58012	41 53 N, 70 30 W	2 May 1943
CG 83415	Off France	21 June 1944
CG 83421	26 14 N, 79 05 W	30 June 1943
CG 83471	Off France	21 June 1944
ACACIA	Caribbean Sea	15 March 1942
ALEXANDER HAMILTON	Off Iceland	29 January 1942
BEDLOE	Off Cape Hatteras	14 September 1944
BODEGA	Gulf of Mexico	20 December 1943
CATAMOUNT	Off Ambrose Light, New York	27 March 1943
DOW	Caribbean Sea	15 October 1943
ESCANABA	60 50 N, 52 00 W	13 June 1943
JACKSON	Off North Atlantic Coast	14 September 1944
NATSEK	Belle Island Strait	17 December 1942

Name	Location	Date
VINEYARD SOUND	Vineyard Sound	14 September 1944
WILCOX	Off Cape Hatteras	30 September 1943

SEAPLANE TENDERS

GANNET	Off Bermuda	7 June 1942
LANGLEY	South of Java, N.E.I.	27 February 1942
THORNTON	24 24 N, 128 58 E	5 April 1945

MOTOR TORPEDO BOATS

PT 22	North Pacific	11 June 1943
PT 28	Dora Harbor, Alaska	12 January 1943
PT 31	Subic Bay, P. I.	20 January 1942
PT 32	Sulu Sea	13 March 1942
PT 33	Off Pt. Santiago, P. I.	15 December 1941
PT 34	Off Cauit Island, P. I.	9 April 1942
PT 35	At Cebu, P. I.	12 April 1942
PT 37	Off Guadalcanal I., Solomons	1 February 1943
PT 41	Lake Lanao, Mindanao, P. I.	15 April 1942
PT 43	Off Guadalcanal I., Solomons	10 January 1943
PT 44	In South Pacific	11 December 1942
PT 63	Off New Ireland	18 June 1944
PT 67	Off Tufi, New Guinea	17 March 1943
PT 68	New Guinea	1 October 1943
PT 73	Philippines	15 January 1945
PT 77	Off Talin Pt., Luzon, P. I.	1 February 1945
PT 79	Off Talin Pt., Luzon, P. I.	1 February 1945
PT 107	Off New Ireland	18 June 1944
PT 109	In Blackett Straits, Solomons	2 August 1943
PT 110	Off New Guinea	26 January 1944
PT 111	Off Guadalcanal I., Solomons	1 February 1943
PT 112	Off Guadalcanal I., Solomons	10 January 1943
PT 113	Off Buna, New Guinea	8 August 1943
PT 117	Rendova Harbor, Solomons	1 August 1943
PT 118	Vella Lavella, Solomons	7 September 1943
PT 119	Off Tufi, New Guinea	17 March 1943
PT 121	5 S, 151 E	27 March 1944
PT 123	Off Guadalcanal I., Solomons	1 February 1943
PT 133	Off New Guinea	15 July 1944
PT 135	5 29 S, 152 09 E	12 April 1944
PT 136	Vitiaz Strait, New Guinea	17 September 1943
PT 145	New Guinea	4 January 1944
PT 147	New Guinea	19 November 1943
PT 153	Solomons	4 July 1943
PT 158	Off Munda Pt., Solomons	5 July 1943

Name	Location	Date
PT 164	In Rendova Harbor, Solomons	1 August 1943
PT 165	23 45 S, 166 30 E	23 May 1943
PT 166	Solomons	20 July 1943
PT 172	Off Vella Lavella, Solomons	7 September 1943
PT 173	23 45 S, 166 30 E	23 May 1943
PT 193	00 55 S, 134 52 E	25 June 1944
PT 200	41 N, 71 W	22 February 1944
PT 202	43 23 N, 6 43 E	16 August 1944
PT 218	43 23 N, 6 43 E	16 August 1944
PT 219	Off Attu, Aleutians	September 1943
PT 239	Solomons	14 December 1943
PT 247	6 38 S, 156 01 E	5 May 1944
PT 251	Off Bougainville I., Solomons	26 February 1944
PT 279	Off Bougainville I., Solomons	11 February 1944
PT 283	Off Bougainville I., Solomons	17 March 1944
PT 300	Off Mindoro I., P. I.	18 December 1944
PT 301	Off New Guinea	7 November 1944
PT 311	43 N, 9 E	18 November 1944
PT 320	Off Leyte, P. I.	5 November 1944
PT 321	San Isidoro Bay, P. I.	11 November 1944
PT 322	Off New Guinea	23 November 1943
PT 323	10 33 N, 125 14 E	10 December 1944
PT 337	Hansa Bay, New Guinea	7 March 1944
PT 338	12 06 N, 121 23 E	28 January 1945
PT 339	Off Biak, New Guinea	27 May 1944
PT 346	Off New Britain	29 April 1944
PT 347	Off New Britain	29 April 1944
PT 353	5 S, 151 E	27 March 1944
PT 363	Kaoe Bay, Halmahera, N.E.I.	25 November 1944
PT 368	Off Halmahera, N.E.I.	11 October 1944
PT 371	2 05 N, 127 51 E	19 September 1944
PT 493	In Surigao Strait, P. I.	25 October 1944
PT 509	English Channel	9 August 1944
PT 555	Off Cape Couronne, Mediterranean	23 August 1944

TANK LANDING SHIPS

Name	Location	Date
LST 6	In Seine River, France	18 November 1944
LST 43	Pearl Harbor	21 May 1944
LST 69	Pearl Harbor	21 May 1944
LST 158	Off Licata, Sicily	11 July 1943
LST 167	At Vella Lavella	25 September 1943
LST 179	Pearl Harbor	21 May 1944
LST 203	Near Nanumea, Union Islands	1 October 1943
LST 228	In Azores	20 January 1944

Name	Location	Date
LST 282	Off southern France	15 August 1944
LST 313	At Gela, Sicily	10 July 1943
LST 314	49 43 N, 00 52 W	9 June 1944
LST 318	Off Caronia, Sicily	9 August 1943
LST 333	36 59 N, 4 01 E	22 June 1943
LST 342	9 03 S, 158 11 E	18 July 1943
LST 348	40 57 N, 13 14 E	20 February 1944
LST 349	Off Ponza, Italy	26 February 1944
LST 353	Pearl Harbor	21 May 1944
LST 359	42 N, 19 W	20 December 1944
LST 376	Off northern France	9 June 1944
LST 396	8 18 S, 156 55 E	18 August 1943
LST 447	26 9 N, 127 18 E	6 April 1945
LST 448	Off Vella Lavella, Solomons	1 October 1943
LST 460	11 10 N, 121 11 E	21 December 1944
LST 472	Off Mindoro, P. I.	15 December 1944
LST 480	At Pearl Harbor	21 May 1944
LST 493	50 20 N, 4 09 W	12 April 1945
LST 496	Off northern France	11 June 1944
LST 499	Off northern France	8 June 1944
LST 507	50 29 N, 2 52 W	28 April 1944
LST 523	Off northern France	19 June 1944
LST 531	50 29 N, 2 52 W	28 April 1944
LST 563	Southwest of Mexico	22 December 1944
LST 577	8 1 N, 130 22 E	11 February 1945
LST 675	Off Okinawa	4 April 1945
LST 738	Off Mindoro, P. I.	15 December 1944
LST 749	11 10 N, 121 11 E	21 December 1944
LST 750	Off Negros, P. I.	28 December 1944
LST 808	Off Ie Shima	20 May 1945
LST 906	At Leghorn, Italy	18 October 1944
LST 921	In English Channel	14 August 1944

MEDIUM LANDING SHIPS

Name	Location	Date
LSM 12	Off Okinawa	4 April 1945
LSM 20	10 12 N, 125 19 E	5 December 1944
LSM 59	Off Okinawa	21 June 1945
LSM 135	Off Okinawa	25 May 1945
LSM 149	At Sansapor, New Guinea	5 December 1944
LSM 190	26 35 N, 127 10 E	4 May 1945
LSM 194	Off Okinawa	4 May 1945
LSM 195	Off Okinawa	3 May 1945
LSM 318	10 56 N, 124 38 E	7 December 1944

TANK LANDING CRAFT

Name	Location	Date
LCT 19	Off Salerno, Italy	15 September 1943
LCT 21	Off Oran	1 January 1943
LCT 23	At Algiers	3 May 1943
LCT 25	Off northern France	6 June 1944
LCT 26	41 4 N, 13 30 E	25 February 1944
LCT 27	Off northern France	6 June 1944
LCT 28	In Mediterranean	30 May 1943
LCT 30	Off northern France	6 June 1944
LCT 35	Off Anzio, Italy	15 February 1944
LCT 36	Off Naples, Italy	26 February 1944
LCT 66	At Pearl Harbor	12 April 1945
LCT 71	53 38 N, 146 5 W	11 September 1943
LCT 147	Off northern France	June 1944
LCT 154	37 8 N, 10 58 E	31 August 1943
LCT 175	4 27 N, 133 40 E	21 February 1945
LCT 182	Solomons	7 August 1944
LCT 185	Off Bizerte, Tunisia	24 January 1944
LCT 196	Off Salerno, Italy	27 September 1943
LCT 197	Off northern France	6 June 1944
LCT 200	Off northern France	June 1944
LCT 208	Off Algeria	20 June 1943
LCT 209	Off northern France	10 June 1944
LCT 215	Off Salerno, Italy	1943
LCT 220	At Anzio, Italy	13 February 1944
LCT 241	Off Salerno, Italy	15 September 1943
LCT 242	Off Naples, Italy	2 December 1943
LCT 244	Off northern France	8 June 1944
LCT 253	On passage to Tarawa	21 January 1945
LCT 293	In English Channel	11 October 1944
LCT 294	Off northern France	6 June 1944
LCT 305	Off northern France	6 June 1944
LCT 311	Off Bizerte, Tunisia	9 August 1943
LCT 315	At Eniwetok Atoll	23 March 1944
LCT 319	At Kiska	27 August 1943
LCT 332	Off northern France	6 June 1944
LCT 340	36 49 N, 11 55 E	9 February 1944
LCT 342	Off Salerno, Italy	29 September 1943
LCT 352	At Pearl Harbor	12 April 1945
LCT 362	Off northern France	6 June 1944
LCT 364	Off northern France	6 June 1944
LCT 366	53 1 N, 152 W	9 September 1943
LCT 413	Off northern France	June 1944

APPENDIX C

Name	Location	Date
LCT 458	Off northern France	7 June 1944
LCT 459	Off western France	19 September 1944
LCT 486	Off northern France	7 June 1944
LCT 496	English Channel	2 October 1943
LCT 548	At Portsmouth, England	October 1944
LCT 555	Off northern France	6 June 1944
LCT 572	Off northern France	June 1944
LCT 579	Off Palau	4 October 1944
LCT 582	In Azores	22 January 1944
LCT 593	Off northern France	6 June 1944
LCT 597	Off northern France	6 June 1944
LCT 612	Off northern France	6 June 1944
LCT 703	Off northern France	6 June 1944
LCT 713	Off northern France	June 1944
LCT 714	Off northern France	June 1944
LCT 777	Off northern France	6 June 1944
LCT 823	Off Palau	27 September 1944
LCT 961	Pearl Harbor	21 May 1944
LCT 963	Pearl Harbor	21 May 1944
LCT 983	Pearl Harbor	21 May 1944
LCT 984	20 N, 157 W	15 May 1944
LCT 988	20 N, 157 W	15 May 1944
LCT 995	At Guam	21 April 1945
LCT 1029	At Iwo Jima	2 March 1945
LCT 1050	Off Ie Shima, Ryukyus	27 July 1945
LCT 1075	Off Leyte, P. I.	10 December 1944
LCT 1090	Off Luzon, P. I.	26 March 1945
LCT 1151	1 N, 138 36 E	26 January 1945
LCT 1358	Off California	4 May 1945

INFANTRY LANDING CRAFT

Name	Location	Date
LCI 1	At Bizerte, Tunisia	17 August 1943
LCI 20	Off Anzio, Italy	22 January 1944
LCI 32	Off Anzio, Italy	26 January 1944
LCI 82	Off Okinawa	4 April 1945
LCI 85	Off northern France	6 June 1944
LCI 91	Off northern France	6 June 1944
LCI 92	Off northern France	6 June 1944
LCI 93	Off northern France	6 June 1944
LCI 219	Off northern France	11 June 1944
LCI 232	Off northern France	6 June 1944
LCI 339	Off New Guinea	4 September 1943
LCI 365	Off Luzon, P. I.	10 January 1945
LCI 416	Off northern France	9 June 1944

Name	Location	Date
LCI 459	Off Palau	19 September 1944
LCI 468	13 28 N, 148 18 E	17 June 1944
LCI 474	Off Iwo Jima	17 February 1945
LCI 497	Off northern France	6 June 1944
LCI 553	Off northern France	6 June 1944
LCI 600	In Ulithi, Carolines	12 January 1945
LCI 684	Off Samar, P.I.	12 November 1944
LCI 974	16 6 N, 120 14 E	10 January 1945
LCI 1065	Off Leyte, P. I.	24 October 1944

SUPPORT LANDING CRAFT

Name	Location	Date
LCS 7	Off Luzon, P. I.	16 February 1945
LCS 15	27 20 N, 127 10 E	22 April 1945
LCS 26	Off Luzon, P. I.	16 February 1945
LCS 33	Off Okinawa	12 April 1945
LCS 49	Off Luzon, P. I.	16 February 1945
LCS 127	Off California	5 March 1945

TUGS

Name	Location	Date
ATR 15	49 N, 00 26 W	19 June 1944
ATR 98	44 05 N, 24 08 W	12 April 1944
GENESEE	At Corregidor, P. I.	5 May 1942
GREBE	South of Fiji Islands	5 December 1942
NAPA	At Bataan, P. I.	8 April 1942
NAUSET	40 38 N, 14 38 E	9 September 1943
NAVAJO	Off New Hebrides	11 September 1943
PARTRIDGE	Off northern France	11 June 1944
SEMINOLE	Off Tulagi I., Solomons	25 October 1942
SONOMA	At Leyte, P. I.	24 October 1944

TANKERS

Name	Location	Date
KANAWHA	9 10 S, 160 12 E	7 April 1943
MISSISSINEWA	10 6 N, 139 43 E	20 November 1944
NECHES	21 1 N, 160 6 W	23 January 1942
NEOSHO	Coral Sea	7 May 1942
PECOS	14 30 S, 106 30 E	1 March 1942
SHEEPSCOT	Off Iwo Jima	6 June 1945

TROOP TRANSPORTS

Name	Location	Date
APc 21	Off New Britain	17 December 1943
APc 35	Off New Georgia, Solomons	22 September 1943
BARRY	Off Okinawa	25 May 1945

APPENDIX C

Name	Location	Date
BATES	Off Okinawa	25 May 1945
COLHOUN	9 24 S, 160 1 E	30 August 1942
DICKERSON	Off Okinawa	2 April 1945
EDWARD RUTLEDGE	Off Morocco	12 November 1942
GEORGE F. ELLIOTT	Off Guadalcanal I., Solomons	8 August 1942
GREGORY	Off Guadalcanal I., Solomons	5 September 1942
HUGH L. SCOTT	Off Morocco	12 November 1942
JOHN PENN	Off Guadalcanal I., Solomons	13 August 1943
JOSEPH HEWES	Off Morocco	11 November 1942
LEEDSTOWN	Off Algiers	9 November 1942
LITTLE	Solomons	5 September 1942
MC CAWLEY	8 25 S, 157 28 E	30 June 1943
MC KEAN	6 31 S, 154 52 E	17 November 1943
NOA	7 1 N, 134 30 E	12 September 1944
SUSAN B. ANTHONY	49 32 N, 00 48 W	7 June 1944
TASKER H. BLISS	Off Morocco	12 November 1942
THOMAS STONE	37 31 N, 00 00 E	7 November 1942
WARD	10 51 N, 124 32 E	7 December 1944

DISTRICT PATROL CRAFT

Name	Location	Date
YP 16	Philippines	December 1941
YP 17	Philippines	December 1941
YP 26	In Canal Zone	19 November 1942
YP 47	Off Staten Island, New York	26 April 1943
YP 72	At Adak, Aleutians	22 February 1943
YP 73	In Kodiak Harbor, Alaska	15 January 1945
YP 74	54 23 N, 164 10 W	6 September 1942
YP 77	Off Atlantic Coast	28 April 1942
YP 88	At Amchitka, Aleutians	28 October 1943
YP 94	56 32 N, 154 22 W	18 February 1945
YP 95	At Adak, Aleutians	1 May 1944
YP 97	Philippines	March 1942
YP 128	Off Monterey, California	30 June 1942
YP 183	On west coast of Hawaii	12 January 1943
YP 205	18 30 N, 65 00 W	1 November 1942
YP 235	In Gulf of Mexico	1 April 1943
YP 270	25 30 N, 112 06 W	30 June 1942
YP 277	East of Hawaii	23 May 1942
YP 279	Off Townsville, Australia	5 September 1943
YP 281	16 53 S, 177 18 W	9 January 1944
YP 284	Off Guadalcanal I., Solomons	25 October 1942
YP 331	24 56 N, 81 58 W	23 March 1944
YP 336	In Delaware River	23 February 1943
YP 345	Southeast of Midway	31 October 1942

Name	Location	Date
YP 346	In South Pacific	9 September 1942
YP 383	8 22 N, 79 29 W	24 November 1944
YP 387	39 N, 75 W	20 May 1942
YP 389	Off Cape Hatteras	19 June 1942
YP 405	In Caribbean Sea	20 November 1942
YP 422	Off New Caledonia	23 April 1943
YP 426	31 59 N, 80 48 W	16 December 1943
YP 438	At Port Everglades, Fla.	20 March 1943
YP 453	In the Bahamas	15 April 1943
YP 481	At Charleston, S. C.	25 April 1943
YP 492	Off east Florida	8 January 1943
YP 577	Great Lakes	23 January 1943

MISCELLANEOUS DISTRICT CRAFT

Name	Location	Date
YA 52	Philippines	1942
YA 59	Philippines	1942
YA 65	Philippines	1942
YAG 2	Philippines	1942
YAG 3	Philippines	1942
YAG 4	Philippines	1942
YAG 17	36 57 N, 76 13 W	14 September 1944
YC 178	Philippines	1942
YC 181	Philippines	1942
YC 523	Off Portsmouth, N. H.	24 February 1944
YC 537	Philippines	1942
YC 643	Philippines	1942
YC 644	Philippines	1942
YC 646	Philippines	1942
YC 647	Philippines	1942
YC 648	Philippines	1942
YC 649	Philippines	1942
YC 652	Philippines	1942
YC 653	Philippines	1942
YC 654	Philippines	1942
YC 664	Guam	1942
YC 665	Guam	1942
YC 666	Guam	1942
YC 667	Guam	1942
YC 668	Guam	1942
YC 669	Philippines	1942
YC 670	Guam	1942
YC 671	Guam	1942

APPENDIX C

Name	Location	Date
YC 672	Guam	1942
YC 673	Guam	1942
YC 674	Guam	1942
YC 683	Philippines	1942
YC 685	Guam	1942
YC 693	Alaska	February 1945
YC 714	Philippines	1942
YC 715	Philippines	1942
YC 716	Philippines	1942
YC 717	Guam	1942
YC 718	Guam	1942
YC 857	Off Cape Cod, Mass.	12 November 1943
YC 869	Off Imperial Beach, Calif.	23 March 1943
YC 886	Guantanamo	3 February 1943
YC 887	Guantanamo	3 February 1943
YC 891	Off Key West, Fla.	18 April 1943
YC 898	Off Key West, Fla.	29 September 1942
YC 899	Off Key West, Fla.	29 September 1942
YC 912	In North Pacific	13 January 1945
YC 961	At Biorka Island	May 1945
YC 970	In Puget Sound, Wash.	14 August 1943
YC 1272	Near San Pedro	June 1945
YC 1278	Off Atlantic coast	10 March 1943
YCF 23	En route to Eniwetok	March 1945
YCF 29	En route to Eniwetok	March 1945
YCF 36	En route to Eniwetok	March 1945
YCF 37	En route to Eniwetok	March 1945
YCF 42	34 47 N, 75 5 W	December 1944
YCF 59	Off Delaware	January 1945
YCK 1	Wake Island	1942
YCK 2	45 47 N, 58 57 W	5 November 1943
YCK 8	Off Key West, Fla.	13 December 1943
YD 19	Philippines	1942
YD 47	Philippines	1942
YD 56	Philippines	1942
YD 60	Philippines	1942
YDG 4	Off New Caledonia	1 October 1943
YF 86	Philippines	1942
YF 177	Philippines	1942

Name	Location	Date
YF 178	Philippines	1942
YF 179	Philippines	1942
YF 180	Philippines	1942
YF 181	Philippines	1942
YF 212	Philippines	1942
YF 223	Philippines	1942
YF 224	Philippines	1942
YF 230	Philippines	1942
YF 317	Philippines	1942
YF 401	35 7 N, 69 W	20 June 1943
YF 415	42 24 N, 70 36 W	11 May 1944
YF 487	In Caribbean	18 July 1943
YF 575	Off Atlantic City, N. J.	6 May 1943
YF 579	At San Francisco	20 September 1943
YF 724	Off Farallones	22 March 1945
YF 725	Off Farallones	22 March 1945
YF 777	At Eniwetok	6 August 1945
YF 926	En route Pearl Harbor	8 March 1945
SAN FELIPE	Philippines	1942
SANTA RITA	Philippines	1942
ROSAL	Philippines	1942
CAMIA	Philippines	1942
DAPDAP	Philippines	1942
RIVERA	Philippines	1942
MAGDALENA	Philippines	1942
YACAL	Philippines	1942
DEWEY DRYDOCK	At Bataan, P. I.	10 April 1942
YFD 20	Off California	31 January 1943
YG 39	10 10 N, 79 51 W	27 September 1944
YG 44	At Pearl Harbor	7 February 1945
YM 4	Philippines	1942
YM 13	Guam	1942
YMS 14	In Boston Harbor	11 January 1945
YMS 19	Off Palau	24 September 1944
YMS 21	43 6 N, 5 54 E	1 September 1944
YMS 24	43 23 N, 6 43 E	16 August 1944
YMS 30	41 23 N, 12 45 E	25 January 1944
YMS 39	1 19 S, 116 49 E	26 June 1945
YMS 48	14 25 N, 120 34 E	14 February 1945

APPENDIX C

Name	Location	Date
YMS 50	Off Java, N.E.I.	18 June 1945
YMS 70	In Leyte Gulf, P. I.	17 October 1944
YMS 71	4 58 N, 119 47 E	3 April 1945
YMS 84	Off Balikpapan, Borneo	9 July 1945
YMS 98	Off Okinawa	16 September 1945
YMS 103	26 13 N, 127 54 E	8 April 1945
YMS 127	In Aleutians	10 January 1944
YMS 133	Off Oregon Coast	21 February 1943
YMS 304	Off northern France	30 July 1944
YMS 341	Off Okinawa	16 September 1945
YMS 350	Off Cherbourg	2 July 1944
YMS 365	1 18 S, 116 50 E	26 June 1945
YMS 378	49 33 N, 1 13 W	30 July 1944
YMS 385	Off Ulithi, Caroline Islands	1 October 1944
YMS 409	Off Atlantic Coast	12 September 1944
YMS 421	Off Okinawa	16 September 1945
YMS 472	Off Okinawa	16 September 1945
YMS 481	Off Tarakan, Borneo	2 May 1945
YO 41	Philippines	1942
YO 42	Philippines	1942
YO 64	Philippines	January 1942
YO 156	At Sitka, Alaska	May 1945
YO 157	At Sitka, Alaska	May 1945
YO 159	Off New Hebrides	14 January 1944
YPD 22	Philippines	1942
YPK 6	Philippines	1942
YPK 7	Philippines	1942
YR 43	In Gulf of Alaska	28 March 1945
YRC 4	Philippines	1942
YSP 41	Philippines	1942
YSP 42	Philippines	1942
YSP 43	Philippines	1942
YSP 44	Philippines	1942
YSP 45	Philippines	1942
YSP 46	Philippines	1942
YSP 47	Philippines	1942
YSP 48	Philippines	1942
YSP 49	Philippines	1942

Name	Location	Date
YSP 50	Philippines	1942
YSR 2	Philippines	1942
BANAAG	Philippines	1942
IONA	Philippines	1942
MERCEDES	Philippines	1942
VAGA	At Corregidor, P. I.	5 May 1942
YT 198	Off Anzio, Italy	18 February 1944
YT 247	14 14 N, 158 59 W	5 April 1944
SHAHAKA	27 21 N, 136 29 W	9 May 1944
YTM 467	Marshall or Gilbert Islands	March 1944
YW 50	Guam	1942
YW 54	Philippines	1942
YW 55	Guam	1942
YW 58	Guam	1942

CARGO VESSELS

Name	Location	Date
ALUDRA	11 26 S, 162 E	23 June 1943
DEIMOS	11 26 S, 162 E	23 June 1943
POLLUX	Off Newfoundland Coast	18 February 1942
SERPENS	At Guadalcanal I., Solomons	29 January 1945

MISCELLANEOUS AUXILIARIES

Name	Location	Date
AILANTHUS	In Aleutians	26 February 1944
ASPHALT	At Saipan	6 October 1944
ATIK	36 N, 70 W	26 March 1942
CANOPUS	At Bataan, P. I.	10 April 1942
CYTHERA	Off Atlantic Coast	May 1942
EXTRACTOR	In Marianas	24 January 1945
MACAW	At Midway Channel	12 February 1944
MOONSTONE	Off Delaware Capes	16 October 1943
MOUNT HOOD	At Manus, Admiralty Islands	10 November 1944
MUSKEGET	In North Atlantic Ocean	September 1942
NIAGARA	In Solomons	23 May 1943
PIGEON	At Corregidor, P. I.	3 May 1942
PONTIAC	Off Halifax, Nova Scotia	30 January 1945
PORCUPINE	At Mindoro, P. I.	30 December 1944
REDWING	37 22 N, 9 55 E	28 June 1943
RESCUER	In Aleutians	1 January 1943

APPENDIX C

Name	Location	Date
ROBERT BARNES	Guam	December 1941
RONAKI	Off eastern Australia	18 June 1943
UTAH	Pearl Harbor	7 December 1941
ex FISHERIES	At Corregidor, P. I.	5 May 1942
ex MARYANN	At Corregidor, P. I.	5 May 1942
ex PERRY	At Corregidor, P. I.	5 May 1952
DCH 1	En route to Pearl Harbor	8 December 1941
AFD 13	Off Okinawa	16 September 1945

In the above list the dates are those of the effective loss; that is, the date of the attack or damage which resulted in loss, rather than that of sinking.

www.ingramcontent.com/pod-product-compliance
Lightning Source LLC
Chambersburg PA
CBHW080741250426
43671CB00038B/2648